MW01156537

PANES OF THE GLASS CEILING

More than fifty years of civil rights legislation and movements have not ended employment discrimination. This book reframes the discourse about the "glass ceiling" that women face with respect to workplace inequality. It explores the unspoken, societally held beliefs that underlie and engender workplace behaviour and failures of the law, policy, and human nature that contribute "panes" and ("pains") to the "glass ceiling." Each chapter identifies an "unspoken belief" and connects it with failures of law, policy, and human nature. It then describes the resulting harm and shows how this belief is not imagined or operating in a vacuum, but is pervasive throughout popular culture and society. By giving voice to previously unvoiced – even taboo – beliefs, we can better address and confront them and the problems they cause.

Kerri Lynn Stone is Professor of Law at the Florida International University College of Law. Named a "Top Scholar" by FIU, she has published extensively on issues of employment discrimination. She graduated from Columbia College, Columbia University with a BA magna cum laude, and from New York University School of Law.

Panes of the Glass Ceiling

THE UNSPOKEN BELIEFS BEHIND THE LAW'S FAILURE TO HELP WOMEN ACHIEVE PROFESSIONAL PARITY

KERRI LYNN STONE

Florida International University

CAMBRIDGE
UNIVERSITY PRESS

CAMBRIDGE
UNIVERSITY PRESS

University Printing House, Cambridge CB2 8BS, United Kingdom

One Liberty Plaza, 20th Floor, New York, NY 10006, USA

477 Williamstown Road, Port Melbourne, VIC 3207, Australia

314–321, 3rd Floor, Plot 3, Splendor Forum, Jasola District Centre, New Delhi – 110025, India

103 Penang Road, #05–06/07, Visioncrest Commercial, Singapore 238467

Cambridge University Press is part of the University of Cambridge.

It furthers the University's mission by disseminating knowledge in the pursuit of education, learning, and research at the highest international levels of excellence.

www.cambridge.org
Information on this title: www.cambridge.org/9781108427593
DOI: 10.1017/9781108551793

© Kerri Lynn Stone 2022

This publication is in copyright. Subject to statutory exception and to the provisions of relevant collective licensing agreements, no reproduction of any part may take place without the written permission of Cambridge University Press.

First published 2022

A catalogue record for this publication is available from the British Library.

Library of Congress Cataloging-in-Publication Data
NAMES: Stone, Kerri Lynn, author.
TITLE: Panes of the glass ceiling : the unspoken beliefs behind the law's failure to help women achieve professional parity / Kerri Lynn Stone, Florida International University.
DESCRIPTION: Cambridge, United Kingdom ; New York, NY : Cambridge University Press, 2022. | Includes index.
IDENTIFIERS: LCCN 2021045752 (print) | LCCN 2021045753 (ebook) | ISBN 9781108427593 (hardback) | ISBN 9781108446464 (paperback) | ISBN 9781108551793 (ebook)
SUBJECTS: LCSH: Sex discrimination in employment – Law and legislation. | Women – Employment – Law and legislation. | Sex discrimination against women – Law and legislation.
CLASSIFICATION: LCC K1772 .S76 2022 (print) | LCC K1772 (ebook) | DDC 344.01/4133–dc23/eng/20211006
LC record available at https://lccn.loc.gov/2021045752
LC ebook record available at https://lccn.loc.gov/2021045753

ISBN 978-1-108-42759-3 Hardback

Cambridge University Press has no responsibility for the persistence or accuracy of URLs for external or third-party internet websites referred to in this publication and does not guarantee that any content on such websites is, or will remain, accurate or appropriate.

This book is dedicated to Joshua Matthew, Dylan Jacob, and Marlee Dina, with more love than they can fathom. They know exactly why.

Contents

Acknowledgments

Cori Ann Varsallone-Gordon, Karina Bodnieks, Jennifer Santos, Alexis Hanson, Amaia Sanz de Acedo, Shannon Crosby, and, especially, the BIG SIX: Yina Cabrera, Dawn Doughty, Samantha Gonzalez, Devon Hoffman, Kyle MacDonald, and Michelle Sola.

Attribution

Many of the ideas set forth in this book have been drawn from my previously published articles, which include, all in the name Kerri Lynn Stone: *Clarifying Stereotyping*, 59 U. KAN. L. REV. 591 (2011); *Lessons from the Dolphins/Richie Incognito Saga*, 14 NEV. L. J. 723 (2014); *Decoding Civility*, 28 BERKELEY J. GENDER L. & JUST. 185 (2013); *Taking in Strays: A Critique of the Stray Comment Doctrine in Employment Discrimination Law*, 77 MO. L. REV. 149 (2012); *For Shame: When High Profile Shaming Is the Only Way to Get Things Discussed and Done*, 48 CONN. L. REV. 1 (2016); *From Queen Bees and Wannabes to Worker Bees: Why Gender Consideration Should Inform the Emerging Law of Workplace Bullying*, 65 N.Y.U. ANN SURV. AM. L. 35 (2009); *License to Harass: Holding Defendants Accountable for Retaining Recidivist Harassers*, 41 AKRON L. REV. 1059 (2008); and *Shortcuts in Employment Discrimination Law*, 56 ST. LOUIS U. L. J. 111 (2011). Certain stories that begin chapters of this book represent loose compilations of anecdotal stories I have collected through interviews and discussions over the years and certain key facts about the speakers and their stories have been changed to protect the anonymity of the parties. They are presented for illustrative purposes and to facilitate discussion when this book is used in an educational setting. Quotes used therein are thus not necessarily always actual quotes but are there to indicate that the narrative is being told from a first-person perspective.

Introduction

"I left the workforce to have a baby. But when I thought about going back, I realized how unpleasant it was for me there. The culture was so miserable. And I knew there'd be no slack given to parent the baby—ever. So, I chose not to go back."

"Nobody hits on me. There's a line with them. But it still feels like a locker room in there sometimes."

"They never said, 'you've lost your spark since the baby.' But they just stopped giving me the good assignments from the good partners."

"He's a jerk to everyone. It's not like he highlights the fact that I'm a woman when he screams at me. I'm just not cut out for this."

"I was assigned a formal mentor along with everyone else, and we have lunch when we're supposed to, but everyone knows that the career-making partners select the people that they gel with socially."

"When my class entered the firm as first years, the women outnumbered the men. Now it's just a few years later, and I'm tired of always being the only woman in the room."

"I knew then that anything I said was going to come across as shrill, angry, and overly ambitious, but if a guy said what I needed to say, he could pull it off."

We have seen, heard, and even experienced contemporary sex discrimination in the workplace. We know what it looks like, and yet, we seem somehow amused and surprised when we realize that others can relate. We share blog posts, memes, and cartoons online about the coded messages we receive, the unspoken, knowing glances we exchange, and the universal feelings of helplessness and frustration that we experience because we know better. We know that something is amiss, and we know that what is happening isn't right. But we also know that it is legally permissible (or that the cards would, at the very least, be stacked against us if we were to attempt to bring a claim). People with little to no knowledge of, or experience with, the law nonetheless instinctively realize that what's happening is "too hard to prove" or just somehow "alright" because they know from their experiences in the world that these sorts of

1

things continue, typically unchecked, and are not really societally frowned upon; they're just the way things go. In fact, that's why women commiserate over the memes and cartoons that depict these things with other women[1] – because, somehow, we know that while some of us "get it," others are oblivious to what is occurring. And there's something very telling about that.

People who have studied the law of discrimination, of course, realize what is happening. They realize that the law's strictures, limitations, and omissions – coupled with the courts' constructions and interpretations of the law and promulgation of doctrines to adjudicate cases brought under it – have simply failed to capture a great deal of what has befallen women in the workplace for as long as the law prohibiting workplace discrimination because of sex has been in effect. And they see that what befalls women in the workplace has largely changed over the years, as more overt discrimination and harassment have become socially recognized as taboo. Consciousness and behaviors have changed, even as attitudes and, more importantly, workplace demographics may not have changed as rapidly or as drastically. The result? A contemporary American workplace governed by outmoded, poorly interpreted laws with gaping holes that fail to capture much of what is occurring within it, and a resultant power structure that, by and large, finds women woefully under-represented in its highest levels.

---

[1]   The author does not seek to minimize sex or other discrimination against anyone who does not, for any reason, identify as a woman. While this book is about workplace discrimination against women, portions of it may have great applicability to many who do not identify as such. Cf. Peter Blanck et al., *Diversity and Inclusion in the American Legal Profession: First Phase Findings from a National Study of Lawyers with Disabilities and Lawyers Who Identify as LGBTQ+*, 23 U. D.C. L. Rev. 23 (2020); Shirley Lin, *Dehumanization "Because of Sex": The Multiaxial Approach to the Rights of Sexual Minorities*, 24 Lewis & Clark L. Rev. 731, 732 (2020). Similarly, the subject of intersectionality when it comes to race, color, religion, or other protected classes is raised throughout the book because it is inextricably linked with many women's experiences. The subject of race and workplace discrimination is one of the utmost significance and, while much has been written on the subject, there is much more work to do – especially when it comes to providing an exposition of the unspoken beliefs that undergird racism in the workplace and its abhorrent effects. This book focuses mainly on sex discrimination, but the following is a mere sliver of the rich literature available and simply a jumping-off point for those who wish to study discrimination and intersectionality in the workplace: James Thuo Gathii, *Writing Race and Identity in a Global Context: What Crt and Twail Can Learn from Each Other*, 67 UCLA L. Rev. 1610, 1628 (2021); Joan C. Williams et al., *Beyond Implicit Bias: Litigating Race and Gender Employment Discrimination Using Data from the Workplace Experiences Survey*, 72 Hastings L.J. 337 (2020); Devon W. Carbado & Cheryl I. Harris, *Intersectionality at 30: Mapping the Margins of Anti-essentialism, Intersectionality, and Dominance Theory*, 132 Harv. L. Rev. 2193 (2019); Serena Mayeri, *Intersectionality and Title VII: A Brief (Pre-)history*, 95 B.U. L. Rev. 713 (2015).

We know the story all too well. In 1964, in the midst of the Civil Rights Movement, Congress passed Title VII of the Civil Rights Act. It prohibited, among other things, discrimination against women in the workplace, meaning that employers of a certain size were forbidden from treating women differently from men with respect to the terms, privileges, and conditions of their employment "because of sex."[2] This occurred against a rather dramatic backdrop and a bleak landscape; in 1964, there were fewer women in the workforce, and very few of those women held leadership positions. In 1967, 14.8 million women had full-time jobs, compared to 36.6 million men.[3] At that time, only 15 percent of those women held management positions.[4] The premise of Title VII of the Civil Rights Act was simple: systemic and societal discrimination must not operate to divest individuals of the right to pursue happiness and the American dream by interfering with their workplace and professional prospects. Mandated inclusion would compel equality of opportunity and make the workforce look truly representative of all those who seek to participate in it.

This, however, has not been the case. For fifty-plus years, Title VII and other civil rights laws have been used to vindicate the rights of victims of discrimination. Both federal and state legislatures have updated and amended the laws, and the courts have set about interpreting them in ways that aim to achieve the ends sought by their architects. And yet, still, women make up 46.5 percent of the workforce and less than 8 percent of its top leadership.[5] This book is about viewing the failure of society and those entrusted with running its regulatory institutions to confer upon women parity and equality with men with respect to power, prestige, and compensation in the workplace. This failure is all too often handily dismissed and ascribed to a singular or monolithic cause or issue, like "work–life balance."[6] In reality, a multiplicity of legal, behavioral, and psychological phenomena join forces to prematurely and disproportionately winnow out and siphon off female employees from the corporate ladder

---

[2] *See* Title VII of the Civil Rights Act of 1964, 42 U.S.C. § 2000e.
[3] Dr. Robert Groves, *Women in the Workforce*, UNITED STATES CENSUS BUREAU (Aug. 12, 2011), www.census.gov/newsroom/pdf/women_workforce_slides.pdf.
[4] *Id.* at 11.
[5] *The Conundrum of the Glass Ceiling*, ECONOMIST (Jul. 21, 2005), www.economist.com/node/4197626.
[6] *See* Sarah Green Carmichael, *Ambitious Women Face More Obstacles Than Just Work-Life Balance*, HARV. BUS. REV. (Sept. 5, 2013), https://hbr.org/2013/09/ambitious-women-face-more-obst; Kimberly Seals Allers, *Rethinking Work-Life Balance for Women of Color*, SLATE (Mar. 5, 2018, 10:00 AM), https://slate.com/human-interest/2018/03/for-women-of-color-work-life-balance-is-a-different-kind-of-problem.html.

and the workplace generally before they can attain the same status and power as men at the helm of employer enterprises.

The expression "glass ceiling" is ubiquitous. For decades, it has been used to describe an invisible or transparent barrier to the ascension or promotion of women into positions of greater power, influence, and compensation in the workplace. The phrase conjures up a palpably powerful metaphor. Women trying to ascend the corporate ladder may be fooled at its bottom, unable to perceive the impervious but transparent barrier at all, but they will invariably progress to the point at which they make contact with it and are obstructed. Then, thanks to its translucence, they will be able to see up into the upper echelons of the organization, but remain unable to transcend the barrier and gain access.

The term "glass ceiling" was initially coined in 1984 by magazine editor Gay Bryant.[7] In 1986, it debuted in a WALL STREET JOURNAL article entitled, "The Glass Ceiling: Why Women Can't Seem to Break the Invisible Barrier That Blocks Them from the Top Jobs," and then soon found its way into the titles of scholarly articles, often by feminist academics.[8] The term was seen as perfectly encapsulating the phenomenon whereby, despite the passage of the Civil Rights Act of 1964 and the widespread education of society about sex discrimination and sexual harassment, sex inequality persists in the American workplace when it comes to everything from promotion to compensation. And despite the repeated refrains that women are tired of making pennies on the dollar as compared with men doing the same jobs, and being taken less seriously as colleagues, supervisors, or bosses than are their male counterparts, the rift between the sexes when it comes to power, prestige, influence, and compensation has continued, sometimes deepening with the passage of time.

In 1991, the federal government established a "Glass Ceiling Commission" charged with examining the barriers of (1) skills honing and development; (2) the hiring of management and supervisory employees; and (3) reward and compensation systems.[9] The Glass Ceiling Commission, which consisted of twenty-one members and was chaired by the Secretary of Labor, was disbanded in 1996, but the intractable problem of the glass ceiling did not disappear with it.[10] Interestingly, as it has persisted, those who study it have started to challenge the metaphor of the glass ceiling, arguing that it

---

[7]   Manish Rana, *Glass Ceiling*, www.scribd.com/document/176204299/Glass-Ceiling (last visited Jun. 10, 2020).

[8]   *The Conundrum of the Glass Ceiling, supra* note 5.

[9]   *Id.*

[10] Glass Ceiling Commission, DIGITALCOMMONS@ILR, https://digitalcommons .ilr.cornell.edu/glassceiling/ (last visited Jun. 10, 2020).

misguidedly depicts a singular obstruction in the pipeline of a career trajectory, rather than what it is: the complex, subtle tapestry made of factors that present themselves in the workplace, the legislatures, and the courts.[11]

This book asserts that the glass ceiling is not made up of one translucent piece of glass, and it posits several distinct problems with a body of law and its interpretation that fail to capture what it sets out to capture and to ensure parity for women in the workplace. Each issue, viewed in isolation, may not seem like a wide-reaching phenomenon. But combined, just like panes of clear glass when laid one on top of another, they eventually form a thick and opaque barrier through which light has trouble penetrating. The glass ceiling becomes murkier, cloudier, and more impenetrable. And the most insidious part of these "panes," or flaws in the law and/or its interpretation, is that many stem from one or more unspoken beliefs that inhere in hearts, minds, and society, but elude exposition because they are so often left unsaid.

Many Americans may not know who Todd Akin is, but few can forget the phrase that he infamously made famous in the summer of 2012: "legitimate rape."[12] Questioned about his stance on abortion in cases of rape, the former Congressman shot back that pregnancy following a rape would be "really rare," noting that "if it's a legitimate rape, the female body has ways to try to shut that whole thing down."[13] By daring to qualify the word "rape" with the word "legitimate," Akin gave voice to the taboo and unspoken belief that there is such a thing as "illegitimate rape," where the word "rape" is applied, but consent is somehow not truly withheld. While this notion is appalling, it being voiced is what truly shocked so many people. The law surrounding gender equality is rife with "unspoken beliefs" that many, if not most people

---

[11] *See* Zoe Williams, *The Glass Ceiling: A Metaphor That Needs to Be Smashed*, GUARDIAN (Jul. 27, 2016), www.theguardian.com/us-news/2016/jul/27/hillary-clinton-glass-ceiling-metaphor-that-needs-to-be-smashed ("[T]he phrase ['glass ceiling'] stuck ... it spawned a whole raft of related executive hurdles made of glass"); *Glasloft/Glass Ceiling*, GILL GATFIELD (2015), www.gillgatfield.com/projects-exhibitions/glasloft-glass-ceiling/ ("The elusive 'glass ceiling' is not transparent, a singular high barrier or a level playing field. It is a structural membrane with multifaceted and toughened components, in multiple dimensions."); Jenna Goudreau, *A New Obstacle for Professional Women: The Glass Escalator*, FORBES (May 12, 2012, 2:28 PM), www.forbes.com/sites/jennagoudreau/2012/05/21/a-new-obstacle-for-professional-women-the-glass-escalator/#3506d2a41135 ("[W]omen started flooding the labor market and taking on the male-dominated corporate world, they then hit a glass ceiling. ... Now, they must contend with yet another advancement obstacle, the 'glass escalator.'").

[12] David Cohen, *Earlier: Akin: "Legitimate Rape" Rarely Leads to Pregnancy*, POLITICO (Aug. 19, 2012), www.politico.com/story/2012/08/akin-legitimate-rape-victims-dont-get-pregnant-079864.

[13] *Id.*

would feel uncomfortable expressing publicly, but which need to be challenged. This book argues that these beliefs have given rise to inconsistencies and fallibilities in the law, vulnerabilities in the interpretation of the law, and the failure of those who make, interpret, and enforce the law to capture the entire spectrum of behavior and beliefs that subordinate women's rights to men's.

There are gaping holes in every layer of netting in the legal system meant to capture the root causes of workplace sex inequality. These holes can be best explained by a series of beliefs, largely unspoken in polite society, about women, their place in society, and those who would discriminate against or harass them. The laws themselves, as written, often evince flaws and fail to provide the protections, accommodations, or guarantees that would be most conducive to the successful recruitment, retention, and promotion of women in the workplace. On another level, both the interpretations of those laws and the doctrines crafted by judges to aid in the adjudication of cases brought under those laws are full of inconsistencies undergirded by unspoken beliefs.[14] Finally, the absence of certain laws and protections shows society's failure to grapple with and accept the existence of certain behaviors and cultures in the workplace that are antithetical to the recruitment, retention, and promotion of talented women in the workplace. This book will be organized by unspoken beliefs and the phenomena engendered by each one. Each chapter will contain illustrative examples and hypotheticals, an exposition of the unspoken belief addressed, with its manifestations in the law and the U.S. legal system, and the legal and social science research to contextualize that particular "pane" of the glass ceiling, before concluding with takeaways. Takeaways may include some useful ways of thinking about, or addressing, the problems outlined in a chapter, but at a minimum, they will provide parting thoughts or summaries as to how we might identify and confront each belief.

Throughout the book, there will be snippets or recaps of interviews conducted and discussions had with working women to highlight or illustrate points being made. In the interest of preserving the privacy and/or anonymity of these women, identifying details about their identities have been changed,

---

[14] *See, e.g.*, EEOC v. Catastrophe Mgmt. Sols. 852 F.3d 1018 (11th Cir. 2016) (finding that a company asking an African American woman to cut her dreadlocks was not discrimination because it was not an "immutable characteristic of race"); Tse v. N. Y. Univ., No. 10 Civ 7207 (DAB), 2013 WL 5288848, at *44 (S.D.N.Y. Sept. 19, 2013) (finding that two stray comments were insufficient to survive the defendant's motion for summary judgment).

and some stories have been altered or blended. They are included to enhance classroom discussion when this book is used in an academic context.[15]

LEGAL BACKGROUND: A QUICK PRIMER

Before we get into this litany of unspoken beliefs, it is important to understand the current state of employment discrimination law. Employment in the United States is essentially at-will.[16] This means that in almost every state (Montana is a notable and singular exception),[17] the background presumption underlying every employment relationship at its inception is that employees serve at the will of their employers. This means that, in theory, employees may be fired at any juncture and for any reason, no matter how arbitrary. Similarly, employees are free to leave employment at their pleasure.

Atop this background presumption are several things that may overwrite it. One may be a contractual arrangement between the employer and the employee that may guarantee, among other things, that the employee may not be fired, or may not be fired except for cause, for a specified period of time. Interestingly, because of the law's aversion to anything resembling compelled servitude, an employer who breaches such a contract may be forced to reinstate the terminated employee, but an employee who quits her job in contravention of such an agreement will not be ordered by a court to return to work against her will, though she may owe the employer damages for the breach.[18]

Another thing that may be engrafted atop the at-will presumption is legislation or case law that mandates that an employer[19] may not fire an employee

---

[15] *See supra* disclaimer in note 1 regarding interviews and dialogue.

[16] *Employment-at-Will Doctrine*, CORNELL L SCH., www.law.cornell.edu/wex/employment-at-will_doctrine (last visited Feb. 5, 2020).

[17] Montana's Wrongful Discharge from Employment Act (WDEA) grants some employees the right to be terminated only for just or good cause after a minimal probationary period. MONT. CODE. ANN. § 39-2-904 (2019).

[18] *See, e.g.*, Thurston v. Box Edler Cty., 892, P.2d 1034, 1040 (Utah 1995) ("Reinstatement may be considered as a remedy by a trial court when fashioning a remedy for breach of an employment contract."); Bacon v. Karr, 139, So. 2d 166, 170 (Fla. 2d DCA 1962) ("Although courts will not compel specific performance of personal service contracts, an employee may be held liable in appropriate proceedings for breach of his contract with his employer."); Bali v. Christiana Care Health Servs., C.A. No. 16433 NC, 1999 Del. Ch. LEXIS 128, at *9 n.5 (Ch. Jun. 16, 1999) ("Any order of specific performance against the employee would raise substantial, if not insurmountable, objections under the Thirteenth Amendment to the United States Constitution . . ..").

[19] The fifteen-employee requirement is a jurisdictional threshold in a Title VII employment discrimination case. Civil Rights Act of 1964, § 701 et seq., as amended, 42 U.S.C. § 2000e.

because of that employee's protected activity or protected class status. So, for example, an employee who works for an employer subject to Title VII – the federal centerpiece of workplace civil rights laws – may not be terminated or otherwise discriminated against with respect to workplace terms, conditions, or privileges "because of" her race, sex, religion, color, or national origin.[20] These are referred to as protected classes. Under other federal statutes, disability, age, and veteran's status are protected classes.[21] Although much of what this book discusses and critiques is salient and applicable to other protected classes, especially race, because this book is about sex discrimination, instead of referencing "protected class" when discussing the statute, it will usually directly reference sex. Pursuant to the anti-retaliation provisions of Title VII and nearly every other employment law statute, an employee cannot be discriminated against or terminated because of her exercise of rights and other protected activities surrounding the vindication of rights protected under the various statutes.

As Title VII was being crafted and enacted, the nation was still feeling reverberations from the governmentally compelled desegregation of public schools in the 1950s and from the more widespread recognition that societal segregation, like that found at water fountains, on forms of transportation, and beside the lunch counters of America, was more than unconstitutional – it was repugnant. Despite this, however, the American workplace persisted in its near-categorical exclusion of women and other minorities (racial, religious, etc.) from the upper echelons of power, prestige, and compensation.[22] Title VII was enacted to capture the range of discrimination that was occurring in the workplace and operating to exclude these minorities from meaningful participation in the workforce and, thus, in public life. In addition to the more straightforward claim of disparate treatment – that a plaintiff has been treated differently from others because of protected class status in direct contravention of the statute's explicit prohibition – we now also have, via amendment in 1991 and decades of construction by the federal courts, viable claims under Title VII for disparate impact discrimination and harassment.[23]

---

[20] Title VII of the Civil Rights Act of 1964, 42 U.S.C. § 2000e–2(a)(1).

[21] *See, e.g.,* Americans with Disabilities Act of 1990, § 503(a), 42 U.S.C. § 12203(a); Age Discrimination in Employment, 29 U.S.C. § 630; Uniformed Services Employment and Reemployment Rights Act of 1994 (USERRA), 38 U.S.C. §§ 4301–33.

[22] It should be noted that many of the discussions and critiques presented here could apply with at least some force to other minority groups protected by Title VII. This book focuses on the plight of women in the workplace, but it is important to note that African Americans and other racial, religious, and ethnic minorities have been excluded from participation in public life and in the workforce in ways that have required and continued to require great remediation.

[23] Title VII of the Civil Rights Act of 1964, 42 U.S.C. § 2000e-2(a)(1).

This book focuses on sex discrimination in the workplace. However, it is impossible to discuss sexism without discussing racism, and the potently invidious crossroads where they meet: intersectionality. According to a TIME magazine interview with Professor Kimberlé Crenshaw, who coined the term more than thirty years ago,[24] intersectionality is

> a lens, a prism, for seeing the way in which various forms of inequality often operate together and exacerbate each other. We tend to talk about race inequality as separate from inequality based on gender, class, sexuality or immigrant status. What's often missing is how some people are subject to all of these, and the experience is not just the sum of its parts.[25]

The racism that a woman faces doesn't merely combine with the sexism she faces; Professor Crenshaw has said on social media that "[i]ntersectionality is not additive. It's fundamentally reconstructive."[26] Two of the most important, propulsive, and influential social justice movements of our time, Black Lives Matter and #MeToo, are educating people and promoting social justice as this book goes to press, and it is clear that intersectional feminism is key to ensuring true parity for all women. The plague that is racism is also an issue that is undergirded by a host of unspoken beliefs, and these are worthy of much thought and analysis.

The Supreme Court and Congress have recognized that even benign, neutral policies can systemically alter the employment experience for an employee, and that alteration, as experienced, is due to the employee's sex.[27] Thus, pursuant to a disparate impact theory of a discrimination case, a plaintiff may challenge a facially neutral policy or practice that confers a disproportionate or disparate effect upon a protected class.[28] If the plaintiff does this, a court will typically order the cessation of the policy or practice, unless the employer can show that it is a business necessity.[29] Moreover, even if the defendant employer can make that showing, the plaintiff may

---

[24] Kimberlé Crenshaw, *Demarginalizing the Intersection of Race and Sex: A Black Feminist Critique of Antidiscrimination Doctrine, Feminist Theory and Antiracist Politics*, 1989(1), article 8 U. CHI. LEGAL F. 139 (1989).

[25] Katy Steinmetz, *She Coined the Term "Intersectionality" over 30 Years Ago. Here's What It Means to Her Today*, TIME (Feb. 20, 2020, 7:27 AM), https://time.com/5786710/kimberle-crenshaw-intersectionality/.

[26] Kimberlé Crenshaw (@sandylocks), TWITTER (June 26, 2020, 1:41 PM), https://twitter.com/sandylocks/status/1276571389911154688?lang=en.

[27] *See* Dothard v. Rawlinson, 433 U.S. 321 (1977).

[28] Nicholas O. Stephanopoulos, *Disparate Impact, Unified Law*, 128 YALE L. J. 1566, 1597 (2019).

[29] *Id.*

nonetheless identify a less intrusive alternative policy or practice for the court's consideration.[30]

In 1986, the Supreme Court formally recognized that without a concrete adverse action, an employee's conditions of employment may be altered because of her sex by harassment in such a way as to disadvantage her palpably – and actionably – at work, in precisely the way that Title VII was designed to combat.[31] A plaintiff may thus bring a claim for harassment under Title VII, like sexual harassment, for example, by alleging that she was subjected to harassment (which can include sexual advances, ridicule, humiliation, etc.) because of her sex, and that the harassment was sufficiently severe or pervasive so as to alter the conditions of her employment, both as perceived by the plaintiff and as would be perceived by a reasonable person.[32] While there are state and local laws that afford plaintiffs protection akin to that offered by Title VII, this book will focus largely on Title VII as the primary mechanism for using the courts to vindicate women's rights in the workplace. It should be noted that men (and others with nonfemale sex or gender identities) are also victims of sexual harassment and sex-based discrimination in the workplace. However, society's views of people other than women are largely outside the scope of this book. Therefore, in many places, this book will refer to women whereas the applicable phenomenon may also apply to men (or others with nonbinary identities) who have been discriminated against in the workplace. It should also be emphasized that people of all sexes and genders can discriminate and be harassers, even against people who fall within their own protected classes.

As in all areas of law, plaintiffs confront challenges on several levels when attempting to deploy antidiscrimination law.[33] First of all, basic problems of proof persist. After alleging a fact, a plaintiff must make sure that she has the evidence to survive summary judgment.[34] Summary judgment is a motion, usually made by a defendant, that, if granted, would dispose of the entire case after the discovery and exchange of evidence, but before the case goes to trial.[35] For a judge to grant this motion, they must find that even when viewing all of the evidence in the light most favorable to the party opposing the motion

---

[30] *Id.*
[31] Meritor Sav. Bank v. Vinson, 477 U.S. 57 (1986).
[32] *See id.*
[33] Ronald A. Schmidt, *The Plaintiff's Burden in Title VII Disparate Treatment Cases: Discrimination Vel Non*—St. Mary's Honor Center v. Hicks, 113 S. Ct. 2742 (1993), 73 NEB. L. REV. 953 (1994), available at http://digitalcommons.unl.edu/cgi/viewcontent.cgi?article=1624&context=nlr.
[34] Fed. R. Civ. P. 56.
[35] *Id.*

(usually the plaintiff), there is simply not enough there to ever persuade a reasonable juror that that side could prevail.[36] Basically, the defendant usually moves for summary judgment, saying that "even if you look at everything that's debatable or based on credibility in the best light for the plaintiff," because of how the law is written and interpreted, there is no way that they could win. Plaintiffs rarely survive summary judgment in this area of the law. Of approximately 14,000 employment civil rights cases filed annually in federal court, about 18 percent are dismissed on motions for summary judgment, and at trial a mere 2 percent of cases are won by the plaintiff.[37] Some cases eventually settle, typically in a manner that compensates the plaintiff in whole or in part, but those settlements are typically not publicly available.

Second of all, even if a plaintiff does survive summary judgment, and the case moves to trial, meaning that the judge has found that a reasonable juror, construing all of the facts in the light most favorable to the plaintiff, *could* find that the plaintiff should prevail, the strength of the evidence and the credibility of the witnesses need to be strong enough to enable a victory. Thus, cases are like onions, shedding successive layers of skin, but with a core of truth in the middle. There is, of course, what occurred, how what occurred was perceived by witnesses, how credible those witnesses are to others, and what the story sounds like when it hits the ears of the triers of fact, be they judges, juries, or both.

Finally, for a plaintiff to prevail, courts must have interpreted the law in such a way as to afford a given plaintiff a cognizable claim. Many factual claims that might strike an average person as warranting remediation under the law actually do not legally amount to a claim because of the way in which the law is construed and the way in which its contours are drawn. The three branches of government serve discrete functions. The executive branch enforces the law, and the legislative branch puts the law into place, but it is the job of the judicial branch to interpret the law. This means that, in court, people present facts and argue that they fit within the strictures of legal claims as outlined by statutes, and judges determine whether, in fact, they do. Moreover, if the language of a statute is vague, judges supply definitions, clarifications, and constructions as needed. Sometimes, court-created doctrines and law that aid in interpreting a statute need to be interpreted themselves, and courts need to construe other courts' words. So, for example, as stated, the Supreme Court held that "sexual harassment," requiring, among

---

[36] *Id.*; Doe v. C.A.R.S. Protection Plus, Inc., 527 F.3d 358, 362 (3d Cir. 2008).

[37] Ellen Berrey, Laura Beth Nielsen, & Robert L. Nelson, Rights on Trial: How Workplace Discrimination Law Perpetuates Inequality (2017).

other things, "severe or pervasive" harassment, was construed as actionable behavior that comes within the ambit of the prohibitions outlined by Title VII.[38] Subsequent lower court cases then, in turn, had to interpret what, more precisely, was meant by "severe or pervasive." Thus, even if a plaintiff had rock-solid evidence of one instance that she believed to be harassment, to the extent that it failed to meet the standard as construed by these courts, quantitatively or qualitatively, she could not prevail.

But the central, intractable question of interpretation that has beleaguered judges, scholars, and lawyers for more than half a century when it comes to sex discrimination cases brought under Title VII has always been "What, precisely, does 'because of sex' mean?" On one hand, "because of sex" is easy to discern when an employee suffers an adverse action that can be tied to her protected class status via a "smoking gun" admission or even a logical deduction. Sometimes, however, this nexus is more difficult to establish. Likewise, in sexual harassment cases, where the abuse must also be "because of sex," this is readily established where an employee is sexually propositioned or abused with an explicitly sex-based epithet. But sometimes this, too, is less than clear. So, then, what does "because of sex" mean, and what does it take to demonstrate it?

Certainly, invidious, animus-based discrimination ("You are a woman, therefore you are hysterical/inferior/dumber") is a motivation that falls squarely within that term under anyone's construction. A decision-maker who believes that a woman is inherently less capable or intelligent than a man simply because she is a woman is squarely in violation of the law's prohibition. But what about decision-makers who might harbor such beliefs at a level that is so subconscious that they don't even admit to themselves that they hold them? What about one who persists in holding the sexes to different standards with respect to ability, commitment, or even appearance or demeanor, but doesn't explicitly articulate these different standards as such, and merely concludes that one candidate is superior to another without unpacking their reasoning with granularity ("He presents better/is more persuasive/commands respect")?

Title VII's two pivotal words – "because of" – have long stymied judges, scholars, and attorneys alike in various cases. Contouring the parameters of Title VII's coverage presents near-intractable problems when there is such a large gray area along the borders of the statute's coverage, and a veritable tug-of-war ensues across these borders each time a case calls for a determination as to whether something occurred "because of" protected

---

[38]   Meritor Sav. Bank v. Vinson, 477 U.S. 57 (1986).

class status. Each time a court answers the question of coverage, turning a case into an instructive data point around the contentious dividing line between a yes and a no, it seems as though more questions are engendered. By way of example, once the Supreme Court concluded that a woman who was not made a partner by her employer after being deemed by decision-makers to be not feminine, polite, or deferential enough and "too manly" in her affect, appearance, and demeanor could win her Title VII suit because of the sex-based stereotyping that went on, more questions were created for subsequent cases.[39] Did that necessarily confer a cause of action on the next plaintiff making similar arguments? What about a man told that he was too effeminate? A woman told that *she* was too effeminate? A woman who is not given a desired position because, as she is told, she lacks that "Midwestern girl look" that her employer seeks?[40]

Providing another example, once courts established that sexual harassment consisting of sexual overtures or pejorative language that references a victim's sex is "because of sex" and actionable, new questions arose. Since generic vulgarity and "neutral" workplace bullying, evenly meted out, are typically considered to be wholly lawful,[41] how are we to classify "gendered bullying" that does not quite meet the standard for actionable harassment, but nonetheless makes a victim feel demeaned or diminished in the workplace because of her sex?[42]

As courts so frequently intone, Title VII is not a "civility code."[43] Every slight and incivility is not compensable in court; morality and enlightenment are not always to be legislated.[44] However, because social science and psychology inform societal – and should inform judicial – conceptions of things like subconscious prejudice, we know that it is still the case that too many claims with "because of" allegations are dismissed way too readily.[45] The complexities of walking this line often prove to be too much for courts. And this is just the beginning as we set about examining the layers of the "panes" that comprise the glass ceiling. Some "panes" deal with gaps in the legislation; others deal with inauspicious interpretations of the legislation as courts grapple with its complexities and try to fulfill its objectives without overreaching

---

[39] Price Waterhouse v. Hopkins, 490 U.S. 228 (1989).
[40] Lewis v. Heartland Inns of Am. LLC, 591 F.3d 1033 (8th Cir. 2010).
[41] *See* Oncale v. Sundowner Offshore Servs., 523 U.S. 75 (1998).
[42] *See* Reeves v. C. H. Robinson Worldwide Inc., 525 F.3d 1139 (11th Cir. 2008).
[43] Oncale, 523 U.S. at 80.
[44] *See* Kerri Lynn Stone, *Teaching the Post-Sex Generation*, 58 St. Louis L. J. 223, 228 (2013).
[45] *Id.*

and becoming a virtual "super-personnel department" that oversees and second-guesses all actions of Human Resources (HR) departments.

It is important to remember that all of these issues surrounding the law governing sex discrimination come into play only if a lawsuit is actually filed. Filing a sex discrimination or sex harassment lawsuit against one's present or former employer can bring with it immense financial, time, professional, social, and reputational costs. It is unknowable just how many times these factors have inhibited a potential plaintiff from so much as consulting an attorney, let alone committing to file suit. The emotional strain placed upon an employee from the outset of a legal complaint is immense. Fears of retaliation often abound, even though retaliation for opposing a practice, or for participation in a proceeding pursuant to a Title VII complaint are unlawful under Title VII. This is not irrational. To be actionable, a retaliatory action has to be sufficiently severe to deter a reasonable employee from undertaking the plaintiff's course of action. In 2013, only 42 percent of the complaints with a retaliation allegation were found to be actionable.[46] However, even if the employer is ethical, smart, or well-counseled enough not to engage in actionable retaliation, oftentimes petty slights, social alienation, and a palpable overall shift or chill in the workplace climate will ensue. Between this and the time and financial constraints that come with filing and prosecuting a lawsuit, there is an appreciable deterrence factor that contributes to the glass ceiling's imperviousness.

It is also important to recall that even if a suit is filed, often the relevant law, or even sometimes the relevant proof, will not even come into play because of the dynamics that govern settlement. While employers may have somewhat of an impetus to throw some money at what they might perceive as a "nuisance lawsuit," barring a clear violation of the law coupled with solid proof that verges on being a proverbial "smoking gun," it is rare that substantial settlement offers will follow the filing of lawsuits. Employers may be reluctant to offer large settlement offers, or even to settle at all, when they (1) fear the opening of "floodgates" of litigation, and (2) know of the tendency of cases to be dismissed, as discussed above. Thus, employers will tend to either move to dispose of the case via a dismissal or a grant of summary judgment, or offer a very small amount of money for its withdrawal. Attorneys are aware of this, and this leaves many plaintiffs in a position in which they either accept a very small sum of money to retract their claim or face a high probability of the dismissal of their case. The lawyers simply do not want to invest too much time

---

[46] *See Retaliation-Making It Personal*, EEOC, www.eeoc.gov/laws/types/retaliation_considera tions.cfm (last visited Aug. 21, 2021).

or too many resources in something that is likely doomed to fail, especially when weighed against the certainty of a proposed settlement.

Many employees considering suing their employers cannot afford to pay an attorney by the hour and must accept a contingency arrangement, where the attorney takes a percentage of the employee's recovery, if they can get lawyers to take their cases. In light of this, the economics that drive a settlement agreement often boil down to finding the point at which it is worth it to the lawyer to continue versus recouping what she or he has invested.[47] At a more practical level, many interesting cases that could create binding precedent by yielding favorable law for plaintiffs never see the light of day due to settlement dynamics.

With all of these impediments to navigate around, would-be plaintiffs often forgo litigation and simply rely on what we can call legal osmosis, or the knowledge of what the law can theoretically accomplish absorbed by society's collective consciousness and popular culture, which then renders the behavior professionally and socially unacceptable. Case in point: after sexual harassment was deemed violative of Title VII and thus actionable in 1986, things like news reports, "water cooler talk," HR training, and even the featuring of sexual harassment on primetime TV shows helped render things like propositioning and threatening female employees taboo in the workplace even though relatively few victims of sexual harassment actually filed suit against their employers. For numerous practical reasons, many outlined already, this effective "herd immunity" protected many employees from encountering the behavior, or at least protected their ability to speak up to HR about it without actually having to file suit. Then again, this only added to the dearth of opportunities that courts have had to interpret the law in the course of adjudicating claims, creating less law, and affording fewer opportunities to explore difficult cases, nuanced legal points, and boundary-pushing facts.

It is thus easy to see why many of the "panes" of the glass ceiling explored in the following chapters go exasperatingly unfixed. There are simply too few opportunities to aerate new legal arguments or approaches. With every case that is not brought, with every case that settles prematurely, and with every case that is unfairly disposed of too handily by a court, a chance is lost to test, and possibly expand, the parameters of what will be captured by the law. A chance is lost to garner attention for the multitude of unique challenges and hassles that women face at work. And a chance is lost to develop a record that

---

[47] David Sherwyn, *Arbitration of Employment-Discrimination Lawsuits: Legalities, Practicalities, and Realities, Cornell Hotel & Restaurant Admin. Quarterly*, 43(6) (Dec. 2002), 62–72, 64, https://core.ac.uk/download/pdf/145015831.pdf.

would more adequately document the phenomena that include workplace policies, behaviors, and cultures that prematurely winnow women out of the workforce (or suppress their potential advancement), despite their skills, education, and passion for what they do. The statistics and the sometimes stagnant state of reform can make women feel helplessly mired in the status quo. This book seeks to shed some much-needed light on what is wrong with the law and the interpretation of the law governing workplace discrimination against women. Armed with an understanding of how things work generally and the driving force behind the impediments and inertia plaguing the campaign to break or at least start to dismantle the glass ceiling, we can now start to examine some of the layered panes.

Each chapter of this book is an investigation into and an exposition of a "pane" of the glass ceiling – a facet of the law or of workplace behavior that subtly interferes with the retention, advancement, and promotion of talented women in the workplace. This book focuses exclusively on women in the workplace, but there is a rich literature that deals with the very important topic of the plight of racial, religious, and other minorities in the workplace.[48] In fact, many of the points and arguments made here apply with equal force when analyzing the dearth of minorities in the upper echelons of power, prestige, and compensation in the American workforce. Moreover, the issue of intersectionality, when the disadvantage conferred by one's sex, in this case, is compounded by that of other minority statuses, like race, color, or religion, is another topic, as discussed, with a rich literature behind it that is discussed throughout this book. It should be noted that this book focuses largely on the white-collar or professional American workplace. The plight of blue-collar

---

[48] Robert T. Carter & Thomas D. Scheuermann, *Legal and Policy Standards for Addressing Workplace Racism: Employer Liability and Shared Responsibility for Race-Based Traumatic Stress*, 12 U. MD. L.J. RACE, RELIGION, GENDER & CLASS 1, 4–5 (2012) ("Racial discrimination and harassment still exist in the employment setting; we are not living and working in environments that evidence the existence of a 'post-racial America,' but rather the continuation of racism and racial harassment albeit sometimes in different forms."); Alice B. Stock & Christopher S. Chan, *Religious Discrimination in the US Workplace: Is It Getting Better or Worse?*, INT'L BAR ASS'N (Jun. 15, 2015), www.ibanet.org/Article/Detail.aspx?ArticleUid=05 a3130f-07ea-4331-9053-1850007727bd ("[Workplace religious discrimination] claims jumped from two per cent to four per cent of all discrimination claims . . .. These claims are being filed by individuals of numerous religions, including adherents to mainstream Protestant Christian religions as well as Mormons, Jehovah's Witnesses, Seventh-Day Adventists, Jews, Muslims, Sikhs and less well-known religious groups. Experts believe the number of religious discrimination claims will continue to rise."); Natalie Prescott, *English Only at Work, Por Favor*, 9 U. PA. J. LAB. & EMP. L. 445, 453 (2007) ("[S]ome courts have acknowledged that there may be circumstances in which an English-only rule has been crafted or applied such that it discriminates against certain employees on the basis of race or national origin, thereby violating Title VII.").

female workers is one that has some distinct attendant concerns, but one that can also be addressed by some of the analyses in this book.[49]

OVERVIEW OF CHAPTERS

These chapters, as discussed, are organized by the largely unspoken beliefs that underlie the problems being addressed. These beliefs are as insidious as they are precisely because they are tacit. Left unsaid, they create nothing to rail against or even to which to respond. Thus, the damage wrought gets inflicted silently and invisibly. Further, societal acceptance of many of the premises, spoken and unspoken, that underlie what is missing from the law, its inter-pretation, and its dissemination perpetuates them and sanctions much of the behavior that needs regulation. Many people – including those who engage in behaviors that hinder women at work, those in a position to regulate that behavior, lawyers who would take cases, and judges who would adjudicate them, not to mention the affected women, themselves – fail to see what is occurring and fail to understand why what is happening is not captured by existing law. By giving voice to the unspoken beliefs that clearly underlie various defects within behavior, perception, and the law, something palpable is set forth for scrutiny. And that is the first step toward change.

"We see you differently than we see men." We begin with a belief that is really more of a truth. In a world in which the Center for American Women and Politics feels compelled to issue a series of "Topics for [Political] Debate-Watching through a Gender Lens,"[50] to remind debate-watchers to be cogni-zant of, among other things, the types of question posed to and attacks made on female candidates, as opposed to their male opponents, it seems evident that women are perceived differently than men. Indeed, another pane of the glass ceiling is laid through the act of stereotyping women in the workplace, and the law's treatment of this behavior. Stereotyping can actually be a healthy mental function that works to aid the human mind mediate and navigate its confrontations with reality.[51] Humans stereotype to sort their experiences and make sense of the world around them. However, it is well-documented that the stereotyping of women in the workplace, whether it is positive or negative, and

---

[49] The book limits its discussion to U.S. law.

[50] Kelly Ditmar, *Debate-Watching with a Gender Lens*, MEDIUM (Jun. 25, 2019).

[51] C. Neil Macrae and Galen V. Bodenhausen, *Social Cognition: Thinking Categorically about Others*, ANNU. REV. PSYCHOL. (2000), available at www.suz.uzh.ch/dam/jcr:00000000-64a0-5b1c-ffff-ffff9c745ec1/10.19-macrae-bodenhausen-00.pdf; John Stossel and Kristina Kendall, *The Psychology of Stereotypes*, ABC NEWS (Sept. 15, 2006), http://abcnews.go.com/2020/story?id=2442521.

whether it is done consciously or subconsciously, systemically harms individuals and women as a class.[52]

Women are more readily seen as possessing certain negative traits and characteristics, like hysteria and oversensitivity, while simultaneously often being expected to possess others in a way in which men simply are not. It is thus unspoken that women put before decision-makers for hiring, promotion, or anything else are especially prone to experiencing a battery of unspoken assumptions, expectations, and characterizations that will be harmful to them professionally, and the decision-makers may or may not know that they are even harboring these beliefs.[53] The underlying issue, however, lies in the law's treatment of alleged stereotyping, even where these normally tacit beliefs are actually voiced.

With little more than a singular, seminal Supreme Court case about stereotyping to guide them,[54] lower courts have attempted, unsuccessfully, to grapple with allegations of sex discrimination due to underlying stereotyping, and emerge with a consistent, logical jurisprudence. The fact of the matter, however, is that the stereotype doctrine has evolved to essentially mean whatever a given judge wants it to mean in order to achieve the desired ends in a given case.

"We expect you to take your (verbal) punches like a man." On one hand, women are often viewed and depicted differently than are men, or at least held to a disparate standard. On the other hand, ironically, the *actual* sociobiological differences between the sexes might lead to women (as a group) being socialized in a way that makes them more vulnerable to the effects of bullying and viewed in a way that might be making them more susceptible to being targeted for it. Another "pane" of the glass ceiling is the proliferation of equal opportunity bullying in the workplace. Existing law is, of course, violated if women are sexually harassed, either barraged with mistreatment that highlights their sex or even singled out for sex-based abuse. But if men and women alike are subjected to "neutral" abuse that amounts to bullying, Title VII does not come into play, and there is currently no anti-bullying workplace law that has been enacted in any state.[55] This absence of legislation has been explained by several expressed sentiments, like the idea

---

[52]   *See* Cheryl B. Preston, *Subordinated Stills: An Empirical Study of Sexist Print Advertising and Its Implications for Law*, 15 Tex. J. Women & L. 229, 257 (2006) ("Being envisioned as 'girls' and 'girlie' may be fashionable in some circles, but notwithstanding this effort to reclaim and empower these terms, they retain overwhelmingly negative connotations and usages.").

[53]   *Id.*

[54]   *Hopkins*, 490 U.S. 228.

[55]   *See, generally*, FAQ, Healthy Workplace Campaign, www.healthyworkplacebill.org/faq .php (last visited Feb. 12, 2017) (explaining that no state or federal laws exist that address workplace bullying).

that no protected class is harmed by status-neutral bullying, and the notion that attempting to "legislate civility" is overreaching, gratuitous, and even counterproductive in a free market within a democracy.[56]

The problem, however, lies in the unspoken beliefs that materialize around the issue of workplace bullying and attempts at its regulation after it is revealed that bullying disproportionately befalls and disproportionately affects women and other groups: "Bullying only happens to weak people, and if women are disproportionately affected by bullying, it just means that they don't belong in the workplace." Echoes of this sentiment can be heard when model legislation routinely fails to pass upon being introduced around the country and a blind eye is turned to the persistence of women's premature departures from and winnowing out of the workplace due to what they claim is "discomfort with the culture" or "bad experiences" that were not unlawful. The fact is that we need to do little more than examine the disparate socialization of men and women from their childhoods in order to understand why grown women, as a group, tend to absorb, internalize, and respond to workplace bullying differently from the men around them. Even today, as employers, legislators, and others decry the failure of women to attain professional parity with men, the connection between rampant, lawful workplace bullying and the systematic elimination of women from the ranks of corporate leadership is largely ignored.

"Accept 'locker room' and sexist talk." And hand in hand with tacit beliefs about bullying and blindness to its unique effects on women are those about "locker room talk" at work – and the unique alienating and inhibiting effect it can have on women. Crassness at work is nothing new. In fact, with the widespread knowledge of what sexual harassment is that we see today, and training being as pervasive as it is, if anything, there are likely fewer instances of female workers being directly propositioned by supervisors across the board than there once were. But there is a crassness rife in many professional workplaces that is generally not regarded as actionable sexual harassment, even though it quietly erodes the dignity of many women over time. And while some judges have found in certain cases that general sexual crassness can create a hostility toward women that is actionable though it does not target an individual, (1) not all judges agree on this, and both Congress and the Supreme Court have been silent on the matter; (2) because of the tenuous

---

[56] *See Rep. Chris Miller Questions Effectiveness of New Sexual Harassment Legislation*, EAST CENTRAL REPORTER (Aug. 16, 2019), https://eastcentralreporter.com/stories/513001419-rep-chris-miller-questions-effectiveness-of-new-sexual-harassment-legislation ("It's really hard to legislate civility.").

legal status of the "locker room" culture at work, women largely accept it and often fail to so much as complain internally about it; and (3) because society at large has embedded subtle sexism into its lexicon and interactions, the behavior, though uniquely noxious to women, often goes unnoticed and unobjected to.

The unspoken belief that women should acquiesce and "accept locker room talk" at work, as well as the sexually-charged, crass, and misogynistic workplace culture that accompanies it, and if they can't, it's their own fault, has thus become silently etched into popular culture. If you strain, you can hear whispers of it when students discuss workplace regulation and talk about how overreaching by courts and overregulation by Congress happen because "people" are "too sensitive" and "not tough enough," without a mention as to (1) who may be in need of broader constructions of Title VII or why; (2) the structural and societal discrimination against women and others that leads to the common acceptance of words relating to women or to the female anatomy coming to mean negative things generally in a workplace environment; or (3) studies that have shown how the messages embedded in such a belief are absorbed by women.

"You don't operate with full agency." When it comes to sexual harassment jurisprudence, this unspoken belief is pervasive.[57] A somewhat shocking belief, entrenched in centuries of law, was that the "seduction" of another man's wife or daughter was a theft of virtue that belonged not to the woman, but to her husband or father. Shades of it persist in sexual harassment jurisprudence today.[58] In order to establish liability and remove from consideration a powerful affirmative defense otherwise available to a defendant employer, a sexual harassment plaintiff must show, among other things, that she suffered a tangible employment action, like a demotion, firing, etc., usually after she presumably resisted the sexual advances of her harasser. Interestingly, however, in cases in which the victim acquiesces to her harasser, courts have found that, although nothing tangible has happened to her job status, she has suffered a tangible harm sufficient to take the potential defense to liability off the table.[59]

In stark contrast, however, in situations in which the victim is pushed to the brink and departs from her employment on her own, the Supreme Court has held that the defense is still available, even if the departure is deemed to

---

[57]   Lisa Fireston, *Are We Still Condemning Women for Their Sexuality?*, HUFFINGTON POST (Mar. 28, 2012), www.huffingtonpost.com/lisa-firestone/women-and-sex_b_1382892.html.

[58]   *See, e.g.*, Piggott v. Miller, 557 S.W.2d 692 (Mo. Ct. App. 1977); Slawek v. Stroh, 62 Wis. 2d 295, 215 N.W.2d 9 (1974).

[59]   *See Vinson*, 477 U.S. at 59.

be a constructive discharge.[60] A constructive discharge occurs when the law recognizes that any reasonable person would have felt compelled to leave; it is the functional equivalent of a termination.[61] When these two court holdings are held side by side, it becomes clear that while the victims in both scenarios sustain harm right under the employers' noses, only the victim who acquiesces to the advances of her harasser is deemed in need of "rescue." The victim who reaches her breaking point and quits is deemed to have acted volitionally and to be responsible for that choice as a consenting adult, even where the choice to leave is deemed a constructive discharge, and, thus, by definition coerced.

"Women are the downfall of men." When a belief this pernicious is alleged to exist across society, it is important to look at how it might take shape and present itself. When men claim to fear mentoring, working closely with, traveling with, or being out at a social/professional event with women, women are harmed. Many men claim to fear this proximity, and still more silently fear it, but won't admit it. Generally, a man fears that (1) the woman will tempt him into some sort of physical tryst, compromising his integrity in the workplace and/or his marriage/relationship; (2) the woman will falsely accuse him of inappropriate behavior while alone with her; and/or (3) others, seeing them together, will make untoward assumptions about the nature of their relationship.

The refusal to have proximity to women, however, leads to women missing out on opportunities at work that range from invitations to client events and meals outside of the office to quality mentoring. These things, however, are difficult to quantify, and still more difficult to litigate; courts have made it relatively clear that small slights and invisible burdens cannot anchor a lawsuit. The laws that seek to regulate workplace behavior and decision-making aim to stay within the strictures of that which is actual, palpable discrimination. As a result, a Title VII plaintiff bringing a case must have a distinct harm, usually in the form of an "adverse employment action," in order for her case to be legally viable.[62] On one hand, this makes sense; affording legal relief for slights so petty as not to matter would be gratuitous and wasteful. On the other hand, who is to determine what is truly so petty as to be nonexistent or irrelevant, versus what might be salient to one's job and, ultimately, career, but may be difficult to track, document, or prove? So, if a woman works, for example, at a law firm, her termination will be registered

---

[60] Burlington Indus., Inc. v. Ellerth, 524 U.S. 742 (1998).
[61] *Id.*
[62] Title VII of the Civil Rights Act of 1964, 42 U.S.C. § 2000e-2(a)(1).

as an obvious adverse action, but the relative quality of things like the mentoring, assignments, and assistance that she receives will be very difficult to quantify, track, compare, and, ultimately, register as "adverse actions" if she believes that her sex led her to get short shrift relative to her male coworkers.

The seemingly invisible burdens of increased risk and decreased opportunities for learning and advancement can be easily embedded in subjective and necessary choices made to vary assignments, exposure, supervisors, etc. from employee to employee. The belief, even if subconscious, that a male employee has no plans to leave the job or the workforce to have a child or for any other reason, has a family to support, and/or simply has a "bright future" with the employer can readily lead that employer to make a series of choices that can leave a female employee with job dissatisfaction, a narrow skill set, and little to no support, encouragement, or vision of a possible trajectory to the upper echelons of employment.[63] Without a discernible, established "adverse employment action" to anchor it, a female employee's claim will be disposed of handily.[64] And she may be unfairly perceived as petty, herself.

"Just be grateful that you're there." This is the tacit message that no one would admit to sending to women and others, and yet, judging from the way they are so often treated in the workplace, it appears that this is a more widely-held sentiment than would be supposed. Women are, all too often, silently saddled with the "emotional labor" or "housekeeping" of the workplace. From being asked or simply expected to set up or serve food at professional functions when their male colleagues are not, to being asked or simply expected to manage the feelings and expectations of coworkers when others aren't, women too often find their time and energy diverted to making others comfortable, rather than advancing their careers. Worse still, these slights are, too often, imperceptible, and not deemed substantial enough to be actionable or anything other than an employer's normal exercise of discretion.

Until women are freed up to further their professional interests at work and not disproportionately saddled with these types of burden, there is not true equality in the workplace. Moreover, until employers stop looking at women through the trope of their being somehow uniquely responsible for the comfort, aesthetics, and morale of the workplace, women will remain mired in having to transact in emotions, rather than true professional capital in the workplace. And until the law permits a window into this highly problematic,

---

[63] Vicki Schultz, *Taking Sex Discrimination Seriously*, 91 DENV. U.L. REV. 995 (2015).

[64] Autumn George, *"Adverse Employment Action" – How Much Harm Must Be Shown to Sustain a Claim of Discrimination under Title VII?*, 60 MERCER L. REV. 1075, 1079 (2009).

but not highly visible barrier to women's professional success, the glass ceiling will remain firmly intact.

"Don't burden us with your (impending) motherhood." Title VII, especially as amended by the Pregnancy Discrimination Act of 1978, would seem to dictate, and has led many to believe, that women are afforded an affirmative right to be free from pregnancy and motherhood discrimination in the workplace. However, despite the existence of these and other laws and doctrines, there are enough defects and omissions in them, their construction, and their application to render this right compromised. Rather, what is often telegraphed instead is the message that many would never voice: that pregnancy and motherhood are costly, inconvenient, and best kept shielded from sight to the greatest extent possible.

While not all women go on to have children in their lives, most do.[65] Nonetheless, attitudes, workplace policies, and even the laws designed to protect women are fraught with the sentiment that being pregnant, giving birth, or adopting, and taking care of a small child are somehow at odds with the demands of the workplace, or unusual.[66] The lip service given to workplace equality and the facial appeal of the litany of laws and doctrines that are supposed to facilitate the maintenance of a career while becoming and being a parent are belied by the holes in the laws and the words, actions, and attitudes of those charged with abiding by, enforcing, applying, and construing these laws.

"He has a family to support." While some will confess that they have heard these precise words offered as an explanation for why they are not being paid as much as their male colleagues, this sentiment is not commonly expressed in the modern American workplace. But how many subscribe to this reasoning, at least on some level? The pay discrepancy between the sexes has been made clear, based both on national statistics and on individual workplace or industry statistics. But what underlies this? Could it be that, on some level, those charged with setting pay, as well as crafting, enforcing, and applying the laws that purport to compel equal pay for equal work, do subscribe to antiquated beliefs about what a man ought to earn, versus a woman?

Until the fallacious and illogical rationales typically proffered in defense of the status quo are probed and challenged, women will not be able to crack

---

[65] Belinda Luscombe, *No, All Those Strollers Are Not Your Imagination. More American Women Are Having Children*, TIME (Jan. 9, 2018), ("by the end of their childbearing years, 86% of U.S. women have had kids . . ..").

[66] Joan C. Williams, *Deconstructing Gender*, 87 MICH L. REV. 797, 799 (1989).

the glass ceiling. And traditional, facially neutral means of setting salaries, like asking for prior salaries of employees as benchmarks, typically serve to reinforce and replicate old sex-discriminatory patterns more than anything else.

"Bad people don't do good things, and good people frequently say bad things (and employment discrimination plaintiffs can't be fully trusted)." A final "pane" of the glass ceiling emanates from judicial doctrines created and employed to resolve cases at the summary judgment stage. Although most people are not aware of employment discrimination doctrines, the proliferation of doctrines that facilitate the disposition of cases before they are even litigated diminishes women's and other minorities' presence and power. One doctrine, the "stray comments" doctrine, enables judges to essentially disregard speech and behaviors that might have yielded tremendous insight into the mindset of a decision-maker accused of sex discrimination simply because they have been deemed too distant from the precise time, place, and context of the challenged employment decision.[67] So, in other words, a judge may grant summary judgment on a claim of sex discrimination even though the decision-maker at issue made numerous comments and jokes about women's inferiority. This would mean, essentially, that the judge was saying that the case could not even go before a jury because there could never be enough evidence adduced for any reasonable juror to find that the plaintiff was discriminated against because of her sex. This would be the case notwithstanding the jokes and comments, so long as they did not coincide precisely with the alleged discrimination (firing, demotion, etc.) and they were not targeting the plaintiff specifically. The case would be cut off at its knees before it even went to trial.

This kind of disregard of evidence is written nowhere explicitly into the statute; it is a judge-made doctrine that has proliferated unchecked among lower courts. Another such judge-crafted doctrine supposedly aimed at adjudicating cases more consistently and efficiently also facilitates grants of summary judgment, ensuring that cases do not see the light of day but, rather, are foreclosed before they get off the ground: the "same actor inference." Under

---

[67] *See, e.g.*, Johnson v. Grays Harbor Cmty. Hosp., 385 F. App'x 647, 648–49 (9th Cir. 2010) ("These kinds of 'stray remarks' are insufficient as a matter of law to demonstrate discriminatory animus . . ." (citing Merrick v. Farmers Ins. Grp., 892 F.2d 1434, 1438 (9th Cir. 1990))); Ghebreab v. Inova Health Sys., No. 1:16-cv-1088(LMB/JFA), 2017 WL 1520427, at *21 (E.D. Va. Apr. 26, 2017) ("Even if those statements could be authenticated such that they amounted to admissible evidence, three stray comments over a period of two years is insufficient as a matter of law to support an inference of racial animus.").

this doctrine, a presumption is made that one who hired a member of a protected class could not, absent evidence to the contrary and within a prescribed period of time, have discriminated against this person because of her protected class status.[68] This presumption is accorded in spite of many reasons as to why someone who hired an employee may nonetheless harbor conscious or subconscious bias against them because of their protected class status. These two doctrines, not well known to the general public, have been critiqued by legal scholars, but have not really been held up alongside one another for all to see. And once you do, the unspoken belief behind the ways in which courts go about disposing of sex and other discrimination cases summarily emerges with clarity.

The time has come to give voice to the unspoken beliefs that underlie the known and lesser-known wrinkles, omissions, and judgment errors in the law and its interpretation by everyone from employers' internal monitors to the highest court in our land. It is now incumbent upon those who care about workplace equality for women to examine the nexus between unspoken and often encountered societal beliefs and injustices in antidiscrimination law and policy. The chapters that follow attempt to explain and illustrate the nexus for each identified pane of the glass ceiling. Each chapter outlines the belief or range of beliefs being discussed, the "pane," or belief-driven behavior that adds to the glass ceiling; the "pain," or type and extent of the harm done to women; manifestations of the belief(s) discussed in other aspects or contexts of society; and takeaways.

This book is not intended to be a tome or a treatise on all of the root causes and phenomena that comprise or contribute to the glass ceiling. There are countless books and articles that powerfully document and illustrate phenomena like subconscious bias, stereotyping, and even misogyny generally. This book is a compilation of several phenomena that have to do with specific acts or omissions of the judiciary, the legislature, and individuals that seem to be the natural outgrowths of beliefs that have been left largely unspoken in polite society. While there are always hate groups and outliers willing to engage in

---

[68] *See, e.g.*, Grady v. Affiliated Cent., Inc., 130 F.3d 553, 560 (2d Cir. 1997) ("[W]hen the person who made the decision to fire was the same person who made the decision to hire, it is difficult to impute to her an invidious motivation that would be inconsistent with the decision to hire."); Bradley v. Harcourt, Brace & Co., 104 F.3d 267, 270–71 (9th Cir. 1996) ("[W]here the same actor is responsible for both the hiring and the firing of a discrimination plaintiff, and both actions occur within a short period of time, a strong inference arises that there was no discriminatory motive."); Proud v. Stone, 945 F.2d 796, 798 (4th Cir. 1991); *see also* Natasha T. Martin, *Immunity for Hire: How the Same-Actor Doctrine Sustains Discrimination in the Contemporary Workplace*, 40 CONN. L. REV. 1117, 1174 (2008).

overtly misogynistic speech, the more invidious beliefs continue to be those more widely held, consciously or subconsciously, but more unvoiced in society.

It is only by tying these beliefs to these often lesser-known catalysts that spark, enable, or sanction sex discrimination in employment that they can be aerated. This is not to say that every judge who employs a judicial "shortcut" that prematurely excises sex discrimination cases from their docket or every legislator who votes against the enactment of an anti-bullying statute in their state subscribes to the beliefs correlated with these actions in this book. But this book does argue that these beliefs are more widely societally-held than one might think, and that they are too often part of the genesis of (or at least coincide with) these various "panes" of the glass ceiling, as societal beliefs silently seep into policy-making. Moreover, there is typically a range in the scope of a belief. For example, although the people who think that some of the biological aspects of pregnancy and childbirth are "disgusting" or "vile" may very well be a small minority, there are likely many more who are uncomfortable or unfamiliar enough with these biological aspects to hold the unspoken expectation that a woman ought to "snap back" to her old self physically and mentally after pregnancy. This range of beliefs has engendered intolerance for any prolonged time or space for new mothers to care for themselves and their babies, and this is reflected in U.S. policy and lack of policy on the issue.

Moreover, it must be recalled that many beliefs, no matter how offensive or inoffensive, are held at a level that is less than conscious. Subconscious biases and prejudice have long been recognized as detrimental to the professional and other well-being of women. Less than consciously-held beliefs are especially pernicious because people may feel unable to speak about them with even those closest to them at work and at home; they may be ashamed to admit to themselves that they harbor them. Advances in technology and psychology alike have led to the advent of online tests that people can use to attempt to measure their subconscious bias, but (1) some beliefs are way more complex than tests like these allow for; and (2) it is likely the case that many of those who harbor the most bias on any level will not willingly take these tests. So, while we will never be able to truly ascertain how pervasive the beliefs discussed in this book are, exploring their very existence is valuable. This can be done by theorizing about their underlying phenomena whose genesis we may not completely under-stand, like those discussed in this book, and by looking for evidence of their manifestation in the news stories and anecdotes that make up every-day life.

As this book was being finished, HuffPost broke a story that went viral in traditional and on social media.[69] Apparently, in June of 2018, which, as HuffPost astutely pointed out, was the "height" of the #MeToo movement, a powerhouse multinational professional services firm hosted a training for some thirty female executives in New Jersey.[70] As the various headlines screamed, this training was rife with "gender stereotypes":[71] it admonished the women, for example, "not to flaunt their bodies"; it focused on "keeping the company's men happy";[72] and was "sexist" to the point of being "rage-inducing."[73]

Leaked to HuffPost by an outraged attendee, the fifty-plus-page presentation that was supposed to cover "leadership and empowerment"[74] was instead riddled with entreaties to women to learn both to conform to what men expected them to be in the workplace (the feminine stereotypes of good grooming and well-fitting clothes) and to acclimate to the male-dominated workplace culture. Indeed, HuffPost reported that an attendee said she felt that the "message was that women will be penalized ... if they don't adhere to feminine characteristics or if they display more masculine traits."[75]

Rife with unfounded and insulting distinctions between men and women, like the metaphor that women's brains soak in information like pancakes in syrup, rendering them incapable of the neat, compartmentalized focus of men, whose waffle-like brains cordon off discrete squares of thought, the presentation was supposed to facilitate women's navigation of the workplace. Instead, it insulted them (an attendee told HuffPost that she was counseled as to how to confront men without seeming too off-putting or threatening); and it patronized them ("signal fitness and wellness"), even as it objectified them

---

[69] Emily Peck, *Women at Ernst & Young Instructed on How to Dress, Act Nicely around Men*, HuffPost (Oct. 21, 2019), https://tinyurl.com/5ddn4pze.

[70] *Id.*

[71] Allana Akhtar, *An Ernst & Young Seminar Reportedly Suggested Women Have Small Brains and Said They Should Avoid Talking to Men Face-to-Face*, Bus. Insider (Oct. 21, 2019, 5:41 PM), www.businessinsider.com/ernst-and-young-reportedly-hosted-a-training-with-gender-stereotypes.

[72] Cory Doctorow, *Ernst and Young Subjected Women Employees to "Training" about Keeping the Company's Men Happy*, Boingboing (Oct. 22, 2019), https://boingboing.net/2019/10/22/gender-essentialism.html.

[73] Lisette Voytko, *"Rage-Inducing": Sexist Ernst & Young Seminar Draws Women's Reactions*, Forbes (Oct. 21, 2019, 2:14 PM), www.forbes.com/sites/lisettevoytko/2019/10/21/sexist-ernst–young-seminar-draws-rage-inducing-reactions/#255b646152fe.

[74] Peck, *supra* note 69.

[75] *Id.*

("[d]on't flaunt your body—sexuality scrambles the mind" and "don't show skin").[76]

The training even went so far as to identify "invisible rules" for the sexes that consisted of pat, gendered generalizations, such as women "wait[ing] their turn [that never comes] and rais[ing] their hands," "speak[ing] briefly" but "often rambl[ing] and miss[ing] the point," and men "speak[ing] at length" and out of conviction.[77] Moreover, woman were instructed as to how they ought to physically approach a man at work so as not to appear too intimidating and disturb his sensibilities, and to work through what might have been meant by or gained from these "invisible rules."[78] As HuffPost reported, it was not readily apparent from the presentation whether these "'rules' [we]re offered as legitimate expectations or false stereotypes."[79]

While the internet continues to balk at the dated advice that HuffPost reported was given at the presentations, there is no denying the fact that men and women have been asked to play by different rules in workplaces across America for as long as women have been in the workplace. To the extent that these rules are tacit, the unspoken beliefs that underlie them are worth exploring, and voicing these unspoken beliefs may just be their vanquishing.

---

[76] *Id.*
[77] *Id.*
[78] *Id.*
[79] *Id.*

1

"We See You Differently Than We See Men" (But)

I managed a busy worksite. One day, a pipe burst, and I needed authorizations and advice to handle the fallout. I called my supervisor, who was at dinner with friends. He seemed put off by my call, even though I was just following protocol. He brushed me off, and when I called back to follow up with a request for more help, he told me that I needed to calm down. I told him that I was quite calm, handling the situation on the ground, but still needed some assistance, as per protocol. He told me that I was being "dramatic," and that I sounded "upset," and really needed to "calm down." His insistence that I calm down when I was not upset actually started to upset me, but I wasn't about to let him see that. It was only when the situation, which was incredibly stressful, had been handled (no thanks to my supervisor), and I was alone, that I allowed myself to get upset. And it was only after I googled the term "gaslighting," when a friend referenced it in terms of her abusive relationship, that I made the connection and started to understand that it had happened to me at work. That day, and countless other times before.

I also realized that my supervisor, who always accused me of being "sensitive" and "dramatic," when I was neither, was really sensitive—quickly backtracking and disclaiming if he gave me a simple compliment so I would know that he meant no harassment by it. It kind of makes me laugh at how not only was he the one who was sensitive and self-protecting, but how aware he was of harassment that could be discerned from a compliment, but how oblivious he seemed to how much his characterizations of me hurt, and how he would probably never levy them at a man.

—*Vanessa, thirty-four, project manager*

THE BELIEF

We begin this book with an unspoken "belief" that is likely subconsciously held; it is most aptly said to be a description of what people often do without realizing or taking responsibility for it – viewing women (and other marginalized groups) through a certain lens. This is typically done in the process of stereotyping them. People may be stereotyped descriptively, whereupon they

29

are seen as being a certain way more readily than are others. This occurs with women when, for example, a woman is perceived as being "pushy" and "abrasive" when she is assertive at work, whereas a man who acts similarly is perceived as being "strong" or "tough." Women may also be stereotyped prescriptively, whereupon they are *expected* or *anticipated* to be a certain way that others are not. This occurs, for example, when a performance review suggests that a female employee is "not that nurturing," in some capacity, but does not even evaluate a similarly situated man for the same characteristic.

And often the whole notion of stereotyped bias goes unspoken. Implicit sex-based bias is pervasive in the American workplace. A recent study indicated that nearly three-quarters of people surveyed associated "men" with words that connote careers, like "work," "profession," and "business," but associated "women" with words that connote domesticity, like "household," or "family."[1] That study revealed that most people similarly connect "men" with roles like "boss," or "CEO," but connect "women" with roles like "assistant" and "secretary."[2]

Moreover, women are not only more likely to be seen in certain ways that men are not or held to different standards than are men when they are displaying essentially the same traits; they are more likely than their male colleagues are to be viewed through the lens of their personalities or how they make those around them feel.[3] This is evidence of an unspoken belief that women are seen differently on many levels and are, in many ways, held accountable for the way in which those around them feel, in a way that men are simply not. Recently, *Fortune* magazine reported that in personnel reviews, 73.53 percent of the feedback about women consisted of personality-based commentary, using terms like "abrasive," "judgmental," and "strident."[4] In contrast, a mere 2 percent of reviews of men included this sort of commentary.[5]

Stereotyping, as a mental process, is not intrinsically a bad thing. People employ stereotypes all the time as a way of organizing the information and images that the world bombards them with on a daily basis and as a way of

---

[1]   Andrea S. Kramer & Alton B. Harris, *Gender Stereotypes and the Biases They Foster against Women in the Workplace*, THOMSON REUTERS (Jan. 13, 2016), www.legalexecutiveinstitute.com/gender-stereotypes-and-the-biases-they-foster-against-women/.

[2]   *Id.*

[3]   Kieran Snyder, *The Abrasiveness Trap: High-Achieving Men and Women Are Described Differently in Reviews.* FORTUNE (Aug. 26, 2014), https://fortune.com/2014/08/26/performance-review-gender-bias/; Zuhairah Washington et al., *Women of Color Get Less Support at Work. Here's How Managers Can Change That*, HARV. BUS. REV. (Mar. 04, 2019), https://hbr.org/2019/03/women-of-color-get-less-support-at-work-heres-how-managers-can-change-that.

[4]   *Id.*

[5]   *Id.*

mediating their experience and encounters with the world so as to make sense of them. In fact, to the extent that the cultivation of some stereotypes and prejudices is, neurophysiologically, a protective mechanism to defend oneself from harm in one's environment, this mechanism is both rational and beneficial.[6] For example, if someone develops an aversion to a certain fruit after having an allergic reaction when eating it, or becomes hyper-vigilant when crossing an intersection that she has seen cars drive aggressively in before, this is because her brain has taken her past experiences and organized them in such a way as to recall and anticipate danger upon encountering certain triggers. Stereotypes can thus serve as useful schemas and frameworks.

However, when stereotypes are applied to groups of people, they often quickly become invidious, as the perceived traits of an "outgroup" can become enhanced to the point of becoming cartoonish and offensive. As the magnified attributes lend a (typically false) sense of predictability to encounters with group members, they often serve to breed contempt.[7] Moreover, because stereotypes inhere in human cognition on any number of levels of consciousness,[8] and because stereotypes create connections between groups of people and characteristics, irrespective of how nefarious or inauthentic they are,[9] it is easy to see how, in the context of employment discrimination, they can reduce individuals to the crudest, most inauthentic, and hollow constructs of themselves. In this way, stereotypes often render misconceived tendencies and attributes of groups both the fomenters and the indicators of discrimination.[10] And, indeed, when members of underrepresented groups in the workplace, like women, are consistently seen through a lens that renders them viewed as irrational, histrionic, or less capable than men, widespread, systemic discrimination, and exclusion will ensue.[11] In the case of women of

---

[6] Jane Simon, *Prejudice: A Dangerous Defense Mechanism*, HUFFPOST, www.huffpost.com/entry/prejudice-a-dangerous-def_b_7913090 (last updated Dec. 6, 2017).

[7] John F. Dovidio & Michelle R. Hebl, Discrimination at the Level of the Individual: Cognitive and Affective Factors, *in Discrimination at Work: The Psychological and Organizational Bases* 11, 16 (Robert L. Dipboye & Adrienne Colella eds., 2005).

[8] *See* Mahzarin R. Banaji & Anthony G. Greenwald, *Implicit Stereotyping and Prejudice*, 7 THE PSYCHOL. OF PREJUDICE 55, 67–68 (Mark P. Zanna & James M. Olson eds., 1994).

[9] Antony Page, *Batson's Blind Spot: Unconscious Stereotyping and the Peremptory Challenge*, 85 B.U.L. REV. 155, 187–88 (2005).

[10] *See* Louk Hagendoorn & Hub Linssen, *Group Goal Attributions and Stereotypes in Five Former Soviet States*, COMPARATIVE PERSPECTIVES ON RACISM 171, 172–73 (Jessika ter Wal & Maykel Verkuyten eds., 2000).

[11] *See* Debra Cassens Weiss, *Why More than 75% of Minority Female Lawyers Leave Law Firms within 5 Years*, A.B.A. J.–L. NEWS NOW (Jul. 22, 2009, 9:41 AM), www.abajournal.com/news/why_more_than_75_of_minority_female_lawyers_leave_law_firms_within_5_years/.

color or other groups who experience intersectionality, this harm will only be magnified.[12]

This discrimination may take many forms, some of which are actionable and some of which are not. Much depends on what is left unspoken versus what is made explicit. So, for example, if a woman is fired by someone who says, "You are fired because women are overemotional, and you are a woman," she will likely have a strong case that will either be settled by an employer or get to a jury. However, if that same woman is fired and told that she is overly emotional, without all of the other dots having been connected, her case will be harder to prove, and will likely be disposed of at the summary judgment stage. Moreover, if she, like Vanessa at the beginning of the chapter, is simply told to "calm down" on a regular basis, she likely will not even see her own situation as coming within the ambit of what is actionable. This can be the case even if she or others do not believe that she is unduly riled up and/or if men are not spoken to in that manner, irrespective of how they act. Nevertheless, being seen through this lens may very well spring from the same stereotyped and prejudicial beliefs as those which, when articulated more explicitly, could render the interaction unlawful, either because it is accompanied by an adverse employment action, like a firing, or because it is intoned repeatedly in a manner that is "severe or pervasive," and thus constitutes sexual harassment. The experience of being seen through this lens, even when the nexus to unlawful stereotyping is less than explicit, can also erode a woman's sense of well-being in the workplace, just as in actionable cases.

THE PANE

There are really two parts to the way in which this "belief" in, or practice of, stereotyping women in the workplace filters into the law and operates to create "panes" of the glass ceiling. First, the actual stereotyping occurs in workplaces, tacit, silent, and sometimes so surreptitious as to render the people doing it oblivious to the fact that they are doing it. Second, the way in which the antidiscrimination laws have been interpreted and applied by courts and the ways that courts do and don't permit sex discrimination cases to be adjudicated allow the stereotyping to elude capture by the law.

---

[12] *Id.*; J. Camille Hall et al., *Black Women Talk about Workplace Stress and How They Cope*, 43 J. OF BLACK STUD. 207, 207–26 (2012); Aisha M. B. Holder et al., *Racial Microaggression Experiences and Coping Strategies of Black Women in Corporate Leadership*, 2 QUALITATIVE PSYCHOL. 164, 164–80 (2015).

Stereotyping in the Workplace

There is a host of academic literature that connects women's underrepresentation everywhere from corporate boards[13] to whole swaths of professions (like those in STEM),[14] to equity and leadership positions in business,[15] medicine,[16] or government,[17] to science – and, specifically, the science of how they are perceived and how that perception affects their treatment at work.[18] In fact, numerous studies have shown that when it comes to raw skill in most areas, as well as some intangibles, like empathy, competitiveness, and affability, which are hard to measure but ingredients for success by most metrics, women score as well as or better than men.[19] However, studies show that when variables are controlled and the only differences among candidates are markers like names, people, from STEM professors[20] to decision-makers in employment, show a bias toward males and maleness.[21]

A 2017 study published in the *Harvard Business Review* sought to draw conclusions from the difference between promotion rates of men and

---

[13]   Neysa Dillon-Brown, *Women and Minorities Are Still Underrepresented in the Boardroom*, CORP. BD. MEMBER (last visited Jan. 12, 2020), https://boardmember.com/women-minorities -underrepresented-board/.

[14]   Whitney H. Beeler, Reshma Jagsi, & Susan L. Solomon, *541 Report Cards Show That Women Are Still Underrepresented in STEM Fields*, STAT (Sept. 5, 2019), www.statnews.com/2019/09/ 05/stem-report-cards-women-underrepresented/.

[15]   Judith Warner, Nora Ellmann, & Diana Boesch, *The Women's Leadership Gap*, CTR. FOR AM. PROGRESS (Nov. 20, 2018), www.americanprogress.org/issues/women/reports/2018/11/20/ 461273/womens-leadership-gap-2/.

[16]   *Research Shows Underrepresentation of Women Continues within Society Presidents*, AM. COLL. OF CARDIOLOGY (Jan. 7, 2019), www.acc.org/latest-in-cardiology/articles/2019/01/07/ 14/50/research-shows-underrepresentation-of-women-continues-within-society-presidents.

[17]   *Women in Government: Quick Take*, CATALYST (Dec. 9, 2019), www.catalyst.org/research/ women-in-government/.

[18]   Stefanie K. Johnson, *What the Science Actually Says about Gender Gaps in the Workplace*, HARV. BUS. REV. (Aug. 17, 2017), https://hbr.org/2017/08/what-the-science-actually-says-about -gender-gaps-in-the-workplace.

[19]   Jack Zenger & Joseph Folkman, *Research: Women Score Higher Than Men in Most Leadership Skills*, HARV. BUS. REV. (Jun. 25, 2019), https://hbr.org/2019/06/research-women- score-higher-than-men-in-most-leadership-skills.

[20]   Corinne A. Moss-Racusin, John F. Dovidio, Victoria L. Brescoll, Mark J. Graham, & Jo Handelsman, *Science Faculty's Subtle Gender Biases Favor Male Students*, PNAS (Oct. 9, 2012), www.pnas.org/content/109/41/16474.full.

[21]   Kramer & Harris, *supra* note 1; Danica Dodds, *Gender Stereotyping in the Workplace and the Discrimination It Creates*, TODAY'S WORKPLACE (Dec. 1, 2006), www.todaysworkplace.org/ 2006/12/01/gender-stereotyping-in-the-workplace-and-the-discrimination-it-creates-danica- dodds/; Zeynep Ilgaz, *Small Ways Leaders Alienate Female Employees through Gender-Biased Criticism*, FORBES (Mar. 3, 2015), www.forbes.com/sites/ellevate/2015/03/03/small-ways- leaders-alienate-female-employees-through-gender-biased-criticism/#63e6f7d66459.

women at a company by looking at the behavior and treatment of promotion candidates employed by a large, multinational firm, whose upper echelons of management were disproportionately occupied by men.[22] Women, by contrast, comprised 35–40 percent of entry-level employees, but a scant 20 percent of the two highest seniority levels of management. The study relied on the collection of data pertaining to workplace meetings and communications, as well as in-person behavior tracking capable of measuring everything from communication patterns to employees' movement and proximity to various other employees.[23]

The study found that whereas the researchers had anticipated that they would find gulfs of difference between the behaviors of the sexes that could arguably predicate outcomes, like being proactive in seeking access to higher-ups, this was not the case.[24] The researchers found that men were promoted more often than women, not due to differences in their behavior, as there were no real differences in behavior, but due to differences in their respective treatment by those situated to mentor and advance them professionally.[25] To illustrate the phenomenon they saw, the researchers provided the example of mentoring programs that aim to facilitate networking between talented female employees and management, and the way in which "[i]f women talk to leadership at similar rates as men, then the problem isn't lack of access but how those conversations are viewed."[26]

This, as the researchers noted, meant that popular appeals, exhortations, and even admonishments issued to women to "lean in," lest they be left behind professionally, may be misplaced and, arguably, unfair.[27] The invisible piece of this is, of course, that women are arguably, as a class, treated differently because they are *perceived* differently, or even viewed through a different lens so that descriptively, and even prescriptively, attributes and attitudes wholly outside of their control are projected onto them, to their detriment.

Stereotypes and the Law

But, the occurrence of stereotyping is only part of the problem. The real problem occurs when the law fails to deal effectively with it. In effect, this

---

[22] Stephen Turban et al., *A Study Used Sensors to Show That Men and Women Are Treated Differently at Work*, HARV. BUS. REV. (Oct. 23, 2017), https://hbr.org/2017/10/a-study-used-sensors-to-show-that-men-and-women-are-treated-differently-at-work
[23] *Id.*
[24] *Id.*
[25] *Id.*
[26] *Id.*
[27] *Id.*

renders all kinds of unspoken beliefs about women – and what they are and aren't and what they should and should not be – potent, and as invincible as they are invisible. After the enactment of Title VII, the law grappled for decades with what it meant to be discriminated against "because of" sex. From the outset, it seemed clear that an admission that a decision-maker was moved to make a decision about a woman because she was a woman and this colored how he saw her ("I didn't choose her because she is a woman, and women can't handle that type of work"), was unlawful under Title VII.

But there were a host of other scenarios about which very little would be clear. What if a commonly invoked trope or stereotype about a protected class was applied to a candidate ("she is too hysterical and sensitive"), but the connection to the class is not explicit? What if an expectation is crafted with an eye toward a sex-based stereotype ("she is not nurturing enough"), but the nexus to the class is tacit? What if a sex-based, stereotyped comment can be written off readily as a simple misspeak ("I said she was too macho, but I just meant that she was abrasive and off-putting to our customers")? Obviously, if a decision-maker admits that he has not judged or would not judge a man similarly, the unlawful disparate treatment is readily apparent and actionable. But what if there are no comparators, because no men are admitted to have been deemed capable of the same judgment ("If I thought a man were too abrasive, I'd fire him too, but I have not seen that")? How explicit do all of the often-unspoken thoughts and connections bound up in a stereotype have to be before the law can start to capture or weigh what is voiced? And what about all that goes unvoiced?

Because unexpressed stereotypes tint the lens with which people view others and taint perceptions as silently as they do invidiously, there are relatively few "stereotyping" cases on the books to begin with. To be sure, some, where the stereotype is expressed and serves as a smoking gun of sorts, most settle quickly so as to ward off an expensive, embarrassing trial. But most are likely simply not brought, either because the employee is unaware that she has been stereotyped or because, although she suspects that she has, she or her attorney knows that there is not enough evidence for a viable case. Where a sex discrimination case is brought with a stereotype that is uttered, but remains somewhat attenuated from the plaintiff's sex, courts are typically not willing to permit the evidence to proceed to a jury.[28]

---

[28] Bianchi v. City of Philadelphia, 183 F. Supp. 2d 726, 736–37 (E.D. Pa. 2002); Betz v. Temple Health Sys., No. 15-cv-00727, 2015 WL 4713661 (E.D. Pa. Aug. 7, 2015).

The Supreme Court Speaks: Hopkins

In 1989, the Supreme Court decided the most famous case to address stereo-typing in the workplace: *Price Waterhouse* v. *Hopkins*.[29] That case centered on Ann Hopkins, who, in 1982 made an unsuccessful bid for partnership at the accounting firm of Price Waterhouse[30] and subsequently resigned from her employment there.[31] The comments and evaluations that undergirded the partnership process showed that those doing the selection found, as they were entitled to do, that Hopkins was difficult to work with. As the Supreme Court stated:

> On too many occasions ... Hopkins' aggressiveness ... spilled over into abrasiveness. Staff members seem to have borne the brunt of [her] brusque-ness. Long before her bid for partnership, partners evaluating her work had counseled her to improve her relations with staff members. Although later evaluations indicate an improvement, [her] perceived shortcomings in this important area eventually doomed her bid for partnership. Virtually all of the partners' negative remarks about Hopkins — even those of partners supporting her — had to do with her "interpersonal skills." Both "[s]upporters and oppon-ents of her candidacy ... indicated that she was sometimes overly aggressive, unduly harsh, difficult to work with and impatient with staff."[32]

However, whether it was a product of the times, the workplace culture of that employer, or both, there was evidence that Hopkins, as a woman, likely had a tougher road to partnership than the men around her. For one thing, at the time, Price Waterhouse had 662 partners nationwide, only 7 of whom were women.[33] For another thing, despite the fact that eighty-eight candidates were proposed for partnership that year, Hopkins was the only woman among them.[34]

Moreover, by many objective measures of success, Hopkins seemed to be the ideal partner. The Supreme Court recalled that the partners from her office, "[i]n a jointly prepared statement supporting her candidacy, ... show-cased her successful 2-year effort to secure a $25 million contract with the Department of State, labeling it 'an outstanding performance' and one that Hopkins carried out 'virtually at the partner level.'"[35] The statement

---

[29] Price Waterhouse v. Hopkins, 490 U.S. 228 (1989).
[30] *Id.* at 233.
[31] *Id.* at 233 n.1.
[32] *Id.* at 233.
[33] *Id.*
[34] *Id.*
[35] *Id.* at 234.

characterized Hopkins as "an outstanding professional" with a "deft touch, strong character, independence and integrity."[36] In fact, even the district judge who adjudicated Hopkins's case initially found that she had "played a key role in Price Waterhouse's successful effort to win a multi-million dollar [*sic*] contract with the Department of State" and that Hopkins "had no difficulty dealing with clients and her clients appear to have been very pleased with her work."[37]

The Supreme Court noted, however, that in written comments about Hopkins's candidacy, "[o]ne partner described her as 'macho'; a second suggested that she 'overcompensated for being a woman'; and a third advised her to take 'a course at charm school.'"[38] Several partners criticized her use of profanity, and another partner posited that those partners objected to this only "because it's a lady using foul language."[39] Even a champion of Hopkins explained that she "ha[d] matured from a tough-talking somewhat masculine hard-nosed mgr [*sic*] to an authoritative, formidable, but much more appealing lady ptr [*sic*] candidate."[40] However, it was, as the Supreme Court recited,

> the man who . . . bore responsibility for explaining to Hopkins the reasons for the Policy Board's decision to place her candidacy on hold who delivered the *coup de grace*: in order to improve her chances for partnership, [he] advised, Hopkins should "walk more femininely, talk more femininely, dress more femininely, wear make-up, have her hair styled, and wear jewelry."[41]

Also working in Hopkins's favor were the district court finding that past partner candidates at Price Waterhouse had been "evaluated in sex-based terms" and a renowned social psychologist's testimony "that the partnership selection process at Price Waterhouse was likely influenced by sex stereotyping."[42] The Court was brought to the inexorable conclusion that unlawful sex stereotyping had seeped into the decision-making process: "Hopkins' uniqueness (as the only woman in the pool of candidates) and the subjectivity of the evaluations made it likely that sharply critical remarks such as these were the product of sex stereotyping . . . ."[43]

Noting that "we are beyond the day when an employer could evaluate employees by assuming or insisting that they matched the stereotype

---

[36] *Id.*
[37] *Id.*
[38] *Id.* at 245.
[39] *Id.*
[40] *Id.*
[41] *Id.*
[42] *Id.* at 236.
[43] *Id.*

associated with their group," the Court emphasized that Congress's intent in enacting Title VII was to "strike at the entire spectrum of disparate treatment of men and women resulting from sex stereotypes." The Court explained: "In the specific context of sex stereotyping, an employer who acts on the basis of a belief that a woman cannot be aggressive, or that she must not be, has acted on the basis of gender." Therefore, the Court noted: "An employer who objects to aggressiveness in women but whose positions require this trait places women in an intolerable and impermissible catch 22: out of a job if they behave aggressively and out of a job if they do not. Title VII lifts women out of this bind."[44]

That said, the Court held that stereotyped comments in the workplace "do not inevitably prove that gender played a part in a particular employment decision."[45] Instead, the plaintiff retains the burden of demonstrating that her employer "actually relied on her gender in making its decision."[46] In Hopkins's case, the Court found that Price Waterhouse was incorrect when it contended that, armed with the comments, all Hopkins could demonstrate, at best, was "discrimination in the air."[47] Rather, the Court observed, this was a case of "discrimination brought to ground and visited upon an employee."[48]

However, the Court did little to refine stereotype doctrine, or when, precisely, reliance on a stereotype in one's comments would yield employer liability. The Court declined to limit the myriad "possible ways of proving that stereotyping played a motivating role in an employment decision," and declined to "decid[e] here which specific facts, 'standing alone, would or would not establish a plaintiff's case . . . .'"[49] In fact, after observing that the expert testimony on stereotyping was "merely icing on Hopkins' cake," the Court took a we'll-know-it-when-we-see-it approach to ascertaining liability from sex stereotyping:

> It takes no special training to discern sex stereotyping in a description of an aggressive female employee as requiring "a course at charm school." Nor, turning to Thomas Beyer's memorable advice to Hopkins, does it require expertise in psychology to know that, if an employee's flawed "interpersonal skills" can be corrected by a soft-hued suit or a new shade of lipstick, perhaps it is the employee's sex and not her interpersonal skills that has drawn the criticism.[50]

---

[44]   *Id.* at 250.
[45]   *Id.* at 251.
[46]   *Id.*
[47]   *Id.* at 241.
[48]   *Id.*
[49]   *Id.* at 251.
[50]   *Id.* at 254.

[E]ven if we knew that Hopkins had "personality problems," this would not tell us that the partners who cast their evaluations of Hopkins in sex-based terms would have criticized her as sharply (or criticized her at all) if she had been a man . . . . We sit not to determine whether Ms. Hopkins is nice, but to decide whether the partners reacted negatively to her personality because she is a woman.[51]

Confusion in the Wake of Hopkins: A Muddled Legacy

Hopkins was a relatively straightforward case of sex-based discrimination. Once one saw the numbers and demographics involved in the case, and once one heard the things that were said in the course of judging the plaintiff's candidacy, this could not be plausibly denied. But more difficult sex discrimination cases abounded, in which there were legitimate questions as to whether the same comment would have been said to a man, or whether what was said to a female plaintiff could have been unfortunately worded and reflect thinking much more innocuous than what she read into it. Once the comments become less heavy-handed and the defendant's employment statistics become less indicative of overall inequality of opportunity, the arguments become more robust and plausible in both directions.

And *Hopkins*, revisited by lower courts armed with little else, didn't offer a lot of clear guidance on how to navigate these murkier waters. These courts seemed to struggle, and continue to struggle with how to apply the law when sex-based stereotyping is alleged. What has resulted is a failure of courts to create, in *Hopkins*'s wake, a coherent legal doctrine of stereotyping evidence that would cement its legacy. There seem to be few, if any, clear-cut rules about how, why, or even when a stereotyped comment can carry a plaintiff past the summary judgment stage of a case. And to underscore this point, one need not look past the fractured opinions of judges adjudicating the same case, whether this takes the form of a majority circuit of appeals court opinion with a strident dissent, or a district court decision that is summarily reversed on appeal due to a contrasting view of the law of stereotyping. A few examples below illustrate this.

Courts have reached results that cannot necessarily be reconciled with one another. Armed with the understanding that the Supreme Court said that sex-stereotyped comments were evidence of discrimination,[52] but apparently unclear as to when a statement derives from a sex stereotype or how much

---

[51] *Id.* at 258.
[52] *Id.* at 256.

other evidence of discrimination is needed for a case to survive summary judgment, courts have come up confused.[53] And they have tended to err on the side of refusing to see the connection between comments and their largely unspoken nexus to sex stereotyping that would evince sex discrimination.[54]

"No Basis to Impute Sex-Bias Based on Words"

In a 2012 First Circuit Court of Appeals case[55] in which the plaintiff posited what she termed evidence of sex stereotyping, she claimed, among other things, "that various officials described [her] as 'fragile,' 'immature,' 'unable to handle complex and sensitive issues,' engaged in 'twisting the truth,' and exhibiting 'lack of judgment.'"[56] The court, however, refused to let her case go to trial, noting that while the words were "admittedly unflattering," they were "without exception gender-neutral."[57]

Similarly, in a 2016 district court case,[58] the plaintiff argued that her employers "unlawfully made stereotypical assumptions about [her] 'interpersonal skills,'" and that their descriptions of her illustrated their "disfavor of assertiveness in female candidates."[59] She alleged that she had been described as "impulsive" and as one who would "challenge a decision," noting a "bias against [her] assertiveness, which would not have been viewed negatively in a male candidate."[60] The court, however, dismissed her case, highlighting her failure to "point[] to any comments . . . of . . . explicit stereotyping."[61]

In a 2011 district court case,[62] the plaintiff, who had been denied a promotion to assistant head custodian by the school district for which she worked because, she was told, she "did not present as an authoritative figure," argued that this "was a veiled way of saying that [the] Plaintiff's appearance was too feminine for a supervisory position."[63] The court, however, rejected

---

[53] *See* Smith v. City of Salem, 378 F.3d 566, 572 (6th Cir. 2004); Evans v. Georgia Regional Hospital, 850 F.3d 1248, 1253 (11th Cir. 2017).

[54] *See, e.g.,* Prowel v. Wise Bus. Forms, Inc., No. 2:06-cv-259, 2007 WL 2702664 (W.D. Pa. Sept. 13, 2007), *affirmed in part, vacated in part, remanded by* Prowel v. Wise Bus. Forms, Inc., 579 F.2d 285 (3d Cir. 2009).

[55] Morales-Cruz v. Univ. of Puerto Rico, 676 F.3d 220, 224–26 (1st Cir. 2012).

[56] *Id.* at 225.

[57] *Id.*

[58] Fanelli v. New York, 200 F. Supp. 3d 363, 374–75 (E.D.N.Y. 2016).

[59] *Id.* at 374.

[60] *Id.*

[61] *Id.*

[62] DeVito v. Valley Stream Central High School Dist. No. 09–CV–0287(JS)(ARL), 2011 WL 3471552 (E.D.N.Y. Aug. 3, 2011).

[63] *Id.*

this theory as being too tacit, noting that what was said did not intimate that the plaintiff was too feminine for the promotion and failed to express a sex stereotype in the way that calling Ann Hopkins "macho" did.[64] Pointing to another case[65] in which a professor whose adverse employment action was accompanied by her being called "nice" and "nurturing" found her case derailed, the court noted that neither these words nor the term "authoritative figure" were "code words for gender bias."[66] Because the stereotypes were left largely unspoken, the allegation of their hanging in the air or coloring the lens through which the plaintiffs were seen would not get to a jury. The court observed "an utter lack of evidence that [the] Defendants actually perceived her as more feminine-appearing than anyone else," and that there was an absence of "testimony from anyone other than herself that [the] Plaintiff . . . embodied an accentuated femininity vis-à-vis the 'matronly' [candidate who got the promotion]."[67]

In another district court case, a state-employed conservation officer alleged that a supervisor said that women were manipulative, and that she, specifically, was manipulative, and that this supervisor had been part of a team that determined that she was to be transferred and disciplined for something.[68] The court rejected her arguments, deciding, among other things, that while the supervisor's "comments may unfairly stereotype women, they are not direct evidence that he intended to discriminate against [her] by transferring or suspending her based on her sex."[69] The court said that infusing a sexist reading into his words would be wrong because the "comment was more critical of [her] specific behavior than of her sex or gender."[70]

The Third Circuit Court of Appeals handily disposed of a case in which the plaintiff claimed he was stereotyped as "'rude' or 'arrogant' or 'self-centered,'" because these "terms do not have any inherent gender-specific meaning, and ascribe no pejorative characteristic to [him] based upon an invidious gender stereotype."[71] And a district court in Connecticut rejected a sex discrimination plaintiff's argument that words used by her supervisors like "'moody[,]' 'difficult to get along with[,]' 'going off on her own[,]' [and] 'doing her own thing'

[64] *Id.* at *3.
[65] Weinstock v. Columbia University, 224 F.3d 33 (2d Cir. 2000).
[66] *Id.* at 44.
[67] *DeVito*, 2011 WL 3471552 at *3 (E.D.N.Y. Aug. 3, 2011).
[68] Miller v. Dep't of Natural Res., 2006 U.S. Dist. LEXIS 23145, at *28 (W.D. Mich. Apr. 24, 2006).
[69] *Id.* at *17.
[70] *Id.* at *29 (citing Lautermilch v. Findlay City Schs., 314 F.3d 271, 276 (6th Cir. 2003)).
[71] Kahan v. Slippery Rock Univ. of Pennsylvania, 50 F. Supp. 3d 667, 690–91 (W.D. Pa. 2014), aff'd, 664 F. App'x 170 (3d Cir. 2016).

[we]re ... stereotypical code words ... frequently used to describe a female working in an all-male environment." The court reasoned that "the stereo-typed remarks in [the plaintiff's cited] cases had plain gender connotations, in contrast with the remarks [she] identifies here."[72]

But even calling someone "macho" is not necessarily enough to compel a court to adjudge the case viable. In 2002, a federal appellate court[73] affirmed the disposal of a case brought by a male substitute teacher who had been fired because decision-makers believed that he was "acting inappropriately with young people, tutoring a female student at his home, telling inappropriate jokes in the classroom, and commenting on the size of a female teacher's breasts," among other inappropriate comments.[74] Upon his termination, he was told by the principal that he was, in fact, "too macho."[75] The court found that, quite simply, when viewed against the backdrop of the plaintiff's mis-deeds, the case could not survive because no reasonable juror could possibly find in his favor.[76]

However, even there, a strident, thoughtful dissent emphasized that rather than being properly characterized as "offhand" by the majority, the "macho" comment was, in fact, potentially quite telling.[77] After all, the dissent reasoned, the word literally meant like "a tough guy," and it explicitly "refers exclusively to behaviors or qualities associated with the male gender."[78] Noting the need to discern sex as a substantial motivating factor in the decision, not whether the plaintiff was an ideal teacher, the dissent likened his case to that of Ann Hopkins, observing that they were both essentially called too manly, and that "[u]nder either scenario the plaintiff is suffering sex discrimination by the application of harmful gender stereotypes."[79]

As shown below, this perspective from the dissent has found favor with some federal judges as well.

"We Can Read between the Lines"

A district court in New York denied a defendant employer summary judgment and allowed a sex discrimination plaintiff's case to advance to a jury for

---

[72] Delgado v. City of Stamford, No. 3:11-CV-01735-VAB, 2015 WL 6675534, at *21 (D. Conn. Nov. 2, 2015).
[73] Lautermilch v. Findlay City Schools, 314 F.3d 271, 273 (6th Cir. 2003).
[74] Id. at 273.
[75] Id. at 274.
[76] Id. at 276.
[77] Lautermilch v. Findlay City Schools, 314 F.3d 271, 276 (6th Cir. 2003) (Moore, J., dissenting).
[78] Id. at 273.
[79] Id. at 278.

a resolution of "legitimate factual questions as to whether [a supervisor] treated female employees differently than males," where there was "third party witness testimony that [he] was dismissive of female branch managers' suggestions," and a note from him in the plaintiff's file in which he "wonder-[ed] whether she manage[d] the branch 'on emotions.'"[80] Clearly, the judge could see how a reasonable juror could infer sex discrimination, even where the supervisor conveyed these unspoken beliefs through stereotypes, rather than stating them explicitly.

In 2009, the Second Circuit Court of Appeals reversed a grant of summary judgment, resurrecting a case in which a supervisor terminating a male employee who had been accused of sexual harassment told him, "[Y]ou probably did what she said you did because you're a male and nobody would believe you anyway."[81] The court there found that the supervisor looked to have "defended his decision to credit [the] allegations of sexual harassment by pointing to the propensity of men, as a group, to sexually harass women."[82] Interestingly, there, the court below had initially summarily disposed of the case, reasoning that the decision had invariably been reached on lawful grounds, and that the comment was, to any reasonable juror, a misspeak or afterthought that could garner no insight into the motivation of the firing.[83] The appellate court, however, saw the sex stereotyping as an integral insight into how the decision had been reached.

Finally, in a 2010 case, the Eighth Circuit held that plaintiff Brenna Lewis's sex discrimination case should have been permitted to proceed to trial where, she claimed, she had performed well at her job as a hotel front desk clerk, only to lose out on a promotion to a full-time front desk position due to unlawful sex stereotyping.[84] Lewis alleged that once supervisors saw her "Ellen DeGeneres kind of look,"[85] which, she said, was "slightly more masculine," word circulated among them that she was not a "'good fit' for the front desk."[86] Ultimately, Lewis alleged, she was believed to "lack[] the 'Midwestern girl

---

[80] Jankousky v. N. Fork Bancorporation, Inc., No. 08 CIV. 1858 PAC, 2011 WL 1118602, at *8 (S.D.N.Y. Mar. 23, 2011).

[81] Sassaman v. Gamache, 566 F.3d 307, 311 (2d Cir. 2009).

[82] *Id.* at 313.

[83] *See* Seim v. Three Eagles Commc'ns, Inc., No. 09-CV-3071-DEO, 2011 WL 2149061, at *3 (N.D. Iowa Jun. 1, 2011); Lewis v. Heartland Inns of Am., L.L.C., 591 F.3d 1033, 1041 (quoting Simmons v. New Pub. Sch. Dist. No. Eight, 251 F.3d 1210, 1214–15 (8th Cir. 2001)); Dawson v. H&H Elec., Inc., No. 4:14CV00583 SWW, 2015 WL 5437101, at *4 (E. D. Ark. Sept. 15, 2015).

[84] *Lewis*, 591 F.3d 1033.

[85] *Id.* at 1036.

[86] *Id.*

look'" needed for the job, and fired for not being "pretty" enough.[87] Her legal argument was that her employer imposed a tacit requirement "that a female employee conform to gender stereotypes."[88]

The district court below,[89] however, had initially disposed of the case, noting that Lewis could not show any men who had been adjudged differently than she had on her suitability for the job. The Court of Appeals, however, resurrected the case, comparing Lewis to Ann Hopkins and noting that, like Hopkins, "Lewis alleges that her employer found her unsuited for her job not because of her qualifications or her performance on the job, but because her appearance did not comport with its preferred feminine stereotype."[90] It held that *Hopkins* had established the unlawfulness of adverse employment actions premised on an employee's "gender non-conforming behavior and appearance."[91] However, one of the three judges on the appellate panel dissented, maintaining that the holding of *Hopkins* had been distorted by the majority's reading and application of it.[92] The judge noted that "an employer's decision to hire or fire based on a person's physical appearance is not discrimination 'because of . . . sex' unless it is a pretext for disadvantaging women candidates."[93]

The divergence of judges, even when working on the same case, as to how and when to properly read *Hopkins* as aiding a plaintiff adducing evidence of sex-stereotyping shows just how muddled the legacy of this case remains.

Sexual Orientation and Gender Nonconformity Cases Highlight Courts' Temporary Confusion about Hopkins's Legacy

Brenna Lewis's case may exemplify some of the dynamics of sex discrimination cases brought by LGBTQIA+ community members under a sexual nonconformity/stereotyping theory. While nothing was said regarding Ms. Lewis's sexuality or LGBTQIA+ status, the Court of Appeals did note:

> Lewis describes her own appearance as "slightly more masculine," and [it has been] characterized [] as "an Ellen DeGeneres kind of look." Lewis prefers to wear loose fitting clothing, including men's button[-]down shirts and slacks.

---

[87] *Id.* at 1039.
[88] *Id.* at 1038.
[89] Lewis v. Heartland Inns of Am., L.L.C. 585 F. Supp. 2d 1046 (S.D. Iowa 2008).
[90] *Lewis*, 591 F.3d at 1038.
[91] *Id.* at 1039.
[92] *Id.* at 1043 (Loken, J., dissenting).
[93] *Id.* at 1043.

She avoids makeup and wore her hair short at the time. Lewis has been mistaken for a male and referred to as "tomboyish."[94]

Many female members of the LGBTQIA+ community who have brought sex discrimination suits have described themselves as having been discriminated against for being more masculine-looking, among other things.[95] Prior to the 2020 Supreme Court case *Bostock v. Clayton County*, the question of whether discrimination because of LGBTQIA+ class status amounted to discrimination because of sex starkly divided courts.[96] Many courts, as one court put it, "routinely rejected attempts to use a sex-stereotyping theory to bring under Title VII what is in essence a claim for discrimination on the basis of sexual orientation."[97] Other courts, however, instead of seeing these claims as an attempt to bootstrap around the contours of Title VII, saw sex-stereotyping theory as the perfect vehicle for many of these plaintiffs,[98] whose narratives do not read much differently from that of Ann Hopkins's, in terms of their having been harassed and discriminated against for being too feminine for men or too masculine for women.

On June 15, 2020, the Supreme Court held in *Bostock* that an employer who terminates an employee because she is homosexual or transgender violates Title VII's prohibition against discrimination "because of" sex.[99] To employers who have tried to argue that discrimination against individuals because of their sexual orientation or gender nonconformity is not discrimination because of sex, the Court responded plainly that it is, irrespective of "what an employer might call its discriminatory practice, how others might label it, or what else might motivate it."[100] As the Court reasoned, it is an impossible task to explain sexual orientation or transgender discrimination without making explicit reference to individuals' sex status.[101] Because of the evolution of antidiscrimination jurisprudence, this conclusion was virtually inevitable.

---

[94] *Id.* at 1036.
[95] *See, e.g.*, Doe v. Casino, 381 F. Supp. 3d 425, 437 (E.D. Pa. 2019).
[96] Evans v. Georgia Regional Hospital, 850 F.3d 1248 (11th Cir. 2017).
[97] Pambianchi v. Arkansas Tech Univ., 95 F. Supp. 3d 1101, 1114 (E.D. Ark. 2015) (citing Vickers v. Fairfield Med. Ctr., 453 F.3d 757, 763 (6th Cir. 2006)); Dawson v. Bumble & Bumble, 398 F.3d 211, 218 (2d Cir. 2005); Bibby, 260 F.3d at 264; Spearman v. Ford Motor Co., 231 F.3d 1080, 1085–87 (7th Cir. 2000).
[98] *See* Smith v. City of Salem 378 F.3d 566 (6th Cir. 2004); Valentine Ge v. Dun & Bradstreet, Inc., No. 6:15-CV-1029-ORL-41GJK, 2017 U.S. Dist. LEXIS 9497, 2017 WL 347582, at *4 (M.D. Fla. Jan. 24, 2017); Lopez v. River Oaks Imaging & Diagnostic Grp., Inc., 542 F. Supp. 2d 653, 660 (S.D. Tex. 2008).
[99] Bostock v. Clayton Cty., No. 17–1618, 2020 WL 3146686, at *18 (U.S. Jun. 15, 2020).
[100] *Id.* at *2.
[101] *Id.* at *13.

Courts' Rejection of Social Framework Evidence

Another layer of this "pane" of the glass ceiling is packaged in the form of courts' rejection of something called social framework evidence. Essentially, when decision-makers persist in seeing women (or any protected class) differently, but without being explicit, a culture of subtle and silent discrimination can pervade a workplace. What can happen is that women are habitually passed over for promotion or other opportunities, held to different or double standards, and relegated to certain assignments, roles, and interactions in the workplace.[102] Because stereotyping often happens so wordlessly and through the prism of what looks like legitimate, thoughtful determinations ("We picked the best people for the committee"; "She didn't come across as well as he did"; "He just happened to hit it off with that client/mentor/partner"), the discriminatory culture may not be discernible until you pull back and take in the big picture.

And as long as there is no "smoking gun" and there is plausibility behind each discrete decision, it may not be ascertainable to a court adjudicating any singular case that anything is amiss. Yes, the law recognizes the cognizability of so-called systemic disparate treatment, and it dispenses with the intent requirement in the case of disparate impact cases; but both of those kinds of claims require the plaintiff or plaintiffs to set forth a discrete policy or practice that engendered the discrimination of which they complain. And, yes, plaintiffs may join together to bring a class action suit; but, to be certified as a class, plaintiffs must posit commonalities in the law or facts that unite their cases.

But what happens when types of decisions and decision-makers themselves are spread out across a company, or even across the country, and identifying one concrete policy or practice with precision is not possible? What happens when a diffuse array of inequities and indignities stems from widespread, tacit stereotyping that has silently seeped into a corporate or workplace culture?

In 2001, a woman named Betty Dukes filed a class action lawsuit against Walmart, the country's largest employer, on behalf of herself and women who worked for Walmart across the country and across various professional levels of promotion.[103] They alleged that structurally and culturally ingrained bias pervaded Wal-Mart's corporate culture and systemically hindered their advancement, retention, and pay equality at Walmart.[104] Specifically, they

---

[102] *See* Danielle D. Dickens & Ernest L. Chavez, *Navigating the Workplace: The Costs and Benefits of Shifting Identities at Work among Early Career U.S. Black Women*, 78 Sex Roles 760–74 (2018).

[103] Dukes v. Wal-Mart Stores, Inc., 603 F.3d 571 (9th Cir. 2010).

[104] *Id.*

alleged that female employees were routinely passed over for promotions and raises that they should have been awarded.[105] The plaintiffs argued "that their local managers' discretion over pay and promotions is exercised disproportionately in favor of men, leading to an unlawful disparate impact on female employees."[106] Wal-Mart, however, claimed that the class ought not be certified because the plaintiffs could not show that a single corporate policy impacted the whole putative class.[107] To counter, the plaintiffs sought to introduce the testimony of an organizational psychologist who could point to the structural and organizational mechanisms by which the discrimination took place, such as the wide discretion afforded supervisors in compensation and promotion decisions.[108]

The case made its way all the way up to the Supreme Court on appeal, but it was eventually dismissed in 2011 because, as the Supreme Court saw it:

> The crux of this case is commonality—the rule requiring a plaintiff to show that "there are questions of law or fact common to the class." ... Commonality requires the plaintiff to demonstrate that the class members "have suffered the same injury" .... Their claims must depend upon a common contention—for example, the assertion of discriminatory bias on the part of the same supervisor. That common contention, moreover, must be of such a nature that it is capable of class wide resolution—which means that determination of its truth or falsity will resolve an issue that is central to the validity of each one of the claims in one stroke .... Here respondents wish to sue about literally millions of employment decisions at once. Without some glue holding the alleged reasons for all those decisions together, it will be impossible to say that examination of all the class members' claims for relief will produce a common answer to the crucial question why was I disfavored.[109]

Moreover, when the plaintiffs tried to argue that they opposed Wal-Mart's corporate policy of affording discretion to make employment decisions to its supervisors, the Supreme Court called this "just the opposite of a uniform employment practice that would provide the commonality needed for a class action," because it was "a policy against having uniform employment practices," and, in actuality, a quite "common and presumptively reasonable way of doing business—one that ... 'should itself raise no inference of

---

[105] *Id.*
[106] Wal-Mart Stores, Inc. v. Dukes, 564 U.S. 338, 345 (2011).
[107] *Id.*
[108] *Id.*
[109] *Id.* at 339, 352 338.

discriminatory conduct.'"[110] In other words, scattered amidst widespread and virtually unfettered discretion to make decisions, an allegedly culturally ingrained, stereotype-based systemic bias could not be put on trial at all, let alone successfully vanquished by the law. Since the alleged stereotyping went on in many people's heads across time, space, and contexts, it derived invincibility from its invisibility.

The plaintiffs had tried to present evidence that would backlight what they alleged were these near-invisible threads that interlaced to create the corporate culture in which they were submerged. To do this, they presented what they called a "social framework analysis," conducted by a sociologist, Dr. William Bielby, who, as the Supreme Court described it, looked at "Wal–Mart's 'culture' and personnel practices," and "[r]elying on 'social framework' analysis, . . . testified that Wal-Mart has a 'strong corporate culture,' that makes it 'vulnerable' to 'gender bias.'"[111]

The Supreme Court, however, rejected this analysis, observing that Dr. Bielby failed to "determine with any specificity how regularly stereotypes play a meaningful role in employment decisions at Wal-Mart," and, "[a]t his deposition[,] . . . conceded that he could not calculate whether 0.5 percent or 95 percent of the employment decisions at Wal-Mart might be determined by stereotyped thinking."[112] The Supreme Court concluded:

> Bielby's testimony does nothing to advance [the] respondents' case, because "whether 0.5 percent or 95 percent of the employment decisions at Wal-Mart might be determined by stereotyped thinking" is the essential question on which respondents' theory of commonality depends. If Bielby admittedly has no answer to that question, we can safely disregard what he has to say. It is worlds away from "significant proof" that Wal-Mart "operated under a general policy of discrimination."[113]

---

[110]   *Id.* at 355.

[111]   *Id.* at 354.

[112]   *Id.*

[113]   *Id; see also* Annika L. Jones, *Implicit Bias as Social-Framework Evidence in Employment Discrimination*, 165 PENN. L. REV. 1221 (2017); Roger W. Reinsch & Sonia Goltz, *You Can't Get There from Here: Implications of the Wal-Mart v. Dukes Decision for Addressing Second-Generation Discrimination*, 9 NW. J.L. & SOC. POL'Y 264, 274 (2014) ("Prior to Dukes, social framework testimony had been used in many types of discrimination cases, and social science experts were key in providing evidence of commonality for class certification. The Supreme Court's rejection of the social framework testimony was a big blow to the viability of class action discrimination suits. After Dukes, courts are less likely to accept general evidence of bias as a basis for fulfilling the commonality requirement mandated in Rule 23(a)(2)."); Megan Whitehill, *Better Safe Than Subjective: The Problematic Intersection of Pre-hire Social Networking Checks and Title VII Employment Discrimination*, 85 TEMP. L. REV. 229 (2012); Melissa Hart & Paul M. Secunda, *A Matter of Context: Social Framework Evidence*

The Supreme Court essentially did away with a type of evidence and of analysis that could have proven useful in this case and others. This is unfortunate because social framework evidence had the potential to really help a trier grapple with the enormity of the looming invisible shadow that is stereotyping embedded in corporate culture. In fact, the Supreme Court was explicit not only in its rejection of the speculation necessarily wrapped up in social framework theory and testimony, but also of the idea that the pervasive stereotyping alleged to have embedded itself in the corporate culture could have existed at all, stating: "In a company of Wal-Mart's size and geographical scope, it is quite unbelievable that all managers would exercise their discretion in a common way without some common direction."[114] The Supreme Court also took note of the criticism that Dr. Bielby's work received "from the very scholars on whose conclusions he relies for his social-framework analysis."[115]

With the social framework theory testimony off the table, the Supreme Court went on to reject the plaintiffs' proffer of statistical evidence because "[m]erely showing that [a] policy of discretion has produced an overall sex-based disparity does not suffice," since "[o]ther than the bare existence of delegated discretion, [the plaintiffs] have identified no 'specific employment practice'—much less one that ties all their 1.5 million claims together."[116] It observed that, invariably, "[s]ome managers will claim that the availability of women, or qualified women, or interested women, in their stores' area does not mirror the national or regional statistics. And almost all of them will claim to have been applying some sex-neutral, performance-based criteria—whose nature and effects will differ from store to store."[117] The Supreme Court rejected the anecdotal evidence as well, noting that "about 1 affidavit for every 12,500 class members—relating to only some 235 out of Wal-Mart's 3,400 stores," was simply too diffuse and insignificant to "demonstrate that the entire company 'operates under a general policy of discrimination.'"[118]

The Supreme Court, however, was sharply divided on the question of this putative class's commonality. Justice Ginsburg, in a partial dissent, observed that the plaintiffs' evidence "suggests that gender bias suffused Wal-Mart's company culture," and that "[m]anagers, like all humankind, may be prey to

---

in *Employment Discrimination Class Actions*, 78 Fordham L. Rev. 37 (2009), available at http://scholar.law.colorado.edu/articles/253.
[114] Wal-Mart Stores, Inc. v. Dukes, 564 U.S. 338, 356 (2011).
[115] *Id.* at 346.
[116] *Id.* at 357.
[117] *Id.*
[118] *Id.* at 358 n.9.

biases of which they are unaware."[119] "The risk of discrimination is heightened when those managers are predominantly of one sex, and are steeped in a corporate culture that perpetuates gender stereotypes."[120]

Very few cases since *Dukes* have even referenced social framework evidence, though some have been receptive to it.[121] Many plaintiffs, however, have seen their proffered social framework theory evidence rejected, often with nods to *Dukes*.[122] These include a case in which the lead plaintiff alleged that her employer essentially ran a "boys' club" at work.[123] Courts remain relatively divided about the admissibility of social framework testimony,[124] with *Dukes* having dealt it a heavy blow, though the case left it theoretically available going forward. A new lawsuit filed by nearly 100 female past and present employees of Wal-Mart on February 1, 2019, alleges that the company has abused and discriminated against them, and withheld raises and promotions from them.[125] Many of these women were part of the originally proposed class in *Dukes*.[126]

---

[119]   *Id.* at 371 (Ginsburg, J., dissenting).

[120]   *Id.* at 373 (Ginsburg, J., dissenting).

[121]   *See, e.g.,* Van v. Ford Motor Co., No. 14-CV-8708, 2018 WL 4635649, at *13 (N.D. Ill. Sept. 27, 2018).

[122]   Kassman v. KPMG LLP, 416 F. Supp. 3d 252, 258 (S.D.N.Y. 2018), *leave to appeal denied,* No. 18–3728, 2019 WL 2498769 (2d Cir. Mar. 19, 2019) ("As Plaintiffs provide insufficient evidence of 'some glue' holding together the reasons for the countless individual employment decisions they challenge, the motion for class certification is denied."); Maciel v. Thomas J. Hastings Properties, Inc., No. CV 10–12167-JCB, 2012 WL 13047595, at *5 (D. Mass. Nov. 30, 2012).

[123]   Lindsley v. Omni Hotels Mgmt. Corp., No. 3:17-CV-2942-B, 2019 WL 2743892, at *12 (N.D. Tex. Jul. 1, 2019).

[124]   *See* Childers v. Trustees of the Univ. of Pennsylvania, No. CV 14–2439, 2016 WL 1086669, at *5–6 (E.D. Pa. Mar. 21, 2016) ("Courts are divided about whether testimony of this type is admissible or not. On the one hand, those that exclude it tend to reason that general testimony on stereotyping does not 'fit' the case closely enough and that laboratory findings about unconscious stereotyping are too far removed from carefully considered employment decisions to be helpful to juries."); *see also* Karlo v. Pittsburgh Glass Works, LLC, 2:10-cv-1283, 2015 WL 4232600 (W.D. Pa. Jul. 13, 2015); EEOC v. Bloomberg L.P., No. 07–8383, 2010 WL 3466370, at *16 (S.D.N.Y. Aug. 31, 2015) (showing that courts that allow social stereotyping testimony note that jurors are not necessarily knowledgeable about stereotyping and what factors can facilitate impermissible stereotyping and hold that the testimony can give jurors a context within which to evaluate the evidence); Merrill v. M.I.T.C.H. Charter Sch. Tigard, 2001 WL 1457461 (D. Or. Apr. 4, 2011).

[125]   Chavie Lieber, *Walmart Just Got Hit with a Major Gender Discrimination Lawsuit,* Vox (Feb. 15, 2019), www.vox.com/the-goods/2019/2/15/18223752/walmart-gender-discrimination-class-action-lawsuit-2019.

[126]   *Id.*

THE PAIN/MANIFESTATIONS

The pain of stereotyping is plain to see. It pervades individual decision-making and workplace cultures alike. The ABA Journal website has reported that nearly 75 percent of female lawyers of color leave their law firms within five years of commencing work because of challenges like "unwanted or unfair critical attention" and institutional discrimination.[127] As these women reported, this discrimination resulted in things like their being denied opportunities to get things like high-profile assignments and important client engagements.[128]

The pain of courts' difficulty construing *Hopkins* is readily discernible as well. In most cases, stereotyped thoughts are likely not voiced because they are considered taboo. In the infrequent instances in which they are voiced, many courts are too willing to discount stereotyped remarks brought to them by plaintiffs as "stray," or somehow unintended misspeaks that do not reflect the speaker's mindset. This brushing off of potentially actionable comments effectively kills the claim and prevents a trier from using the comments as a potential window into what occurred. This conveys a strong message.

This may seem axiomatic – that the law should not permit cases to go forward where there is no concrete evidence of unlawful stereotyping except that which the plaintiffs ask to be read into ostensibly neutral descriptions or characterizations. "She is very abrasive." "He lacks motivation." To be sure, where the plaintiff can establish that certain characteristics are consistently attributed to members of the same protected class by the decision-maker, there should be more consideration given to the weight of that evidence than often is.[129]

But, more often than not, practicalities intervene with such a strategy. Comparators who are seen as precisely similarly situated to plaintiffs are often hard to come by, and courts often require very high levels of precision when plaintiffs attempt to posit comparators. Furthermore, it is often not the case that the same decision-maker is involved in enough of the same stereotype-driven adverse actions or ousters from a single employer, as different employees are evaluated by different supervisors.[130] Finally, where knowledge

---

[127] Weiss, *supra* note 11.

[128] *Id.*

[129] *See* Michael J. Zimmer, *The Emerging Uniform Structure of Disparate Treatment Discrimination Litigation*, 30 GA. L. REV. 563, 619–21 (1996).

[130] *See, e.g.*, Amirmokri v. Baltimore Gas & Elec. Co., 60 F.3d 1126, 1130 (4th Cir. 1995) (indicating that hirer-firer identity was satisfied if the same company was involved in both decisions); Lowe v. J.B. Hunt Transport, Inc., 963 F.2d 173, 174 (8th Cir. 1992) (considering evidence that

of the law and social pressure have pushed discrimination deeper under-
ground and where savvy people will typically not voice the entirety of
a stereotype, so as not to run afoul of the law, deployed stereotypes will more
often be unvoiced or partially voiced than explicitly stated.

Courts' resistance to social framework evidence is problematic as well.
Many times, plaintiffs are being discriminated against because of sex, but
there is no one smoking gun or singular practice to point to. So long as
decision-makers are diffused across corporate, geographic, or other boundaries, there is no concrete, discrete practice, policy, or systemic mechanism
to attack. So long as the complaints vary and range from non-promotions to
unequal pay, to harassment, there is no reason why a court should not insist
that each claim be made to stand or fall in a factual vacuum, devoid of
context. So long as discrimination is subtle and stereotyped beliefs go
unvoiced and the courts refuse to permit a jury to even opt to make the
inferential leap to a finding of discrimination, cases are not filed, or are
doomed to fail.

Scholars have observed that the conflict between those who would advance
social framework testimony and those who would see it as too limited to be
probative is emblematic of the larger debate surrounding the regulation of
workplace discrimination: prescriptively, should the law attempt to capture
bias that is unvoiced, less than conscious, or otherwise too subtle to yield the
concrete, "smoking gun" evidence that many would like to see required?[131]
Stereotyping is very often, as discussed, too difficult to prove under existing
law, and even when potentially insight-yielding words are uttered, if they are
not explicit or well-timed enough, the strictures of the law, as it is currently
interpreted, typically dispose of the cases.

Sometimes, the only way to get to the truth is to look at the larger, integrated
picture. This is where social framework evidence could come into play. This
evidence, typically consisting of an expert brought into a case to supplement
its record with testimony, is not about the case's own facts. Rather, it is about,
as one judge recited, "general social science research on the operation of
stereotyping and bias in decision making and [the court] will examine the
policies and practices operating in the workplace at issue to identify those that
research has shown will tend to increase or limit the likely impact of these

the "same people" or "same company officials" hired and fired the plaintiff in less than two
years "compelling . . . in light of the weakness of the plaintiff's evidence otherwise"); *see also*
Natasha T. Martin, *Immunity for Hire: How the Same-Actor Doctrine Sustains Discrimination
in the Contemporary Workplace*, 40 CONN. L. REV. 1117 n.68 (2008).
[131]   Hart & Secunda, *supra* note 113, 39–70.

factors."[132] Because of the expert's dearth of first-hand knowledge of the specific workplace at issue, some judges and scholars have become ardent opponents of this evidence's admission. However, some judges have touted this evidence as invaluable, especially in the context of class action litigation. They value the evidence's ability to inform and animate the triers' understanding of the evidence of the large-scale culture and dynamics of the workplace, so as to possibly help them discern unlawful motivations where they are suppressed or otherwise unspoken.

TAKEAWAYS

Psychologist John Bargh has said that "stereotypes are categories that have gone too far."[133] They are not intrinsically bad things, but they can be catastrophic in the workplace. There are no truly simple solutions to the intractable problem of stereotyping pervading the culture of a workplace, and the separate problem of what the law is to do with allegations that this occurred.

Scrubbing a workplace of stereotypes may not be entirely possible. Numerous researches examining stereotypes have found them to be "sticky," noting that sensitivity exercises or trainings often prove ineffective, and can even backfire by stoking resentment, especially if they are compulsory.[134] Behavioral economist Iris Bohnet has advocated for sweeping, systemic change among employers who want to ensure a diverse workplace as free as possible from the intrusion of bias, like overhauling educational and job performance assessments and revamping hiring practices and protocols.[135] Indeed, trainings and bias reduction programs are tempting resorts, but diversity training alone may be ineffective; studies and anecdotal reports have concluded that compulsory training alone may fail if the stereotype persists outside of the workplace.[136]

[132] Phipps v. Wal-Mart Stores, Inc., No. 3:12–01009, 2016 WL 10649206, at *3 (M.D. Tenn. Nov. 18, 2016).

[133] Annie Murphy Paul, *Where Bias Begins: The Truth about Stereotypes*, PSYCHOL. TODAY (May–Jun. 1998) at 53 (quoting John Bargh).

[134] Tiina Likki, *Why Gender Stereotypes Are So Hard to Fight at Work*, WORKPLACE (Jun. 29, 2018), https://greatergood.berkeley.edu/article/item/why_gender_stereotypes_are_so_hard_to_fight_at_work.

[135] Alisa Yu, *How Can Organizations Promote Gender Equality? Iris Bohnet on "What Works,"* BEHAVIORAL SCIENTIST (May 3, 2016), https://behavioralscientist.org/how-can-organizations-promote-gender-equality-iris-bohnet-on-what-works/.

[136] Julia Carpenter, *When Workplace Trainings Can Backfire*, CNN MONEY (Jan. 29, 2018, 2:01 PM), https://money.cnn.com/2018/01/29/pf/diversity-harassment-trainings/index.html.

That is, when such training is even permitted. In mid-2020, while the country was still reeling from the coronavirus pandemic and the horrific murders and injustices that helped to propel the Black Lives Matter movement into the national spotlight, President Trump issued an Executive Order that actually prohibited executive departments and agencies, uniformed services, federal contractors, and federal grant recipients from running or participating in what he termed "divisive" diversity training. Specifically critical of how the supposed "different vision of America that is grounded in hierarchies based on collective social and political identities rather than in the inherent and equal dignity of every person as an individual," the Order sought to erase notions of white privilege, critical race theory, and unconscious bias from the curricula of government contractors. Violators face contracts that can be "canceled, terminated, or suspended in whole or in part and the contractor may be declared ineligible for further Government contracts."

The spring and summer of 2020 had seen the abject, ineffable anguish of the murders of George Floyd, Breonna Taylor, and so many others, as well as other horrific racial injustices against African Americans, precipitate an outpouring of pain and anger in response. On the heels of this unrest came even more waves of violence and discrimination directed at Asian Americans.[137] Many have noted the cruel irony to silencing discussion about promoting the reckonings that could help advance and engender racial and other equality.[138]

One strategy deployed by attorneys in cases in which very subtle or ineffable stereotyping is believed to be at play has been asking the court to take judicial notice of the connection between a protected class and a negative stereotypical attribute. Judicial notice is a court's acknowledgment of the existence of a fact or phenomenon, outside of the record of a given case. This is not unprecedented. The Second Circuit has taken judicial notice of the "demeaning ethnic stereotype that Jews are 'cheap.'"[139] With a reference to *Hopkins*,

---

[137]   Kimmy Yam, *Anti-Asian Hate Crimes Increased by Nearly 150% in 2020, Mostly in N.Y. and L.A., New Report Says*, NBC NEWS (Mar. 9, 2021, 3:37 PM), www.nbcnews.com/news/asian-america /anti-asian-hate-crimes-increased-nearly-150-2020-mostly-n-n1260264; FACT SHEET: ANTI-ASIAN PREJUDICE MARCH 2020, CALIFORNIA STATE UNIVERSITY, SAN BERNADINO: CENTER FOR THE STUDY OF HATE & EXTREMISM, www.csusb.edu/sites/default/files/ FACT%20SHEET-%20Anti-Asian%20Hate%202020%203.2.21.pdf (last visited Aug. 23, 2021).

[138]   *See, e.g.*, Matthew S. Schwartz, *Trump Tells Agencies to End Trainings on "White Privilege" and "Critical Race Theory,"* NPR (Sep. 5, 2020, 4:31 PM), www.npr.org/2020/09/05/9100534 96/trump-tells-agencies-to-end-trainings-on-white-privilege-and-critical-race-theor.

[139]   Back v. Hastings on Hudson Union Free Sch. Dist., 365 F.3d 107, 120 n.10 (2d Cir. 2004) (quoting Mandell v. Cty. of Suffolk, 316 F.3d 368, 378 (2d Cir. 2003)).

a district court in the Second Circuit has noted: "'Just as "[i]t takes no special training to discern sex stereotyping in a description of an aggressive female employee as requiring 'a course at charm school,' so it takes no special training to discern stereotyping" and disapproval in the view that a Jewish doctor's success is attributable to conspiratorial clannishness rather than to his own individual work.'"[140]

With the same reference, the Second Circuit has observed: "Just as '[i]t takes no special training to discern sex stereotyping in a description of an aggressive female employee as requiring "a course at charm school',"... so it takes no special training to discern stereotyping in the view that a woman cannot 'be a good mother' and have a job that requires long hours, or in the statement that a mother who received tenure 'would not show the same level of commitment [she] had shown because [she] had little ones at home.'"[141] In fact, numerous federal judges across the country have taken judicial notice of the fact that childcare responsibilities within a family have been ascribed to women, stereotypically, by society in order to carve out Title VII protection for the subset of women that have small children.[142] Even the Supreme Court has observed that the FMLA was enacted because "stereo-type-based beliefs about the allocation of family duties remained firmly rooted [in society]."[143]

On the other hand, judges have found that remarks alleged to be stereotyped required too much of an inferential leap to even put before a jury. The Second Circuit refused to let a female professor denied tenure take her case to a jury where she alleged that, among other things, the use of the words "nice" and "nurturing" to describe her were stereotyped and coded, reflective of the biased lens through which they saw and dismissed her.[144] The court found that these were "simply not qualities that are stereotypically female."[145] While the dissent favored looking at the larger context of how and when women were

---

[140] Sandler v. Montefiore Health Sys., Inc., No. 16-CV-2258 (JPO), 2018 WL 4636835, at *8 (S.D. N.Y. Sept. 27, 2018) (quoting Price Waterhouse v. Hopkins, 490 U.S. 228, 256 (1989)).

[141] Back v. Hastings on Hudson Union Free Sch. Dist., 365 F.3d 107, 119–21 (2d Cir. 2004).

[142] Zambrano-Lamhaouhi v. New York City Bd. of Educ., 866 F. Supp. 2d 147, 172 (E.D.N.Y. 2011) (citing cases that have "taken judicial notice of the real-world prevalence of the stereotype that pregnant women and young mothers will make undesirable employees," and noting that "The frequency of such stereotypes has been confirmed in numerous studies."); Chadwick v. WellPoint, Inc., 561 F.3d 38, 48 (1st Cir. 2009) (invoking the "common stereotype about the job performance of women with children."); Santiago–Ramos v. Centennial P.R. Wireless Corp., 217 F.3d 46, 57 (1st Cir. 2000); Sheehan v. Donlen Corp., 173 F.3d 1039, 1044–45 (7th Cir. 1999).

[143] Hibbs, 538 U.S. at 730, 123 S. Ct. 1972.

[144] Weinstock v. Columbia Univ., 224 F.3d 33, 44–45 (2d Cir. 2000).

[145] *Id.* at 44.

promoted at the university and permitting a jury to take a nuanced look at her claim, the court clung to very literal, unnuanced meanings of these words, claiming:

> Any reasonable person of either sex would like to be considered "nice," .... Nor can "nurturing" possibly be the basis for a Title VII action. The two primary definitions of the verb "nurture" are "to supply with food, nourishment, and protection" and "to train by or as if by instruction." Webster's Third International Dictionary (1961). These are definitions that are in no way stereotypically female. ... It is simply not objectively reasonable to label these innocuous words as semaphores for discrimination. To do so would preclude tenure committees from ever discussing a candidate's positive personal attributes as a teacher. Niceness and nurturing are not, after all, bad qualities to have in a teacher's mentoring capacity—particularly of undergraduates.[146]

A district court in Illinois declined a race discrimination plaintiff's request to acknowledge and give voice to the abhorrent "stereotype of African-Americans" as "a lazy people who prefer the dole to work."[147] The court recited the Federal Rule of Evidence's mandate that it only "take judicial notice of a fact 'not subject to reasonable dispute in that it is either (1) generally known within the territorial jurisdiction of the trial court or (2) capable of accurate and ready determination by resort to sources whose accuracy cannot reasonably be questioned.'"[148] The court did this in the course of inexplicably determining that while the comment that an employer was "going to fire your black ass, you're defrauding the government," was "offensive," it failed to help prove that the termination was because of race.[149] Interestingly, the Second Circuit refused to credit the stereotype that a woman dressed in pants is dressed "more masculinely."[150] Courts can and should be better when it comes to the integration of real world behavior, sentiment, and nuance in existing legal frameworks.

At the end of the day, courts' selectiveness and rigidity when it comes to allowing the unspoken nuance, tone, and meaning of stereotyped comments to help propel a case to a jury hinder Title VII's ability to effectuate equality. Courts' taking judicial notice of the fact that certain "benign" or "innocuous" words can, in certain contexts, help establish discrimination would be very

---

[146] *Id.* at 44.
[147] Johnson v. Brown, No. 93C3489, 1998 WL 142375, at *10 (N.D. Ill. Mar. 19, 1998).
[148] *Id.*
[149] *Id.*
[150] Zalewska v. County of Sullivan, 316 F.3d 314, 323 (2d Cir. 2003).

helpful. However, this approach, while championed by scholars,[151] has not been successful in litigation. There are scarcely any federal cases that mention the terms "stereotype" and "judicial notice" in the same sentence, and most of the ones that do address family responsibility discrimination, a rare recognized doctrine that derives from judicial notice of societal stereotyping.

Whether it be through taking judicial notice of what goes on in the real world, allowing for the presentation of evidence and experts that inject insight into the dynamics of the workplace, or generally being more vigilant about not prematurely foreclosing a case before it gets to a jury, there is much that courts can do to enable "reading between the lines" when it comes to evidence of stereotyping in discrimination cases. There is often much conveyed by the tacit insinuations of certain phrases, terms, and indignities levied at specific individuals. Until courts acknowledge the richness of this potential, and stop foreclosing cases, pretrial, in which cryptic or coded speech bespeaks discrimination, the unspoken beliefs bound up in stereotyping will continue to elide the law.

[151] Stephanie Bornstein, *Unifying Antidiscrimination Law through Stereotype Theory*, 20 LEWIS & CLARK L. REV. 919, 945–46 (2016).

2

"We Expect You to Take Your (Verbal) Punches Like a Man" (And)

I was one of those students in law school who felt like if you were tough and smart and hardworking enough, nothing could bring you down. I did not let sexism stand in the way of my getting into a top law school, and I did not let my male classmates intimidate me from getting top grades. When we discussed bullying in law school and its potential effect on women, I was actually embarrassed. After all, what makes you more vulnerable and less competent than being part of a group that's perceived as being so weak and incapable of rolling with the punches that it's asking for special consideration? When we discussed harassment, power dynamics, and the workplace in school, I was proud, as a woman, to raise my hand and comment on how the beauty of a free society and employment at will was that a person was empowered to move if he or she felt that the atmosphere was too "rough," and how it wasn't entirely clear that it was best or fair for an employer to have to retain an employee who couldn't acclimate to the culture . . . or who basically couldn't hack it. It was undeniably harsh, but so, I reasoned, was the real world that beckoned my peers and me. If a job didn't work out, a capable person got a new one.

And then I graduated school and confronted the real world. And here's the thing, it wasn't even as bad as it could have been. I had my own office with a door. I worked in white-collar environments. I was never propositioned or hit on. I was certainly never threatened that I would lose my job if I didn't acquiesce to physical advances. In fact, most of what I was subjected to seems to me now[,] as an informed attorney, perfectly legal. Multiple partners at my firm were known for being brutal to work for—and some were crass to top it off. They were relentlessly derisive and abusive to the point that I often needed to retreat to my office to gather myself together during the course of a day. They broke me. I started looking for a new job.

I think back now to my smug retorts to the victims in cases and hypotheticals that we read about in law school, and I cringe. People who worked on loading docks. People who were crammed into crowded break rooms after long hours of abuse, some physical, some mental and verbal, while standing on assembly lines. People who didn't speak English or made minimum wage, or both. From the safety of my seat in a law school classroom in which respect for me and for who I was, was mandated and artificial, it was so easy to speak and think in absolutes. My definition of words like "strong," and "tough," and even "good," have changed so much in such a short time. My perspectives on things like one's locus of control and what one can legitimately assume credit or blame for have shifted radically. And I have become more humble, more compassionate, and more self-aware.

—*Alison, twenty-nine, attorney*

THE BELIEF

The belief that women in the workplace should simply toughen up and "take bullying like a man," though largely unexpressed, helps to obscure a major reason that many women find themselves disadvantaged at work and even prematurely winnowed out of their workplace. As will be discussed, status-neutral bullying is wholly lawful everywhere in the United States, except for Puerto Rico, which, just in the summer of 2020, passed the Act to Prohibit and Prevent Workplace Harassment in Puerto Rico, which prohibits status-blind bullying in the workplace that is "malicious[,] . . . unwanted, repetitive and abusive, arbitrary, unreasonable or capricious, not related to legitimate business interests, and that infringes on constitutionally protected rights, such as the protection against attacks to the employee's reputation or private life, among others."[1]

There is evidence that such bullying confers unique and disproportionate harm on women and other minorities in the workplace. Some of this harm is easily calculable and some is not so easily ascertained. To be sure, this harm is discernible when women are looked at as a group and the picture is painted with a broad brush; there are certainly many women who handle bullying in ways that advantage them over men, as well as many men who struggle to thrive in a culture in which bullying is rife. However, in the aggregate, lawful, status-blind bullying harms women, as a group, uniquely and in a multitude of ways.

An entire book could be written about workplace bullying; several outstanding ones have been.[2] Though many say the term is hard to pin to a definition, there are several excellent and clear definitions. According to Professor David

[1] Juan Felipe Santos et al., *Puerto Rico Becomes First Jurisdiction to Adopt Law Against Workplace Bullying*, JACKSON LEWIS (Aug. 7, 2020), www.jacksonlewis.com/publication/pue rto-rico-becomes-first-jurisdiction-adopt-law-against-workplace-bullying; 2020 P.R. LAWS 90.

[2] WORKPLACE BULLYING: SYMPTOMS AND SOLUTIONS (Noreen Tehrani ed., 2012); ANDREA NEEDHAM, WORKPLACE BULLYING: A COSTLY BUSINESS SECRET (2004); DAVID LEADS, WORKPLACE BULLYING: HOW TO SURVIVE AND THRIVE WITH A BULLY BOSS (2014).

Yamada, workplace bullying is "the intentional infliction of a hostile work environment upon an employee by a coworker or coworkers, typically through a combination of verbal and nonverbal behaviors."[3] For his part, Gary Namie, the industrial psychologist, educator, and founder of the nonprofit US Workplace Bullying Institute (WBI), describes workplace bullying as the "repeated mistreatment by one or more perpetrators of an individual or group" who are "driven by a need to control other people."[4] Social psychologist and professor Loraleigh Keashly says that a hallmark of workplace bullying, which is perpetrated mainly by higher-up employees, is "hostile verbal and nonverbal, nonphysical behaviors directed at a person(s) such that the target's sense of him/herself as a competent person and worker is negatively affected."[5]

Recent studies on this veritable plague in the American workplace indicate that the vast resources spent on this problem each year, including on sick days and stress-related ill-health, are both immense and grossly underestimated.[6] Further, since employment is generally presumed to be at will, unless workplace bullying can be shown to be some kind of actionable harassment under Title VII or another law, absent the enactment of a statute, it is perfectly lawful. It is estimated that antidiscrimination laws are properly invoked in a scant 20 percent of workplace bullying episodes.[7]

This is not to say that individual employers cannot undertake to regulate or even outright ban it themselves, and some choose to. However, in many cases, employers do not wish to penalize or ban a behavior that may be exhibited by those who may be among the most successful at what they do. And studies have shown that traits that correlate with bullying behaviors also correlate with

---

[3]   David C. Yamada, *The Phenomenon of "Workplace Bullying" and the Need for Status-Blind Hostile Work Environment Protection*, 88 Georgetown L. J. 475 (2000).

[4]   Gary Namie, *The Challenge of Workplace Bullying*, 34 Emp. Rel. Today 43, 45 (2007).

[5]   Loraleigh Keashly, *Emotional Abuse in the Workplace: Conceptual and Empirical Issues*, 1 J. Emotional Abuse 85, 87 (1998).

[6]   Jana P. Grimm, *Workplace Bullying: Its Costs and Prevention*, Steptoe & Johnson: Lab. & Emp. Essentials (Aug. 27, 2015), www.lexisnexis.com/legalnewsroom/labor-employment/b/labor-employment-top-blogs/archive/2015/08/27/workplace-bullying-its-costs-and-prevention.aspx; Janet Fowler, *Financial Impacts of Workplace Bullying*, Investopedia (Jul. 16, 2012), www.investopedia.com/financial-edge/0712/financial-impacts-of-workplace-bullying.aspx; Judith Lynn Fisher-Blando, Workplace Bullying: Aggressive Behavior and Its Effect on Job Satisfaction and Productivity (Feb. 2008) (unpublished PhD dissertation, Univ. of Phx.).

[7]   Gary Namie, *2007 WBI U.S. Workplace Bullying Survey*, Workplace Bullying Inst., (Sept. 2007), https://workplacebullying.org/multi/pdf/WBIsurvey2007.pdf.

professional and business success.[8] Indeed, those who engage in abusive behavior at work often receive positive feedback on their work and win praise in their evaluation. This has traditionally been ascribed to their ability to be both charming and manipulative. A 2013 study conducted collaboratively by researchers in the United States, Germany, and China attempted to explain why bullies thrive professionally, even as employers strive to deter and eradicate bullying.[9] The study showed a "strong correlation between bullying, social competence, and positive job evaluations."[10] Specifically, the study found that when bullying tendencies and political astuteness were combined in one individual, that individual performed better, bolstering the researchers' theory that individuals may wield abusive behavior as a tool of sorts to attract support and resources to help them attain success.[11] As an article in the *Washington Post* surmised, "maybe the typical work environment – one too often built on rigid hierarchies and coercion – promotes it. Today's cutthroat job market and demanding performance expectations surely makes [*sic*] it worse. But just like bullying in the classroom, such behavior in the office can ravage an otherwise well-functioning workplace."[12]

Scholars, for their part, have long described (and bemoaned) the "masculinization" of the workplace, whereby historically masculine behavioral norms and male attributes are prized and dominate, and those who do not take on or perform them struggle to successfully navigate the terrain of the workplace.[13] Masculinities, then, make up the invisible structure that subordinates the traditionally feminine to the traditionally masculine. Tacit entrenching of sex stereotypes and privileging of masculine or "macho" behaviors like aggression, objectification, and competitiveness operate invisibly to maintain a sexist hegemony in the workplace.[14] Being aggressive, even

---

[8] Darren C. Treadway et al., *Political Skill and the Job Performance of Bullies*, 28 J. MANAGERIAL PSYCHOL. 273 (2013); Helen LaVan & Marty Martin, *Bullying in the U.S. Workplace: Normative and Process-Oriented Ethical Approaches*, 83 J. BUS. ETHICS 147 (2008).

[9] Treadway, *supra* note 8, at 3.

[10] *Id.*

[11] *Id.*

[12] Jena McGregor, *Why Bullies Succeed at Work*, WASH. POST (May 20, 2013), www .washingtonpost.com/news/on-leadership/wp/2013/05/20/why-bullies-succeed-at-work-2/?noredirect=on&utm_term=.4267124a675e.

[13] Kerri Lynn Stone, *From Queen Bees and Wannabes to Worker Bees: Why Gender Considerations Should Inform the Emerging Law of Workplace Bullying*, 65 N.Y.U ANN. SURV. AM. L. 35 (2009); Ann C. McGinley, *Creating Masculine Identities: Bullying and Harassment "Because of Sex,"* 78 U. COLO. L. REV. 1151 (2008).

[14] ANN C. McGINLEY, MASCULINITY AT WORK: EMPLOYMENT DISCRIMINATION THROUGH A DIFFERENT LENS (2016); Jennifer L. Berdahl, Peter Glick, & Marianne Cooper, *How Masculinity Contests Undermine Organizations, and What to Do*

to the point of perhaps being abusive and antisocial, can actually *advance* one's career in an industry or in a workplace, to the extent that many American girls find having been educated and socialized in a more typically feminine way to be a liability.[15]

According to Professor Ann C. McGinley:

> Masculinities are not merely practices by individual actors. Rather, masculine identities and norms are associated with the very definition of work, the identity of certain jobs as feminine and masculine, and the value attributed to those jobs. These practices harm women at work, permitting powerful heterosexual white men to define what work is, while denying that the workplace is gendered.[16]

Grown women at work may have been taught as children, explicitly or implicitly, to appease and be "nice" in the face of cruelty or abuse, rather than to "duke it out" with the bully, verbally or otherwise, to win respect and save face. Studies show that women, as a group, tend to be more conflict-averse and more concerned with maintaining peaceful relationships than are men.[17] By contrast, they may be navigating a hostile or bullying environment alongside men who were taught to absorb and respond to bullying in ways that may be more favored within the structural norms of the workplace.

And these differences when it comes to how the sexes tend to absorb workplace bullying, as well as abuse and criticism, most likely have their genesis in the disparate ways in which boys and girls are socialized in their formative years, both formally and informally. Although a lot of research on sex and childhood, as well as adolescent socialization and dynamics, is highly anecdotal, there is support for the notion that there are firmly entrenched differences between the ways in which boys and girls tend to confront and engage with bullying.[18] Boys tend to be better taught to stand up to those who

About It, HARV. BUS. REV. (Nov. 2, 2018), https://hbr.org/2018/11/how-masculinity-contests-undermine-organizations-and-what-to-do-about-it.

[15] See Ruchika Tulshyan, *Speaking Up As a Woman of Color at Work*, FORBES (Feb. 10, 2015), www.forbes.com/sites/ruchikatulshyan/2015/02/10/speaking-up-as-a-woman-of-color-at-work/#c14b222ea3.

[16] Ann C. McGinley, *Masculinities at Work*, 83 OR. L. REV. 359, 365 (2004).

[17] Mark H. David et al., *Gender Differences in Responding to Conflict in the Workplace: Evidence from a Large Sample of Working Adults*, 63 SEX ROLES 500–01 (2010); Audrey Nelson, *Women, Conflict and Mixed Messages*, PSYCHOLOGY TODAY (Oct. 12, 2018), www.psychologytoday.com/us/blog/he-speaks-she-speaks/201810/women-conflict-and-mixed-messages.

[18] MARY PIPHER, REVIVING OPHELIA: SAVING THE SELVES OF ADOLESCENT GIRLS (1994); RACHEL SIMMONS, ODD GIRL SPEAKS OUT: GIRLS WRITE ABOUT BULLIES, CLIQUES,

challenge them and perhaps even walk off arm in arm with an aggressor once it's all been "left on the field." Girls, on the other hand, have historically tended to absorb the message that they ought to remain "nice," and noncon-frontational, and that it would be almost unseemly to show anger, raise their voices, or push back against a bully, especially in a professional setting. Thus, as research has continually shown, while boys may be more likely than girls to "duke out" their problems verbally or physically on the playground, their conflicts are more likely to reach a point of resolution.[19] Girls, on the other hand, may lean toward outward civility and politeness, even in the midst of conflict, but their most scathing and vicious battles may play out behind one another's backs, on social media and through deploying third parties as "weapons," either by using them as channels of gossip or by turning them on their opponents.

Rosalind Wiseman's 2002 book *Queen Bees and Wannabes* sets forth a good deal of research positing that there are inherent differences between the ways in which boys and girls are socialized to engage with bullies, conflict, abuse, and one another.[20] The studies demonstrate that while the boys surveyed claimed to have been hit, pushed, or slapped more often than did the girls, the girls reported being bullied through the use of rumors and sexual com-ments more frequently than the boys did.[21] Moreover, male adolescents were shown to engage in more direct conflict than girls, whether they were physical or verbal altercations, but female adolescents, when fighting with and bullying one another, tended to deploy more subtle, sometimes clandestine tactics, like spreading rumors or gossiping.[22] Opting for less face-to-face fighting, girls also engaged more frequently in passive-aggressive behaviors, like "hijacking online screen names of others and sending out cruel and fraudulent e-mails and internet instant messages, subscribing victims to or enrolling them in pornographic or embarrassing websites or schemes, and sending notes to others purporting to be the victim in order to damage the victim's social standing."[23]

POPULARITY, AND JEALOUSY (2004) [hereinafter ODD GIRL SPEAKS OUT]; ROSALIND WISEMAN, QUEEN BEES AND WANNABES: HELPING YOUR DAUGHTER SURVIVE CLIQUES, GOSSIP, BOYFRIENDS, AND OTHER REALITIES OF ADOLESCENCE (2002).

[19] *See* Carolyn Pope Edwards et al., *Socialization of Boys and Girls in Natural Contexts*, 1 ENCYCLOPEDIA OF SEX & GENDER 34, 38 (2003).

[20] WISEMAN, *supra* note 18.

[21] *Id.*

[22] *Id.*

[23] Stone, *supra* note 13, at 51; ODD GIRL SPEAKS OUT, *supra* note 18 (detailing the experiences of 300 girls as related to being bullied or bullying).

Interestingly, bullied boys were shown to be more likely than bullied girls to engage parental involvement at school to address the bullying.[24] This appears to indicate that boys will tend to voluntarily identify as victims and seek redress for their problems through formal channels, whereas girls may be more prone to permitting shame or fear to prevent open and direct resolution of the problem. In Rachel Simmons's 2011 book *Odd Girl Out: The Hidden Culture of Aggression in Girls, Revised and Updated*, she relates conversations that she had with 300 girls, aged 9 to 15, about how they handled relational aggression.[25] Having discussed the experience of bullying and being bullied with these girls, Simmons concluded that, essentially, girls are educated by the people and the influences surrounding them to believe that their anger is not palatable to those around them. They are, she conveys, made to feel as though unless they are visually and otherwise appealing at all times, as well as obedient, they will be rejected for their unseemliness.[26]

Therefore, the females' responses to abusive and bullying behavior inflicted by their peers contained more "socially acceptable," passive-aggressive responses. For example, the girls were prone to hiding anger, giving others the "silent treatment," expressing their feelings, but indirectly, spreading rumors and gossip about others in person or online, becoming depressed, cutting or otherwise harming themselves, or developing eating disorders. Even when the females did confess that they "ganged up" after being bullied, it was not to engage in direct conflict and combat the behavior but to threaten to disengage completely and to end their friendship with the bully or bullies.[27] According to Simmons, an overwhelming number of the girls avoided direct conflict out of fear that it would cause others to hate or abandon them.[28] Simmons quotes one of the girls, who maintained that boys "don't stab you in the back" because "[w]ith guys there's no drama. It's less complicated."[29]

Simmons argues that, faced with mistreatment, girls often repress their anger until the point at which they "burst with rage," because "if something's wrong, good girls had better hide it."[30] She observes that society often turns a blind eye toward girls' cruelty and aggressiveness with other girls, with little more than platitudes like "[g]irls will be girls," or "[i]t's a phase all girls go

---

[24]   Stone, *supra* note 13, at 51.
[25]   RACHEL SIMMONS, ODD GIRL OUT: THE HIDDEN CULTURE OF AGGRESSION IN GIRLS, REVISED AND UPDATED (2011).
[26]   *Id.*
[27]   Stone, *supra* note 13, at 52.
[28]   ODD GIRL SPEAKS OUT, *supra* note 18, at 5.
[29]   *Id.*
[30]   *Id.*

through."[31] Ensuingly, she says, "most girls suffer alone," and "[w]hen 'good' girls deny their own anger and punish the ones who don't, they empower the culture that is forcing them to be nice all the time."[32]

Many others have echoed these views on young girls' socialization. As Soraya Chemaly recently said, most women, reflecting on their youth, cannot recall "any conversations with authority figures or role models about how to think about . . . anger or what to do with it."[33] She added in her book: "As girls, we are not taught to acknowledge or manage our anger so much as to fear, ignore, hide, and transform it."[34]

There is no reason to think that growing up and leaving the playground behind for the workplace means eschewing these distinct learned beliefs and socialized behaviors. These girls are likely to become women who, in greater numbers than their male counterparts, amidst the quiet erosion of their dignity over time, will self-select out of promotions and opportunities and perhaps eliminate themselves from the workplace entirely.[35]

And yet, it is a largely unspoken belief that women – despite the nexus between sex (and other protected statuses) and the impact of bullying on a career trajectory and well-being in the workplace – should simply take workplace bullying and abuse the way men do, or admit that they don't have what it takes to thrive in a given workplace.

THE PANE

The first behavior that is spurred by this belief is the bullying itself. In a 2017 study, the WBI found that 19 percent of Americans were bullied in the workplace while another 19 percent witnessed others being bullied.[36] A staggering 61 percent of Americans are aware of abusive conduct in the workplace, with 60.4 million Americans affected by it.[37] The study showed that some 29 percent of victims remain silent.[38] Further, 70 percent of perpetrators were men, but 60 percent of workplace bullying targets were

[31] *Id.*

[32] *Id.*

[33] Meghna Chakrabarti, *"Rage Becomes Her": The Current Conversation around Women's Anger*, WBUR (Sept. 12, 2018), www.wbur.org/onpoint/2018/09/12/rage-becomes-her-soraya-chemaly.

[34] SORAYA CHEMALY, RAGE BECOMES HER: THE POWER OF WOMEN'S ANGER (2018).

[35] Stone, *supra* note 13, at 53.

[36] Gary Namie, 2017 WBI U.S. *Workplace Bullying Survey*, WORKPLACE BULLYING INST. (Jun. 2017), www.workplacebullying.org/wbiresearch/wbi-2017-survey/.

[37] *Id.* at 3.

[38] *Id.* at 12.

women. Additionally, 40 percent of targets are thought to suffer negative effects on their health as a result of their having been bullied.[39]

As for bullies in the workplace, 61 percent of them are bosses and 63 percent operate alone, rather than in tandem with others.[40] Further, 71 percent of employer reactions are harmful to targets and some 60 percent of co-worker reactions are harmful to targets.[41] In fact, in the course of staving off bullying, some 60 percent of targets lose their original jobs.[42] And, as will be discussed, while 77 percent of Americans support enacting a new law to aid in the fight against workplace bullying, and a couple of states have passed training/education statutes, only Puerto Rico has passed a true anti-workplace bullying statute.[43]

The next behavior that is spurred by the belief that women should simply buck up[44] and withstand bullying the way men do[45] is adherence to corporate cultures that do little to curb bullies or stem their behavior, despite the fact that many employers have written policies that aim to deter or ban bullying behaviors in the workplace. All too often, workplace managers, Human Resources departments, and supervisors, in the moments when bullying is experienced or reported, fail to take the proper action, whether that amounts to formal redress or an off-the-cuff expression of disapproval. A 2014 study showed that 72 percent of employers denied, discounted, rationalized, or defended behavior when employees reported workplace bullying.[46] Indeed, in many cases, the target of the bullying may even experience retribution, whether it is more overt, like being mocked further, not being selected to work on an important project, or not being invited to an important professional event or opportunity; or more subtle, like being shunned socially.

---

[39]   *Id.* at 8.
[40]   *Id.* at 10.
[41]   *Id.* at 14.
[42]   *Id.* at 18.
[43]   2020 P.R. LAWS 90; CAL. GOV'T CODE § 12950.1 (DEERING, LEXIS through 2021 Reg. Sess.); UTAH CODE ANN. § 67-19-44 (LEXIS through 2021 First Special Sess.).
[44]   Amy Epstein Gluck, *Women Are Just "Too Sensitive" – Or Could It Be Sexual Harassment?*, FISHER BROYLES (Mar. 2016), http://employmentdiscrimination.fisherbroyles.com/2016/03/women-are-just-too-sensitive-or-could-it-be-sexual-harassment/ ("Martinez allegedly told his female CCO that another female employee should be 'hogtied' as well as raped into submission. When the CCO objected to such comments, Martinez, raised in Spain, allegedly said that American women were too sensitive.").
[45]   *See* Victoria Ward, *Women Should "Toughen Up" Former Lib Dem Spin Doctor Says*, TELEGRAPH (Feb. 28, 2013), www.telegraph.co.uk/news/politics/9899316/Women-should-toughen-up-former-Lib-Dem-spin-doctor-says.html ("It's tough for men and women. There's a lot of bullying, there's a lot of nastiness, there's a lot of appalling behaviour that you'd never get away with outside politics so you do have to toughen up a little bit.").
[46]   Gary Namie, *2014 WBI U.S. Workplace Bullying Survey February 2014*, WORKPLACE BULLYING INST. (2014), www.workplacebullying.org/wbiresearch/wbi-2014-us-survey/.

One of the biggest observable behaviors and/or phenomena that looks to be driven by the belief that women and men alike should just take their (verbal) punches is the failure of Congress or any state legislature to pass anti-bullying legislation for the workplace.

Since 2003, twenty-nine states and two territories have introduced some version of the WBI's model anti-workplace bullying Healthy Workplace Bill,[47] which was conceived of and written by Professor David Yamada. Despite these attempts, the legislation has only been enacted in Puerto Rico.[48] This Bill, as per the Healthy Workplace Campaign that promotes it, does multiple things to thoughtfully contour what should be deemed regulable behavior, without opening up proverbial floodgates of litigation. These things include (1) furnishing a precise definition of an "abusive work environment," affording a "high standard for misconduct," (2) demanding that a putative plaintiff provide proof of health harm by licensed professional, (3) insulating conscientious employers from the risk of vicarious liability in circumstances where internal correction and prevention protocols are operational, (4) providing employers with a reason to punish or fire offenders, (5) requiring that plaintiffs bring suit using private attorneys, and (6) correcting loopholes and gaps in extant civil rights legislation.[49]

Workers, for their part, can seek redress against the bully directly, as well as hold their employers accountable for workplace abuse. The Bill lists as examples of abusive behavior, among other things, "verbal abuse, threatening, intimidating or humiliating behaviors (including nonverbal), or work interference – sabotage – which prevents work from getting done, or some combination of one or more."[50]

THE PAIN

The "pain" of both workplace bullying and the societal belief that women should be forced to endure it, despite the sex-based disadvantage it confers, is immense. In terms of the bullying itself, female victims of workplace bullying may look lazy or disengaged to others. They may be more likely to leave the job or even the workforce altogether, and they may not even be able to identify precisely how or why they were essentially forced out. Having normalized the

---

[47] *The Healthy Workplace Campaign FAQ*, HEALTHY WORKPLACE BILL, www .healthyworkplacebill.org/faq.php (last visited Jan. 13, 2020).

[48] 2020 P.R. LAWS 90.

[49] *Quick Facts About the Healthy Workplace Bill*, HEALTHY WORKPLACE BILL, https://healthy workplacebill.org/bill/ (last visited Feb. 4, 2020).

[50] *The Healthy Workplace Campaign*, HEALTHY WORKPLACE BILL, https://healthyworkplace bill.org/problem/ (last visited Jan. 13, 2020).

lawful, bullying behavior in their own minds, and even having seen how men were bullied too, they may not identify as readily as victims of something wrong or with sex-discriminatory outcomes. In fact, due to the general unpleasantness and toxicity of their workplaces, they may even convince themselves that they simply "opted out" of something that they couldn't "hack."

A lot of research, largely ignored, underscores the conclusion that women, as a group, absorb and respond to bullying and abuse in the workplace differently from men.[51] Even the aftermath and effects of workplace bullying support the narrative that women are disproportionately affected by it. According to the 2014 WBI study, bullying "targets lose their jobs at a much higher rate than perpetrators (82 [percent] vs. 18 [percent])."[52] This is a sad commentary on the impact of workplace bullying, but it is far from the whole story. The study goes on to illustrate a key component of workplace gender inequality: "When bullies are men[,] regardless of the target[']s gender[,] the loss rate is equally high. However, when bullies are women, women targets lose their jobs 89 [percent] of the time.[53] Notably women bullies, as perpetrators, suffer the highest job loss rate (30 [percent]) of any gender pairing."[54]

In terms of the unique harm imparted to women, it bears noting that in addition to women learning everything from behavioral expectations to defense mechanisms that disadvantage them, evidence shows that they may simply have less of a taste for an abuse-fueled workplace than their male colleagues. More prone to shrink back, avoid the toxic atmosphere, or simply leave, women may have less tolerance for bullying than their male counterparts. Indeed, recent reports say that female victims of workplace bullying took twice as much sick leave as their colleagues who were not targeted.[55] Further, female victims of workplace bullying were found to be more likely to use antidepressants than were their colleagues.[56] While concerns involving child-rearing or the perennial lament of "work–life balance" are often cited as

---

[51] Escartín Solanelles et al., *Workplace Bullying or Mobbing: Gender Similarities and Differences in Its Perceived Severity*, 28 REVISTA DE PSICOLOGÍA SOCIAL 211 (2013); Tine L. Mundbjerg Eriksen et al., *Long-Term Consequences of Workplace Bullying on Sickness Absence*, 43 LAB. & ECON. 129 (2016).

[52] Namie, *supra* note 46, at 8.

[53] *Id.*

[54] *Id.*

[55] Zawn Villines, *Study: Men and Women React Differently to Workplace Bullying*, GOOD THERAPY (Dec. 28, 2016), www.goodtherapy.org/blog/study-men-and-women-react-differently-to-workplace-bullying-1228161; R. Rugulies, U. Bultmann, B. Aust, & H. Burr, *Psychosocial Work Environment and Incidence of Severe Depressive Symptoms: Prospective Findings from a 5-Year Follow-Up of the Danish Work Environment Cohort Study*, 163 AM. J. EPIDEMIOLOGY 877–87 (2006).

[56] Villines, *supra* note 55.

reasons why women choose to leave their workplace or even the workforce altogether in the prime of their careers, there may be more to these stories. How many women who opt out of the workforce after a major event like a wedding or a birth might not make that choice if they weren't so dissatisfied with the climate and interactions at their workplace?

There is much anecdotal and documented evidence of workplace dissatisfaction among women due to workplace abuse, bullying, or hostility. In a 2015 LinkedIn.com survey of more than 4,000 women who recently switched employers, work–life balance concerns did not even make the top three reasons reported for departure.[57] In fact, the three top reasons – a "concern for the lack of advancement opportunity," a "dissatisfaction with senior leadership," and a "dissatisfaction with the work environment/culture" – point toward the fault lying with corporate cultures, rather than with individuals' inabilities to manage their professional and personal responsibilities.[58]

Despite this, many women asked about their own or others' exodus from the workforce habitually revert to tying women's departures to "family concerns." We only sometimes hear someone articulate that they felt driven from the workforce by an abusive climate. When people discuss the exodus of women from the workplace, they can tend to overly-ascribe it to "family and work/life balancing issues." There is a dearth of research in this area, but a 2016 survey in the United Kingdom about why women choose to leave the workforce sheds some light.[59] The survey reveals that while many women leave the workforce when they want to start a family, this is typically not the reason for the departure.[60] Most of the women attributed their exit to things like not feeling that they could compete on a level playing field at work, or advance as they would wish, yet, because the "manifestation" of that feeling is, often, leaving the workforce to have children, employers often fail to discern the true motivation for the flight, focusing instead on the exit itself.[61]

These women surveyed reported to the researchers that they opted to have children because of the impediments placed in their way at work, and figured that, in the face of these impediments, "they might as well do it now." According to the researchers, this flies in the face of notions that women are

[57] Allison Schnidman *Why Women Are Leaving Their Jobs (Your First Guess Is Wrong)*, LINKEDIN: TALENT BLOG (Nov. 5, 2015), https://business.linkedin.com/talent-solutions/blog/trends-and-research/2015/why-women-are-leaving-their-jobs-your-first-guess-is-wrong.
[58] *Id.*
[59] Nicky Acuna Ocana, *Event Blog: Why Do Women Really Leave the Workforce?*, AMBITION (Feb. 5, 2016), www.ambition.co.uk/blog/2016/02/event-blog-why-do-women-really-leave-the-workforce.
[60] *Id.*
[61] *Id.*

actively choosing not to return to work after having children because of the way in which work would interfere with child-rearing. What is actually happening, they explain, is that women do not return because the prospect of doing so seems too daunting due to a lack of flexible options for work and work support, as well as the backlash they anticipate if they work fewer hours than they did previously.[62]

In the United States, there may be an over-attribution of this exodus to "work–life balance" concerns (which are also valid), with bullying and workplace abuse conspiring to alienate and drive women out of the workforce in droves, in many cases. According to a 2016 Fortune.com article, despite the fact that some in the media are quick to tie the "leaky pipeline" – referring to the fact that (as per a 2012 McKinsey study), while women have 53 percent of entry-level jobs, this funnels down to 37 percent of mid-level manager jobs and a scant 26 percent of senior management jobs – to women's higher rates of "burnout," desire to start a family, and feelings of being "overwhelmed," this may not be an accurate depiction.[63] Rather, the International Consortium for Executive Development Research has found that the number one reason for women aged about thirty leaving their workplace was finding a more lucrative job, followed by a dearth of opportunities to develop professionally, and not having enough meaningful work. And, indeed, a 2014 study by the Harvard Business Review shows that only one in ten women leave the workplace to start a family.[64] Popular beliefs about women, the "leaky pipeline," and workplace cultures seem to be quite misplaced.

According to Professor Ann McGinley, research that has rendered "visible the structures and practices that damage women ... at work ... is valuable because it contradicts the notion that women 'choose' to work in less equal positions."[65] Along these lines, an understanding of workplace bullying's adverse and disproportionate impact on women can go a long way toward disabusing society of the notion that so many women are "opting" to depart the workplace just as they hit what could be their prime professional years.[66]

---

[62] *Id.*

[63] Valentina Zarya, *What Everyone Gets Wrong About Why Millennial Women Quit Their Jobs*, Fortune (Mar. 16, 2013, 3:16 PM), https://fortune.com/2016/03/16/millennial-women-quit-jobs/.

[64] *Id.*

[65] Ann C. McGinley, *Reproducing Gender on Law School Faculties*, 172 Scholarly Works 99 (2009).

[66] *Prevent Sexual Harassment in Your State*, Nat'l Women's L. Ctr., https://nwlc.org/wp-content/uploads/2019/09/Prevent-Sexual-Harassment-In-Your-State.pdf (last visited Feb. 4, 2020).

The Yerkes-Dodson Law says that when a workplace's level of stress is either extremely high or extremely low, productivity will be relatively low.[67] This is intuitive, but the fact remains that the costs of workplace bullying are both incredibly difficult to estimate and higher than most people realize. From sick days taken from its effects, to the less visible costs of things like lost productivity, morale, and loyalty, to the costs of repeatedly training and acclimating new employees due to high turnover, workplace bullying exacts a huge toll.

In the past few years, Americans have seen high profile sports figures like tennis star Serena Williams[68] and Miami Dolphins player Jonathan Martin[69] publicly call out what may be termed their "workplace" bullying, and this may or may not have moved the needle on how intractable a problem Americans find workplace bullying to be. Interestingly, in both of these athletes' cases, they are people of color, and the bullying took the form of some kind of gendered and/or racialized attack on them. This highlights how closely tied protected class status and being targeted for bullying can be.

In Williams's case, she called out Russian tennis federation president Shamil Tarpischev in 2014 for "bullying" sexist and racist comments directed at her and her sister, Venus.[70] Among other comments, Tarpischev referred to the women as "the Williams brothers," and said "it's scary when you really look at them,"[71] on Russian television. While he was disciplined for this by the Women's Tennis Association (WTA) and suffered other professional consequences, the fact that people as powerful and revered as the Williams sisters could be targeted for bullying shows how invidious and pervasive the problem is.

As for Jonathan Martin, in 2013 he played professional football for the Miami Dolphins, and it looked like he had it all. A Stanford graduate who had majored in classics, the Dolphins' starting right tackle abruptly

[67] *The Leader's Edge: Playground Bullies, Corporate Counterparts Share Same Traits*, Bizwest (Mar. 8, 2002), http://bizwest.com/2002/03/08/the-leaders-edge-playground-bullies-corporate-counterparts-share-same-traits/.

[68] Vivek Saxena, *Serena Williams Claims Sexism, Called "Spoiled Brat" After Temper Tantrums Cost Her Victory*, BPR (Sept. 9, 2018), www.bizpacreview.com/2018/09/09/serena-williams-claims-sexism-called-spoiled-brat-after-temper-tantrums-cost-her-victory-672360.

[69] Ryan Van Bibber, *The Worst of the Richie Incognito/Jonathan Martin Report*, SBNation (Feb. 14, 2014, 11:27 AM), www.sbnation.com/nfl/2014/2/14/5411608/worst-of-the-richie-incognito-jonathan-martin-report-miami-dolphins.

[70] *Shamil Tarpischev Fined, Banned Year*, ESPN (Oct. 17, 2014), www.espn.com/tennis/story/_/id/11718876/russian-tennis-federation-president-shamil-tarpischev-sanctioned-serena-venus-williams-gender-comments.

[71] Des Bieler, *Russian Tennis Official Slammed for "Williams Brothers" Crack*, Wash. Post (Oct. 18, 2014, 12:16 AM), www.washingtonpost.com/news/early-lead/wp/2014/10/18/russian-tennis-official-slammed-for-williams-brothers-crack/.

abandoned his burgeoning career as an offensive lineman on October 28, 2013. The fabulously well-paid and famous Martin, who stood 6 feet 5 inches and weighed 312 pounds, left the Dolphins, and retired from professional football 2 years later. He alleged that he had simply been beaten down by relentless gendered, racial, crass, physical, and emotional abuse and horrific hazing at the hands of his teammates and other Dolphins employees. His heart-breaking correspondence with his mother, revealed in a later report compiled by a well-known law firm, told the story of his distress and agony at the hands of his tormentors:

> I have really severe depression. There are many instances where I can't get out of bed . . . . I'm really embarrassed to talk about it with anyone in person, I tried to with you when I was home but I couldn't do it . . .. Anyways, I really do wanna take care of it, because it is debilitating & keeps me from reaching my potential in all facets of life . . . .
>
>   Sometimes I very badly want to quit football . . . . I am deeply troubled, I have been lying to myself saying that eventually I'll get over it. I won't . . . . I really am getting increasingly tempted to just get in my car and leave Miami, live by myself for months or a year or two off the grid. But something holds me back every time, because part of me still loves football. But I am losing touch with that part more and more every day.[72]

Both of these high-profile stories illustrate not only that workplace bullying happens at all levels of employment but also how devastating the results can be, even for those who already have fame, fortune, and accomplishments behind them. A simple internet search reveals numerous memorials, foundations, and even speaking tours devoted to educating others about the effects of workplace bullying, which has resulted in suicide on occasion.[73]

   It is also impossible to ignore the link between the cruelest things that were said to and about Williams and Martin during and in the wake of these incidents and the fact that they are both African American. A teammate is alleged to have used racial slurs against Martin during the course of his

---

[72]   Paul, Weiss, Rifkind, Wharton & Garrison LLP, *Report to the National Football League Concerning Issues of Workplace Conduct at the Miami Dolphins* (Feb. 14, 2014), https://workplacebullying.org/multi/pdf/PaulWeissReport.pdf.

[73]   *See, e.g.*, Arash Emamzadeh, *Workplace Bullying: Causes, Effects, and Prevention*, PSYCHOL. TODAY (Sept. 27, 2018), www.psychologytoday.com/us/blog/finding-new-home/201809/workplace-bullying-causes-effects-and-prevention; Christian Jarrett, *Workplace Bullying Is More Harmful than We Realised*, WORKLIFE (Jan. 6, 2020), www.bbc.com/worklife/article/20191219-workplace-bullying-is-more-harmful-than-we-realised; Sherri Gordon, *The Effects of Workplace Bullying*, VERY WELL MIND, www.verywellmind.com/what-are-the-effects-of-workplace-bullying-460628 (updated Mar. 10, 2020).

bullying;[74] Tarpischev received widespread backlash for his comments,[75] which were construed by most, including Williams, herself, as racist.[76] This underscores the magnification of the scope and harm of bullying when intersectionality is at play. The identity of the victim should always be relevant when assessing the harm conferred by workplace bullying.

MANIFESTATIONS

Evidence of the belief that everyone, including women, just needs to toughen up, irrespective of the sex differential implicated by bullying, abounds. It is seen (and often expressed) in school classrooms when the policy of policing bullying and harassment is debated; on the floor of legislatures weighing the pros and cons of legislation that would render workplace bullying unlawful; and sometimes around watercoolers and family dinner tables, when high-profile events like the Miami Dolphins/ Jonathan Martin scandal thrust the subject onto a grander stage and into the spotlight. Most people stop short of saying that if women specifically can't acclimate, then they don't belong at work, but when the absolutist language that says that *anyone* who can't "fit in" shouldn't be there meets the absence of recognition that the culture of a particular workplace is inherently abusive or "rough," the result speaks for itself. And another pane of the glass ceiling is revealed.

Examples of this "toughen up" attitude being ascribed to those who set the tone in every field, from industry to politics, abound as well. In 2018, advertising CEO Gustavo Martinez stepped down from the multinational advertising and public relations company that employed him, embattled after a lawsuit filed against him.[77] According to the allegations in the lawsuit, he had made very derogatory and racist statements to the media, as well as to his employees. He was also alleged to have acted and spoken violently toward employees.

[74] Victor Mather, *Richie Incognito Accused of Using Racial Slurs in Game*, N.Y. Times (Jan. 8, 2018), www.nytimes.com/2018/01/08/sports/football/richie-incognito-racist-slurs-yannick-ngakoue.html.

[75] *Shamil Tarpischev Fined, supra* note 70.

[76] *Serena: Comments "In a Way Bullying"*, ESPN (Oct. 19, 2014), www.espn.com/tennis/story/_/id/11726918/serena-williams-responds-russian-tennis-federation-official-comments-supports-suspension.

[77] Megan Graham, *Gustavo Martinez Out at WPP Two Years After Johnson Lawsuit*, AdAge (Jun. 7, 2018), https://adage.com/article/agency-news/gustavo-martinez-wpp-years-johnson-lawsuit-filed/313776.

According to the allegations in the suit, which ignited fierce discourse, ousters, and other initiatives within the advertising industry, Martinez said that American women were too sensitive.[78]

President Donald Trump's son, Donald Trump Jr., famously said in a 2013 interview about women who complained about sexual harassment in the workplace: "If you can't handle some of the basic stuff that's become a problem in the workforce today, then you don't belong in the workforce . . . . Like, you should go maybe teach kindergarten. I think it's a respectable position."[79] Many in the United States seem to concur with this, as do many across the globe, male and female alike. Jo Phillips, the former press secretary to British Liberal Democrat Paddy Ashdown, has been quoted as saying that men and women alike need to understand that when one enters the political arena, "you're going into a very tough world." Noting that "[t]here's a lot of bullying, there's a lot of nastiness, there's a lot of appalling behavior that you'd never get away with outside politics," she admonished female politicians to "toughen up a little bit," observing that, compared with other women in the workforce, female politicians are fortunate to be "in a better place to do something about it. You are in a position, having had to toughen up to get where you are in the first place."[80]

And Britain's John Major's former press secretary, Sheila Gunn, came under fire in 2013, when she answered questions about whether female aspiring politicians ought to "toughen up" by exhorting women to "find ways of coping with it and coping with that sort of inappropriate behaviour," and "to be sisterly, [by] mak[ing] sure that they pass on comments to each other and maybe take formal complaints." Twitter comments left for her in the wake of this interview were not kind, as commenters said things like: "Not really sure why it's all down to women to 'toughen up' – surely men have a role to play in treating women as equals," and "Jo Phillips and Sheila Gunn telling us that women in politics will encounter sexual harassment and should 'toughen up'. I despair."[81]

---

[78] Amy Epstein Gluck, *Women Are Just "Too Sensitive" – Or Could It Be Sexual Harassment,* Fisher Broyles LLP (Mar. 18, 2016), http://employmentdiscrimination.fisherbroyles.com /2016/03/women-are-just-too-sensitive-or-could-it-be-sexual-harassment/.

[79] Libby Nelson, *Donald Trump Jr.: If Women Can't Handle Sexual Harassment, They Should Be "Kindergarten Teachers",* Vox (Oct. 14, 2016, 12:40 PM), www.vox.com/2016/10/14/132849 64/donald-trump-jr-sexual-harassment.

[80] Marie Claire, *Women Should "Toughen Up" to Deal with Sexual Harassment in Politics, Says Former Spin Doctor,* Marie Claire (Feb. 28, 2013, 4:27 PM), www.marieclaire.co.uk/news/ former-spin-doctor-says-women-should-toughen-up-to-deal-with-sexual-harassment-in-politics -128219.

[81] Victoria Ward, *Women Should "Toughen Up", Former Lib Dem Spin Doctor Says,* Telegraph (Feb. 28, 2013, 9:03 AM), www.telegraph.co.uk/news/politics/9899316/Women- should-toughen-up-former-Lib-Dem-spin-doctor-says.html.

The internet and women's magazines are rife with articles admonishing women who are "too sensitive" to "toughen up" at work for their own benefit.[82] Far fewer articles seek to reproach men uniquely and similarly. And try to count the innumerable memes, story or article titles, or T-shirts flooding the marketplace that exhort women to "Act Like a Lady; Think Like a Boss," or, worse, "Act Like a Lady; Think Like a Man." It's pop-psychology peddling the notion that womanhood and being a competent, strong, capable leader are mutually exclusive.

TAKEAWAYS

Workplace bullying and the notion that taking issue with it makes one weak or petty are much bigger components of the glass ceiling than most people realize. The idea that "neutral" bullying is truly neutral and thus affects everyone equally is an insidious myth. Echoes of it are heard each day as legislation is rejected in state after state, as the media and commentators denigrate victims as weak and pathetic, and a "survival of the fittest" mentality continues to be espoused everywhere from the classroom to the boardroom without giving more nuanced thought to the dynamics at play or the systemic effects of the behavior. A 2009 survey conducted by the WBI found that 53.6 percent of employers failed to address the bully, and that, actually, 28.2 percent of bullies were subsequently rewarded or promoted.[83]

Workplace bullying is also insidious; its costs are nearly incalculable. If the United States were like many countries in Europe that passed "anti-mobbing"[84] laws simply because they believed in the value of the "dignitarian workplace," in which the sanctity of workplace well-being is paramount, we would not need to press this point. But since the United States persists in clinging to the outmoded notions that victims of bullying are weak and that bullies' behavior is ultimately harmless to society because those who are "strong enough" will thrive, and the others will somehow move on, it is time to take a different tack. The "equal opportunity bully" who does not seem to

---

[82] Anne Perschel, *Women in Business – Do We Need to Toughen Up?*, 3 PLUSINTERNATIONAL (Nov. 26, 2011), https://3plusinternational.com/2011/11/women-in-business-do-we-need-to-toughen-up/; Paul Keijzer, *How Women Can Be Successful If They Toughen Up*, ENGAGE ASIA WITH PAUL KEIJZER: GENDER INCLUSION (Aug. 2, 2016), www.paulkeijzer.com/women-can-be-successful-toughen-up/; Ward, *supra* note 75, at 13; Nelson, *supra* note 73.

[83] Gary Namie, *(Still) Bullying with Impunity Labor Day Survey* WORKPLACE BULLYING INST. (Sept. 2009).

[84] *Bullying, Harassment and Stress in the Workplace—A European Perspective*, PROSKAUER, www.internationallaborlaw.com/files/2013/01/Bullying-Harassment-and-Stress-in-the-workplace-A-European-Perspective.pdf (last visited Jun. 11, 2019).

run afoul of Title VII should be re-examined as a pane of the glass ceiling for women and other minorities.

Bullying is hard to capture, in many senses. Shame and confusion may render its victims either reluctant or simply unable to see and identify themselves as such. It often occurs behind closed doors or in very subtle ways. Indeed, when done in a context or culture of bullying, otherwise innocuous workplace acts like failing to say hello, altering project assignments or responsibilities, pushing up deadlines, or withholding information can take on new and dark dimensions.[85] There is no way to know how many employees have been prematurely winnowed out of jobs prematurely or unfairly by bullying, but, anecdotally, there is mounting evidence that many people who initially frame their departures as a choice identify as a victim of bully only later, once they have had the benefit of time, insight, education, or the perspective to reframe their experience.

Put simply, the mid-level associate who refrains from calling her mentor unless she absolutely has to because of his unduly harsh and abusive language will almost invariably falter at work. She will receive negative evaluations due to both the resultant poor quality of her work and her failure to avail herself of mentoring. Will this woman make the connection between "her" failure and the bullying? Will the stockbroker who leaves a toxic workplace environment to have a baby and decides never to return realize that, but for how actively unpleasant and hostile her workplace was, she might not have stopped working at that point in her career? After the advertising, executive gets bullied and humiliated in the boardroom and reverts back to her office to deal with her emotions privately behind a closed door, will she parse out the strands of what has occurred and realize that she is not weak for doing so, even if her bosses' inaction makes her look that way in others' eyes? When a recent business school graduate turns down an offer from a prestigious firm because she has been forewarned of its unchecked abusive, "fraternity house" atmosphere, will she realize that she didn't really get to make a choice at all?

With bullying not even made unlawful (except in Puerto Rico), the way sexual harassment is, victims are much more likely to attribute their failure to thrive at work to their own infirmities of character or lack of grit. They are much less likely to ascribe their "choices" to leave to forces outside their own control. As they discern only their own perceived shortcomings, weakness of character, and thinness of skin; they may be blind to others' intolerable behavior that harms them uniquely. They may be so inundated with abuse

---

[85]   Susan Harthill, *Bullying in the Workplace: Lessons from the United Kingdom*, 17 MINN. J. INT'L L. 247, 255–56 (2008).

that they fail to see that, even if it isn't unlawful, it is unethical and inimical to equality. And that's why, when the behavior rises past a certain threshold level (set high and defined well in the Healthy Workplace Bill), it should be unlawful. It is time for legislatures at every level to pass this much-needed legislation with an appreciation for how it will effectuate so much more than healthier workplaces; it will very likely go a long way toward promoting greater diversity in employment.

Resistance to the Healthy Workplace Bill has been attributed to several different things. In the first place, there seems to be a misapprehension, perhaps due to the use of the term "bullying," which is also used in the context of schoolchildren, that bullying is a petty slight that one with properly calibrated maturity and inner strength ought to be able to ward off without state protection or intervention. This concern is misplaced; workplace bullying in the form that the Bill seeks to regulate is nothing short of pernicious. Awareness campaigns highlight tragic suicides and debilitating effects on the health and well-being of many, but they have not been able to move the needle.

Another concern that some have raised is the potential implication of First Amendment concerns with the state regulation of speech. However, this, too, is not a true impediment to the legislation, in light of the facts that (1) Title VII has not been held to offend the First Amendment;[86] and (2) public employees' speech merits Constitutional protection only when it touches upon a matter of public concern,[87] most private employee speech is beyond the bounds of any protection from employers.[88] Still another concern is one that if the Bill were enacted, virtual floodgates of litigation would be opened and the courts would be inundated with claims made by plaintiffs suffering from no more than hurt

---

[86] Robinson v. Jacksonville Shipyards, Inc., 760 F. Supp. 1486, 1535 (M.D. Fla. 1991) (stating "pictures and verbal harassment were not protected speech because they acted as discriminatory conduct in form of hostile environment"); FINDLAW, *Freedom of Speech In the Workplace: The First Amendment Revisited*, https://corporate.findlaw.com/law-library/freedom-of-speech-in-the-workplace-the-first-amendment-revisited.html (last visited Jun. 21, 2019); Eugene Volokh, *Freedom of Speech vs. Workplace Harassment Law – A Growing Conflict: What the Courts Have to Say About Freedom of Speech and Workplace Harassment*, www2.law.ucla.edu/volokh/harass/courts.htm.

[87] Pickering v. Bd. of Ed. of Twp. High Sch. Dist. 205, Will Cty., Illinois, 391 U.S. 563, 574 (1968) (holding that statements by public officials on matters of public concern must be accorded First Amendment protection despite the fact that the statements are directed at their nominal superiors); Garrison v. Louisiana, 379 U.S. 64125 (1964); Wood v. Georgia, 370 U.S. 375 (1962).

[88] U.S. CONST. amend. I.; A. J. Willingham, *The First Amendment Doesn't Guarantee You the Rights You Think It Does*, CNN POST (Sept. 6, 2018, 7:36 PM), www.cnn.com/2017/04/27/politics/first-amendment-explainer-trnd/index.html.

feelings following petty slights.[89] This, too, is misplaced. Unlike Title VII, which the courts have held does not require a showing of concrete psychological harm for the plaintiff to recover, the Healthy Workplace Act requires "proof of health harm by licensed health or mental health professionals."[90] A simple reading of these requirements and the limitations on damages, along with attorneys' preexisting professional duties and the financial disincentives to bringing weak claims, should deter the filing of frivolous claims.[91]

Significantly, in the wake of the passage of the legislation, there is reason to believe that much of the flagrant, egregious bullying that we see today would likely abate somewhat. With an understanding that women, as a group, are often not socialized in ways that equip them to grapple with workplace bullying in ways that are as pleasing to their employers as their male colleagues' attempts, legislators could pass legislation to effectuate equality in the workplace as well. But as long as it remains an unspoken, unchallenged belief that "neutral" bullying is a mainstay of employment that has truly neutral effects, and that women must simply "toughen up" to meet it rather than taking issue with it, another pane in this glass ceiling has been firmly affixed.

---

[89] Eric Welter, *Workplace Bullying Legislation (aka "Employment Lawyer Full-Employment Act")*, CASETEXT (Feb. 7, 2008), https://casetext.com/analysis/workplace-bullying-legislation-aka-employment-lawyer-full-employment-act; *see* Michael Arria, *Workplace Bullying Affects Nearly Half of US Workers. It's Time We Did Something About It*, TRUTH OUT (Jan. 11, 2018), https://truthout.org/articles/workplace-bullying-affects-nearly-half-of-us-workers-it-s-time-we-did-something-about-it/.

[90] *Quick Facts About the Healthy Workplace Bill*, HEALTHY WORKPLACE BILL, https://healthy workplacebill.org/bill/ (last visited Jun. 11, 2019).

[91] David C. Yamada, *Crafting a Legislative Response to Workplace Bullying*, 8 EMP. RTS. & EMP. POL'Y J. 475, 478, 484 (2004).

3

"Accept 'Locker Room' and Sexist Talk" (But)

There were only five partners, and they were all pretty young. They never harassed me; I mean, they never hit on me. They were actually all married. But the way they spoke about women! Our opposing counsel on one case was female, and Michael had a host of unflattering and sexually derogatory nicknames for her. One was even a play on her last name. Once, she sent us a very aggressive motion with very little time for us to respond, and he made a bunch of comments about how she had him "bent over" and was violating him. Another female associate cut her hair once, and he joked that drastic appearance changes needed to be run by him first—especially if they involved cutting one's hair "above her bra strap." I don't think he realized how uncomfortable he made me or any of the other women in the office. After all, he never hit on or insulted any of us, and even the comments about us, like the one about her cutting her hair, weren't super sexual, super graphic, or super regular. One thing I knew as a lawyer was that there just wasn't enough 'there, there' for him to have committed any actionable sexual harassment. I just knew that I was feeling less and less comfortable at work.

—Samantha, twenty-five, summer associate

THE BELIEF

The (unspoken) belief that women in the workplace should "accept locker room talk" as something that not only goes on but may be perfectly fine in their working environments does not seem at first blush like one that the typical American workplace would want to be transmitting in modern times. After all, what is often termed "locker room talk," while not necessarily that which rises to the level of unlawful sexual harassment targeted at a particular subject, is considered crass and demeaning to or objectifying of women generally. It can be incredibly noxious and inimical to the comfort and progress of women and men in a workplace. Further, the very terming of this speech as "locker room talk" conveys the notions that (1) it is natural, common, and understandable; (2) there is a natural physical space (the locker room) and an ideological space for it in the world where it is sanctioned/given sanctuary; and (3) to the extent that it is (over)heard, it is just harmless speech that has escaped from the locker room and should not be surprising. In other words, "boys will be boys." Some may even hold the belief that letting employees let their hair down in this manner builds camaraderie.

The phrase "locker room talk" gained new notoriety in 2016, when then presidential candidate Donald Trump responded to the release of the now-infamous 2005 "Access Hollywood" tape that captured him speaking candidly with host Billy Bush about what could amount to the idea of sexually assaulting women. Upon being confronted with the tape, Trump was quoted as responding: "This was locker room talk. I'm not proud of it . . . . Yes, I'm very embarrassed by it, and I hate it, but it's locker room talk."[1] Critics subsequently attacked Trump and his supporters for attempting to normalize something – a mode of speaking about women outside their presence – that ought not be normalized. Some criticized what Trump said as even beyond the bounds of "locker room talk," since the vast majority of men would consider it to be deviant behavior even in an informal single-sex setting like a gym locker room.[2]

Whether used to describe speech that would describe sexual assault or that would demean or defame a specific woman, or even to describe generally sexist, hostile language that evinces disrespect for women, the concept of acceptable "locker room talk" would seem to be anathema to modern notions of ensuring equality in the workplace, and the strands of a workplace of mental well-being, accountability, and respect that undergird it.[3] Indeed, company after company and employer after employer seem to be following the modern trend of training and encouraging employees to report frowned-upon crass,

---

[1] Sally Jenkins, *Donald Trump's Idea of "Locker Room Talk" Is as Demeaning to Men as It Is to Women*, WASH. POST (Oct. 10, 2016), www.washingtonpost.com/sports/redskins/donald-trumps-idea-of-locker-room-talk-is-as-demeaning-to-men-as-it-is-to-women/2016/10/10/7e34718a-8eee-11e6-a6a3-d50061aa9fae_story.html.

[2] *See, e.g.*, Richard Pérez-Peña, *Men Say Trump's Remarks on Sex and Women Are Beyond the Pale*, N.Y. TIMES (Oct. 8, 2016), www.nytimes.com/2016/10/09/us/politics/men-say-trumps-remarks-on-sex-and-women-are-beyond-the-pale.html; Associated Press, *Athletes Respond to Trump's Usage of "Locker Room Talk,"* NBC SPORTS (Oct. 10, 2016, 3:39 PM), www.nbcsports.com/bayarea/home-page/athletes-respond-trumps-usage-locker-room-talk.

[3] A. Downing, *#MeToo: When Sexual Harassment in the Workplace Leaves You Feeling Powerless*, ROOT (Dec. 1, 2017), www.theroot.com/metoo-when-sexual-harassment-in-the-workplace-leaves-1820860452.

inappropriate overtures and discussions that would tend to make men or women uncomfortable, whether or not they are unlawful.

However, the superficial public relations and public statements of employers do not tell the whole story. In order for the message that locker room talk is not acceptable at work to truly take hold, more would need to be happening on a larger scale; the day-to-day cultures of workplaces and unspoken cues given to workers would have to transform. And, ultimately, although the law is a floor and not a ceiling – meaning that employers are typically free to legislate beyond what the law requires, but not free to suspend requirements imposed by the law – until the law, itself, is written or interpreted to render discouraged behavior to be unlawful, not much will change.

THE PANE

The message that women at work must simply put up with "locker room talk" can be found everywhere. And some scholars and commentators have gone so far as to criticize extant workplace law and regulation for over-sanitizing workplace speech and relationships.

When rampant locker room talk is given sanction at work, whole swaths of industries or physical places become hotbeds of sex and other discrimination.[4] Their cultures foment discrimination and harassment by permitting and encouraging demeaning and objectifying speech and behavior. From Wall Street to Silicon Valley, from "tech and startup" industries (and the cited "culture of sexism and discrimination" alleged at workplaces in Silicon Valley such as Tesla and Uber[5]) to funds and finance,[6] to entertainment,[7] and news,[8] it seems as though every day there is a new lawsuit, exposé, or social movement exposing not merely bad actors violating the laws designed to ensure equality

---

[4] *See* Erica T. G. Warren, *[Opinion] Dear Executive Men, Your Sexual Behavior Is Costing Us Both*, BLACK ENTERPRISE (Mar. 22, 2018), www.blackenterprise.com/executive-men-sexual-bahvior/.

[5] *See* Nicole Spector, *After Sexual Harassment Claims at Uber and Tesla, Is Silicon Valley Prone to Discrimination?*, NBC NEWS (Mar. 9, 2017), www.nbcnews.com/tech/tech-news/after-sexual-harassment-claims-uber-tesla-silicon-valley-prone-discrimination-n731236.

[6] *See* Sonya Dreizler, *When Locker Room Talk Is Office Talk and Women's Bodies Are for Touching*, SOLUTIONS WITH SONYA (Oct. 27, 2019), www.solutionswithsonya.com/news/2019/10/26/do-better-office-behavior.

[7] Claire Fallon & Emma Gray, *For Women Behind the Camera, Sexual Harassment Is Part of the Job*, HUFFPOST (Mar. 15, 2018), www.huffpost.com/entry/women-film-crew-member-sexual-harassment_n_5aa81eeee4b001c8bf147bf8.

[8] Soraya Chemaly, *"Locker Room" Language Encourages Rape Culture, Even If It Stays Private*, QUARTZ (Oct. 13, 2016), https://qz.com/806386/donald-trumps-lewd-access-hollywood-video-locker-room-language-encourages-rape-culture/.

but a whole culture that foments, facilitates, and ultimately protects abuse and subjugation. This culture is built upon, in many instances, a foundation of unchecked, demeaning workplace speech and interactions.

The unspoken belief that women should have to put up with locker room talk translates into several discrete challenges to equality seen in the law and in the workplace itself. One such challenge is in the actual law and its interpretation, which often allows speech and behavior inimical to workplace equality to elide capture. Another is workplace cultures that, often in contravention of their own promulgated regulations, tolerate or even encourage toxic environments.

The Supreme Court famously confirmed in 1989 that "discrimination in the air" was not actionable, but that once that discrimination was "grounded" and "visited upon" an employee, it became actionable.[9] This signaled strongly that the laws mandating equality and forbidding harassment required a certain degree of concreteness and directedness to be invoked. So, directly propositioning or continually insulting a woman in a sexually derogatory way is paradigmatic sexual harassment, but more subtle or indirect behavior and language can persist and remain unchecked.

There are many ways to fall just short of sexual harassment (and other legal discrimination standards) and still create an environment in which women become disproportionately disadvantaged. From the hanging of sexually graphic images in the office,[10] to the playing of Howard Stern and other explicit radio shows,[11] to the simple use of phrases that allude to sexual acts or parts of anatomy in order to convey a sentiment,[12] to banter that demeans women, to sexually explicit language or gendered slurs used to convey otherwise workplace-appropriate thoughts and ideas (one junior associate recalls working for a law firm partner who would say things like, "Wow, they are really asking you to bend over having you turn in that brief so early").[13]

What is particularly problematic is that much of what alienates and discomforts women and others is simply a function of structurally embedded notions in society of what is funny or descriptive. In other words, phrases used to describe everything from feeling professionally outmaneuvered to being

[9]   *Hopkins*, 490 U.S. at 251.
[10] Reeves v. C. H. Robinson Worldwide, Inc., 594 F.3d 798, 805 (11th Cir. 2010).
[11] *Id.* at 804.
[12] *Id.*
[13] *See* Kerri Lynn Stone, *Decoding Civility*, 28 BERKELEY J. GENDER L. & JUST. 185 (2013); *see also* Cardin v. Via Tropical Fruits, Inc., No. 88–14201, 1993 U.S. Dist. LEXIS 16302, at *24–25, n.4 (S.D. Fla. Jul. 9, 1993); Jenson v. Eveleth Taconite Co., 824 F. Supp. 847, 880 (D. Minn. 1993); Andrews v. City of Philadelphia, 895 F.2d 1469, 1485 (3d Cir. 1990); Tunis v. Corning Glass Works, 747 F. Supp. 951, 959 (S.D.N.Y. 1990).

frustrated with how something is going are rife with sexually explicit terminology, much of which is sex-specific. Whether it is the colloquial use of words for female genitalia to describe someone weak or to insult someone, the act of sex used as a protracted metaphor to describe being taken advantage of or defeated, or the use of the word "bitch" to alternately insult a petty, vicious woman or demean a man as weak or servile, the harm conferred upon women is often packaged in a way that is so familiar that it may be glossed over. The cultural association between this language and these ideas are so cemented as to render users unconscious of their real meaning, but palpable, in that women are consistently depicted as "others" to whom things are done.[14]

"It's weird," says Raquel, a thirty-five-year old financial associate. "The men in the room don't hear the words the way that I do. They hear my boss complaining about someone on the other side of a deal or a regulatory agency, and they hear the substance of the complaint. But I hear the words he uses, and it's so belittling to me as a woman." Work experiences such as those described by Raquel expose the limits of the law to offer a remedy. Courts need to draw lines of delineation when determining when alleged harassment is (1) truly "because of sex" and (2) "severe or pervasive" enough to be actionable, and things like tone, emphasis, or context of usage can get obscured when evidence is collected and proffered.[15] Much of what we colloquially refer to as "locker room talk" goes uncaptured by these standards as applied by courts. And this happens because the speech at issue is so structurally embedded into cultural norms of humor and conversation that it is seen as too nuanced, subtle, or otherwise innocuous to violate the law.

This inadequacy is not well known to or well understood by many people. Many people erroneously believe that there is such a thing as "sexual harassment," unmoored from law. They imagine that, as Justice Stewart once famously quipped about obscenity, they or anyone else would "know it if they saw it,"[16] and that there are unambiguous laws in place to vindicate victims and to deter would-be harassers. In fact, those finding facts and interpreting the law too often fail to recognize when less targeted, less sexual language nonetheless creates an atmosphere that is demeaning to women.

The belief that women should simply resign themselves to locker room talk at work exists in the actual workplace as well as in the courts. While many

---

[14] *See* Emily Smith Cardineau, *Words of Wisdom: How Workplace Language Influences Gender Equality*, CAKE & ARROW (Oct. 16, 2017), https://cakeandarrow.com/newsfeed/2017/10/words-of-wisdom-workplace-language-gender-equality/.

[15] *See e.g.*, Pipkins v. City of Temple Terrace, 267 F.3d 1197, 1200 (11th Cir. 2001); Succar v. Dade Cty. Sch. Bd., 229 F.3d 1343, 1345 (11th Cir. 2000).

[16] Jacobellis v. Ohio, 378 U.S. 184, 197 (Stewart, J., concurring).

companies – according to their corporate handbooks, policies, and public statements – forbid speech and behavior that demeans a group, like women, without fostering a corporate ethos or culture that does the same, it is all to no avail. "If you look at our employee handbook, we are not supposed to use vulgar or obscene language or language that is jargon for body parts or sex acts," says Maria, a floor supervisor, "[b]ut no one ever enforces that, and it's actually done so much by the higher-ups that it would be unthinkable to complain about it."

Many judges seem to fear that capturing locker room talk and other less obvious harassment would be overreaching that effectively transforms Title VII into, as the courts recite, a "civility code."[17] However, judges must employ diligence to ensure that what is occurring is not, in fact, affecting women uniquely. They must apply a more critical eye toward the structural sexism that seeps into common slang, interactions, humor, and entertainment, lest they screen out cases that do allege discriminatory behavior.

On one hand, it must be recognized that, at some point, references are simply too attenuated from their origins, and behaviors are simply unmoored from their larger societal contexts. Title VII was not intended to transform Human Resources executives and federal judges into "thought police" ready to remedy sexism even where it does not exist and is not felt. Title VII is not a civility code, but there is a widening chasm between this theoretical stopping point and judges' often dismissive, narrowly crafted, uninformed interpretations of "because of sex." This chasm exists on many levels. It knocks out the cases of the actual litigants, but the reverberations of each of these decisions are also felt when they fuel lawyers' beliefs that these cases are not worthwhile, employers' understandings of the law and their consequent disregard for employee complaints, and society's larger beliefs about what is and is not taboo behavior.

For a very long time after the recognition of sexual harassment as a cause of action in 1986, cases where plaintiffs were not directly targeted were viewed as having diminished evidence, if they even had enough at all. For example, in 1997 in *Gleason* v. *Mesirow Financial, Inc.*, the Seventh Circuit Court of Appeals pointed out that much of the harassment alleged by the plaintiff was

---

[17]   Oncale v. Sundowner Offshore Services, Inc., 523 U.S. 75, 80 (1998); Faragher v. City of Boca Raton, 524 U.S. 775 (1998); Burlington Northern & Santa Fe Ry. v. White, 548 U.S. 53, 68 (2006) ("Title VII of the Civil Rights Act of 1964 (Title VII) does not set forth a general civility code for the American workplace . . . [J]udicial standards for sexual harassment must 'filter out complaints attacking the ordinary tribulations of the workplace, such as the sporadic use of abusive language, gender-related jokes, and occasional teasing.'") (quoting *Faragher*, 524 U.S. at 788).

experienced not by the plaintiff, herself, but by "female customers, [her] female relatives when they visited or called the office, or other female employees."[18] While the court acknowledged that these experiences would retain "some relevance in demonstrating the existence of a hostile work environment," it declared that "the impact of 'second-hand harassment' is obviously not as great as the impact of harassment directed at the plaintiff."[19] In this case, the court concluded that while both sexes may have experienced a hostile environment at the plaintiff's workplace, "that environment was not more hostile for women than for men."[20] The court concluded this despite the fact that the plaintiff alleged that, in her presence, her alleged harasser referred to "female customers as 'bitchy' or 'dumb,' on occasion[,] appeared to be ogling other female employees, flirted with [her] female relatives, and ... commented on the anatomy of one of [her] co-workers."[21] While the court described this behavior as "off-color, juvenile[,] and inappropriate," it framed the relevant query as whether the plaintiff, "particularly when this alleged behavior was directed at others and not herself, could rationally consider herself at a disadvantage in relation to her male co-workers by virtue of being a woman," and concluded that she could not.[22]

This was far from the only court to perceive a plaintiff's showing as diminished or insufficient where the sexually hostile environment alleged consisted largely or entirely of comments and behavior directed at others in the presence of the plaintiff.[23] Interestingly, the California Supreme Court held that "[a] hostile work environment sexual harassment claim by a plaintiff who was not personally subjected to offensive remarks and touching requires 'an even higher showing' than a claim by one who had been sexually harassed without suffering tangible job detriment: such a plaintiff must 'establish that the sexually harassing conduct permeated [her] direct work environment.'"[24] The Sixth Circuit Court of Appeals noted that even where one's work

---

[18] Gleason v. Mesirow Fin., 118 F.3d 1134, 1144–45 (7th Cir. 1997).

[19] *Id.*

[20] *Id.*

[21] *Id.*

[22] *Id.*

[23] Black v. Zaring Homes, Inc., 104 F.3d 822, 826 (6th Cir. 1997); Jackson v. Racine Cty., No. 02-C-936, 02-C-1262, 02-C-1263, 2005 WL 2291025 (E.D. Wis. 2005); Brennan v. Townsend & O'Leary Enters., Inc., 199 Cal. App. 4th 1336, 1358 (2011); EEOC v. Evans Fruit Co., 2013 U.S. Dist. LEXIS 23289 (E.D. Wash., 2013); Stewart v. FCC, 279 F. Supp. 3d 209 (D.D.C. 2017).

[24] Lyle v. Warner Bros. Television Productions, 38 Cal. 4th 264, 285 (2006) (quoting Fisher v. San Pedro Peninsula Hospital 214 Cal.App.3d 590, 608 (1989)); *see also* Brill v. Lante Corp., 119 F.3d 1266, 1274 (7th Cir. 1997): ("The 'locker room' atmosphere in San Jose that Brill painted in her deposition consisted of remarks directed at [another woman], not her ....").

environment was impacted by the harassment of others "because of sex," the court should remain mindful that the "severe or pervasive" standard may very well not be met and that "Title VII was 'not designed to purge the workplace of vulgarity.'"[25]

Courts have also taken it upon themselves to dispose of cases, rather than permit them to get to a jury, based on highly subjective standards crafted on the fly. These standards could consist of a glib assessment of how raunchy a comment or behavior was or wasn't, without any evaluation of the effect on a woman of hearing the comments or witnessing the behavior at work.

In 1995, the Seventh Circuit overturned a jury verdict awarded to a plaintiff who alleged that her harasser would

> 1. call her "pretty girl," as in "There's always a pretty girl giving me something to sign off on." 2. Once, when she was wearing a leather skirt, he made a grunting sound that sounded like "um um um" as she turned to leave his office. 3. Once when she commented on how hot his office was, he raised his eyebrows and said, "Not until you stepped your foot in here." 4. Once when the announcement "May I have your attention, please" was broadcast over the public-address system, [he] stopped at [her] desk and said, "You know what that means, don't you? All pretty girls run around naked." 5. He once called [her] a "tilly," explaining that he uses the term for all women. 6. He once told her that his wife had told him he had "better clean up my act" and "better think of you as Ms. Anita Hill." 7. When asked by [her] why he had left the office Christmas Party early, [he] replied that there were so many pretty girls there that he "didn't want to lose control, so I thought I'd better leave." 8. Once when she complained that his office was "smokey" from cigarette smoke, [he] replied, "Oh really? Were we dancing, like in a nightclub?" 9. When she asked him whether he had gotten his wife a Valentine's Day card, he responded that he had not but he should because it was lonely in his hotel room (his wife had not yet moved to Chicago) and all he had for company was his pillow. Then [he] looked ostentatiously at his hand. The gesture was intended to suggest masturbation.[26]

The court concluded that "these incidents, spread over seven months," could not possibly reasonably add up to sexual harassment, even though the case had already been tried, and a jury had already concluded that they did.[27]

The court, in taking it upon itself to declare that the case's outcome was not legally tenable, declared: "The concept of sexual harassment is designed to

---

[25] *Black*, 104 F.3d at 826 (quoting Baskerville v. Culligan Int'l Co., 50 F.3d 428, 430 (7th Cir. 1995)).

[26] *Baskerville*, 50 F.3d at 430.

[27] *Id.*

protect working women from the kind of male attentions that can make the workplace hellish for women," but "[i]t is not designed to purge the workplace of vulgarity."[28] Declaring that "[d]rawing the line is not always easy," the court made the delineation nonetheless: "On one side lie sexual assaults; other physical contact, whether amorous or hostile, for which there is no consent express or implied; uninvited sexual solicitations; intimidating words or acts; obscene language or gestures; pornographic pictures. . . . On the other side lies the occasional vulgar banter, tinged with sexual innuendo, of coarse or boorish workers."[29] While the court conceded that the line was not a "bright" one, and that when the issue of which side of the line harbors unlawful behavior is debatable, a jury should take it up, and not be questioned, it nonetheless concluded that this case was not "within the area of uncertainty," and that the alleged harasser was not, as a matter of law, a sexual harasser.[30] The court was able to get to what it felt was this inexorable conclusion because, among other things, "[t]he comment about Anita Hill was the opposite of solicitation, the implication being that he would get into trouble if he didn't keep his distance."[31] It also added:

> He never touched the plaintiff. He did not invite her, explicitly or by implication, to have sex with him, or to go out on a date with him. He made no threats. He did not expose himself, or show her dirty pictures. He never said anything to her that could not be repeated on primetime television. . . . Some of his repartée, such as, "Not until you stepped your foot in here," or, "Were we dancing, like in a nightclub?," has the sexual charge of an Abbott and Costello movie. The reference to masturbation completes the impression of a man whose sense of humor took final shape in adolescence. It is no doubt distasteful to a sensitive woman to have such a silly man as one's boss, but only a woman of Victorian delicacy—a woman mysteriously aloof from contemporary American popular culture in all its sex-saturated vulgarity—would find Hall's patter substantially more distressing than the heat and cigarette smoke of which the plaintiff does not complain.[32]

The court so found, as a matter of law, while purporting to remain "mindful of the dangers that lurk in trying to assess the impact of words without taking account of gesture, inflection, the physical propinquity of speaker and hearer, the presence or absence of other persons, and other aspects of context."[33]

[28] *Id.*
[29] *Id.*
[30] *Id.* at 431.
[31] *Id.*
[32] *Id.*
[33] *Id.*

However, the court handily disposed of the case – a case that had just been won before a jury – as it noted that the plaintiff and her accused harasser "were never alone outside the office, and there is no suggestion of any other contextual feature of their conversations that might make Hall a harasser."[34]

In 1997, the Seventh Circuit in another case also dismissed gendered acts, like a "manager telling [a plaintiff] he disapproved of premarital sex and another yelling at her while 'towering' over her," as "not appear[ing] to have anything to do with her sex, and for that matter ... not [being] particularly sexual in nature, either."[35] As recently as 2010, a district court in that same circuit used the plaintiff's "admissions" that "none of the conduct cited in her complaints was directed towards her, and at no time did she feel discriminated against because she was female," to dismiss her claims, without a word to what might be going on to spark her claim or consideration of how her workplace might have been transformed for her "because of" her sex. The court emphasized that her "complaints reference conversations she overheard around the workplace amongst subordinates or fellow supervisors. She was infrequently, if ever, a participant in these vulgar conversations and was never the subject of them."[36]

A 2013 *en banc* (fully constituted) decision out of the Eleventh Circuit should have been a watershed decision that moved the goalposts when it comes to construing the "because of" requirement of Title VII.[37] However, the past few years have shown that subsequent courts have largely, often spuriously cabined it to its precise facts.[38] Its facts and the decision's analysis

---

[34]   *Id.*

[35]   Brill v. Lante Corp., 119 F.3d 1266, 1274 (7th Cir. 1997).

[36]   Taylor v. ABT Elecs., Inc., No. 05 C 576, 2010 U.S. Dist. LEXIS 3147 at *7–9 (N.D. Ill. Jan. 15, 2010); *see also* Kortan v. Cal. Youth Auth., 217 F.3d 1104, 1100 (9th Cir. 2000) (stating that while "[t]here is no question that [her supervisor's] comments were offensive[,] ... the comments were about other people. He never directed a sexual insult to [Plaintiff]"); Anderson v. State, No. CV06-00817-PHZ-NVW, 2007 U.S. Dist. LEXIS 36399 at *28–29 (D. Ariz. May 15, 2007) (holding that the plaintiff is not entitled to trial on claims of sexual harassment where "[Plaintiff] failed to identify any support in her contention that a reasonable woman would find Jones['s] threat to kill another woman's pets 'sufficient or pervasive enough to alter the conditions of her employment,'" and where her "supervisor discussed 'penis myths' with a female coworker on one occasion within earshot.").

[37]   *See* Reeves v. C. H. Robinson Worldwide, Inc., 594 F.3d 798, 803 (11th Cir. 2010).

[38]   *See, e.g.,* McGullam v. Cedar Graphics, Inc., 609 F.3d 70, 85–86 (2d Cir. 2010) (Calabresi, J., concurring) (citing *Reeves* to support that "references to one woman as a 'dog' and as 'bitch[y],' to another woman as being 'on the rag,' and more generically to a 'titty bar' ... appear[] to be the product of a locker-room office culture" but do not insulate the defendant from a hostile work environment claim); Harris v. Mayor of Balt., 429 F. App'x 195, 201 (4th Cir. 2011) (citing *Reeves* as a case "characterizing the use of terms 'whore,' 'bitch,' and 'cunt' as being 'targeted at [a woman's] gender.'").

are, however, instructive. In *Reeves* v. *C. H. Robinson Worldwide, Inc.*, a transportation sales representative who was the only woman working on her sales floor was regularly exposed to a barrage of obscenity and to a workplace inimical to the retention of women.[39] The behavior that she witnessed daily included "language that ... was unusually offensive, even compared to the curse words she heard in the Merchant Marines," though, "while incessant, vulgar, and generally offensive, [it] was not gender-specific."[40] It also included "generally indiscriminate vulgar language and discussions of sexual topics ... such as masturbation and bestiality."[41] Moreover, the plaintiff, while not, herself, a specific target of the abusive language, also regularly heard "a substantial corpus of gender-derogatory language addressed specifically to women as a group in the workplace."[42] As the court recited:

> Her co-workers used such language to refer to or to insult individual females with whom they spoke on the phone or who worked in a separate area of the branch. Although not speaking to Reeves specifically, Reeves said that her male co-workers referred to individuals in the workplace as "bitch," "fucking bitch," "fucking whore," "crack whore," and "cunt." Reeves's co-worker ... frequently shouted the epithets "fucking bitch" or "fucking whore" after hanging up his phone. He also called one woman a "cunt." Indeed, Reeves's supervisor ... often referred to his female colleagues by the term "bitch." Among other examples offered, he ordered Reeves to speak with "that stupid bitch on line 4," and described a former female colleague ... as a "lazy, good-for-nothing bitch." ... [Another] concluded a joke with the punch-line "fuck your sister, and your mother is a whore." Nearly every day, Reeves's co-workers tuned the office radio to a crude morning show. Reeves claimed that this program featured, among other things, regular discussions of women's anatomy, a graphic discussion of how women's nipples harden in the cold, and conversations about the size of women's breasts. It also once advertised a "perverse" bikini contest. On one occasion, Reeves's co-worker ... displayed a pornographic image of a fully naked woman with her legs spread, exposing her vagina, on his computer screen. Her co-workers also regularly sang songs about gender-derogatory topics. Reeves's co-workers singled out ... the only other female employee in the ... branch, for gender-specific ridicule. In Reeves's earshot, albeit out of [her] presence, [the] branch manager ... insulted [her], saying "[s]he may be a bitch, but she can read." [Another worker] also referred to [her] as a "bitch" after she had left the room to use the

[39] *Reeves*, 594 F.3d at 803.
[40] *Id.* at 803–04.
[41] *Id.* at 804.
[42] *Id.*

bathroom. Reeves's co-workers openly discussed [this other woman's] buttocks.[43]

Despite the regularity with which this went on, and despite the plaintiff's frequent complaints about it, nothing seemed to change:

> According to Reeves, this offensive conduct occurred "on a daily basis." She testified that "if you were to pull out a calendar right now and I were to look at, you know, summer of 2001 to spring of '04, I could point at every day of the year that some of this behavior went on. It went on every day." She indicated that "this type of phrase, 'You fucking whore,' was commonplace." Reeves testified that she objected frequently to the crude language, conduct, and radio station to her co-workers. Much of the time, she identified only a generally vulgar and offensive working environment. On occasion, however, she complained about gender-specific offensive behavior, too. Thus, for example, when she heard offensive topics on the radio, Reeves would change the radio station, usually to the "classic rock station," sometimes "twice in one day." Reeves said that when her co-workers used generally offensive terms, she told them that their language was offensive, first orally and then by email. Reeves's co-workers' offensive behavior allegedly persisted unabated. She testified: "It was pretty obvious to me by this time that complaining to co-workers was not bringing about any results. . . . [N]othing would change." Indeed, on one occasion, apparently aware that their conduct offended her, Reeves's co-worker . . . shouted to her, "Ingrid, better wear your earplugs tomorrow," so that a co-worker could behave "any way he liked" on his last day of work. At least once, Reeves complained directly to a co-worker about his gender-specific offensive behavior. Reeves described confronting [a co-worker] when he displayed an explicit image of a naked woman exposing her vagina on his computer screen. Reeves testified that she saw the picture as she walked by [his] desk from the copy machine. Reeves recalled her reaction: "I was really offended by that. I was really upset. And it was very humiliating to me. And I just remember like my hands were like shaking. And . . . I knew I needed to say something to him because I felt that if I didn't say something to him, then he would assume that it's okay." Reeves said that she . . . told him that she "saw that image [he] had on [his] computer. It really is offensive. It ma[de] [her] really uncomfortable." [He] apologized. Because her complaints to her co-workers proved futile, Reeves complained to her branch manager and supervisor . . . . Reeves explained, "[i]t was pretty obvious to me by this time that complaining to co-workers was not bringing about any results. So by about this time, my focus was on upper management." . . . Again, Reeves complained about both non-gender-specific, but generally vulgar behavior, and gender-specific conduct, too. On . . . Reeves's

---

[43] *Id.*

third day in the office, she first complained about [a supervisor's] use of a vulgar reference to a woman. [He] had been speaking with a Japanese customer on the telephone. Reeves recalled listening to [his] frustration rising. He placed the call on hold, looked directly at Reeves, and told her to "talk to that stupid bitch on line 4." After Reeves spoke with the customer, she asked to speak with [him] in his office. In this one-on-one meeting, she explained that the language he had used made her "very uncomfortable." He apologized, but offered that "this is just the way I am, and you will just have to learn to ignore it."[44]

Her subsequent complaints similarly fell on essentially deaf ears, according to the court. As the court recited, after a supervisor "promised that the office could switch to playing less offensive programming, two months later, when Reeves tried once again to turn down the offensive radio station, [the same man] asked her to 'turn it back up a notch' so that he could listen."[45] He would later admit:

[A]lthough he had promised to "pay closer attention" to the language in the office, it "did not stop." He conceded that he never reported her complaints about the offensive language in the office to the corporate office, although it had been his responsibility to do so .... Reeves testified that the offensive language and conduct continued unabated. [He] "laughed at" the offensive language, which Reeves claimed "just encouraged it."[46]

As the plaintiff continually sought to ascend the hierarchy of the organization with her complaints, the court noted, she was consistently ignored. Finally, she resigned and sued. The trial court initially granted summary judgment on her case, meaning that it held that there was not enough there amidst her allegations, arguments, and evidence, to take the case to trial because she could never prevail on her sexual harassment claim. The trial court, pointing to the law's requirement that the harassment be "because of" the plaintiff's sex, held that "both men and women were afforded like treatment," and that, therefore, the plaintiff could not have been "intentionally singled out for adverse treatment because of her sex."[47] It was what an *en banc* appellate court would say in the course of reversing this grant, however, that would transform this case into something groundbreaking.

---

44   *Id.* at 804–05.
45   *Id.* at 806.
46   *Id.*
47   Reeves v. C. H. Robinson Worldwide, Inc., No. 2:06-CV-358-IPJ, 2006 U.S. Dist. LEXIS 97303, *24 (N.D. Ala. Dec. 11, 2006).

The appellate court began by intoning the familiar refrain that "Title VII is not a civility code, and not all profane or sexual language or conduct will constitute discrimination in the terms and conditions of employment."[48] It also took care to note:

> In a case like this, where both gender-specific and general, indiscriminate vulgarity allegedly pervaded the workplace, we reaffirm the bedrock principle that not all objectionable conduct or language amounts to discrimination under Title VII. Although gender-specific language that imposes a change in the terms or conditions of employment based on sex will violate Title VII, general vulgarity or references to sex that are indiscriminate in nature will not, standing alone, generally be actionable. Title VII is not a "general civility code." "Title VII does not prohibit profanity alone, however profane. It does not prohibit harassment alone, however severe and pervasive. Instead, Title VII prohibits discrimination, including harassment that discriminates based on a protected category such as sex."[49]

And the court was mindful in carving out the limits of Title VII's reach, even under what would come to be its construction:

> Title VII does not reach genuine but innocuous differences in the ways men and women routinely interact with members of the same sex and of the opposite sex. The prohibition of harassment on the basis of sex requires neither asexuality nor androgyny in the workplace; it forbids only behavior so objectively offensive as to alter the "conditions" of the victim's employment.[50]

Finally, the court insulated "sexual language and discussions that truly are indiscriminate," noting that they fail to meet the relevant standard because "[t]he Supreme Court has 'never held that workplace harassment, even harassment between men and women, is automatically discrimination because of sex merely because the words used have sexual content or connotations.'"[51] The key here is that this begs the question of what a court, be it in favor of a broad or a narrow construction of Title VII and its reach, will perceive as "truly indiscriminate."

The *Reeves* court reframed the issue that the trial court had used to shut down the plaintiff's case – whether the harassment was "because of sex" – by defining the question before it as whether the plaintiff had been "exposed … to disadvantageous terms or conditions of employment to which members of

---

[48]   *Reeves*, 594 F.3d at 807.
[49]   *Id.* at 809.
[50]   *Id.* at 809 (quoting Oncale v. Sundowner Offshore Servs., 523 U.S. 75, 81 (1998)).
[51]   *Id.* at 809 (quoting *Oncale*, 523 U.S. at 80).

the other sex [were] not exposed," and answering it in the affirmative, even though the plaintiff did not allege that she, herself, was propositioned or disparaged.[52] Noting that "Title VII does not offer boorish employers a free pass to discriminate against their employees specifically on account of gender just because they have tolerated pervasive but indiscriminate profanity as well," the court declared that "the context of offending words or conduct is essential to the Title VII analysis."[53] By way of example, it noted:

> Even gender-specific terms cannot give rise to a cognizable Title VII claim if used in a context that plainly has no reference to gender. Thus, for example, were a frustrated sales representative to shout "Son-of-a-bitch! They lost that truck," the term would bear no reference to gender. In contrast, however, when a co-worker calls a female employee a "bitch," the word is gender-derogatory . . . . [T]he terms "bitch" and "slut" are "more degrading to women than to men."[54]

In the course of this analysis, the court looked to the word's original definition ("the female of the dog") as per Webster's Dictionary; its secondary, more colloquial definition ("a lewd or immoral woman" or "a malicious, spiteful, and domineering woman"); its generally perceived roots ("[c]alling a female colleague a 'bitch' is firmly rooted in gender"); and its often-felt effects ("[i]t is humiliating and degrading based on sex").[55] The court recalled the Supreme Court's admonition that courts evaluating harassment cases look at the totality of the circumstances surrounding words and behavior, noting that "[t]he real social impact of workplace behavior often depends on a constellation of surrounding circumstances, expectations, and relationships which are not fully captured by a simple recitation of the words used or the physical acts performed."[56] The court vowed to "proceed with '[c]ommon sense, and an appropriate sensitivity to social context,'" to distinguish between general office vulgarity and the "conduct which a reasonable person . . . would find severely hostile or abusive."[57]

Significantly, the *Reeves* court eliminated a barrier for many plaintiffs by holding that "words and conduct that are sufficiently gender-specific and either severe or pervasive may s[upport] a claim . . . even if the words are not

---

[52] *Id.* at 809 (quoting Harris v. Forklift Sys., 510 U.S. 17, 25 (1993) (Ginsburg, J., concurring)).
[53] *Id.* at 810.
[54] *Id.*
[55] *Id.*
[56] *Id.* (quoting *Oncale*, 523 U.S. at 81–82).
[57] *Id.* at 811 (quoting *Oncale*, 523 U.S. at 81–82).

directed specifically at the plaintiff."[58] This made much of the plaintiff's "because of sex" argument easy when looking at her facts. The court noted:

> It is enough to hear co-workers on a daily basis refer to female colleagues as "bitches," "whores" and "cunts," to understand that they view women negatively, and in a humiliating or degrading way. The harasser need not close the circle with reference to the plaintiff specifically: "and you are a 'bitch,' too." ... Similarly, words or conduct with sexual content that disparately expose members of one sex to disadvantageous terms or conditions of employment also may support a claim under Title VII .... Evidence that co-workers aimed their insults at a protected group may give rise to the inference of an intent to discriminate on the basis of sex, even when those insults are not directed at the individual employee. A jury could infer the requisite intent to discriminate when that employee complained to her employer about the humiliating and degrading nature of the commentary about women as a group and the conduct persisted unabated.[59]

The court was careful to cabin its holding by noting that "[i]f the environment ... had just involved a generally vulgar workplace whose indiscriminate insults and sexually-laden conversation did not focus on the gender of the victim, we would face a very different case."[60] The case at bar was different, the court maintained, because "a substantial portion of the words and conduct alleged in this case may reasonably be read as gender-specific, derogatory, and humiliating."[61] The court continued: "A reasonable juror could find that this gender-derogatory language and conduct exposed Reeves to 'disadvantageous terms or conditions of employment[,]'" through "repeated and intentional discrimination directed at women as a group, if not at Reeves specifically."[62]

Finally, the court clarified, the defendant could not prevail on its argument, testing the strictures of the "because of" requirement, that since the environment, language, and behavior predated the plaintiff's employment, the harm that she sustained was from abuse that existed wholly independent of her, and therefore could not possibly have been because of her sex.[63] The court rejected the argument as "inconsistent with the central premise of Title VII: [that] workers are to be protected from discrimination on account of gender in the workplace." Rather, the court reaffirmed that the plaintiff's contentions that

[58] *Id.*
[59] *Id.*
[60] *Id.*
[61] *Id.*
[62] *Id.* at 812.
[63] *Id.* at 812–13.

"her conditions of employment were humiliating and degrading in a way that the conditions of her male co-workers' employment were not" constituted a viable question for a jury: "Once Ingrid Reeves entered her workplace, the discriminatory conduct became actionable under the law. Congress has determined that Reeves had a right not to suffer conditions in the workplace that were disparately humiliating, abusive, or degrading."[64]

Similarly, the court flatly rejected the defendant's argument that because many of the gendered terms were used to refer to men and women alike, the plaintiff's harassment could not have been because of her sex.[65] The court noted that the plaintiff's claim of a sexually degrading workplace environment was at least as strong where men were called gendered epithets, noting that "[c]alling a man a 'bitch' belittles him precisely because it belittles women. It implies that the male object of ridicule is a lesser man and feminine, and may not belong in the workplace. Indeed, it insults the man by comparing him to a woman, and thereby, could be taken as humiliating to women as a group as well."[66]

Ultimately, the court summed up its take on the delineation between a generally "rough" environment and one which eroded women's well-being in the workplace precisely because they are women, noting that this "workplace was more than a rough environment—indiscriminately vulgar, profane, and sexual," and that the plaintiff's claims were viable, in that "a jury reasonably could find that it was a workplace that exposed Reeves to disadvantageous terms or conditions of employment to which members of the other sex were not exposed."[67]

At the time that it was published, *Reeves* looked to have held a great potential to dismantle impediments to plaintiffs' sexual harassment claims. However, a look at subsequent citations to the case reveals that it has been cited much more for its background premise that Title VII is not a civility code and for its carve-outs of generic vulgarity from Title VII's reach than for its recognition that a woman may be sexually harassed where she is not directly targeted but merely subjected to the constant demeaning of women.[68] Thus, although the plaintiff "won" in the *Reeves* decision – in that her case was

---

[64] *Id.* at 813.
[65] *Id.*
[66] *Id.*
[67] *Id.* at 813.
[68] *See, e.g.*, Rossi v. Fulton Cty., No. 1:10-CV-4254-RWS-AJB, 2013 U.S. Dist. LEXIS 44781, at *46 (N.D. Ga. Feb. 13, 2013) ("To rise to the level of an actionable Title VII claim, employment decisions must work a material alteration on the terms of employment, as opposed to being merely petty slights or trivial annoyances."); Kavanaugh v. Miami-Dade Cty., 775 F. Supp. 2d 1361, 1370 (S.D. Fla. 2011) (citing Reeves as support for the following: "courts have applied liability for more egregious conduct, such as when the name-calling was highly offensive,

resurrected and allowed to proceed past the summary judgment stage –
subsequent courts have seized upon what they presume to be the bedrock
presumptions underlying the analysis, noting the carve-outs and disclaimers to
highlight the limits of Title VII's reach, and construing the "because of"
requirement narrowly.

In one 2013 case,[69] the district, or trial, court was asked to review a jury verdict
for a sexual harassment plaintiff of $700,000. Basically, the facts were to be
construed as they had been by the jury, and unless the relevant law had been
misapprehended or otherwise misapplied by the judge presenting the jury with
questions, the verdict was to stand. In this particular case, the court reviewed
what it described as "twelve single-occurring incidents of [the]harassment" of
a female firefighter.[70] These incidents included her being told, in front of
instructors and co-workers, that "she basically took somebody else's spot, she
shouldn't be here," having her clothes and personal items thrown on the floor
after she accidentally placed them in the wrong holding space, and having
a bathing suit that she needed for training go missing from her unlocked locker
for two weeks, only to be found covered in a white substance that she assumed
was semen.[71] Other incidents included her receiving a call that "her bra was
hanging in the station," being called "bimbo" and a "cunt," workplace comments to the effect that she was promiscuous, and an incident whereupon she
was given a broomstick handle, labeled "Smart Lock" (Smart was her last name),
to use as a wedge for the door in her station's female restroom after requesting
a lock when she was walked in on by a male colleague while in the shower.[72]

The judge in the case went ahead and nullified the jury award for this
plaintiff, and perhaps the most telling insight into the judge's mindset in so
doing came when the judge recounted an incident in which the plaintiff's co-
worker refused to ride with her, saying "I am not going to work with that cunt."[73]
The judge immediately followed this recital with the notation that "Ms. Smart
concedes that it was she specifically that some of her co-workers did not want to
ride with and that they had ridden with other female firefighters."[74] This is very

---

frequent in nature, or occurring for an extended period of time."); EEOC v. Jomar Transp.,
Inc., No. 1:13-CV-3143-ODE, 2014 U.S. Dist. LEXIS 187898, *10 (N.D. Ga. Aug. 12, 2014);
Livingston v. Marion Bank & Tr. Co., 30 F. Supp. 3d 1285, 1301 (N.D. Ala. 2014); DeLeon
v. ST Mobile Aero. Eng'g, Inc., 684 F. Supp. 2d 1301, 1321–22 (S.D. Ala. 2010).

[69]   Smart v. City of Miami Beach, Fla., 933 F. Supp. 2d 1366, 1373–76 (S.D. Fla. 2013), *aff'd*, 567
F. App'x 820 (11th Cir. 2014).

[70]   *Id.* at 1373.

[71]   *Id.* at 1373–74.

[72]   *Id.* at 1374–75.

[73]   *Id.* at 1375.

[74]   *Id.*

telling; the judge appeared to voice the belief that the "because of sex" facet of the analysis was somehow diminished or mitigated because those who singled her out with a derogatory gendered epithet were somehow tolerant of riding with other women. One is left wondering whether this signifies that the incident was somehow not "because of" her sex. Thus, the court found, "the few, single-occurring instances of sex or gender-based harassment [the] Plaintiff suffered is [*sic*] simply legally insufficient to maintain a sexual harassment claim,"[75] meaning that the jury verdict, as a matter of law, could not possibly stand.

Moreover, the court went to the lengths of attempting to flesh out, from this package of treatment that had already persuaded a jury that the plaintiff was sexually harassed, which of the incidents were truly "sexual" and "gender-based" harassment. Rather than view the events, as the jury did, as one inextricably intertwined campaign of harassment, the judge did what many judges do and attempted to "slice and dice" the evidence[76] in order to winnow it down to something too tenuous and diffuse to substantiate the belief that it was, in fact, "because of sex," and thus capable of supporting the verdict.[77] Ironically, and not insignificantly, the case that the court cited for the proposition that "[i]n a case like this, where both gender-specific and general, indiscriminate [harassment] allegedly pervaded the workplace, we reaffirm the bedrock principle that not all objectionable conduct or language amounts to discrimination under Title VII," was *Reeves*.[78]

This court, as have others, appropriated *Reeves*'s soundbites, even as it upended its premise that one's working environment and well-being at work may be rocked to their core because of one's sex, without many of the hallmarks of harassment that courts had once sought. In any event, the *Smart* court toppled the jury's verdict, noting that "[o]nly a handful of the incidents [the] Plaintiff encountered – the bathing suit possibly containing semen, being called a 'bimbo' and a 'cunt,' having a male co-worker walk in during a shower, and being called promiscuous – can arguably be considered events that are sexual or gender-based. . . . Therefore," the court concluded, "many of the events elicited at trial cannot be considered in the determination of whether the sexual harassment Ms. Smart claims to have been subjected to was severe or pervasive." In other words, the evidence, once shorn away and disaggregated from its core, could not meet the standard.

---

[75] *Id.*
[76] Michael Zimmer, *Slicing & Dicing of Individual Disparate Treatment Law*, 61 LA. L. REV. 577 (2001).
[77] *Smart*, 933 F. Supp. 2d at 1376–78.
[78] *Id.* at 1376.

This is not the only recent case to invoke *Reeves* while disaggregating evidence to strip away the notion that too many elements in an environment or campaign of abuse were simply not occurring "because of sex." In 2013, the Sixth Circuit Court of Appeals invoked *Reeves* as it noted that, "in this case, on the other hand, the pornography was visible but not directed at [the plaintiff], . . . and the only sex-based remarks directed at her were made by one co-worker . . . in a single incident."[79] The plaintiff in that case had alleged that she, a woman of color, had suffered disparate treatment from her white male colleagues.[80] She also alleged that she was told at work that

> she was a Democrat only because she was a black woman; that unmarried women cannot "have the love of God in their heart[s]"; and that this country should "get rid of Jesse Jackson and Al Sharpton because without those two 'monkeys' the country 'would be a whole lot better'" . . . [and] that if she returned to school, she would not have to pay for her education because she was a single black mother.[81]

She also alleged that she was asked "why black people cannot name their children 'stuff that people can pronounce, like John or Sue.'" And told that "black people should 'go back to where [they] came from.'"[82]

Interestingly, the above was described by the court as a "single racist and sexist confrontation,"[83] and the term "intersectionality," which describes the overlapping and compounded harm that comes from being discriminated against as a member of two or more discrete protected classes,[84] is nowhere to be found in the opinion. The case was cut off at the knees and would never get to a jury. Courts have persisted in dismissing evidence as not "because of sex" where it is nuanced, subtle, or not overtly sexually aggressive. In December 2016, a district court, intent on excising from a harassment analysis the claimed hostility a plaintiff alleged to have endured after she reported her alleged harasser for harassment, asserted:

> [F]rom all that can be discerned from the record, after [his] reassignment, no words were ever exchanged between them. Plaintiff insists that [he] continued to "harass" her in that, when she would see him, he allegedly would

---

[79]　Williams v. CSX Transp. Co., 533 F. App'x 637, 642 (6th Cir. 2013).

[80]　*Id.* at 638.

[81]　*Id.* at 638–39.

[82]　*Id.* at 639.

[83]　*Id.* at 638.

[84]　Kimberlé Crenshaw, *Demarginalizing the Intersection of Race and Sex: A Black Feminist Critique of Antidiscrimination Doctrine, Feminist Theory and Antiracist Politics*, U. Chi. Legal F. 139 (1989).

stare and look at her with "angry" and "mean" looks. But such subtle, non-verbal "harassment" is distinctly different both in its *form* and *severity* from the repeated, overtly graphic sexual remarks and displays Plaintiff purportedly endured working alongside [him], before the VA intervened. Indeed, there is nothing in the record to support that [his] post-transfer "harassment" was based specifically on sex or gender. Rather, according to Plaintiff, Troupe began giving her stares, glares, and dirty looks immediately after he became aware she had *reported him to VA managers for sexual harassment.*[85]

It is clear that whether sexist or locker room talk takes the form of demeaning, objectifying, or sexually humiliating women, there is too much of it, and too much that has been found tolerable in the workplace.

THE PAIN

Some 82 percent of women and 74 percent of men report hearing sexist comments at work. In the face of this widespread normalization of sexist and locker room talk comes the realization that more significant than any of the above cases is their widespread impact on the legal market and on the workplaces of America. Victims of sexually charged or sexually hostile workplaces who are not personally targeted often do not see themselves as victims and blame their lack of enthusiasm for, and accomplishment at, the workplace on themselves.[86] Attorneys to whom such cases are brought might very well become more likely to reject those cases, or, at the very least, assign lower value to them, because of the way prior decisions have set their expectations.

The harms – social and dignitary, among others – that flow to women from locker room talk are incalculable. As activist Betty Ann Heggie put it, "[o]nce you have obscenely torn a woman apart with bro-talk, an insidious web of disrespect is woven. It becomes difficult to promote her and even more difficult to work for her. In short, it limits her opportunities."[87] Indeed, in the wake of the resurgence of the phrase "locker room talk" after the 2016

---

[85] Ike v. United States Dep't of Veterans Affairs, No. 2:16-CV-0406-JEO, 2016 WL 7094707, at *13 (N.D. Ala. Dec. 6, 2016) (emphasis in original).

[86] Kathi Miner-Rubino & Lilia M. Cortina, *Beyond Targets: Consequences of Vicarious Exposure to Misogyny at Work*, 92 J. OF APPLIED PSYCHOL., 1254, 1264 (2007) ("the more that both male and female employees observed uncivil and sexually harassing behavior directed toward female coworkers, the lower their psychological well-being and job satisfaction. Declines in psychological well-being, in turn, related to lower physical well-being, higher job burnout, and more thoughts about quitting. Lower job satisfaction was also linked with higher burnout, lower affective organizational commitment, and greater turnover intention.").

[87] Betty A. Heggie, *Why "Locker Room Talk" Hurts Both Men and Women*, HUFFPOST (Dec. 5, 2016), www.huffingtonpost.ca/betty-ann-heggie/trump-locker-room-talk_b_13372750.html.

Donald Trump revelation, commentator after commentator attempted to calculate the harm done by "locker room" talk to women. These commentators pointed out everything from locker room talk's role in the precipitation of rape culture to its ability to normalize sexual assault, to its effect of demeaning women, both in the eyes of others and in their own. This is to say nothing of the toll that a demeaning environment can take on a woman's job performance.

The failure of judges to construe the law in a manner that achieves its objective of ensuring workplace equality through parity in the privileges, terms, and conditions of employment occurs for several reasons. It occurs because the law has not kept pace with the social science research explaining that there is a quiet but palpable erosion of dignity that occurs when women are continually subjected to, and expected to work within a workplace culture that objectifies, demeans, and ultimately undermines their sex. It has also not kept pace with the reality that many women subjected to such a culture will experience effects that range from a loss of confidence, to a decline in work quality, to a general aversion to being at or doing their jobs. Thus, women become winnowed out of the workplace, be it by a "choice" they think they've made, which was actually *made for them*, bad performance or attendance records, or a slow, generalized fatigue that causes their careers to "stall."

MANIFESTATIONS

The unspoken belief or sentiment that women should put up with locker room talk at work is reinforced by several instances of current events in society. In addition to President Trump's having adverted to "locker room talk" in such a way as to normalize it, many others have as well.

And we should not forget about the many examples of a silent sexist workplace culture that tacitly normalized locker room talk and a toxic work environment, that only became drawn into sharper focus when a dissenter tried to shine a light on it and object. In 2018, many were talking about software engineer Shannon Lubetich who exited her job with a parting memo that decried what she perceived as her employer's lapses when it came to issues of diversity and sexism.[88] News outlet cheddar.com picked up the story, noting both that these issues plagued and reverberated within the tech industry at large and that executives from that company had acknowledged to the news

---

[88] Alex Heath, *Former Snap Employee Questions Company's Culture and Diversity*, CHEDDAR (May 29, 2018), https://cheddar.com/media/inside-snap-employee-concerns-raise-questions-about-culture-and-diversity.

outlet that it aimed to be a place where all felt respected, but that much work remained to be done.

Cheddar.com reported that, in addition to a host of issues dealing with diversity and inclusion, the sex-based issues that Lubetich mentioned included a corporate party at which scantily clad female models were paid to appear, a former executive who allegedly used sexist and other inappropriate language and humor at work, and "macho competitions and male-dominated turf wars," references to a "co-ed soccer league for employees as 'boys' night," and "hot tub parties after work where alcohol flowed freely." These all conspired to create what Lubetich termed a "pervading sexist vibe" that employees had foisted on them at work. And while the outlet did report that the employer had made robust efforts at remediating much of what Lubetich described, the entire tech industry seems to be beleaguered by accusations that women, as well as other minority employees, have, for quite some time, felt as though they were tacitly informed on a daily basis that they needed to accept that "locker room talk" and a toxic culture would festoon around them, both inside and outside of their presence.

TAKEAWAYS

There is tremendous power in voicing this largely unspoken belief. From those who supervise, to those who run Human Resources and Compliance departments, to lawyers who would litigate such cases, to judges, legislators, and others who could act to expand the confines of the law to include what truly harms women at work "because of their sex" – but don't. Whether it is voiced partially in a law school classroom, or runs silently and unnoticed through the mind of a decision-maker in a court or a legislature, the most invidious part of this unspoken belief is the failure of those who integrate it into their world views to acknowledge and broadcast that fact so that a response to it may be generated.

And that response must be carefully crafted. On one hand, narrow, literal interpretations of evidence that excise off from consideration all but the most direct affronts allow harm to be done to women "because of" their sex at work. On the other hand, even the *Reeves* court acknowledged that Title VII was not meant to mobilize "thought police" who would prosecute all instances of incivility, banter, or slang at work. So, what is to be done? First off, those who write, interpret, argue, and think and write about the law need to be aware of the unspoken belief that so many hold that "women should be able to handle a sexually-charged, crass, workplace culture, and if they can't, it's their own fault." And we need to rethink it and the premises that underlie it. Buried in the decisions that unnecessarily restrict evidence without allowing it to get to a trier of fact are invaluable lessons.

Many women who work in a pervasively sexually hostile environment do not identify as victims of harassment or discrimination simply because the behavior is not specifically targeted at them. This failure to identify should not be preclusive or dispositive of the question of harassment, either when a woman does file suit nonetheless, or when she complains to HR that she is uncomfortable. Judges and attorneys can open the law up to be more receptive to claims that certain language, behaviors, or even exposure to visual, electronic, or radio media during the workday may be as corrosive to a woman's sense of well-being at work as being directly propositioned. They can better factor in the damage done to a woman by continually witnessing others' harassment or by hearing language that demeans women generally. They can become more culturally attuned to the features of the context in which workplace interactions occur – the context that they claim to value so much – the inflections, the word choices, the postures of those interacting, and even if they don't carry the day for a case ultimately, these things can be recognized as relevant and put before a trier of fact more frequently than they are.

This will trickle down to the monitoring and compliance practices of employers internally.[89] To the extent that this does not happen, HR professionals and employer management, if proactive and committed to equality in the workplace, can pick up the mantle. Responsiveness to complaints, disciplinary action, workplace policies, and workplace training can be sharply tuned to factor in the myriad ways in which the demeaning of other women or of women in general, can erode a woman's self-worth, career trajectory, and sense of well-being in the workplace. Specifically, when a company commits to discipline or fire a harasser, whether or not the person who complains is his direct victim, more potential harassers are deterred, irrespective of whether the complainant would have a viable case in court that would survive summary judgment. When a rain-maker is disciplined or fired for an action which may or may not render the employer liable for harassment under the current construction of the law, the reverberations are felt throughout that workplace – and potentially in many others. When training makes employees aware that certain language or behavior is intolerable, it is less likely to occur. Gone

---

[89]   *See* Joan C. Williams, Marina Multhaup, Su Li, & Rachel Korn, *You Can't Change What You Can't See: Interrupting Racial and Gender Bias in the Legal Profession*, A.B.A. (Nov. 1, 2018), www.americanbar.org/content/dam/aba/administrative/women/you-cant-change-what-you-cant-see-print.pdf; *see also* Chris Newlands & Madison Marriage, *Women in Asset Management: Battling a Culture of "Subtle Sexism,"* FIN. TIMES (Nov. 29, 2014), www.ft.com/content/11585c1a-76ff-11e4-8273-00144feabdco#axzz3RQWBBxjy.

should be the days when employees are forced to watch awkward, dated videos about asking subordinates for sex in exchange for promotions. Training needs to keep pace with the times. The nuances of harassment and its effects should be informed by the latest research and relayed in keeping with how they most often present in real life. Employers should also be aware that the law is a floor, rather than a ceiling; they are free to legislate beyond the bare requirements of the law when it comes to dignity and respect in workplace interactions.

Finally, everyday people can voice a response to this and other unspoken beliefs. Awareness, not only by those who would perpetrate wrongs in the workplace but by bystanders, can make a difference. For every person who has seen an amusing meme about "mansplaining" – the patronizing, condescending explanation of basic things by men to women – on Facebook, and jokingly calls out a co-worker for doing it, a positive chilling effect on subtle harassment may be felt. For every person who has read an article on the Internet about the origins of certain crass phrases and their effect on women and self-edits the next time he is tempted to use a choice expression, a similar chilling effect may be felt. No; the widespread problem of the alienation of women from workplace cultures will not be remedied with a few simple word choices or some chiding, but the key here is awareness. To the extent that much of what goes on can be subtle enough that the victims, themselves, may not even identify as such,[90] to the extent that courts have been resistant to being educated about the effects of things that they consider petty or inconsequential,[91] and to the extent that for women who are ultimately forced out of a workplace by forces that they can't wholly identify, it has been, in effect, death by a thousand papercuts,[92] this kind of grassroots awareness may be the best bet. It should be

---

[90] MERIT SYSTEMS PROTECTION BOARD, REPORT ON SEXUAL HARASSMENT IN THE FEDERAL WORKPLACE, 96th Cong. (Sept. 1980) (submitted to the H.R. Subcomm. on Investigations of the Comm. on Post Office and Civil Service); *see also* Frank J. Till, *Sexual Harassment: A Report on the Sexual Harassment of Students*, NAT'L ADVISORY COUNCIL ON WOMEN'S EDUCATIONAL PROGRAMS, U.S. DEP'T. OF EDU. (Aug. 1980); CATHERINE A. MACKINNON, SEXUAL HARASSMENT OF WORKING WOMEN (1979); Claire Safran, *What Men Do to Women on the Job*, REDBOOK, 149 (Nov. 1976).

[91] *See* Morehouse v. Berkshire Gas Co., 989 F. Supp. 54 (D. Mass. 1997); Lewis v. Johnston, 908-CV-482 TJM ATB, 2010 WL 1268024, at *2 (N.D.N.Y. Apr. 1, 2010) ("Plaintiff's allegations that he may be the victim of future harassment or harm by DOCS employees do not amount to irreparable harm."); ANJA ANGELICA CHAN, WOMEN AND SEXUAL HARASSMENT: A PRACTICAL GUIDE TO THE LEGAL PROTECTIONS OF TITLE VII AND THE HOSTILE ENVIRONMENT CLAIM (1994).

[92] *Wage & Leadership Gaps*, CATALYZE SEATTLE (2019), www.catalyzeseattle.org/wage-leadership-gaps (last visited Jun. 21, 2018); *1000 Adult Interviews*, HUFFINGTON POST, http://big.assets.huffingtonpost.com/toplines_harassment_0819202013.pdf (last visited Jun. 21, 2018); Joni Hersch, *Compensating Differentials for Sexual Harassment*, AM. ECON. REV. (May 3, 2011), www.aeaweb.org/issues/196.

recalled that at one point in history, it was socially acceptable, if not downright amusing to many, to have propositioned or otherwise pursued one's secretary or female co-workers. Only after years of corporate compliance trainings, news headlines about sexual harassment on big stages, like the Clarence Thomas/ Anita Hill case, and even "very special" or themed episodes of popular TV shows that decided to tackle the issue, did it really seep into the public consciousness that it is socially taboo to engage in such behavior. There is no telling how many instances of harassment have been prevented by the knowledge of the shame or consequences that might have accompanied them, regardless of how many cases would have actually been filed. Subtle actions that demean women in ways that may or may not make it to a jury, but erode women's ability to thrive at work nonetheless are the next frontier. And with the advent of social media and the accessibility that it provides to all to educate themselves and to have information delivered in palatable, interesting ways, it may just be easier than ever to disseminate critical understandings about gender dynamics, language, and professionalism.

A number of blogs, social media pages, and online groups share individuals' narratives and exposition of the harm, subtle and otherwise, done to them and the protected classes to which they belong. While some people prefer to read scientific and other journals that publish studies and research, and others prefer short "pop culture" articles that reference them, many, no doubt, benefit from seeing the experiences and reactions of others in print. The trick is to connect the alienation of women from crass corporate or "locker room" culture to the unspoken belief that underlies it, to voice that belief, and to generate a response to it at every level.

What should it mean for abuse to be so sex-neutral as to elide capture by the statute? Are we to look at the words used and their dictionary definitions? Are we to infuse any cultural context into the abuse? Take note of how turns of phrase came into being? Their literal meaning? How much of their literal meaning seeps into how they are heard and absorbed by their targets? By others? The effect of the abuse on protected groups historically? Much of this work has not even been done by courts, let alone deemed relevant and allowed to enter legal analysis.

4

"You Don't Operate with Full Agency" (But)

At my law firm, I and my female friends are assigned "mentors." When we compare notes, we find that they come in one of only a few varieties. We get lectured to by senior women who tell us how hard things were for them to advance, and we get lots of personal comments, (I guess because they feel close to us, they can make them?) about "how we come across," in our demeanor and appearance. Like, they tell us to be "put together and professional," but not "too much," looks- and dress-wise, and confident, but not arrogant, in our interactions[.] I think they mean well. Sometimes, I feel like they are even nervous for us and looking out for us to protect us from a danger that they know we don't even fully understand yet.

The men, I have noticed, don't seem to have people bother talking with them so much about how they "come off," but they seem to, from what I have heard, more often get the "inside scoop" on things like which cool, new cases they should ask to be assigned to. Many of my male colleagues who are friends tell me that so-and-so is taking them "under his wing," and advising them about and recommending them to the "inside track," where gaining certain experiences and catching the eye of the right people get you staffed on certain cases and on the right "track" to advancement.

When I do get mentored by the older, male partners, I feel as though they talk more "at" me than "to me," the way they do to the men. I hear a lot of war stories as a captive audience, and sometimes even get compliments on what a good "lunch companion" I am. The men, though, sometimes seated around the same table, seem to get more offers and invitations for events and opportunities. It's not that we don't get any, and it's not that I think anyone doesn't mean well toward all of the junior associates. It's just that the actual words, actions, and results are, by and large, different for us.

—Nicole, twenty-eight, attorney

THE BELIEF

This chapter focuses on the unspoken belief that women do not move through the world with full agency to make their own decisions, but, rather, have to be regulated, watched, and even "rescued" in ways that men do not. This belief seems to express itself in many of the ways in which society and the law hold women accountable as adults with full agency for their actions, except, it appears, when it comes to sex and attraction – in and outside of the workplace. This inconsistent behavior is inexplicable – unless you impute it to the unspoken belief.

Going back centuries, women have too often lacked basic rights, such as voting, land ownership, and many others. While women were viewed across large swaths of society as being less physically and mentally capable than men, they were traditionally not able to plead their relative capacity,[1] agency, or ability in order to renounce or undo their actions legally. In other words, their perceived lack of agency, ability, and capacity was a sword that could be used against them, but never a shield that, as with others perceived to lack capacity or to have been susceptible to coercion or over-persuasion, could protect or rescue them from a contract or other legal decision. There was a large exception to this, though. While, historically, women could not, typically, renounce their actions, once taken, or disclaim ownership of their decisions by dint of their sex, this was not the case when it came to decisions that involved sexual relations. Indeed, the law used to afford recourse to those, like her father or husband, who surrounded a woman who had been "seduced"; she was not seen through the lens of the law as owning her own sexuality.[2]

Today, we see women in the workplace railing daily against the cliché that they somehow require more regulation than do men as to how they dress or comport themselves.[3] They are admonished to be less "emotional," and "mentored" to be more "professional." Human Resources officials and supervisors try to walk the precarious line between not appearing sexist and reinforcing the nearly ineffable ideal of the appearance of the "professional woman" – feminine enough to avoid making those around her uneasy, but covered-up enough, in multiple ways, to avoid arousing unwanted attention.[4] We see women trying to navigate dress codes, dating, or anti-fraternization policies in the office that were

---

[1] The power to create or enter into a legal relation under the same circumstances in which a normal person would have the power to create or enter into such relation. *Capacity*, BLACK LAW'S DICTIONARY (5th ed., 2016).

[2] *See* Joanna Grossman, *Is the Tort of Wrongful Seduction Still Viable? A North Carolina Court Will Get the Chance to Decide*, FINDLAW (Feb. 11, 2003), https://supreme.findlaw.com/legal-commentary/is-the-tort-of-wrongful-seduction-still-viable.html.

[3] Aditi Shrikant, *The Unspoken Rules of Workplace Attire for Women*, REWIRE (Aug. 7, 2018), www.rewire.org/work/unspoken-rules-workplace-attire-women/.

[4] Caroline Turner, *Can "Feminine" Women Make It to the Top?*, FORBES (Oct. 24, 2012, 10:21 PM), www.forbes.com/sites/womensmedia/2012/10/24/can-feminine-women-make-it-to-the-top /#171e884f27b7.

crafted against the backdrop of paternalistic laws and ideals.[5] And all too often, we see some men, for their part, fearful of navigating these same spaces.[6] Worried about seeming patronizing or being seen as overregulating with too many policies and too much "advice," many men deputize female HR officials and female mentors to dispense the "advice" and enforce the policies. "My law firm mentor was Latina and female like me," says Jennifer, thirty-two, an attorney.

> I guess because of that, she felt free to take me out to lunch and "remind" me not to wear jewelry that was too big, clothing that anyone would think is too tight, or colors that were too bright. I dressed very professionally at work, but she always seemed nervous for me, like even though I was fine objectively, I could still give people the "wrong idea" about myself—or maybe other Latinas too? . . . Looking back, it was so offensive, but she seemed like she was trying to be helpful, and I wasn't in law school choosing my friends; I was at work, and I felt I needed to get in line.

We also see that those who craft and enforce appearance, behavior, and "professionalism" standards often do so with the noxious belief that women lack agency and with the discriminatory suspicion that women will invariably paint themselves as victims while seeking recourse for alleged violations of their rights. They may, the belief goes, do this in or out of court, as victims who have been seduced by power and lack agency. Viewed through this lens and from a defensive posture, as they often are, female employees can thus trigger vigilance and apprehension in those charged with regulation, oversight, and peacekeeping in the workplace.

Viewed with such suspicion, women can have a hard time being seen as autonomous, self-made, accomplished people. Whereas an accomplished male may be more likely to be seen as a "rising star," or a "catch" that the employer was lucky to hire, an equally accomplished woman may be more likely to be seen as having or needing an older, more accomplished person – often a man – as her "mentor" or "sponsor" as she rises through the ranks.[7]

---

[5] *See* Shrikant, *supra* note 3.

[6] *See* Courtney Conley, *How Corporate America's Diversity Initiatives Continue to Fail Black Women*, CNBC (Jul. 1, 2020, 2:11 PM), www.cnbc.com/2020/07/01/how-corporate-americas-diversity-initiatives-continue-to-fail-black-women.html?__source=sharebar| twitter&par=sharebar.

[7] *See* Rania H. Anderson, *Challenging Our Gendered Idea of Mentorship*, HARV. BUS. REV. (Jan. 6, 2020), https://hbr.org/2020/01/challenging-our-gendered-idea-of-mentorship; Brittney Oliver, *For Black Women, the Biggest Workplace Barrier Begins at Entry-Level*, ESSENCE (Oct. 15, 2019), www.essence.com/news/money-career/for-black-women-the-biggest-systematic-workplace-barrier-begins-at-entry-level/.

With this sponsor or mentor to groom and vouch for her, she is seen to obtain the credibility and publicity that she isn't viewed to have been able to garner for herself. And so we see women combating the pervasive idea that only if they are "smart," "special," or "lucky" will they somehow be "discovered," "chosen," or "rescued" by men at work in a way that permits them to thrive and advance.[8]

With both men and women finding success in American workplaces, is this subtle, unvoiced dynamic easily proven? Clearly not. But a searching look at the sheer numerical disparities – discussed earlier – between men and women when it comes to those who attain the highest level of power, compensation, and prestige tells a powerful story that persists despite social, legal, and political movements to correct it.[9] Beyond the numbers, women's own reflections when they pause to consider not just *that* they ascended but *how* they ascended professionally, are illustrative.[10] "Almost every time we hire or promote someone with 'buzz' or 'cachet,' it turns out to be a male recruit," says Courtney, a forty-one-year-old editor.

> When a woman gets hired, the sense is, more often, "She deserves a chance," or "She has potential." It's all positive when we hire or promote, so no one really unpacks what they're thinking in the executive suite, but if you really listen to the buzz and do a comparison [between the sexes], you can really see the difference in the approach.

Once ensconced in a position, women often complain of feeling patronized and talked down to at work in ways that hurt not only how they feel but how they are perceived. One need not look beyond the increasing number of headlines exposing and decrying the casual advice, written protocols, and other regulations that have been demeaning and patronizing women in the workplace.[11] Emboldened, perhaps by recent social movements, women have been more readily coming forward with these stories and painting a picture of

---

[8]   *Cf.* Jessica Miller-Merrell, *Three Things Women Need to Be Successful in the Workplace*, WORKOLOGY (May 23, 2017), https://workology.com/three-things-women-successful-workplace/.

[9]   According to the Center for American Progress, women make up a mere 20 percent of high-level officers, executives, and managers in high-tech American businesses; 22.7 percent of law firm partners; 32 percent of full professors; 30 percent of college presidents; and 12.5 percent of Fortune 500 chief financial officers. Judith Warner, Nora Ellmann, & Diana Boesch, *The Women's Leadership Gap*, CTR. FOR AM. PROGRESS (Nov. 20, 2018, 9:04 AM), www .americanprogress.org/issues/women/reports/2018/11/20/461273/womens-leadership-gap-2/.

[10]   *See* Samara Lynn, *Black Women Less Likely to Be Promoted, Receive Recognition for Accomplishments*, BLACK ENTER. (Aug. 22, 2019), www.blackenterprise.com/black-women-less-likely-to-be-promoted-receive-recognition-for-accomplishments/.

[11]   *See, e.g.*, Frances Dodds, *10 Behaviors People Find Condescending*, ENTREPRENEUR (Feb. 12, 2020), www.entrepreneur.com/article/346238.

a landscape in which they have truly been viewed as simultaneously having and meriting less personal autonomy in the workplace.[12] Women are having wardrobe restrictions dictated to them in a way in which men are not. As will be discussed, even the law of sexual harassment is, on some level, operating to "rescue" women, rather than viewing them as fully autonomous people.

THE PANE

"Wanting" – Being Seen (and Spoken to) as Less Autonomous and More in Need of Personal Scrutiny

This unspoken belief that women don't operate with full agency is telegraphed by a range of people, from judges to HR officials, every day and creates yet another pane of the glass ceiling.[13] The fact is that women get punished by being seen more negatively for exhibiting the same ambitious, assertive behaviors as men, but *also* get punished for "holding back" and being too demure or withdrawn at work.[14] This is often referred to as a classic "double bind" ensuring that women cannot advance as easily as men do, and garner far more criticism and corrections than do their male peers.[15] Because these "punishments" may not be articulated, but may, rather, manifest themselves in the subconscious of a decision-maker or evaluator, they can go unnoticed, and women can be left with the feeling that they are seen as warranting more correction, regulation, and professional grooming than their male peers.

Moreover, research has demonstrated that when something called benevolent sexism takes hold, the misperception that women ought to be more "protected" at work can insulate them from receiving more challenging, "stretch" assignments that can be career advancing.[16] Similarly, the feedback that women are given at

---

[12] Susan Chira, *The Universal Phenomenon of Men Interrupting Women*, N.Y. TIMES (Jun. 14, 2017), www.nytimes.com/2017/06/14/business/women-sexism-work-huffington-kamala-harris.html; Reni Eddo-Lodge, *You're Talked to as If You Are a Junior—Employees on Workplace Racism*, GUARDIAN (Sept. 26, 2017), www.theguardian.com/inequality/2017/sep/2 6/employees-on-workplace-racism-under-representation-bame.

[13] Kerri Lynn Stone, *Consenting Adults? Why Women Who Submit to Supervisory Sexual Harassment Are Faring Better in Court Than Those Who Say No … and Why They Shouldn't*, 20 YALE J.L. & FEMINISM 25, 67–68 (2008).

[14] Herminia Ibarra, Robin J. Ely, & Deborah M. Kolb, *Women Rising: The Unseen Barriers*, HARV. BUS. REV. (Sept. 2013), https://hbr.org/2013/09/women-rising-the-unseen-barriers.

[15] *See The Double-Bind Dilemma for Women in Leadership*, CATALYST (Aug. 2, 2018), www .catalyst.org/research/infographic-the-double-bind-dilemma-for-women-in-leadership/.

[16] *Women Need a Network of Champions*, CTR. FOR CREATIVE LEADERSHIP, www.ccl.org/ar ticles/leading-effectively-articles/why-women-need-a-network-of-champions/ (last visited

work, compared with that given to men, has been found by studies to be relatively unfocused, personal in nature, and generally unhelpful.[17]

Over-Mentored but Under-Sponsored? The Opportunity Gap as a Reflection of a Belief

Though women are seen as having a need for more rescues, they are, ironically, less likely than their male peers to actually have a meaningful champion at work. While mentors may impart advice and have beneficent intentions toward their mentees, sponsors can be critical for all workers, as they, as per FAST COMPANY magazine, "promote, protect, prepare, and push" those whom they sponsor.[18] Citing examples of famous women in business, government, and public service whose high-profile male sponsors were vital to their situation in their companies, like Facebook CEO Sheryl Sandberg and U.S. Attorney General Loretta Lynch, FAST COMPANY nonetheless bemoaned the fact that women are 54 percent less likely than are their male peers to have a sponsor to help them advance.[19] In any event, if a sponsor is, as the *Harvard Business Review* says, "a person who has power and will use it for you," women not only lack this more than men but are seen as needing it more than men do.[20] And if women in the workplace are, as the *Harvard Business Review* concludes, "over-mentored and under-sponsored," that means that while they are targeted for advice and help, they are not, ultimately, thrust into the spotlight, supported, or meaningfully helped to ascend the power structure of the workplace.[21] Studies show that men benefit more meaningfully from mentoring when metrics like promotions are used.[22]

It only makes sense that with the demographics of workplace power being what they are and always have been, an employee of *either* sex is typically better off, salary-wise, with a workplace sponsor or advocate. Additionally, it only makes sense that, generally speaking, the more powerful an employee's mentor or

Dec. 29, 2019); Eden B. King et al., *Benevolent Sexism at Work: Gender Differences in the Distribution of Challenging Developmental Experiences*, 38 J. OF MGMT. 1835, 1835–66 (2010).

[17] *Id.*

[18] Sava Berhané, *Why Women Need Career Sponsors More Than Mentors*, FAST CO. (Aug. 15, 2015), www.fastcompany.com/3050430/why-women-need-career-sponsors-more-than-mentors.

[19] *Id.*

[20] Herminia Iberra, *A Lack of Sponsorship Is Keeping Women from Advancing into Leadership*, HARV. BUS. REV. (Aug. 19, 2019), https://hbr.org/2019/08/a-lack-of-sponsorship-is-keeping-women-from-advancing-into-leadership.

[21] Id.

[22] Herminia Ibarra, Nancy M. Carter, & Christine Silva, *Why Men Still Get More Promotions Than Women*, HARV. BUS. REV (Sept. 2010), https://hbr.org/2010/09/why-men-still-get-more-promotions-than-women.

sponsor, the better that employee will fare at work. Unfortunately, to the extent that sex, race, and other structural discrimination has left women, and particularly women of color, out of many of the highest ranks of employment, this is highly problematic. Men's mentors tend to be more senior and/or influential, and men are "talked at" less and promoted more. Women, especially women of color, are less likely to have such an experience and such a proponent; recent research shows as much.[23] Where people seek out those most like themselves to connect with at work, and where workplace power is disproportionately concentrated in the hands of white men, inequality will invariably self-replicate. According to the *Harvard Business Review*, men are more likely than are their female peers to get jobs that candidates must be situated "in line" to get, and what's more, as per a 2012 study of top business school alumni, men were more likely than women to have budget responsibility of more than ten million dollars and direct reports.[24] The study also revealed that the projects run by men had budgets twice as large as those run by women, and headcounts three times as big, and that while only a quarter of the women surveyed reported getting much coveted "C-suite visibility" on their projects, a full third of the men surveyed claimed that they did.[25]

Dress Codes: More Selective Scrutiny and Overregulation

Women being seen as lacking agency manifests itself in other ways at work. In recent years, there has been more and more of an outcry nationwide over office dress codes alleged to be patronizing and sexist. People are calling out the frequency and extent to which women's dress at work, whether it is supposed to be more professional or more casual, is regulated as compared with men's. Dress codes for men are typically broad and brief (like "dress pants, not made from denim"), while those for women can go on for pages with granular, often patronizing specificity.[26] And while men have typically been urged away from certain looks that women are permitted – like donning makeup, long hair, or earrings – most of the complaints of sexism and of the disparate burden conferred on the sexes by these codes have come from women.[27]

---

[23] Rebecca Greenfield, *The White-Male Mentorship Premium*, BLOOMBERG (Aug. 9, 2019, 4:00 AM), www.bloomberg.com/news/articles/2019-08-09/white-male-mentorship-brings-a-pre mium-and-it-s-hurting-women.

[24] Iberra, *supra* note 20.

[25] *Id.*

[26] *See, e.g., Grooming Guidelines/Dress Code Guidelines & Standards* SAFEWAY, (2008), www .careersatsafeway.com/wp-content/uploads/2012/11/Store-Dress-Code-All-Divisions.pdf.

[27] *Id.*

Some of the underlying thought strands on this selective overregulation can likely be found in the promulgation of student dress codes and the criticisms that they have engendered. With critics levying attacks against student dress codes being crafted for the purpose of protecting boys from the distraction and temptation of girls and their bodies,[28] it is easy to hear the echoes of the overregulation of women in the workplace when it comes to the style and modesty of their dress. And just as school dress code critics have urged administrators to place more of an onus on boys to control their thoughts and urges, than on girls to measure hemlines and strap thickness,[29] workplace scholars and observers have followed suit. Although one could argue that this standard line of purported reasoning cuts against the view that women, not men, lack agency, the school administrators' argument that they are imposing dress codes on girls since the boys lack agency to concentrate on schoolwork and not female bodies doesn't pass the smell test, given all that we know about how society feels about women and the imposition of shame on women for not repressing their (perceived) sexuality sufficiently (which changes based on the setting). It seems far more likely that schools want to send a subtle message to girls that they need to thread the needle and finely tune their level of sexuality throughout life to avoid being shamed.[30]

Fortunately, companies are generally scaling back on, or generally treading lighter when it comes to office dress codes and women.[31] That said, workplace dress codes, even in offices, persist in dictating to women when it comes to things like heel height, makeup, and the way in which clothing fits. Women are

---

[28] *See* Talia Lakritz, *18 Times Students and Parents Said School Dress Codes Went Too Far*, INSIDER (Feb 14, 2019), www.insider.com/school-dress-code-rules-controversy-2018-8; *Parents Outraged after Daughter, 9, Told Tank Top "Distracts" Boys at School*, NZ HERALD (Aug. 30, 2019), www.nzherald.co.nz/lifestyle/news/article.cfm?c_id=6&objec tid=12263617; Cecilia D'Anastasio & Student Nation, *Girls Speak Out Against Sexist School Dress Codes*, THE NATION, Aug. 27, 2014, www.thenation.com/article/girls-speak-out-against-sexist-school-dress-codes/; Donna St. George, *Are Leggings Too Distracting? A Mom Takes on a "Sexist" School Dress Code*, WASH. POST (Nov. 5, 2016).

[29] *See, e.g.*, Meredith J. Harbach, *Sexualization, Sex Discrimination, and Public School Dress Codes*, 50 U. RICH. L. REV. 1039 (2016); Autumn Spencer, *School Assembly Blames Girls for Distracting Boys from Learning*, MOTHERLY (May 5, 2016), www.mother.ly/parenting/school-assembly-blames-girls-for-distracting-boys-for-learning.

[30] *See* Harbach, *supra* note 29; Deborah M. Ahrens & Andrew M. Siegel, *Of Dress and Redress: Student Dress Restrictions in Constitutional Law and Culture*, 54 HARV. C.R.-C. L. L. REV.49, 99–100 (2019); Li Zhou, *The Sexism of School Dress Codes*, THE ATLANTIC (Oct. 20, 2015), www.theatlantic.com/education/archive/2015/10/school-dress-codes-are-problematic/410962/; Spencer, *supra* note 29; S. Suresh, *How Should Society View a Woman's Body?*, FAIR OBSERVER (Nov. 10, 2018), www.fairobserver.com/region/north_america/womens-dress-code-sexism-sexual-harassment-feminism-news-54131/.

[31] *See* Mirande Valbrune, *Gender-Based Dress Codes: Human Resources, Diversity and Legal Impact*, FORBES (Sept. 28, 2018), www.forbes.com/sites/forbeshumanresourcescouncil/2018/09/28/gender-based-dress-codes-human-resources-diversity-and-legal-impact/#420d4e294f53.

often admonished to look "pulled together," while not wearing clothes or accessories that are "too loud" or "too flashy."[32] They may be discreetly advised through whispers or be issued formal policies that try to convey a "look." The conventional wisdom imparted in many professional environments, even if casually, is that women's clothes should fit well, but not too tightly, their hair ought not be gray, and they should wear heels that are high, but not too high. All in all, the details of women's appearance seem to be much more finely regulated than do men's, across the board, and even a national trend that turns toward more "business casual" dress codes at work has not done much to change this.

Further, these codes are far more punishing when it comes to women of color,[33] transgender individuals,[34] and others who, as Carmen Rios specified for Everyday Feminism, "aren't supposed to be comfortable when ... being professional."[35] A whole new layer of imposition exists if a woman becomes a victim of intersectional discrimination,[36] and is held to standards disprate from those imposed on men. An example of this is when African American women are told that their natural hair, untreated or styled certain ways, is somehow "unprofessional."[37] Much has been written about this racist, pernicious treatment of African American women that has been permitted to go on

---

[32] *See* Dana Wilkie, *When Do Dress Codes That Perpetuate Gender Stereotypes Cross the Line?*, SHRM (Mar. 18, 2019), www.shrm.org/resourcesandtools/hr-topics/employee-relations/pages/gender-discrimination-in-dress-codes.aspx.

[33] *The CROWN Research Study*, DOVE, www.thecrownact.com/research (last visited Jan. 19, 2020) (finding that African American women are 30 percent more likely to be made aware of "formal workplace appearance policy," and are 1.5 times "more likely to be sent home from the workplace because of their hair.").

[34] *See* Katelyn Burns, *Here's What Trans People Really Think of Your Dress Code*, EVERYDAY FEMINISM (Nov. 8, 2017), https://everydayfeminism.com/2017/11/trans-dress-code/.

[35] *See, e.g.*, *Legal Enforcement Guidance on Race Discrimination on the Basis of Hair*, NYC HUMAN RIGHTS (Feb. 2019), www1.nyc.gov/assets/cchr/downloads/pdf/Hair-Guidance.pdf ("A grooming policy to maintain a 'neat and orderly' appearance that prohibits locs or cornrows is discriminatory against Black people because it presumes that these hairstyles, which are commonly associated with Black people, are inherently messy or disorderly.").

[36] Michael Haberman, *What Is Intersectional Discrimination and Why Should You Care?*, OMEGA HR SOLUTIONS INC. (Jun. 30, 2016), http://omegahrsolutions.com/2016/06/what-is-intersectional-discrimination-and-why-should-you-care.html (Intersectional discrimination "occurs when someone is discriminated against because of the combination of two or more protected bases (e.g. national origin and race).").

[37] *See* D. Wendy Greene, *Splitting Hairs: The Eleventh Circuit's Take on Workplace Bans Against Black Women's Natural Hair in EEOC v. Catastrophe Management Solutions*, 71 U. MIAMI L. REV. 987, 999–1000 (2017), available at: http://repository.law.miami.edu/umlr/vol71/iss4/5; D. Wendy Greene, *Black Women Can't Have Blonde Hair ... in the Workplace*, 14 J. OF GENDER, RACE & JUST. 405 (2011); EEOC v. Catastrophe Mgmt. Solutions, 852 F.3d 1018, 1021–23 (11th Cir. 2016).

for so long,[38] and although some areas, like New York City[39] and California,[40] have passed laws to combat this discrimination, there remains a long way to go.

Many cases challenging the sexism and paternalism of sex-based dress and grooming codes under Title VII are brought as sex stereotyping cases.[41] As discussed in Chapter 1, in 1989, the Supreme Court held that employers may not premise job evaluations or requirements that can lead to adverse actions on sex-based stereotypes that confer disparate standards on the sexes.[42] Since then, sex stereotyping cases have continued to stymie courts and produce wildly varying, unpredictable results.[43]

Some of the most exciting movements in the law recently have been in cases brought by homosexual and transgender employees. Most recently, we have seen that, though historically thwarted in their attempts to show Title VII violations even when sex-based appearance and other stereotyped standards were applied to them, homosexual and transgender plaintiffs have succeeded before the Supreme Court in arguing their coverage under Title VII.[44] The Court stated that it is "impossible to discriminate against a person for being homosexual or transgender without discriminating against that individual based on sex."[45] The Supreme Court expressly declined to comment on the applicability of its holding to dress codes, reserving that question for another day.[46]

---

[38] Greene, Splitting Hairs, *supra* note 37; Greene, Black Women Can't Have Blonde Hair, *supra* note 37; D. Wendy Greene, *A Multidimensional Analysis of What Not to Wear in the Workplace: Hijabs and Natural Hair*, 8 FIU L. Rev. 333 (2013), available at: https://ecollec tions.law.fiu.edu/lawreview/vol8/iss2/8.

[39] N.Y. Exec. Law § 292 (McKinney 2019); NYC Commission on Human Rights, NYC *Commission on Human Rights Legal Enforcement Guidance on Race Discrimination on the Basis of Hair* (Feb. 2019), www1.nyc.gov/assets/cchr/downloads/pdf/Hair-Guidance.pdf.

[40] Cal. Gov't Code § 212.1 (2019); Jason N. W. Plowman & Erica H. Gruver, *California Bans Discrimination against Natural Hair*, Nat'l L. Rev. (Jul. 12, 2019), www.natlawreview.com /article/california-bans-discrimination-against-natural-hair.

[41] Jespersen v. Harrah's Operating Co., 444 F.3d 1104, 1106, 1113 (9th Cir. 2006) (claiming that the grooming policy requiring women to wear make-up was sex-stereotyping in violation of Title VII); Schiavo v. Marina Dist. Development Co., 442 N.J. Super. 346 360–61 (N.J. Super. Ct. App. Div. 2014) (claiming that the casino's requirements to maintain weight proportionate to height, to have clean hair that is naturally styled and tasteful, and to wear professional make-up constituted sex-stereotyping in violation of Title VII).

[42] Price Waterhouse v. Hopkins, 490 U.S. 228, 251, 109 S. Ct. 1775, 1791, 104 L. Ed. 2d 268 (1989) (holding that "we are beyond the day when an employer could evaluate employees by assuming or insisting that they matched the stereotype associate with their group.").

[43] *See* Nelson v. James H. Knight DDS, P.C., 834 N.W.2d 64, 77 (Iowa 2013).

[44] Bostock v. Clayton Cty., No. 17–1618, 2020 WL 3146686, at *1 (U.S. Jun. 15, 2020).

[45] *Id.* at *7.

[46] *Id.* at *18 ("The employers worry that our decision will sweep beyond Title VII to other federal or state laws that prohibit sex discrimination. And, under Title VII itself, they say sex-

However, when it comes to sex stereotyping cases brought by women complaining about dress or grooming codes, courts have traditionally upheld these codes.[47] They have done so in several ways. Some courts have invoked the employer's unfettered prerogative to manage its workplace as it sees fit and dictate its corporate image.[48] Others have intoned the refrain that the courts should not sit in judgment of the minute day-to-day details of the businesses, like "super-personnel departments."[49] Still others have invoked societal grooming norms for the sexes as part of their rationale.

Notable among these cases is *Jespersen* v. *Harrah's*, in which the Ninth Circuit held that Harrah's Casino did not engage in sex-based discrimination in violation of Title VII when it promulgated sex-differentiated grooming standards which required women, among other things, to wear makeup, nail polish, and stockings; and have their hair "teased, curled, or styled," while requiring substantially less of men in terms of the cost and time to be invested in compliance.[50] The court pointed out that nothing about the stereotyped requirements impeded the plaintiff's ability to perform her job, and maintained that the requirements were different, but imposed substantially the same burden on the sexes,[51] an argument that many scholars and commentators took issue with.[52] While that case has generated much criticism,[53] courts in other jurisdictions have come to the opposite conclusion about the unlawfulness of appearance codes and requirements rooted in sex stereotypes – like that of wearing makeup, for example; other courts seem to adhere to

segregated bathrooms, locker rooms, and dress codes will prove unsustainable after our decision today. But none of these other laws are before us; we have not had the benefit of adversarial testing about the meaning of their terms, and we do not prejudge any such question today ... Whether other policies and practices might or might not qualify as unlawful discrimination or find justifications under other provisions of Title VII are questions for future cases, not these.").

47 *See, e.g.*, Creed v. Family Express Corp., 2009 U.S. Dist. LEXIS 237 (N.D. Ind. Jan. 5, 2009).
48 *See, e.g.*, Lanigan v. Bartlett & Co. Grain, 466 F. Supp. 1388, 1392 (W.D. Mo. 1979) ("The decision to project a certain image as one aspect of company policy is the employer's prerogative which employees may accept or reject. If they choose to reject the policy, they are subject to such sanctions as deemed appropriate by the company.").
49 *See* Kiel v. Select Artificials, Inc., 169 F.3d 1131, 1136 (8th Cir. 1999) (quoting Hutson v. McDonnell Douglas Corp., 63 F.3d 771, 781 (8th Cir. 1995)).
50 Jespersen v. Harrah's Operating Co., 444 F.3d 1104 (9th Cir. 2006) (*en banc*).
51 *Id.* at 1106.
52 *See* Leslie Harris, *Ninth Circuit Holds That Women Can Be Fired for Refusing to Wear Makeup*, 120 HARV. L. REV 651 (2006); Dianne Avery, *The Great American Makeover: The Sexing Up and Dumbing Down of Women's Work after Jespersen v. Harrah's Operating Company*, 49 U.S.F.L. REV. 1 (2007).
53 *Id.*

a "different but substantially equal burden is passable" standard when it comes to these kinds of challenge.[54]

The persistence and the sanctioning of dress and grooming codes seem to stem from the unspoken belief that women operate without agency and require additional regulation to ensure that they are attired and groomed professionally enough for the workplace. The codes, both formal and informal, written and unspoken, prop up a hierarchy in which women, in addition to being evaluated on the merits of their job performance, as men are, are held up against an intricate set of guidelines pertaining to their appearance and demeanor. These expectations, often unspoken but typically higher and more numerous for women, disproportionately filter women's overall evaluations through the lens of their aesthetic.

Sexual "Submission" at Work and the Romance of Rescue?

Back in 1992, Professor Hilary Schor wrote wryly and presciently of the irresistible trope of "sexual harassment and happy endings" as she saw it unfolding in popular culture, unwittingly both mirroring and forging the narratives of beloved literature and films.[55] She wrote that the trope of the imposing, "angry masters and modest, patient, 'romantic' women" is captivating because it achieves something "really important for our culture. It mystifies power. It romanticizes the abuse of power, and it teaches women to consent to things they otherwise might never allow."[56] And citing pieces of the "plotlines" of everything from Anita Hill's saga as it played out in Justice Thomas's hearings to *Jane Eyre*, to *Cinderella*, to *Working Girl*, Professor Schor posited that when a woman minimizes her own or another woman's abuse or exploitation, or allows herself to be flattered, and ultimately "rescued" by or from her abuser, this dark but strangely alluring trope is playing out and becoming normalized.[57]

Professor Schor argued that these tales seduce the cultural consciousness with the promise of comfort for victims as they navigate the world and a desired happy (or at least more palatable) ending, as well as a certain amount of – strangely enough – empowerment.[58] But as popular culture bought into the

---

[54] Higgins v. New Balance Athletic Shoe, Inc., 194 F.3d 252, 261 n.4 (1st Cir. 1999); Rosa v. Park West Bank & Trust Co., 214 F.3d 213 (1st Cir. 2000); Smith v. City of Salem, Ohio, 378 F.3d 566, 574 (6th Cir. 2004).

[55] Hilary M. Schor, *Storytelling in Washington, D.C.: Fables of Love, Power, and Consent in Sexual Harassment Stories*, 65 S. CAL. L. REV. 1347, 1348–49 (1992).

[56] *Id.*

[57] *Id.*

[58] *Id.*

comforting notion that those around us could not possibly be all bad, and must on some level have our best interests in mind, its members – often women – subsequently lost the resolve to stand up for themselves. As Professor Schor presciently put it, stories of the "romance of patriarchal power" make it "harder to stand up and say, yes, this happened to me too and it wasn't about love. They make it harder for us to believe our friends when they come to us and say it happened to me."[59] It is likely that this darkly alluring, saccharine trope that society has been fed has affected not only individuals but the institutions charged with regulating behavior and vindicating individuals' rights. Specifically, it may have pervaded and influenced how courts have chosen to grapple with sexual harassment cases, and the "submission cases" in particular.

The "submission" sexual harassment cases are those in which a plaintiff alleges that, faced with the coercive threats of a supervisor, she submitted to his overtures and sustained the harm of that coerced submission. And it is the courts' treatment of these cases that highlights a disparity between the way plaintiffs alleging that they acquiesced to their harasser's demands are treated and the treatment of plaintiffs alleging they were harassed to the point of feeling compelled to quit. At the root of this disparity arguably lies the unspoken belief that women lack agency and, specifically, do not truly possess or control their own sexuality. As per the Supreme Court, the "decision" to leave employment after harassment without trying to report and rectify things through official channels is treated as a decision for which the victim is responsible.[60] The "decision" to acquiesce to a supervisor's overtures without, similarly, affording the employer notice and a chance to remediate the situation has been treated by courts as a coerced harm from which the victim requires rescue.[61]

As discussed, ordinarily, where a sexual harassment plaintiff sustains a "tangible employment action," they need prove only that harassment occurred, and they will win their case, without the defendant being able to interpose an affirmative defense. The Supreme Court has set forth a nonexhaustive list of tangible employment actions including things like firings, nonselections, and demotions – things that require that an official employer decision be made at a level beyond the harasser and thus officially sanctioned by the employer.[62] According to the Supreme Court, these actions indicate that the power of the enterprise was brought to bear upon the

---

[59] *Id.* at 1349.
[60] *See, e.g.*, Pa. State Police v. Suders, 542 U.S. 129, 147 (2004).
[61] Jin v. Metropolitan Life Ins. Co., 295 F.3d 335, 352 (2d Cir. 2002); Holly D. v. Calif. Inst. of Tech., 339 F.3d 1158, 1173 (9th Cir. 2003).
[62] *See* Burlington Indus., Inc. v. Ellerth, 524 U.S. 742, 761 (1998).

harassment victim, and that the situation wasn't merely one in which a single harassing supervisor "went rogue," so to speak, denying the employer the opportunity to step in and remediate the situation.[63] This is significant because, as discussed in this chapter, the affirmative defense that employers can interpose in cases in which no tangible employment action exists permits them to argue that (1) they had channels of recourse and remediation for harassment in place, but (2) the plaintiff failed to complain of the harassment so as to avail herself of them.

While courts differ on this issue, several prominent federal courts, including the Second[64] and Ninth Circuits,[65] have held that in the "submission" cases, where a plaintiff acquiesces and "submits" to relations with the individual she later names as her harasser, the sheer act of the relations is to be construed as a tangible employment action. This means that where a plaintiff submits to relations with her harasser without affording her employer a chance to step in, the courts construe that in such a way as to insulate her from a claim-killing affirmative defense, and thus "rescue" her from her predicament.

But this stands in stark contrast to the Supreme Court's handling of allegations of a constructive discharge in the context of a harassment claim. Essentially, a constructive discharge is when an employer does all but fire an employee. A constructive discharge is the functional equivalent of a formal discharge, and it is recognized by the law when an employer stops short of formally firing an employee but makes working conditions so objectively intolerable for the employee that any reasonable person in their shoes would feel compelled to resign. In 2004, the Supreme Court held that a constructive discharge is not considered to be a tangible employment action.[66] The Court reasoned, among other things, that a constructive discharge would not have been ratified by the employer, and thus, it would be unfair to equate one to an "official" act like a termination.

This means that a victim of harassment whose life was made so objectively intolerable at work that she felt compelled to resign and did so without resorting to her employer's policies for help first could not prevail. Her claim would invariably fall prey to the affirmative defense that she "chose" to leave without alerting her employer to the problem. This would be so despite the fact that, as per the definition of constructive discharge, she wouldn't really have made much of a "choice" at all. Ironically, though, the

---

[63] *Id.* at 762.
[64] *Jin*, 295 F.3d 335.
[65] *Holly D.*, 339 F.3d at 1158.
[66] Pa. State Police v. Suders, 542 U.S. at 149, 152.

coerced "choice" to submit or acquiesce to the physical requests of a harasser is certainly no less of a "choice" than that of leaving a job because one feels forced out (a constructive discharge). The coerced "choice" to submit occurs just as much behind closed doors, and just as much under the employer's nose, and without a chance for the employer to interject and correct things, as does a constructive discharge.

Society is left to think about this disparity, especially in light of the Supreme Court's mandate that defense-killing tangible employment actions ought to be limited to "the acts most likely to be brought home to the employer, the measures over which the employer can exercise greatest control ... [and] official acts of the enterprise."[67] Is it possible that this is undergirded by the unspoken notion that women have less agency when it comes to the realms of their lives that involve sexual relations, and are in need of rescue or redemption by the law when they submit to relations inherently coerced by a workplace power disparity? Has the law bought into the idea that the coerced decision to submit without seeking recourse for harassment through official channels is somehow more of a "harm" and less of a "choice" than the "choice" to quit employment altogether because of a constructive discharge (which is not really volitional at all)?

And yet this resonates with the way women and their agency are viewed through the lens of the law. As discussed, women were held to their word legally when they signed contracts, sold property, etc., under any amount of inherent coercion short of fraud or unconscionability. However, rights of action surrounding women's "virtue" and "seduction" treated them as unaccountably susceptible to nearly any amount of coercion and conferred rights of action not upon them, but upon their fathers or husbands.

As one federal court said in 2010, the plaintiff's acquiescence is best seen as "a term or condition of her employment."[68] This court went on to note that, as other courts had said before, "requiring an employee to engage in unwanted sex acts is one of the most pernicious and oppressive forms of sexual harassment that occur in the workplace."[69] In other words, though the Supreme Court has said that being made to feel as though you must leave your job is something that, paradoxically, you must decide and do on your own,

---

[67] *Id.* at 148.

[68] Shields v. FedEx Customer Info. Servs., Inc., No. 1:09-CV-309, 2010 WL 11538009, at *6 (S.D. Ohio W.D. Oct. 10, 2010).

[69] *Id.* (citing Jin v. Metropolitan Life Ins. Co., 310 F.3d 84, 94 (2d Cir. 2002)); *see also Holly D.,* 339 F.3d at 1158.

submission is seen as a seduction or manipulation in which the harassment plaintiff, typically a woman, has her will overborne.

And the perceived insidiousness of the physical relations, though agreed to when they occurred, seems to horrify courts more than the various harms that plaintiffs sustain in the course of constructive discharges. As the federal court quoted above put it, a submission plaintiff sustains the direct injury of the "physical and emotional damage resulting from performance of unwanted sexual acts as a condition of employment," and agreed with another court that this kind of injury "is as tangible as an injury can be."[70]

To drive home the point, in the 2004 Supreme Court case where it was held that a constructive discharge was not a tangible employment action,[71] the plaintiff had alleged that she was constructively discharged when, as the Third Circuit explained, on her final day of work, "the officers [with whom the plaintiff worked] attempted to set her up on a false charge of theft."[72] As the Third Circuit noted, construing the facts in the light most favorable to the plaintiff:

> The concealment of her test results in a set of drawers in the women's locker room, the use of theft detection powder to catch one of their own inside the station, and the excessive and humiliating treatment that [the plaintiff] suffered when she was handcuffed and photographed all point to a pattern of conduct designed to find some way to terminate Suders . . .. [F]alse charges of misconduct are tantamount to threats or suggestions of discharge. Attacking someone with a false charge of theft seems a most effective way of suggesting that an employee will be fired or should leave voluntarily.[73]

All of this was not enough to move the needle for the Supreme Court when it came to discerning a concrete harm that would stave off the interposition of the defense. But when it came to federal courts determining the open issue of submission as a tangible employment action, even after 2004, several courts have insisted on rendering these claims invulnerable to the affirmative defense that typically cuts off constructive discharge cases at the knees. This essentially "rescues" the victims where physical relations occurred. Courts seem to be acting with the unspoken belief that women are somewhat bereft of agency when it comes to having consented to an inherently coercive workplace relationship in a way in which they are not similarly bankrupt when it comes to other, at least equally intolerable behavior.

---

[70]   *Shields*, 2010 WL 11538009, at *6 (citing *Holly D.*, 339 F.3d at 1171).
[71]   Pa. State Police v. Suders, 542 U.S. at 149, 152.
[72]   Suders v. Easton, 325 F.3d 432, 446 (3d Cir. 2003).
[73]   *Id.* at 447.

We are left to wonder exactly what is going on in terms of the unspoken beliefs that underlie this disparity. Does the law extend something akin to sympathy to women who submit to physical relations, such that it will read a remediable deprivation of will into that consent; whereas it has less sympathy for those who quietly resist harassment until one day they simply leave? Or is it less about sympathy than it is about a determination that a rescue or redemption is needed after submission, whereas none is needed for those who simply walk away? Is the law, on some unspoken level, acting to protect and favor those women viewed as "desirable" enough to be propositioned, but requiring victims of other types of harassment to fend for themselves if they cannot report and work through their issues in the system, as the affirmative defense requires?

THE PAIN

Tremendous harm flows from individuals, courts, and legislatures acting on the unspoken belief that women lack agency, relative to men, when it comes to various aspects of their lives. There are hundreds of articles and blogs online addressing the issues of how everything from typical office temperatures (they tend to be too cold),[74] to imbalanced, overly specific, and convoluted dress codes, take an undue toll on women by presenting conditions that are inimical to their ease and comfort.

For example, there is no shortage of research that demonstrates how typical dress and grooming codes are far more onerous for women, who must shoulder the burden of having to expend more time, money, care, and thought on their appearance before they even set foot in the workplace than do men. This research establishes that dress and/or grooming codes are more onerous for women in both professional workplaces, like accounting firms, and more traditionally "blue collar" workplaces, like restaurants and casinos.[75] From the time to the money invested in purchasing makeup, and from the energy to the self-consciousness put into appearing "put together" with respect to hair, makeup, and accessories, onerous requirements and expectations can deplete

---

[74] *See, e.g.,* Susan Davis & Audrey Nguyen, *Study Shows Freezing Office Temperatures Affect Women's Productivity,* NPR (May 26, 2019), www.npr.org/2019/05/26/727108363/how-office-temperature-affects-cognitive-performance; Aimee Picchi, *Why Cold Offices May Have a Chilling Impact on Women,* CBS NEWS (May 23, 2019), www.cbsnews.com/news/why-cold-offices-may-have-a-chilling-impact-on-women/.

[75] *See* Madeleine Holden, *Being a Woman in the Workplace Means Getting Pressured to Wear Makeup on the Job,* ALLURE (Aug. 15, 2017), www.allure.com/story/women-pressured-to-wear-makeup-at-work-as-a-double-standard.

women's valuable time, money, and other resources that could be otherwise poured into themselves and their work.[76]

This is all made no easier by the fact that research shows that everyone from supervisors to clients may incorporate an additional layer of appearance evaluation into their overall assessment of women in a way that they simply do not do with men.[77] This layer is challenging to capture because it is difficult to discern and, thus, to police. In most fields, there is an unspoken expectation that women, more than men, should be fit, youthful, and attractive, but not overly sexualized. Polished, but not harsh or intimidating. These standards, though, are typically either wholly unvoiced or expressed as copiously intricate codes for women that stand in stark contrast to those for men, which are usually succinct and reserve much discretion to the men. Research also establishes that even when guidance on things like wearing makeup or traditionally feminine clothing is not expressly incorporated into any formal policies, codes, or manuals, whispered admonitions and even silent judgments make them seem screamed.[78] Informal conversations and the reality of a workplace's culture can send a louder message than anything that is written in a formal policy.

Bookstores and the internet are replete with columns, manuals, articles, and books – humorous and ironic, as well as all too serious – dedicated to helping women find "nonthreatening leadership strategies" (this is actually a humorous book title),[79] endure casual sexism and other indignities with grace and humor, and otherwise navigate a sexist workplace terrain.[80] Women are counseled throughout popular culture and media that their colleagues' egos are as much an obstacle to sidestep as are any other professional foibles. This, itself, is evidence of how frequently women are presumptively assumed to lack gravitas and agency.

Moreover, everyone from Forbes[81] to lifehacker.com,[82] it seems, wants (or sees the need) to furnish guidance as to gracefully "shutting down"

---

[76] *Id.*

[77] Naomi Ellemers, *Looks Do Matter, Especially for Women, and Also at Work*, PSYCHOL. TODAY (Sept. 7, 2018), www.psychologytoday.com/us/blog/social-climates/201809/looks-do-matter-especially-women-and-also-work.

[78] *See* Aditi Shrikant, *The Unspoken Rules of Workplace Attire for Women*, REWIRE (Aug. 7, 2018), www.rewire.org/unspoken-rules-workplace-attire-women/.

[79] SARAH COOPER, HOW TO BE SUCCESSFUL WITHOUT HURTING MEN'S FEELINGS: NON-THREATENING LEADERSHIP STRATEGIES FOR WOMEN (2018).

[80] *See* JESSICA BENNETT, FEMINIST FIGHT CLUB: AN OFFICE SURVIVAL MANUAL FOR A SEXIST WORKPLACE (2016); *see also* JOAN C. WILLIAMS, WHAT WORKS FOR WOMEN AT WORK: FOUR PATTERNS WORKING WOMEN NEED TO KNOW (2014).

[81] Kristi Hedges, 5 *Ways to Shut Down Mansplaining*, FORBES (Feb. 26, 2018), www.forbes.com /sites/work-in-progress/2018/02/26/5-ways-to-shut-down-mansplaining/#4bd16e0a589e.

[82] Emily Price, *How to Deal with Mansplaining at Work*, LIFEHACKER (Sept. 10, 2017), https:// lifehacker.com/1803767659.

a phenomenon termed "mansplaining," whereby someone, often cast as a man, condescends while explaining something to a woman with the express (and impliedly sex-based) assumption that he knows more about the subject than she does. Extricating oneself from this or other disrespectful treatment at work, which women are forced to do far more often than are men,[83] is regarded as nothing less than an artform that is at once equal parts wit, smarts, humor, and deflection, so that one can (often in front of others) maintain or reclaim respect and dignity without losing goodwill. This act is performative and, simply put, exhausting. It exhausts a person's time and energy. It may even exhaust the goodwill others afford them, inasmuch as needing to confront someone trying to diminish you, no matter how cordial the conversation, may result in your coming across as hostile, defensive, or self-conscious. Women are already uniquely viewed through a prism that renders them more susceptible to being seen as or judged for having these emotions. But teaching them to "rescue" themselves, rather than bringing awareness to, or otherwise stemming, the problem, does not acknowledge or honor their agency.

These losses may be difficult to discern at all, let alone quantify, but the importance of leveling the playing field, or at least being aware of the ways in which it is inherently tilted when it comes to issues like perception, dignity, and respect across the board cannot be overstated. When promotions, raises, client assignments, or other workplace selections are made, it is crucial that decision-makers operate with a concept of these unspoken beliefs and the projections and perceptions that they may engender – "he seems more authoritative," or "she seems too emotional and defensive," or "she's not ready; she's not put together." Though all of these and other sentiments cannot always be unpacked, dismantled, and derived optimally to avoid harm, an overarching awareness of what factors might be at play in precipitating these and other judgments can go a long way toward mitigating some of these harms.

The Supreme Court was likely wrong to hold that, even where a harassing supervisor makes a harassee's life so objectively intolerable at work that she quits without giving the employer notice of what is going on, the affirmative defense can be interposed and potentially kill the claim.[84] However, since the Supreme Court has held as it has, there is no reason for courts to carve out a unique holding in submission scenarios yet unaddressed by the Supreme Court – all because of the unique "harm" that is said to come from the

---

[83] *See* Janice Gassam, *How Mansplaining Is Negatively Impacting Your Workplace—and What You Can Do to Prevent It*, FORBES (Jan. 7, 2019), www.forbes.com/sites/janicegassam/2019/01/07/how-mansplaining-is-negatively-impacting-your-workplace-and-how-to-prevent-it/#4c45a66013f1.

[84] Pa. State Police v. Suders, 542 U.S. at 149, 152.

physical encounter. If women were regarded as having full and free agency, there would be no reason to treat a coerced, but not physically forced, sexual encounter differently from a coerced, but not physically forced, flight from the job. The finding, as a matter of law, that any reasonable person would have left employment immediately (as is the case with a constructive discharge) is actually at least as compelling than the stark fact that a physical encounter took place at the request of a supervisor without the employee's resort to the employer for redress. The law's implicit denial that women have as much autonomy and agency when it comes to nonphysically forced sexual coercion driven by a power disparity as they do when it comes to irresistible coercion in any other context (which could involve anything from bullying to physical abuse) could be seen as an affront to women. In fact, in the 2004 Supreme Court opinion discussed earlier, the plaintiff alleged that she was, among other things, handcuffed to a wall while being framed for a theft she did not commit.[85] And, still, the Court framed her resignation as a choice.

MANIFESTATIONS

Another area in which employers seem to telegraph the paternalistic notion that female employees require curbing and regulation that male employees do not is in dating and fraternization policies and views. According to a 2009 study that appeared in the *Western Journal of Communication*, a majority of workers view workplace romances negatively, despite the fact that many have been a party to one.[86] And, saliently, the survey found that these negative views of the majority take the shape of workers focusing their disdain and ire at the woman in a heterosexual workplace romance. The study found that workers impute a motivation of professional gain or advancement to women in workplace romances, but ascribe purer motivations of ego or love to men similarly involved. Other studies have confirmed that women are also more likely than their male colleagues to be gossiped about at the office as a result of a workplace romance.[87]

Societal manifestations of the unspoken belief that women operate with less agency than do men (especially when it comes to sex and sexuality) abound and have abounded for centuries. Long before courts split inconsistently on

---

[85] *Id.*

[86] Sean M. Horan & Rebecca M. Chory, *When Work and Love Mix: Perceptions of Peers in Workplace Romances*, W. J. COMM. 349, 350 (2009).

[87] *See* David C. Watson, *Gender Differences in Gossip and Friendship*, 67 SEX ROLES 494, 495 (2012); Peggy Drexler, *The Truth about Office Romance*, FORBES (Apr. 7, 2014), www .forbes.com/sites/peggydrexler/2014/04/07/the-truth-about-office-romance/#61bad1186673.

the law's handling of submission versus constructive discharge, American law separated out women's sexuality as an aspect of their lives that they were seen as less able to control than others – and one that they did not even necessarily possess for themselves. When the topic of women's consent and the validity of that consent came up in civil cases in courts, historically, judges did not take issue with the premise that women (where permitted to do so) could and did operate with full volition and agency. However, when women's consent was put at issue in the context of cases that dealt with sex and seduction, courts took a very different tack.

Looking at courts' treatment of women's consent in civil cases historically, there is a bifurcation between cases in which it was alleged that consent was undermined by seduction and those in which it was alleged that consent was subverted by other constraints or pressures. Historically, proclaimed victims of coercion who sought to have their rendering of consent essentially "undone" by courts – men and women alike – have had to adduce evidence of some sort of immediate threat of grave harm before a court would absolve them of responsibility.[88]

Contract law doctrines like undue influence, in which one claims that their consent was procured through an exploitation of their relative vulnerability via over-persuasion, or duress, in which an unlawful threat is alleged to have induced one to act as they normally would not have, have historically been applied to the claims of men and women even-handedly. In fact, courts have not, historically, been wild about the idea of invalidating contracts by nullifying the consent of either party. This is so even though judges understand that consent is often engendered by coercive pressures, which include financial, social, and even professional inducements and constraints.

U.S. courts have long held that women were more than capable of giving valid consent, despite the fact that different pressures and constraints may have compelled their decisions. For example, in one case from 1910, a woman tried to fight the reformation of a deed that she and her husband had signed by claiming that "she did not join in the execution of the bond for title, and that she did not sign the deed of her own free will, but that her signature and acknowledgment thereto was obtained by [the] coercion and undue influence of her husband."[89] The court rejected her argument, noting: "She was unwilling to sign the deed; but, inasmuch as she could not get the money therefore without signing it, she permitted her great desire for the money to overcome

---

[88] *See* Stone, *supra* note 13, at 24, 61).
[89] Bell v. Castelberry, 96 Ark. 564, 565–66 (1910).

her will. This was not an undue influence exerted upon her, or an involuntary act upon her part."[90]

The tortured and complex relationship between women and consent as seen through history's lens, however, shows that women have traditionally been perceived by the law as capable of giving meaningful consent – except when it came to sexual or physical relations. Then, there is evidence that women were not always perceived by the law as fully possessing the agency one would normally ascribe to an adult. Indeed, as far back as the thirteenth century in England, the Anglican Church set up courts that adjudicated cases of adultery, which was punishable by public embarrassment. However, even if a woman committed adultery voluntarily, her husband possessed the power to bring the case, which was termed "theft of chattels," as though her physical relations were disembodied from her and entirely outside of her control.[91]

At a certain point, secular courts started to hear what became known as "seduction" cases in instances of infidelity. In these cases, a married woman's cause of action for being "seduced" belonged to her husband. Moreover, the cause of action's premise evolved such that the trespass being adjudicated was no longer related to physical property but rather to an intangible right that he possessed via his marriage contract. An unmarried woman's cause of action typically resided with her father or fiancé,[92] and, in terms of criminal charges brought against men for engaging in relations with unmarried women, the women's consent was not typically factored into an assessment of guilt.

According to one scholar, this "might be explained as the law's desire to protect the woman's chastity even when she, presumably incorrectly, had determined not to protect it," but a less benign rationale would be the law's positing of the "ownership interest of the dominant social group (men) being asserted in the law to prevent the owned members of the oppressed group (women) from determining the course of their own bodily integrity. Such an act of self-determination would threaten the ownership rights of men, as a group, over women, as a group."[93]

Modern courts continue to note that, even though coercive forces are present, consent given absent an illegitimate threat from which there is no

---

[90]   *Id.* at 568.
[91]   *See* Damian Corless, *When a Wife Was Her Man's Chattel*, INDEPENDENT (Jan 4. 2015), www .independent.ie/life/when-a-wife-was-her-mans-chattel-30871468.html.
[92]   *See* Joanna Grossman, *Is the Tort of Wrongful Seduction Still Viable? A North Carolina Court Will Get the Chance to Decide*, FINDLAW (Feb. 11, 2003), https://supreme.findlaw.com/legal-commentary/is-the-tort-of-wrongful-seduction-still-viable.html.
[93]   Keith M. Harrison, *Law, Order, and the Consent Defense*, 12 ST. LOUIS U. PUB. L. REV. 477, 490 (1993).

way out ought not lose its force.[94] Similarly, when a person is accused of a crime and argues that they were forced to behave as they did so as to absolve themselves of criminal guilt, absent extraordinary circumstances, they are responsible for their actions.[95] Women, like men, must typically, in such cases, prove, at a minimum, an "immediate threat of death or serious bodily injury, a well-grounded fear that the threat would be carried out if [s]he did not commit the crime in question and the absence of any reasonable opportunity to escape the threatened harm without committing the offense."[96]

Even the Restatement of Agency provides that the torts committed by a person that were dictated to them by a principal will not serve to be a viable defense, and that even "[t]he fact that the agent acts under physical or economic duress used by his principal does not relieve him from liability for causing harm to another."[97] As the Supreme Court acknowledged when it rejected a constructive discharge as a tangible employment action, "[u]nlike an actual termination . . . [a] constructive discharge involves both an employee's decision to leave and precipitating conduct: The former involves no official action . . . ."[98]

Even in criminal cases brought against battered women where, for example, "failure to protect" charges are brought against women with children who were also abused, the notion that forces outside of their control were brought to bear upon them so as to absolve them of guilt is relatively foreign to the law.[99] Although battered women with children are seemingly defendants who are among the most vulnerable in society and the most likely to be placed under circumstances in which they may be able to claim that they bore no legal responsibility for certain acts or omissions, duress is rarely used as a criminal defense for them, and where it is, it is rarely successful. In other words, criminal law views women, even under the direst of circumstances, as resourceful adults with ample agency to seek redress where it is needed.

Yet, somehow, despite all of this, when modern law examines allegations of sexual harassment where the plaintiff submitted to her harasser's demands without resort to or even notifying the employer for redress of the situation, some courts inexplicably "cancel" consent summarily. And even though that subversion of consent may operate to benefit individual sexual harassment

---

94   *Id.*

95   *See* Stone, *supra* note 13, at 24, 65.

96   *Id.*

97   *Id.* (quoting Restatement (Second) of Agency § 343 cmt. e. (1958)).

98   Pa. State Police v. Suders, 542 U.S. at 148.

99   *See, e.g.,* V. Pualani Enos, *Prosecuting Battered Mothers: State Laws' Failure to Protect Battered Women and Abused Children,* 19 HARV. WOMEN'S L.J. 229, 237–257 (1996).

plaintiffs (most of whom are female) by rendering their claims invulnerable to the interposition of the affirmative defense, it does not benefit women as a group. The denial of women's agency when it comes to consent is particularly pernicious in other contexts. It seems important to mention rape cases here, although it bears underscoring that in the submission sexual harassment cases discussed, physical coercion and/or assault were not a factor. In the context of rape cases in this country, rape shield laws needed to be enacted in order to address the aggressiveness with which women's agency was assailed. Indeed, defendants' attorneys aggressively question victims about clothing, behavior, and other things that they may use to subvert the victim's agency and call her lack or withdrawal of consent into question.

In the United States, the twentieth century was marked by various law and policy-based denunciations of extra- or premarital sex – from laws that curtailed the rights of those born outside of wedlock,[100] to denials of opportunities to single parents,[101] to the denial of access to contraception to the unmarried.[102] The modern-day outlier treatment of submission sexual harassment cases is distinguished from other sexual harassment cases occurring in the context of power disparities, and the coercion that is fostered or enabled by them typifies the law's treatment of women's sexual autonomy. If a woman is tortured and coerced into fleeing her job, the law tells her that she should have resorted to her employer if she hoped to bring a claim, but if she is coerced by threats and a power disparity into physical intimacy that she later uses as the basis of a claim, the law "rescues" her claim by insulating it from the interposition of the affirmative defense, citing the unique "harm" that her coerced consent caused her.

Whatever one's stance on whether the affirmative defense should exist in sexual harassment cases, or how it should be applied, it hardly seems fair for the law not to recognize the quiet desperation of those who feel that they have no choice but to leave their jobs in the face of harassment, but to (in some cases) trumpet the perceived unique harm of those victims willing to comply with what is being asked of them to retain their employment status. The difference in treatment is inexplicable – unless one subscribes to the belief that women do not have full agency in all circumstances.

---

[100]   See Stephen D. Sugarman, *What Is a "Family"? Conflicting Messages from Our Public Programs*, 42 FAMILY LAW QUARTERLY 231, 232–235 (2008).
[101]   *Id.*
[102]   See Kirsten M. J. Thompson, *A Brief History of Birth Control in the U.S.*, OUR BODIES OUR SELVES (Dec. 13, 2013), www.ourbodiesourselves.org/book-excerpts/health-article/a-brief-history-of-birth-control/.

TAKEAWAYS

The takeaways here are somewhat tricky. Since nobody credible is really out there saying that women, as a sex, are less self-possessed or have less agency than men do, it is a hard concept to wrangle with. What we can do is examine our law and our workplaces for signs that women are being dictated to, "rescued," or otherwise infantilized or somehow treated as more fragile than men. Overly dictatorial dress and grooming codes might be a good place to start. The fiction that courts like the Ninth Circuit Court of Appeals in *Jespersen* have created, whereby wildly disparate burdens attendant to dress or grooming are rationalized as different but equal, should be rejected by courts in the future. To the extent that women really are sustaining a much more onerous imposition, this should be addressed by the law. Even outside the courtroom, employers can do much to help their female employees by rethinking how much disparate scrutiny and judgment goes into their formal and informal expectations and evaluations of employees.

Mary Barra, who famously rose from a factory floor inspector to become the CEO of General Motors, famously reduced the corporate behemoth's dress code from ten pages to two words: "Dress appropriately."[103] According to Barra, she was immediately reproached by a senior director, whom she had to assuage. As she put it: "What I realized is that you really need to make sure your managers are empowered—because if they cannot handle 'dress appropriately,' what other decisions can they handle? And I realized that often, if you have a lot of overly prescriptive policies and procedures, people will live down to them."[104]

While employers do retain the managerial prerogative to dictate nearly all aspects of their corporate image, consciously thinking about not being patronizing toward women in the workplace can go a long way when formulating policies and when thinking about the unspoken messages that are transmitted to employees as well. Employers should incorporate the topic of women's agency into corporate and compliance training to the extent that they can, so that as corporate needs regarding things like professionalism and image are factored into things like the formulation of an appearance code, the need to refrain from insulting, alienating, or belittling any group, including women, is reinforced as well. Perhaps a company that thought it needed a ten-page policy

---

[103] Leah Fessler, *GM's Dress Code Is Only Two Words*, QUARTZ AT WORK (Apr. 3, 2018), https://qz.com/work/1242801/gms-dress-code-is-only-two-words/.

[104] *Id.*

really would fare better, in many respects, with one that is much more succinct.

At its core, the unspoken belief that women do not possess full agency is so diffused across contexts and so deeply embedded in thoughts and actions as to disappear altogether often. Merely considering the ideas set forth here may cause an individual to reframe her thoughts about a female employee at work needing to be "discovered," as opposed to "recognized" (as a male employee might be thought to be) or "taught how to dress," as opposed to being seen primarily for the substance of her work, as a man might be.

Our nation's history of denying women their sexual agency and autonomy should not be forgotten when law is crafted either. The treatment of submission cases in courts is, as discussed, split, and not often cited by feminists as in need of particular reform. However, when it is juxtaposed with the law's treatment of harassment victims who are constructively discharged (as dictated by the Supreme Court), it, too, reveals an almost subconscious message about women that likely won't benefit them in the long term.

5

"Women Are the Downfall of Men" (So)

So, the new partner in my department is so worried about somehow being labeled a sexual harasser that he's constantly making pithy, passive-aggressive jokes about the #MeToo movement and dodging having to spend time with women in the office—any women. Every time a new headline emerges about another powerful man resigning from his job or being forced out due to allegations of sexual misconduct, he has to bring it up, fiddle with his wedding ring, and make some comment about staying happily married and out of trouble. It's annoying, like he's protesting too much, but it's harmless. Except it's not, because I've noticed that when I go to his office to review a memo, my reviews are perfunctory, quick, and peppered with comments about how we'd better leave the door open and how he doesn't want to "upset" me. Meanwhile, my male colleagues get lots of time with him behind closed doors, and I know that he's tougher on their work. They're learning how to write the way he likes things done, and they're progressing while I am stagnating.

—Chloe, thirty-three, attorney

THE BELIEF

The unspoken belief that "women are the downfall of men" actually subsumes an array of underlying beliefs, depending on how and why it motivates men to step back when it comes to the comprehensive inclusion of women in mentoring and instruction, professional networking opportunities – and everything in between. Perhaps this view was most pronouncedly *not* spoken when Mike Pence famously said in 2002 that he would never be seen dining alone with a woman who was not his wife.[1] This immediately sparked conversation and debate about just how many men felt it was "safer," for any number of reasons,

---

[1] Aaron Blake, *Mike Pence Doesn't Dine Alone with Other Women. And We're All Shocked*, WASH. POST (Mar. 30, 2017), www.washingtonpost.com/news/the-fix/wp/2017/03/30/mike-pence-doesnt-dine-alone-with-other-women-and-were-all-shocked/?utm_term=.8b7037e25ef6.

to keep a certain measure of distance between themselves and the women with whom they worked.

Interestingly, when the *Washington Post* reported on Mike Pence's statement about never dining with another woman who is not his wife or attending events at which alcohol is being served without his wife, it was actually the resurfacing of a comment that he had initially made to *The Hill* in 2002.[2] Only this time, the speaker was now the Vice President of the United States, and the political climate in which it was examined, still reeling from the #MeToo movement and its political and professional fallout, was more conducive to its critical evaluation.[3]

And while some critiqued his statements as uniquely disadvantageous to the women around him professionally, it seems as though these voices were nearly drowned out by the din of voices that concurred with him and resonated with the same almost fear of being alone with women. As more and more men in American workplaces began to nervously joke about leaving the door open when a woman enters their offices, especially when it's going to be one-on-one, "just to be safe," it became evident that perhaps the Vice President had voiced, or at least tapped into, an old, unspoken belief that, indeed, "women are the downfall of men."

Bloomberg News, among other outlets, documented this phenomenon, and as it put it in late 2018:

> No more dinners with female colleagues. Don't sit next to them on flights. Book hotel rooms on different floors. Avoid one-on-one meetings. In fact, as a wealth adviser put it, just hiring a woman these days is "an unknown risk." What if she takes something he said the wrong way? Across Wall Street, men are adopting controversial strategies for the #MeToo era and, in the process, making life even harder for women.[4]

Also, in late 2018, the *Baltimore Sun* asked, point-blank: "Has #MeToo made men wary of working closely with women?" along with numerous other news outlets posing similar questions.[5] That same year, the *New York Times* seemed

---

[2] *Id.*

[3] Genevieve Zingg, *Mike Pence's Rule Is Not a Solution to Sexual Assault*, HuffPost (Dec. 20, 2017), www.huffingtonpost.ca/genevieve-zingg/mike-pences-rule-is-not-a-solution-to-sexual-assault_a_23308908/.

[4] Gillian Tan & Katia Porzecanski, *Wall Street Rule for the #MeToo Era: Avoid Women at All Cost*, Bloomberg (Dec. 3, 2018), www.bloomberg.com/news/articles/2018-12-03/a-wall-street-rule-for-the-metoo-era-avoid-women-at-all-cost.

[5] Jean Marbella, *Has #MeToo Made Men Wary of Working Closely with Women?*, Balt. Sun (Oct. 8, 2018), www.baltimoresun.com/features/women-to-watch/bs-fe-me-too-men-20180910-story.html.

to give us a definitive answer: "It's Not Just Mike Pence. Americans Are Wary of Being Alone with the Opposite Sex."[6] In that article, the *New York Times* reported on a 2017 Morning Consult poll that it had conducted, which caused it to conclude: "Many men and women are wary of a range of one-on-one situations," with "[a]round a quarter think[ing] private work meetings with colleagues of the opposite sex are inappropriate," and "[n]early two-thirds say[ing] people should take extra caution around members of the opposite sex at work."[7] In fact, most of the women and almost half of the men polled said that it was "unacceptable to have dinner or drinks alone with someone of the opposite sex other than their spouse."[8]

And while this discussion of this formerly taboo topic started in the news, its pervasive extension into everyday workplace discourse amidst half-hearted jokes about being "safe," having "witnesses," and avoiding "trouble," among other things, makes clear that this belief is somewhat widespread, if not somewhat ubiquitous.[9] In late 2018, *Vanity Fair* reported that Wall Street had gone "Full Mike Pence," with "[t]he men of Wall Street ... reportedly refusing to be alone with women, in case they might sexually harass them."[10] But what does the belief that "women are the downfall of men" look like, and what forms does it take?

For some who are more hardened, this belief extends into the notion that women, on some level, are temptresses, ready to lead men down the path of temptation when given the chance, even in a professional context.[11] This taps into all sorts of archaic conceptions of women as seduction personified.[12] Many of those who hold this notion do not trust themselves. But another big part of the belief is that many women, placed in proximity to men by virtue of

---

[6]   Claire Cain Miller, *It's Not Just Mike Pence. Americans Are Wary of Being Alone with the Opposite Sex*, N.Y. TIMES (Jul. 1, 2017), www.nytimes.com/2017/07/01/upshot/members-of-the-opposite-sex-at-work-gender-study.html.

[7]   *Id.*

[8]   *Id.*

[9]   Lulu Garcia-Navarro, *When Black Women's Stories of Sexual Abuse Are Excluded from the National Narrative*, NPR (Dec. 3, 2017, 8:08 AM), www.npr.org/2017/12/03/568133048/women-of-color-and-sexual-harassment; P.R. Lockhart, *Women of Color in Low-Wage Jobs Are Being Overlooked in the #MeToo Moment*, VOX (Dec. 19, 2017, 4:10 PM), www.vox.com/identities/2017/12/19/16620918/sexual-harassment-low-wages-minority-women.

[10] Bess Levin, *Wall Street Goes Full Mike Pence to Avoid #MeToo Accusations*, VANITY FAIR (Dec. 3, 2018), www.vanityfair.com/news/2018/12/wall-street-goes-full-mike-pence-to-avoid-metoo-accusations.

[11] Jia Tolentino, *Mike Pence's Marriage and the Beliefs That Keep Women from Power*, NEW YORKER (Mar. 31, 2017), www.newyorker.com/culture/jia-tolentino/mike-pences-marriage-and-the-beliefs-that-keep-women-from-power.

[12] *Id.*

their professional or workplace endeavors, will participate in fraternization that goes beyond professional engagement. When Pence's statement resurfaced in 2017, many noted its similarity to the so-called "Billy Graham Rule," pursuant to which, as per the Reverend, a man ought be wary of too much socialization with a woman that is not his wife.[13] Graham's "rule" is said to have come from a long-standing fear that he had of being "set up," whereby he would step into a hotel room that he had booked, only to discover a naked woman, determined to bring down his ministry, lying on his bed with a photographer nearby.[14]

For others who believe, on some level, that a woman, or women, may be their downfall, there is less worry about their being led into temptation, and more concern about women as false accusers, setting traps for men, and then deploying their own credibility or their ties to a popular movement to destroy a man's reputation or career.[15] For some, maybe this belief is fed by a paranoia of sorts – or a sense that they've ascended too far in their career to be brought down by a woman lying in wait to harm them. Indeed, *Vanity Fair* reported that practices of professional men on business trips doing things like refusing to be seated next to women or booking rooms on different floors from female colleagues are becoming more widespread, and quoted a former managing director at Morgan Stanley as saying that the #MeToo movement has, for these men, conjured up "a sense of walking on eggshells."[16]

For still others, the belief is not about anything they think that they will succumb to or do, themselves. Nor is it about anything that a woman will do or try to do when alone with them. They fear what the "optics" of being behind a closed door, or out to a professional lunch or dinner, with a woman can do to bring about their downfall – in other words, what the misperceptions and misapprehensions of others – from their own wives and families, to their colleagues, to the public at large – could do to their good names and career trajectories.[17]

---

[13] Monica Hesse, *The "Billy Graham Rule" Doesn't Honor Your Wife. It Demeans Her – and All Women*, WASH. POST (Jul. 11, 2019), www.washingtonpost.com/lifestyle/style/the-billy-graham-rule-doesnt-honor-your-wife-it-demeans-her--and-all-women/2019/07/11/c1ac14e6-a380-11e9-bd56-eac6bbo2do1d_story.html.

[14] Tim Funk, *Mike Pence Follows "Billy Graham Rule" – Created to Avoid "Naked Lady with Photographer,"* CHARLOTTE OBSERVER (Apr. 4, 2017), www.charlotteobserver.com/living/re ligion/article142611599.html.

[15] Joana Piacenza, *A Year Into #MeToo, Public Worried about False Allegations*, MORNING CONSULT (Oct. 11, 2018), https://morningconsult.com/2018/10/11/a-year-into-metoo-public-worried-about-false-allegations/.

[16] Levin, *supra* note 10.

[17] Kim Elsesser, *60% of Male Managers Are Uncomfortable in Job-Related Activities with Women – Here's Why*, FORBES (May 17, 2019), www.forbes.com/sites/kimelsesser/2019/05/17/60-of-male-managers-are-uncomfortable-in-job-related-activities-with-women-heres-why/#51b

Irrespective of which form it takes, though, the belief inheres. Women pose a threat. They are a risk and a liability. Women can be your downfall by virtue of their being women. As a man, you protect yourself best by staying at arm's length. Choosing men to be your mentees. Taking men to one-on-one workplace meals or engagements. Keeping the door open and meeting times brief when interacting with women. Remaining guarded. Watching your words. Limiting out-of-office socialization that occurs over phone calls and on weekends when it comes to female colleagues. At the end of the day, the fact that this belief, more than most of the others, has become more acceptable to start to voice publicly, and the fact that many of those who espouse it purport to be doing so in the name of legal compliance and a kind of self-preservation, only serve to make it more pernicious.

THE PANE

At a very basic level, those who subscribe to this belief create distance between themselves and women. They may or may not be conscious of the fact that they hold this belief, but it may be revealed when they are pressed about decisions that they make about things like who to mentor, how to assign mentees to others, who to invite to firm-sponsored banquets or dinners, which employees to introduce or assign to which clients, etc. They may or may not be explicit about the belief, even if it is consciously held – especially once the belief is met with skepticism in popular culture or from colleagues.

To the extent that those who are charged with regulating those in power who may hold this belief (whether they be higher-ups at work, Human Resource officials, legislators, or judges) also subscribe to it, or are at least sympathetic to it, the behavior may be anything from overlooked to legally sanctioned. Some may respect this "keep your distance" rule and think there is virtue in avoiding even the appearance of impropriety, and they may even think that it helps the women involved since it will eliminate the chance of any "legitimate" form of harassment. Even those who do not sympathize with the belief may fail to recognize how pernicious it can be to those looking up at the glass ceiling. A summer 2019 federal court in Puerto Rico recently held that a female plaintiff alleging discrimination, where, she claims, she was not mentored the way her male colleagues were, failed to allege an adverse action significant enough to sue over.[18] The court found that her central

---

00918478c ("Men are more worried about how it looks to meet alone with women or dine alone with women. They don't want to give any hint of impropriety.").

[18] Gautier v. Brennan, No. 17–2275 (CVR), 2019 U.S. Dist. LEXIS 111548, at *27 (D. P.R. Jun. 28, 2019).

responsibilities remained essentially unchanged, as did her salary.[19] The idea that she was being left behind, professionally, by not being adequately mentored, because of her sex, did not resonate with the court as cognizable.[20]

And few seem to appreciate the asymmetry of a "no dining out/spending too much time/professionally socializing with people of the opposite sex" because of heteronormative fears of jealousy. Not only would a belief held by professional women that men should be sidelined from too much one-on-one time with them likely fail to land because it would not be tolerated by society, but it would likely be too impractical for most women to implement in light of the present numbers and power imbalance between the sexes at the highest levels of employment.[21]

THE PAIN

As law professor Joanna Grossman put it: "Vice President Pence's 'never dine alone with a woman' rule isn't honorable. It's probably illegal."[22] Indeed, permitting men to avoid mentoring women and otherwise including them in professional/social events outside of work would all but upend many women's careers and professional prospects.[23] It would also set women as a group back many years.[24] After all, the gross inequality of power, prestige, and compensation across most American workplaces when it comes to the sexes seems to dictate that without male mentors and sponsors, neither men nor women looking for upward mobility would fare very well.[25] But will the law capture the multiple layers of the equality-based problems and harms caused by the belief that, on some level, women are or will be the downfall of men?

At each layer, the failures and frailties of human nature and the law alike conspire to advance and magnify the harm. In the first instance, women report being mentored far less frequently and less intensively than do

---

[19]   *Id.*

[20]   *Id.* at 41.

[21]   Tolentino, *supra* note 11.

[22]   Joanna L. Grossman, *Vice President Pence's "Never Dine Alone with a Woman" Rule Isn't Honorable. It's Probably Illegal*, Vox (Dec. 4, 2017), www.vox.com/the-big-idea/2017/3/31/151 32730/pence-women-alone-rule-graham-discrimination.

[23]   *See* Maya Salam, *What Happens When Men Are Too Afraid to Mentor Women?*, N.Y. Times (Jan. 29, 2019), www.nytimes.com/2019/01/29/us/metoo-men-women-mentors.html; Hesse, *supra* note 13.

[24]   *See* Salam, *supra* note 23.

[25]   Ingrid Fredeen, *Avoiding Women at Work Is Not a Solution, It's Discrimination*, Navex Global (Feb. 12, 2019), www.navexglobal.com/blog/article/avoiding-women-at-work-is-not-a-solution-its-discrimination/; David Smith & Brad Johnson, *When Men Mentor Women*, Harv. Bus. Rev. (Oct. 23, 2018), https://hbr.org/ideacast/2018/10/when-men-mentor-women.

men.[26] This amounts to, in many cases, women receiving less specific guidance than do their male colleagues about precisely how they can go about advancing their careers.[27] Less obvious, perhaps, is the social exclusion that many women report and the professional ramifications that flow from that. So, for example, when a woman fails to receive invitations to things like after-work drinks with coworkers or the chance to use the boss's season tickets, she may quickly realize that these so-called extracurricular activities can be quite central to her being known, trusted, and liked when it comes to everything from work assignments to receiving the benefit of the doubt when things go south in the office.[28] Even more nuanced, and thus easily overlooked and hard to prove, is when potential mentors' failure to extend themselves to women translates into a lack of social bonding. And whether that bonding takes place during the course of a business trip or on a golf course, its absence will likely be felt, in some way, at least, inside the office during working hours.[29] Ultimately, this lack of what is seen by some to amount to no more than discretionary "bonding" likely translates into sharp increases in opportunities, exposure, power, and compensation.[30] Even more importantly, it may take the form of women being less likely to be asked to work on after-hours projects, where more senior people roll up their sleeves and plow through daunting work that can't get done during business hours when the phone calls and emails keep arriving. These may be unparalleled learning and growth opportunities, but they can require team members to spend substantial amounts of time together after hours when others have left the worksite.

---

[26] Sheryl Sandberg, *Sheryl Sandberg Thinks Men Should Mentor Women*, ELLE (Jul. 24, 2018), www.elle.com/culture/career-politics/a22521024/sheryl-workplace-sexual-harassment-mentorship-metoo/.

[27] *See* Salam, *supra* note 23.

[28] Jenna Goudreau, *13 Subtle Ways Women Are Treated Differently at Work*, YAHOO! NEWS (Jun. 27, 2014), www.yahoo.com/news/13-subtle-ways-women-treated-133559035.html ("Getting together to drink, watch the game, or play sports is typically how social bonds are formed at the office and when valuable information, like who's [*sic*]position might be opening up or how to get in the graces of a certain boss, is shared. When women aren't included in these events, says Rhodes, it can marginalize them and limit their knowledge.").

[29] W. Brad Johnson & David G. Smith, *Men Shouldn't Refuse to Be Alone with Female Colleagues*, HARV. BUS. REV. (May 5, 2017), https://hbr.org/2017/05/men-shouldnt-refuse-to-be-alone-with-female-colleagues.

[30] Adam Grant, *Men Are More Afraid to Mentor Women in a Post-Weinstein World. Here Are 3 Reasons to Do It Anyway*, INC. (Feb. 8, 2018), www.inc.com/linkedin/adam-grant/men-afraid-mentor-women-heres-what-we-can-do-adam-grant.html; *see also* Caroline Kitchener, *When It's Hard for Women to Find Male Mentors*, THE ATLANTIC (Aug. 22, 2017), www.theatlantic.com/business/archive/2017/08/women-men-mentorship/537201/.

When women or any other group have less time spent having their work reviewed or being prepared or trained for certain projects than do men, they are more likely to perform poorly.[31] Ultimately, women earn less than men.[32] They occupy grossly disproportionately fewer positions of power and prestige than do men in the workplace.[33] They have fewer meaningful relationships with coworkers or superiors that translate into their being noticed, appreciated, or chosen for opportunities or promotion based on familiarity, as happens so often.[34] This is the first layer of the problem. Because of the societally-held belief that "women are the downfall of men," women are avoided, sometimes to the point of being shunned, and, as a result, lose out to their male colleagues on professional training, relationships, and opportunities.

The next layer of the problem comes when women are either not aware that this is happening or aware of what is going on, but unwilling to approach HR. "It's a hard thing to prove," says Chloe, the attorney quoted at the start of the chapter, "that you aren't getting exactly equal time or time of the same quality. That they're actually too afraid of you to get to know you and teach you the way they do with the men." She continues:

> First of all, you don't know for a fact what is going on behind the doors or at the meals or drinks out. Second of all, even if you did know, in most cases, they're technically doing what they have to do for you. You're assigned a mentor. You're assigned various supervisors. What are you going to say; 'I object to my mentor being a woman'? 'Why don't you hang out with me more'? 'Don't go so easy on me'? It's weird, and it's awkward, and it's not necessarily quantifiable in a way that can be shown to violate the law. And even if it hits a point where you know that you're being explicitly excluded from majorly career-advancing socialization because of your sex and in violation of the law, is complaining in your best interest? Is forced mentoring or socialization going to help or hurt your personal cause after you've complained?

This segues into the next layer of the problem. Even if a woman complains about inequalities engendered by this belief, and her complaints are taken seriously by the employer, she may very well face retaliation from those

---

[31]   Catherine H. Tinsley & Robin J. Ely, *What Most People Get Wrong about Men and Women*, HARV. BUS. REV. (last visited Aug. 1, 2019), https://hbr.org/2018/05/what-most-people-get-wrong-about-men-and-women.

[32]   *Economic News Release*, U.S. DEP'T OF LAB. (last visited Aug. 1, 2019), www.bls.gov/news .release/wkyeng.to3.htm; *The State of the Gender Pay Gap in 2019*, PAYSCALE (last visited Aug. 1, 2019), www.payscale.com/data/gender-pay-gap.

[33]   *The State of the Gender Pay Gap in 2019, supra* note 32.

[34]   Tinsley & Ely, *supra* note 31.

complained about, and the law's prohibition of this retaliation may or may not prove useful. Indeed, Title VII's anti-retaliation provision contains two clauses.[35] The first is the so-called opposition clause, which says that the Act is violated when an employee is retaliated against for opposing practices prohibited by the Act.[36] The second is the so-called participation clause, which says that the Act is violated when an employee is retaliated against for participating in proceedings pursuant to a claim under the Act.[37]

Moreover, even if an employee brings suit over ineffable, sometimes barely tangible things like quality of mentoring or amount of exposure to spheres of influence within the workplace, it is highly unlikely that she will prevail in court.[38] In the first place, where instances of exclusion of most sorts are used to support a claim of sexual harassment or a retaliatory campaign of harassment, courts tend to find that the instances do not rise to the level of actionable harassment.[39] Moreover, where the claim is simply one for discrimination, in

---

[35] Title VII of the Civil Rights Act of 1964, 42 U.S.C. § 2000e-3.

[36] *Id.*

[37] *Id.*

[38] Polsby v. Shalala, 925 F. Supp. 379, 395 (D. Md. 1996) ("[The p]laintiff received mentoring during her fellowship. What she really complains about is that she did not establish as *good* a mentoring relationship as she had hoped and that she found the type and quality of research opportunities disappointing. Disappointment of that type cannot be characterized as denial of a term, condition or privilege of employment. Congress simply cannot legislate that all employment relationships enjoy the best communication or provide the most rewarding learning experience. All Title VII can mandate is that employees receive the basic components of the position."); *see also* Gautier v. Brennan, 2019 U.S. Dist. LEXIS 111548, at *27 (D.P. R. Jun. 28, 2019) (holding that none of the actions taken by the employer, including not mentoring the plaintiff, were adverse employment actions because the plaintiff's main responsibilities did not materially change, nor did her salary, and nothing like a "reassignment with significantly different responsibilities" was made); Tourtellotte v. Eli Lilly & Co., 2013 U.S. Dist. LEXIS 54218, at *43–44 (E.D. Pa. Apr. 15, 2013) (holding that the plaintiff's complaints, including that her employer refused to provide her with a company mentor and failed to invite her to a client dinner, did not rise to the "extreme" conduct needed "to amount to a change in the terms and conditions in employment").

[39] *See* Owen v. Sunstar Acceptance Corp., 1999 U.S. Dist. LEXIS 16932, at *13–16 (S.D. Ala. Oct. 7, 1999) (finding that the plaintiff's harassment claim, consisting of being left out of office lunches and other gatherings and meetings, was not so severe or pervasive that the terms and conditions of her employment had changed. Therefore, the plaintiff did not set forth specific facts showing that there was a genuine issue for trial on her claim of harassment); *see also* Toppert v. Nw. Mech., Inc., 968 F. Supp. 2d 1001, 1018 (S.D. Iowa 2013) (finding that a plaintiff's harassment claim, including the fact that she was left out of decision-making, was simply a claim of a "frustrating and unrewarding" workplace and did not amount to the severity and pervasiveness which would permit a finding that it unreasonably interfered with her work performance); Cox v. GMAC Home Servs., 2004 U.S. Dist. LEXIS 4178, at *39 (S.D. Iowa Mar. 12, 2004) (holding that none of the events that the plaintiff alleged for a claim of harassment, including being left out of the loop in communications and meetings, rose to the level of actionable discriminatory conduct when viewed in isolation; the conduct complained

the absence of an admission that the exclusion is sex-based, courts typically find the claim to be without a sufficient evidentiary basis.[40] And what if a women did sue and win? Would she be more or less likely to be genuinely mentored and included, trained, and looked out for? Or would others in the office brand her a troublemaker, fear her, and just do what they thought they needed to do to stay out of trouble?

And so, complaints are not made. Where they are, they are not likely to advance to legal claims, and they may very well engender additional, retaliatory poor treatment and lack of regard. Where claims do ripen into legal claims that an employee and her lawyer are willing to bring, they are not likely to prevail. Left to languish without what they see as the social and professional support given to their male colleagues, many women simply fall out of contention.[41] Their skill sets and their morale alike suffer, as may their performance. Whether it is by their own (coerced) choice, or a merit-based firing, they may be prematurely siphoned off and winnowed out of the workplace and its highest rungs in huge numbers, as compared with their male counterparts. This transcends their capability and their schools attended or training received. This defies expectations premised on a level playing field.

In the end, it is virtually impossible to quantify the harm that women sustain at the hands of their male colleagues and supervisors who subscribe to this

of was not so severe or pervasive as to be actionable); Beverly v. Genuine Parts Co., 2006 U.S. Dist. LEXIS 27993, at *10, 21 (W.D.N.C. May 8, 2006) (holding that the plaintiff's claim that she worked in a sexually hostile environment, including the fact that she was left out of activities like golf in which male employees were invited to participate, did not constitute conduct that was so severe or pervasive as to create an abusive work environment in violation of Title VII).

[40] *See* Johnson v. Dep't of Pub. Works, 2016 U.S. Dist. LEXIS 36101, at *27–28 (D. Colo. Mar. 21, 2016) (holding that the plaintiff failed to provide an evidentiary basis to support his claim that the reason his employers failed to include him in a mentorship program was discriminatory); Newsome v. IDB Capital Corp., 2016 U.S. Dist. LEXIS 40754, at *58–61 (S.D.N.Y. Mar. 28, 2016) (granting summary judgment to the defendant where the plaintiff complained of discrimination, including the fact that he was left out of mentorship opportunities, because the only evidence in the case was the "conclusory allegations" of the plaintiff); Beverly v. Genuine Parts Co., 2006 U.S. Dist. LEXIS 27993, at *10, 21 (W.D.N.C. May 8, 2006) (holding that a summary judgment should be granted to the defendant because the plaintiff gave no indication that her discrimination allegations, including the fact that she was left out of activities that male employees were invited to, occurred because of her gender); Tourtellotte, 2013 U.S. Dist. LEXIS 54218, at *43–44 (holding that the fact that the plaintiff did not point to any evidence of overtly discriminatory conduct or comment directly targeted to her further supported the conclusion that she failed to demonstrate discriminatory animus).

[41] Gillian Tan & Katia Porzecanski, *Wall Street Rule for the #MeToo Era: Avoid Women at All Cost*, BLOOMBERG (Dec. 3, 2018, 9:59 AM), www.bloomberg.com/news/articles/2018-12-03/a -wall-street-rule-for-the-metoo-era-avoid-women-at-all-cost.

belief. Firstly, the degrees of qualitative difference when it comes to things like mentoring (formal and informal) and professional socializing are small and subjective. Courts have long intoned that they do not want to second-guess employers in the exercise of their managerial prerogative and serve as what they term a "super personnel" office.[42] Thus, when a man is paid more than a woman or promoted instead of a woman, courts can take note of an adverse action having occurred. But when the allegation is that someone received "better mentoring" through a formal system – or even informally – a court may feel as though this sort of assessment is beyond its purview.[43] It is hard to quantify or to articulate the almost imperceptible quality of the closeness of a relationship or the quality of mentoring.

Moreover, even where a woman knows that she has lost out on something like a discretionary meal invitation because of her sex, how is she to quantify the professional harm engendered? Title VII requires an adverse action or a harassing environment. Damages require a showing of harm. It is beyond difficult to prove that in an alternate scenario in which an employee had been adequately mentored, invited to an event, or taken to a meal, concrete benefits would have inured to her.

MANIFESTATIONS

While many of the beliefs in this book remain taboo to voice aloud (hence the notion of confronting unspoken beliefs), the belief, in any of the iterations discussed above, that "women are the downfall of men" is perhaps the most voiced. Further, all too often, when this belief is voiced or acted upon, its adherents are often extolled. Many laud men like Vice President Pence for what are seen as his restraint and his loyalty to his wife.[44] Others have sympathized with the concern that men will be targeted by women with

---

[42] McCoy v. WGN Continental Broadcasting Co., 957 F.2d 368, 373 (7th Cir. 1992); Dale v. Chi. Tribune Co., 797 F.2d 458, 464 (7th Cir. 1986).

[43] *See* Polsby v. Shalala, 925 F. Supp. 379, 395 (D. Md. 1996); Tourtellotte, 2013 U.S. Dist. LEXIS 54218, at *43–44 ("For example, even assuming her male sales partner had a company mentor, Reyes does not provide evidence suggesting that Rowland provided him with the mentor, that having a mentor was a recognized Lilly policy or practice, or that having a mentor is necessary for career advancement. Reyes cannot establish a prima facie case of hostile work environment and summary judgment in Defendant's favor is appropriate.").

[44] Tyler O'Neil, *Liberals Attack Mike Pence for Being Faithful to His Wife*, PJ MEDIA (Mar. 30, 2017), https://pjmedia.com/trending/2017/03/30/liberals-attack-mike-pence-for-being-faithful-to-his-wife/.

whom they are left alone at work, who will fabricate accusations, despite the fact that such manufactured accusations are actually quite rare.[45]

Of even more concern is that many women report men feeling increasingly comfortable articulating, sometimes laughingly, some version of the belief as they quite deliberately leave their office door open during a meeting that would typically be held behind a closed door, cut a meeting short, or explain why a woman is not being invited to something. Voicing the belief, though not always done, seems to be gaining social acceptability, which can further cement women's feelings that they are, in fact, being unabashedly ostracized in a variety of ways.

In 2018, Forbes described a silent backlash to the #MeToo movement, citing several studies concluding that men at work are increasingly frightened of and averse to having too much professional contact with their female coworkers, to the detriment of women seeking workplace advancement.[46] Specifically, a Pew Research Center survey found that 51 percent of adults asked whether they felt as though the increased emphasis on the awareness and prevention of sexual harassment at work created more difficulties for men seeking to interact with women professionally, answered in the affirmative.[47] Forbes has reported on a similar study by SourceMedia that showed that many felt that women would be increasingly excluded from workplace life "in order for men to protect themselves."[48] Finally, an undertaking by Lean In and SurveyMonkey revealed that almost half of male managers surveyed claimed to be "uncomfortable participating in a common work activity with a woman, such as mentoring, working alone, or socializing together," and that men at work with more seniority reported being a shocking five times more likely to think twice about traveling for work with a junior woman than they would be with a junior man.[49]

---

[45]   *Id.*; Karol Markowicz, *"Believe All Women" Makes the "Pence Rule" Just Common Sense*, N.Y. POST (Jul. 14, 2019), https://nypost.com/2019/07/14/believe-all-women-makes-the-pence-rule-just-common-sense/; Julie Borowski (@JulieBorowski), TWITTER (Mar. 30, 2017, 7:30 AM), https://twitter.com/JulieBorowski/status/847458494236065793?ref_src=twsrc%5Etfw%7Ctwcamp%5Etweetembed%7Ctwterm%5E847458494236065793&ref_url=https%3A%2F%2Fpjmedia.com%2Ftrending%2F2017%2F03%2F30%2Fliberals-attack-mike-pence-for-being-faithful-to-his-wife%2F.

[46]   Prudy Gourguechon, *Why in the World Would Men Stop Mentoring Women Post #MeToo?*, FORBES (Aug. 6, 2018), www.forbes.com/sites/prudygourguechon/2018/08/06/why-in-the-world-would-men-stop-mentoring-women-post-metoo/#1bc091e679a5.

[47]   Nikki Graf, *Sexual Harassment at Work in the Era of #MeToo*, PEW RSCH CTR. (Apr. 4, 2018), www.pewsocialtrends.org/2018/04/04/sexual-harassment-at-work-in-the-era-of-metoo/.

[48]   Gourguechon, *supra* note 46.

[49]   *Working Relationships in the #MeToo Era*, LEAN IN (last visited Aug. 1, 2019), https://leanin.org/sexual-harassment-backlash-survey-results#key-finding-1.

And yet, the attitudes that are being termed "backlash" predate both the #MeToo movement and the ill-fated Pence declaration. For example, we have long heard of dress codes promulgated everywhere from airlines, to school dances, and classrooms, where it is explicitly stated that the goal is to keep boys from becoming too "distracted."[50] This rationale, which has been heavily criticized, reinforces the idea that females, from childhood on, are to be held accountable for their having tempted or distracted the males around them. Hence, rather than hold men accountable for their own comportment and self-regulation, many subscribe to the unspoken belief that women are the downfall of men, and are, thus, the ones in need of regulation.[51]

In 2013, an Iowa state case made headlines when a court refused to grant relief to the dental hygienist who was termed "too hot to work."[52] The plaintiff, Melissa Nelson, who was twenty years old when she was hired by her dentist boss, sued under Iowa state law for sex discrimination after she was fired after more than ten years of employment, despite the fact that her boss admitted that she was "a good dental assistant," and the fact that he "generally treated her with respect."[53] According to the court, though Nelson denied that her professional attire was inappropriate, she was fired after her boss complained that "her clothing was too tight and revealing and 'distracting'," and he later admitted that he didn't think it was "good for [him] to see her wearing things that accentuate[d] her body."[54]

---

[50] *See* Talia Lakritz, *18 Times Students and Parents Said School Dress Codes Went Too Far*, INSIDER (Feb. 14, 2019), www.inside.com/school-dress-code-rules-controversy-2018-8; *Parents Outraged after Daughter, 9, Told Tank Top "Distracts" Boys at School*, NZ HERALD (Aug. 30, 2019), www.nzherald.co.nz/lifestyle/news/article.cfm?c_id=6&objec tid=12263617; Cecilia D'Anastasio & Student Nation, *Girls Speak Out against Sexist School Dress Codes*, THE NATION, Aug. 27, 2014, www.thenation.com/article/girls-speak-o ut-against-sexist-school-dress-codes/; Donna St. George, *Are Leggings Too Distracting? A Mom Takes on a "Sexist" School Dress Code*, WASH. POST (Nov. 5, 2016), https://www .washingtonpost.com/local/education/are-leggings-too-distracting-a-mom-takes-on-sexist-sc hool-dress-code/2016/11/05/2c677b00-960e-11e6-bc79-af1cd3d2984b_story.html.

[51] Meredith J. Harbach, *Sexualization, Sex Discrimination, and Public School Dress Codes*, 50 U. RICH. L. REV. 1039, 1044 (2016); Deborah M. Ahrens & Andrew M. Siegel, *Of Dress and Redress: Student Dress Restrictions in Constitutional Law and Culture*, 54 HARV. C.R.-C. L. L. REV. 49, 99–100 (2019); Li Zhou, *The Sexism of School Dress Codes*, THE ATLANTIC (Oct. 20, 2015), www.theatlantic.com/education/archive/2015/10/school-dress-codes-are-problematic/410962/; Autumn Spencer, *School Assembly Blames Girls for Distracting Boys from Learning*, MOTHERLY (May 5, 2016), www.mother.ly/parenting/school-assembly-blames-girls-for-distracting-boys-from-learning; S. Suresh, *How Should Society View a Woman's Body?*, FAIR OBSERVER (Nov. 10, 2018), www.fairobserver.com/region/north_america/wome ns-dress-code-sexism-sexual-harassment-feminism-news-54131/.

[52] Nelson v. James H. Knight DDS, P.C., 834 N.W.2d 64, 77 (Iowa 2013).

[53] *Id.* at 65.

[54] *Id.*

Moreover, as per the court, in the last few months of her employment, Nelson and her boss "started texting each other on both work and personal matters outside the workplace."[55] The court stated that though the subjects of the texts were generally "innocuous," and though "Nelson considered Dr. Knight to be a friend and father figure, and she denie[d] that she ever flirted with him or sought an intimate or sexual relationship with him," she was fired after the dentist's wife discovered that they had been texting and "insisted that her husband terminate Nelson because 'she was a big threat to our marriage'."[56] When she was fired, the court said, her boss made a statement that "their relationship had become a detriment to [his] family and that for the best interests of both . . . the two of them should not work together."[57] The court also noted that the dentist later told Nelson's husband that "he was worried he was getting too personally attached to her," and that "nothing was going on but . . . he feared he would try to have an affair with her down the road if he did not fire her."[58]

The court rejected Nelson's sex discrimination claim, deciding that the answer to the question of "whether an employee who has not engaged in flirtatious conduct may be lawfully terminated simply because the boss's spouse views the relationship between the boss and the employee as a threat to her marriage," was yes.[59] This meant that any professional, highly performing woman who unwittingly evoked the ire or jealousy of her boss's spouse could be targeted and fired without legal consequences, simply because she was viewed as his (potential) downfall, notwithstanding protections that were supposed to be in place to keep her from being discriminated against because of her sex.

The court was careful to delineate between "(1) an isolated employment decision based on personal relations (assuming no coercion . . .), even if the relations would not have existed if the employee had been of the opposite gender, and (2) a decision based on gender itself," noting: "In the former case, the decision is driven entirely by individual feelings and emotions regarding a specific person. Such a decision is not gender-based, nor is it based on factors that might be a proxy for gender."[60] To the extent that this distinction is specious and dances around the idea that an employee who acts and dresses professionally and performs well may lose her job lawfully simply because her

---

[55]   *Id.*
[56]   *Id.* at 65–66.
[57]   *Id.* at 66.
[58]   *Id.*
[59]   *Id.* at 68.
[60]   *Id.* at 70.

boss's spouse is jealous of her, it is an outgrowth of the belief that women are the downfall of men. The court even observed that had the plaintiff proven "that she had been terminated because she did not conform to a particular stereotype, this might be a different case. But the record here does not support that conclusion. It is undisputed, rather, that Nelson was fired because [her boss's wife], unfairly or not, viewed her as a threat to her marriage."[61]

The (as many were quick to point out) all-male court was subsequently bashed in headlines reporting the case.[62] Notably, Nelson's lawyer, Paige Fiedler, was quoted as saying: "We are appalled by the court's ruling and its failure to understand the nature of gender bias .... For the seven men on the Iowa Supreme Court not to 'get it' is shocking and disheartening. It underscores the need for judges on the bench to be diverse in terms of their gender, race and life experiences."[63] Indeed, it is easy to see how the court's conclusion that the decision to terminate Nelson was not "because of sex" belies the unspoken belief that women are the downfall of men. In fact, the dentist's decision to terminate her so as not to upset his wife may even be seen as laudable by some. How could the dentist's honoring his marriage and his wife's feelings contravene the law, many could wonder? But, indeed, if a woman's being told that she is too sexy/pretty, etc. to work is not discrimination because of sex, it is hard to think of what would be. And this case underscores the larger point that women, as well as men, direct discrimination against other women for a variety of reasons.

In the wake of the ousters of powerhouses like Matt Lauer, Charlie Rose, and Harvey Weinstein from their high-profile media and entertainment positions, many were left wondering how behavior deemed so reprehensible could stay shrouded in secrecy for so long.[64] Part of the narrative in virtually every case, for certain, is the way in which the witnesses, the victims, and those surrounding them could be compelled to turn a blind eye by everything from self-doubt, to shame, to sheer intimidation by the immense power these men wielded, at work and within their industries. Perhaps one of the most salient

---

[61] *Id.* at 71.

[62] *See* Gena Kaufman, *Court Says if Your Boss Has a Crush on You, He Can Fire You. WHAT?!*, GLAMOUR (Dec. 26, 2012), www.glamour.com/story/court-says-if-your-boss-has-a; Dana Ford, *Iowa Supreme Court: OK to Fire "Irresistible" Worker*, CNN (Dec. 22, 2012), www.cnn.com /2012/12/21/justice/iowa-irresistible-worker/index.html; Eric M. Strauss, *Iowa Woman Fired for Being Attractive Looks Back and Moves On*, ABC NEWS (Aug. 2, 2013), https://abcnews .go.com/Business/iowa-woman-fired-attractive-back-moves/story?id=19851803.

[63] Ford, *supra* note 62.

[64] *Post-Weinstein, These Are the Powerful Men Facing Sexual Harassment Allegations*, GLAMOUR (May 18, 2019), www.glamour.com/gallery/post-weinstein-these-are-the-powerful-men-facing-sexual-harassment-allegations.

examples of this belief at work is the propagation of the so-called NDA, or nondisclosure agreement, executed either before or during the term of employment. They compel victims into silence about their ordeals. Nondisclosure agreements can also be executed preemptively, prior to and perhaps even in anticipation of sexual harassment or abuse that has yet to occur. This appeared to be the case with Harvey Weinstein, who, it is reported, preemptively made people around him, including employees, sign particularly stringent and sophisticated NDAs.[65] Crafted to protect the perpetrators of sexual abuse and harassment from public embarrassment by the disclosure of details surrounding these events, NDAs typically carry harsh penalties for violations and they are often insisted upon by the accused in order for a victim to procure compensation.[66] These agreements, like all other contracts, vary in many respects, and may also be executed after a court case or informal HR dispute has been settled. For example, according to the *New York Times*, television news host and journalist Bill O'Reilly reached settlement agreements with more than one woman who accused him of sexual harassment.[67] Pursuant to some of these agreements, the women were forced to turn over to him the entirety of their evidence, including diaries and audio recordings.[68]

In early 2020, Democratic presidential candidate Elizabeth Warren famously confronted fellow candidate former New York City mayor Michael Bloomberg about the NDAs that he had executed with women who had previously accused him of sexual harassment.[69] While Bloomberg shot back that the women hadn't accused him of anything worse than telling a joke that they found offensive, Warren, for her part, publicly offered Bloomberg a release and covenant not to sue that she had drafted for him.[70] If he signed it, she said, his accusers would be free to tell their stories without violating any nondisclosure or nondisparagement agreements to which they had been party.[71]

[65]   Marina Fang, *How Harvey Weinstein Used Elaborate Nondisclosure Agreements to Silence Accusers*, HUFFPOST (Nov. 21, 2017), www.huffpost.com/entry/harvey-weinstein-non-disclosure-agreements_n_5a142f45e4b0aa32975dc03b.

[66]   Stacy Perman, *#MeToo Law Restricts Use of Nondisclosure Agreements in Sexual Misconduct Cases*, LA TIMES (last visited Aug. 3, 2019), www.latimes.com/business/hollywood/la-fi-ct-nda-hollywood-20181231-story.html.

[67]   Emily Steel, *How Bill O'Reilly Silenced His Accusers*, N.Y. TIMES (Apr. 4, 2018), www.nytimes.com/2018/04/04/business/media/how-bill-oreilly-silenced-his-accusers.html.

[68]   *Id.*

[69]   DEMOCRATIC DEBATE IN LAS VEGAS (NBC News/MSNBC Broadcast Feb. 19, 2020).

[70]   *Id.*

[71]   *Id.*

Despite the fact that these agreements, like all contracts, are susceptible to being policed or challenged for potential defects, there are relatively few challenges to these agreements, in no small part due to factors like how difficult it is to find an attorney who will take a contract dispute on contingency. The inexplicably sacred place that these NDAs hold in society is what enables them to be weaponized and deployed to silence victims and to shroud sexual misconduct in secrecy. This, in turn, empowers recidivist abusers to obscure and repeat their behavior. Harvey Weinstein, notably, was able to protect his reputation for decades, according to media outlets, by deploying NDAs to shroud his alleged acts and their effects in secrecy.[72] Those who executed the NDAs were contractually bound not to speak to anyone, including friends, family, press, etc., about any aspect of Weinstein's life, including his personal and social activities.[73] Accusers later recounted feeling extremely intimidated and silenced by the NDAs that they had signed; one, in particular, reported that she had refused to speak to a counselor about what she described as Weinstein's attempt to rape her.[74]

Notably, just as many had no idea that men like Cosby and Weinstein had such sordid accusations in their pasts until the proverbial "tipping point" was reached in each of their scandals and victims felt empowered by the revelation of their shared experiences to come forward; many had no idea that NDAs had been tools wielded by serial harassers and abusers to permit them to move forward, professionally and otherwise, from each instance of abuse. In some cases, decades of abuse throughout careers came to light, and the perceived iron-clad untouchability of NDAs – both in terms of their failure to be challenged as a matter of public policy (for systemically harming society) and in terms of individual agreements not being successfully challenged for defects – was to blame. This perceived untouchability may be rooted, on some level, in the societally-held notion that women ought to be able to be kept from toppling powerful men.

In recent years, it has become more evident that, even absent an NDA, egregious workplace abuse by an individual may still be kept secret for periods as long as decades. The silence of many in the know can, unfortunately, also be secured through the vehicles of intimidation, implicit or explicit, and the

---

[72] Robert Mendick & Gordon Rayner, *Non-disclosure Agreements: Everything You Need to Know about NDAs (and Their Misuse)*, TELEGRAPH (Oct. 25, 2018), www.telegraph.co.uk/news/o/non-disclosure-agreements-everything-need-know-ndas-misuse/.

[73] Nicole Einbinder, *What Happens if Someone Breaks a Non-disclosure Agreement?*, FRONTLINE (Mar. 2, 2018), www.pbs.org/wgbh/frontline/article/what-happens-if-someone-breaks-a-non-disclosure-agreement/.

[74] Mendick & Rayner, *supra* note 72.

sheer power of the harasser. Perhaps one of the most shocking things about the spate of recent public accusations against prominent men is simply how long their alleged deeds were allowed to be shrouded in secrecy, while simultaneously known by so many. In early 2020, Olivia Warren, a former clerk of Judge Stephen Reinhardt, a preeminent Ninth Circuit Court of Appeals Judge, known nationwide as the "liberal lion" of the Court, testified before a House Judiciary subcommittee at a hearing on sexual harassment.[75] Shockingly, she recounted numerous instances of sexual harassment and sex-based workplace verbal abuse that she suffered at his hands. But this was just the tip of the iceberg. Soon thereafter, some seventy-two former clerks of this judge, whose tenures as his clerks ranged throughout his tenure as a judge, from 1980 until his death in 2018, issued a statement that declared that they "believe the clerk's testimony that she experienced inappropriate conduct, including sexual harassment," and that they remain "thankful to the clerk for her courage in speaking out about her experience."[76] They continued on to state: "Some of us experienced or witnessed conduct in chambers that we would call sexist, workplace bullying or mistreatment," and to express their desire that "the Judicial Conference—and, if need be, Congress—will take bold steps to ensure that all judges and judicial personnel will be trained in principles of antidiscrimination and anti-harassment; to implement an effective system for reporting and responding to complaints of discrimination and harassment; and to protect law clerks and other personnel from such mistreatment."[77] They lamented that it was "past time to extend the protections of Title VII, or their equivalent, to the judicial branch," and that there could be "no justification for a system in which antidiscrimination law applies to all except those who interpret and enforce it."[78]

It is astounding to think that whatever was known by Judge Reinhardt's successive years' worth of clerks was not known to the general public. It was a secret hiding in plain sight, just as the alleged actions and deeds of producer Harvey Weinstein were, prior to his arrest and 2020 conviction for rape, several decades into his career. The fear that these and other men's power instills in those around them, to keep secrets hidden in plain sight, is staggering. How does a power broker develop such a widespread yet simultaneously unknown reputation for doing such reprehensible things?

---

[75]   Kathryn Rubino, *70+ Former Reinhardt Clerks Come Out in Support of Sexual Harassment Accuser*, ABOVE THE L. (Feb. 21, 2020, 10:02 AM), https://abovethelaw.com/2020/02/reinhardt-clerks/.

[76]   *Id.*

[77]   *Id.*

[78]   *Id.*

Historically, NDAs have not been seen as violative of public policy because, to the extent that they accompany a settlement agreement as a way to dispose of a dispute without formal adjudication, there is no formal admission of guilt or liability on anyone's part.[79] Where accused abusers and/or employers contest guilt or liability, there is legitimacy in confidentiality, just as confidentiality stipulations may accompany any settlement agreement. However, where victims feel coerced into accepting such a settlement, lest they suffer blacklisting or some other professional retaliation, the NDA operates to silence them and to ensure that the accused suffers no harm to his reputation.

With the advent of the #MeToo movement, things look to be changing. There have been renewed calls for courts to look critically at NDAs that might not be enforceable, especially in cases where power inequalities are stark, or where they are being used to mask repeated patterns of harassment and assault.[80] There have even been assertions that NDAs, as a category of contract, offend public policy.[81] In 2019 California's so-called STAND, or Stand Together Against Non-Disclosure Act, took effect.[82] This law renders void any confidentiality clause in settlement agreements executed to resolve claims for, among other things, workplace sexual harassment or discrimination, retaliation for reporting sexual discrimination or harassment, and failure to prevent harassment.[83] Under the law, the person making the claim, however, retains the right to request a term in the settlement agreement that shields his or her identity, as well as facts that could expose it.[84] Tennessee, Washington,

---

[79] Emma J. Roth, *Is a Nondisclosure Agreement Silencing You from Sharing Your "Me Too" Story? 4 Reasons It Might Be Illegal*, ACLU (Jan. 24, 2018, 9:45 AM), www.aclu.org/blog/wo mens-rights/womens-rights-workplace/nondisclosure-agreement-silencing-you-sharing-your-me-too.

[80] *Id. See also* Susan Seager, *NDAs Can't Silence Everyone: Here's When You Can Safely Break a Nondisclosure Agreement*, THE WRAP (Oct. 26, 2017), www.thewrap.com/harvey-weinstein-nda-non-disclsoure-agreements-sexual-harassment-fox-news-gloria-allred/.

[81] Keith Anderson, *Bag the Gag Provision: New Jersey Is the Latest State to Restrict Nondisclosure Agreements in Settlements*, LEXOLOGY: LAB. AND EMP. INSIGHTS BLOG (May 14, 2019), www.lexology.com/library/detail.aspx?g=10fc23d2-cd92-4090-80c1-ed097b0622ec; *see also* Julie Macfarlane, *Should Universities Be Using Non-disclosure Agreements When Employees Are Terminated for Sexual Misconduct?*, MEDIUM (Mar. 18, 2019), https://medium.com/@ProfJulieMac/should-universities-be-using-non-disclosure-agreements-when-employees-are-terminated-for-sexual-bb132f4cdb8.

[82] *California Employers to Face Raft of New #MeToo Laws*, FISHER PHILLIPS (Oct. 1, 2018), www.fisherphillips.com/resources-alerts-california-employers-to-face-raft-of-new.

[83] C.A. CIV PRO CODE § 1001 (2018).

[84] *California Employers to Face Raft of New #MeToo Laws, supra* note 82 ("Because employees themselves may have legitimate privacy concerns, and a desire to protect themselves from unwanted negative attention, the STAND Act contains an exception aimed at allowing claimants to maintain privacy.").

Maryland, Arizona, New Jersey, New York, and Vermont have all introduced laws that restrict the use of nondisclosure agreements in sexual harassment cases by private employers.[85]

TAKEAWAYS

The belief that "women are the downfall of men" can take many forms and be expressed in many ways. However, whether a man is afraid that being alone with a woman in a professional setting will lead him down the path of temptation, will enable her to fabricate false accusations, or will give others something to talk about, it is unlikely that anyone in the workplace would actually come out and say that he fears that a woman will bring about his downfall or topple any of his colleagues. The belief is thus rendered virtually invisible when the lens of the law or social scrutiny tries to ensure workplace equality because it is not factored into the discussion or into the equation when the regulation of workplace behavior is discussed. By understanding that this belief inheres in society, various factions of workplace regulators, from legislators to judges to individuals in the workplace, themselves, can combat its pernicious effects.

This belief and the questions of how and why it systemically harms women in so many ways have been all too absent from meaningful discussions of best practices, legal reform, and workplace equality. Discussing the fears and, some would say, paranoia harbored by so many at workplace harassment training may combat some of the counterproductive takeaways that some develop after listening to all of the behaviors that run afoul of the law. After the headlines made by Pence and others, the statistics that bear out the prevalence of these apprehensions, and those that belie the notion that false accusations of impropriety are common, informed discussions may be quite productive.

Mindfulness of this aspect of the struggle for equality in the workplace on the part of employers' internal regulators, from those who assign mentors and staff assignments to those who evaluate supervisors, can go a long way, as well. On a larger scale, courts ought to account for the fact that seemingly small, nuanced things like the quality of mentoring and "bonding," and impromptu professional interactions spurred by comfort levels, may be eluding scrutiny. Won't some metrics be simply too subjective to invoke, and won't inequality persist? Most certainly. This, like many of the other problems in this book, cannot be solved simply. But a more searching, honest conversation that challenges beliefs and focuses on results is bound to have some utility.

---

[85] *States Move to Limit Workplace Confidentiality Agreements*, CBS NEWS (Aug. 27, 2018), www .cbsnews.com/news/states-move-to-limit-workplace-confidentiality-agreements/.

6

"Just Be Grateful That You're There" (And)

This was the day I had been waiting for . . . for years . . . eight in fact. I had taken my best-lined suit to the dry cleaners, had my hair blown out, and even did yoga that morning to get myself in the right headspace for my final promotion evaluation at my firm. But I'm getting ahead of myself.

The morning of my promotion interview I got dressed, my husband made me a great breakfast and I confidently went to my car and drove to work. I felt great. I was ready. Even during the interview, I thought it was going really well. We were laughing, making jokes, and talking about all the great successes I've achieved as an associate. It was exactly as they say—when you start talking about things other than the job, the interview is going well.

But the feedback from the managing partner wasn't as encouraging as I had thought it would be. In fact, I was taken aback. The managing partner told me that, frankly, he was "put off" by "how much" and how "overwhelming" I was. He said that during the entire interview, he found me to be "kind of overpowering." He said that he believed that he could get "past it," because I was so talented, but that he wanted to let me know that. Ummm . . . thanks?! I have so many questions now.

What is it, exactly, about me that makes me so "overwhelming?" I am all of five foot one. I am pleasant and polite. But I also excel in a field that has traditionally been dominated by men—both nationally and in my firm. Also, what am I supposed to do with this information? Is it supposed to help me? Am I supposed to feel cowed? Beholden? Apologize? Am I supposed to be grateful that he BELIEVED that he could get past it?

I know one thing. I no longer believe that I am at the right firm. I do not need the promotion I was offered. If you have to "get past" who I am (for no discernible reason), and you don't seem to have that problem with similar, affable men, maybe you don't deserve my talent.

—Meghan, thirty-three, brand manager

THE BELIEF

The unspoken belief that women ought simply to be grateful that they are there in the workplace, rather than complaining about perceived wrongs or aspiring to greater workplace power or prestige, is particularly pernicious.[1] The sentiment behind it is inimical to Title VII's goals, and the voicing of such a belief would likely be offensive to a reasonable person today. This is thus perhaps one of the hardest beliefs to write about, since it is arguably one of the beliefs that is most likely to be universally disclaimed and the least likely to be voiced in any way. It may not even be a conscious belief in the mind of most, but it is present, on some level, throughout society and in the workplace, and its impact is felt and seen in numerous problems found in the regulation of workplace behavior.

And perhaps "Just be grateful that you're there" is just one iteration of the belief, which could, perhaps, be better expressed by continuing on to say "And since you are here, we'd be best served if you made sure that all those around you were comfortable, happy, and taken care of." In 2013, Sheryl Sandberg famously exhorted women to "lean in" at work.[2] But to the extent that some men who work around women passively, or silently, resent their presence to begin with, this advice may be harder than might be thought for women to heed as they combat the additional burdens, often invisible, that may be heaped on them. "Leaning in[to]" a climate rife with this resentment and the many burdens and obstacles engendered by it may then be like spitting into a strong, invisible wind.

This belief is likely built upon the notion that women belong in the home, while men belong in the workplace, and that when women are admitted into the workplace, they should respect its norms, regardless of Title VII's protections or goals. Beyond the idea that women should "be grateful," arguably, even more beliefs rooted in this notion may be espoused by men and women alike. For example, for many people of both sexes, the belief persists that having the female member of a heterosexual couple stay at home is a status symbol indicating the financial success of the man (i.e., "we are fortunate that my wife doesn't have to work"). This view can traverse socioeconomic class, as well as education levels and sex, and, whether we like it or not, it persists across segments of society.

More and more heterosexual women are being told by essayists and bloggers that they ought to stop being grateful to their male partners for "helping out" around the house and with the couple's children.[3] This requires a very

[1] Franziska Barczyk, *Stop Being Grateful! Graduation Advice from 12 Women*, N.Y. TIMES (May 31, 2018), www.nytimes.com/2018/05/31/us/abby-wambach-commencement-speeches-women.html; Theresa Suico, *Emotional Labor and Women of Color in the Workplace: A Reality Check*, CITY OF PORTLAND OREGON (last visited Sept. 11, 2020), www .portlandoregon.gov/article/686010.

[2] SHERYL SANDBERG , LEAN IN: WOMEN, WORK AND THE WILL TO LEAD (2013).

[3] *See, e.g.*, Darcy Lockman, *Don't Be Grateful That Dad Does His Share*, THE ATLANTIC (May 7, 2019), www.theatlantic.com/ideas/archive/2019/05/mothers-shouldnt-be-grateful-their-husbands-help/588787/.

necessary reframing of the presupposition that these things are squarely within the purview of the woman's responsibilities to start with, and that anything her male partner does is simply charitable. What we have *not* heard is a similar call for women to stop letting employers make them feel grateful just to occupy their positions at work and to be present in the workplace. But women are made to feel like this constantly, whether it is through their assignment of domestic or menial tasks outside of their job description, the unvoiced expectation that they will perform emotional labor for those around them, or their consignment to roles of professional and emotional support in disproportionate numbers to those of their male colleagues.

THE PANE

The notion that women ought to be so grateful for their seat at the boardroom table that they shouldn't mind shouldering additional burdens is not often voiced, but it is pervasive. These burdens may take the form of enduring a work environment hostile to women, having menial tasks foisted upon them, being held to different standards or having their conduct, demeanor, or dress overregulated.[4] This leads to many concrete disadvantages to women. Coined in 1983 in Arlie Russell Hochschild's book THE MANAGED HEART, the term "emotional labor" refers to a wide range of performative and emotionally regulatory work that most employees have to do at some point in their careers to ensure that their countenance and disposition are appropriate for interactions with clients, supervisors, and colleagues, among others.[5] For example, having to provide good customer service and exhibit "professionalism" at work, to the extent that workers are asked to do these things, demands emotional labor. However, the "pane" of the glass ceiling, or the actual behavior fueled by this belief, can result in, among other things, a disproportionate conferral – both explicitly and implicitly – of "emotional labor" on female employees.

A related, occasionally overlapping term that has sprung up is "office housework," which refers to the actual "housekeeping" tasks that a disproportionate number of women are called upon to do above and beyond what their job descriptions require.[6] According to the WALL STREET

---

4   *See* Ruchika Tulshyan, *Women of Color Get Asked to Do More "Office Housework." Here's How They Can Say No.*, HARV. BUS. REV. (Apr. 6, 2018), https://hbr.org/2018/04/women-of-color-get-asked-to-do-more-office-housework-heres-how-they-can-say-no.

5   ARLIE RUSSELL HOCHSCHILD, THE MANAGED HEART 7 (3rd ed., 2012).

6   Maya Salam, *Women, Stop Volunteering for Office Housework*, N.Y. TIMES (Jul. 19, 2018), www.nytimes.com/2018/07/19/business/women-careers-volunteering-work.html.

JOURNAL, this can include "everything from booking meeting rooms to buying and circulating birthday cards."[7] And, as will be discussed, while women both feel and are made to feel obligated to volunteer for this work in ways that men do and are not, they are also expressly tasked with it disproportionately more often than are their male colleagues. This creates a secondary set of complications, as women must, as others observe them, navigate the precarious line between appearing as agreeable as they are expected to be and simultaneously as strong and boundary-setting as is equally desirous and necessary. Men do not, many feel, need to perform this balancing act nearly so often or with the same heightened, sex-based expectations of their alacrity. Respected more for being assertive and setting boundaries, as well as called upon less to elongate their job duties, men, it is felt, wind up being less saddled with irrelevant tasks that deplete their resources, distract them from advancement, and keep them out of the spotlight and behind the scenes.[8] Sadly, though not surprisingly, women of color are disproportionately saddled with office housework.[9]

As a FAST COMPANY article portrayed the office housework and emotional labor performed by and expected of women in the workplace: "Welcome to being a working woman in the 2010s . . .. [W]e're going to need you to do your part for workplace culture by acting as a sounding board, taking notes during meetings and sending us a recap email, ordering pizza when we work late, and planning office events and birthday parties. Oh, and be sure to clean up the kitchen when you're done."[10] This refers to the largely tacit expectation that women will perform and assume the identity of a caretaker at work. It also adverts to "surface acting," or navigating feelings so as to keep those around them at ease by remaining calm, pleasant, or otherwise comforting at a time when perhaps they do not feel these things. Finally, this passage includes references to what has been alternately termed "invisible labor."[11] This refers to tasks that are so inconsequential and/or unrelated to one's job description

---

7   Rachel Feintzeig, *Don't Ask Me to Do Office Housework!*, WALL ST. J. (Oct. 13, 2019, 5:30 AM), www.wsj.com/articles/dont-ask-me-to-do-office-housework-11570959002.

8   *See* Salam, *supra* note 6; Joan C. Williams, *Sticking Women with the Office Housework*, WASH. POST (Apr. 16, 2014, 11:09 AM), www.washingtonpost.com/news/on-leadership/wp/2014/04/16/sticking-women-with-the-office-housework/.

9   Tulshyan, *supra* note 4.

10 Gwen Moran, *This Is the Cost of Women's Workplace Emotional Labor*, FAST CO. (Oct. 3, 2018), www.fastcompany.com/90241506/women-do-more-emotional-labor-than-men-at-work.

11 Melody Wilding, *How Emotional Labor Affects Women's Careers*, FORBES (Jun. 6, 2018, 8:49 AM), www.forbes.com/sites/melodywilding/2018/06/06/dont-be-the-office-mom-how-emotional-labor-affects-womens-careers/#1b4caf111103; Monica Torres, *How Women Should Say No to Thankless Office Tasks*, HUFFPOST (Jul. 23, 2019), www.huffpost.com/entry/women-serve-coffee-at-work-how-to-say-no_l_5d35c9bfe4b004b6adb352a5.

that they (1) are often assigned outside of the realm of traditional assignments, (2) typically go virtually unnoticed and unappreciated, and (3) do nothing to further the career, reputation, or work of the worker assigned to them.[12]

Emotional Maintenance and Caretaking in the Workplace

A big piece of emotional labor seems to be that a woman at work is responsible for the emotional comfort of those around her. This expectation, while not typically voiced, may materialize in any number of forms. It may show up as an evaluation that criticizes a woman for the poor morale found in the team she is managing in a way that a man would not be criticized, or at least in a way that would not be a focal point of a man's evaluation.[13] It may show up as a constant assumption that in the midst of an interpersonal workplace blowup that may not even involve her, she will insert herself and soothe ruffled feathers. It appears as her (unwanted, unsolicited) assignment to oversee a mentor or summer internship program, while her male colleagues receive higher-profile and more professionally substantive and relevant, less administrative assignments. The tacit expectation is that she, as a woman, transacts largely in the currency of emotions and ought to be charged with the management of things like quelling anger, generating amusement, and establishing interpersonal relationships in the office. It may take the form of male supervisors asking a female supervisor (or woman in HR) to speak with junior female colleagues about their feelings following the receipt of criticism, or the appropriateness of their dress, since the message will be taken differently when delivered by a woman. Even to the extent that a woman who smiles less often or is more dour than most is seen more negatively than a similar man, the unspoken belief conveyed that she should be grateful just to be there is at work.

Women in the workplace report disproportionately being asked to curb their "tone,"[14] written and spoken, and to adjust their countenance to seem more cheerful and accepting of what is happening around them, lest they be seen as "pushy," "abrasive," or "ruthless." In this way, they are, in a manner of

---

[12] Julia Carpenter, *The "Invisible Labor" Still Asked of Women at Work*, CNN MONEY (Oct. 9, 2017, 9:53 AM), https://money.cnn.com/2017/10/18/pf/women-emotional-labor/index.html.

[13] GEMMA HARTLEY, FED UP (2018); Erin Magner, *Could "Emotional Labor at Work Be the Reason You're So Exhausted*, WELL & GOOD (Jun. 13, 2018), www.wellandgood.com/good-advice/emotional-labor-in-the-workplace/.

[14] Kathleen Davis, *The One World Men Never See in Their Performance Reviews*, FAST CO. (Aug. 27, 2014), www.fastcompany.com/3034895/the-one-word-men-never-see-in-their-performance-reviews.

speaking, charged with the maintenance of others' emotional well-being at work. Anecdotally, they report being asked to do things like ceding authority to a man in the room so as to put a client at ease, submit to having their suggestions be passed along by men so as to have them better received, and even addressing personal or interpersonal problems on a workplace team, where necessary, rather than have a man do it. Implicit in this burden is the belief that men have more of an entitlement to their own status and therefore don't need to regulate themselves to the same extent to remain socially and professionally appropriate. Women even report being asked to perform tasks like serving refreshments or taking notes at a meeting, sometimes with express acknowledgment that they are being so asked because they are women.[15]

Being Asked? Volunteering?

The question lingers in popular and scholarly discourse as to whether women are more likely to be assigned or expected to engage in so-called invisible or emotional labor, caretaking, or housekeeping, or if they are more likely than their male colleagues *to have volunteered* for that work.[16] Interesting issues surround this query because, in any event, the disproportionate meting out of emotional labor to women at work seems to be invariably bound up in unspoken sexist societal expectations and the sexist history of the American workplace, which, from its earliest days, either excluded women altogether or relegated them to assistant or administrative roles. Supreme Court Justice Ruth Bader Ginsburg has famously told of graduating near the top of her class from Columbia Law School, only to encounter numerous difficulties securing employment, even as the men who had graduated alongside her received prestigious offers.[17]

Thus, while a woman might be outright told to do things like take notes or pour coffee at meetings, much subsumed within the expectation and assignment of emotional labor will be silent, bound up in unspoken expectations. One of these expectations is that women are somehow responsible for executing the physical housekeeping and domestic tasks that arise in the office, like setting up for or cleaning up after a party, or taking notes at a meeting, and

---

[15]   Kari Paul, *Why Women Should Never Offer to Do Office Housework*, N.Y. POST: LIVING (Oct. 8, 2018, 12:30 PM), https://nypost.com/2018/10/08/why-women-should-never-offer-to-do-office-housework/.

[16]   Salam, *supra* note 6; Paul, *supra* note 15.

[17]   *Ruth Bader Ginsberg*, OYEZ, www.oyez.org/justices/ruth_bader_ginsburg (last visited Jan. 18, 2020); *Ruth Bader Ginsberg*, HISTORY, www.history.com/topics/womens-history/ruth-bader-ginsburg (last updated Nov. 9, 2018).

thereby freeing up male colleagues to interact freely and unencumbered by such tasks.[18]

Sometimes, though, women are simply prevailed upon expressly to "volunteer" for this extra work. In fact, a research study published in the AMERICAN ECONOMIC REVIEW and written up in the HARVARD BUSINESS REVIEW has shown that women are 48 percent more likely than their male colleagues to volunteer when it comes to work that has what the researchers referred to as "low promotability."[19] This refers to thankless work, beyond one's job duties, such as ordering food or physically setting up for a workplace celebration or meal. It also includes other work that typically doesn't invite a lot of glory, recognition, or career advancement for whomever takes it on, such as more administrative tasks, performing service that is considered low prestige, or filling in at something for someone else who usually does it, like answering the phone or taking notes at a meeting. And so it becomes significant, as the researchers found, that women get 44 percent more "asks" for volunteerism than do men in mixed-sex groups; irrespective of the sex of the manager doing the asking, women will get asked more.[20] Moreover, researchers found that a woman asked to volunteer will say yes 76 percent of the time, with just over half of men giving the same response.[21]

Why Women Volunteer

Interestingly, the researchers were able to, from within the context of the study, exclude the possibilities that the women who had volunteered did so because they were in some way either more risk-averse or more altruistic than the men being studied.[22] This led the researchers to press on to find the cause of the women's behavior in volunteering so much more than the men did. They ultimately concluded that the sex-based results of their research stemmed from "a shared understanding or expectation that women would volunteer more than men."[23] This would almost seem to indicate that women in the

---

[18] *See* Elizabeth F. Emens, *Admin*, 103 GEO. L.J. 1409, 1412, 1438 (2015) (discussing how women are disproportionately doing admin work compared to men).

[19] Linda Babcock et al., *Gender Differences in Accepting and Receiving Requests for Tasks with Low Promotability*, 107 AM. ECON. REV. 714 (2017), https://pubs.aeaweb.org/doi/pdfplus/10.1257/aer.20141734; Linda Babcock et al., *Why Women Volunteer for Tasks That Don't Lead to Promotions*, HARV. BUS. REV. (Jul. 16, 2018), https://hbr.org/2018/07/why-women-volunteer-for-tasks-that-dont-lead-to-promotions.

[20] Babcock et al., *Why Women Volunteer for Tasks That Don't Lead to Promotions*, *supra* note 19.

[21] *Id.*

[22] *Id.*

[23] *Id.*

workplace may act as they do simply out of a sense of resignation in the face of their perceived role. Indeed, the researchers found that women and men volunteer equally as often when they are in rooms with only their sex. This would appear to indicate, at least on some level, an awareness on the part of both men and women of this sex-rooted dynamic. The researchers concluded: "Understanding that women volunteer more simply because men are reluctant to do so should also lead men to volunteer more themselves and should empower women to demand fairer treatment."[24]

A Double Bind – with an Audience

The societal expectation component of the sexism attendant in "office housework" cannot be overstated. A 2005 study concluded that, in a classic double-bind scenario, women face penalties if they do office housework because it depletes their focus, time, and energy, and they face penalties if they fail to do it because their work evaluations suffer.[25] And no one, it seems, is immune. Indeed, *Morning Joe* cohost Mika Brzezinski, in a 2013 COSMOPOLITAN article, recalled being told by Massachusetts Senator Elizabeth Warren that back when she was a professor at Harvard Law School, she had often been left "holding the mop" for the men who worked alongside her.[26] This included her assuming the less desirable teaching shifts when the men around her had simply refused to do so. The experience found Warren navigating the tenuous border between, as Brzezinski put it, "paying your dues and knowing when to say no."[27]

Feminist scholar Joan C. Williams echoed this tension and the treacherousness of walking what she called the "political tightrope" in the WASHINGTON POST when she discussed her book WHAT WORKS FOR WOMEN AT WORK.[28] Williams recounted the conversations she had with women who lamented the unequal apportionment of work that was thankless, menial, and administrative, making the nuanced point that refusing to get roped into these tasks while not appearing to be "touchy, humorless or supremely selfish is a particularly tricky balancing act."[29] Maintaining this

---

[24]   *Id.*
[25]   Monica Torres, *Study: Women More Likely to Be Asked and to Do Office Housework*, LADDERS (Jul. 25, 2018), www.theladders.com/career-advice/study-women-more-likely-to-be-asked-and-to-do-office-housework (citing Madeline E. Heilamn & Julie J. Chen, *Same Behavior, Different Consequences: Reaction to Men's and Women's Altruistic Citizenship Behavior*, 90 (3) J. OF APPLIED PSYCHOL. 431–41 (2005)).
[26]   *See* Williams, *supra* note 8.
[27]   *Id.*
[28]   *Id.*
[29]   *Id.*

act ought to be seen as a distinct layer of the harm conferred by the societally coerced "volunteerism" and "asks"; women get judged for their reactions to being asked to do this work as they perform this balancing act for all to see. On one hand, it behooves them to say no, as will be discussed, and by always volunteering and acquiescing, women risk cementing their reputations as the perpetual doers of this work and as too boundaryless. On the other hand, the (unfair and stereotyped) expectations of agreeableness and alacrity that get imposed on women make it nearly impossible to say no without feeling sex-based personal and professional reverberations from others.

THE PAIN

The beliefs that women should happily accept some forms of disparate treatment (or should even endure "locker room" behavior) since they are lucky just to be employed and admitted into a historically male world may be evidenced by phenomena described in many chapters of this book. I will focus on a few here to avoid needless repetition, but it should be recalled that women having to grit their teeth and endure being stereotyped or bombarded with sexual innuendos is an example that bleeds into other chapters.

Emotional, and sometimes physical, housekeeping has been well documented as having its costs. The ever-present expectation that women will take pains – in ways that men do not need to – to ensure that those around them are at ease and to perform the physical housekeeping of the workplace is, obviously, a huge disadvantage to women in the workplace.[30] Often, this housekeeping comes in the form of extra, unpaid work. "I was astonished," says Heather, a forty-one-year-old executive:

> I was asked to head up the firm's mentoring program and told how good I would be at matching people up with just the right mentors, but I wasn't offered any additional compensation or given any less work to do as I devoted countless hours to organizing and administrative work. And when I looked back at the records, I could see that in over twenty-five years of running the program, they had never asked a man to head it. Men at our company get placed on much more high-profile initiatives. The kind that help them to generate business.

[30]   See Cassandra M. Guarino & Victor M. H. Borden, *Faculty Service Loads and Gender: Are Women Taking Care of the Academic Family?*, 58 RES. IN HIGHER EDUC. 672, 672–94 (2017) https://link.springer.com/article/10.1007/s11162-017-9454-2?wt_mc=Internal.Event.1.SEM.ArticleA uthorOnlineFirst; Babcock et al., *Why Women Volunteer for Tasks That Don't Lead to Promotions*, *supra* note 19.

Once again, the numbers bear out the anecdotes. According to Hive's 2018 "State of the Workplace" survey, women are assigned 55 percent of all work, but still manage to complete 10 percent more work than men on average.[31]

This sort of emotional labor and constant pressure for women to make those around them physically and emotionally comfortable is made all the more pernicious because it is typically unspoken. As such, it is hard to prove, or even to become consciously aware of. It thus extracts an enormous toll from women at work, who must so often and disproportionately expend precious physical, mental, and emotional bandwidth on things like whether teacups have been filled in the conference room, the accuracy of meeting notes that no one else has been asked to take, or finding the precise tone with which to communicate, in a way that their male colleagues need not.[32] After all, says Angela, a thirty-one-year-old corporate librarian: "How often do you hear, 'Harvey, you sound awfully worked up over this'? Or 'Brian, I am sensing some hostility here,' or 'Steve, let me know when you're ready to discuss this rationally'? You don't. And it's not like men don't show emotion in the workplace; people just process and respond to theirs differently."

Deana, a forty-two-year-old attorney, adds: "Even when men argue or disagree with one another at work, it's not [typically] patronizing ... It doesn't [usually] devolve into an assessment of their tone or emotions. And because of that, it's going to usually be more respectful, even if it's harsh." Unvoiced, disparate expectations like these will invariably exhaust and distract women mentally and physically, systemically impeding them as a group.

Moreover, this disparate consumption of thought, energy, and time by emotional labor is not fully captured by the law that aims to regulate equality in working conditions between the sexes. In the first place, to the extent that the sex-based expectations that underlie these situations are unvoiced, they will be difficult to prove. Thus, courts will not generally be receptive to being asked to make an inferential leap and conclude that individual instances of inequality were, in fact, sex-based, or even actionable to begin with.[33] The siphoned-off nature of individual situations in individual workplaces and the frequent lack of comparators in various workplace scenarios make it nearly

---

[31] Michaela Rollings, *State of the Workplace*, HIVE (Oct. 1, 2018), https://hive.com/state-of-the-workplace/gender-2018/.

[32] Salam, *supra* note 6.

[33] *See, e.g.,* Byrd v. Auburn Univ. Montgomery, 268 F. App'x 854, 856 (11th Cir. 2008) (noting that "the ordinary tribulations of the workplace and petty slights ... are not actionable"); *Cf.* Oncale v. Sundowner Offshore Servs., 523 U.S. 75, 80, 118 S.Ct. 998, 140 L.Ed.2d 201 (1998) ("Title VII does not prohibit all verbal or physical harassment in the workplace; it is directed only at '*discriminat[ion]* ... because of ... sex.'").

impossible to paint a larger picture for a court that will be admissible for consideration. So, for example, if a female attorney complains about the way in which she is spoken to or evaluated, a judge might well reason that a man placed in her circumstances would be spoken to the same way, when, in fact, this is not the case.

In the second place, courts are typically reluctant to get into the granularity of assessing the parity of things like work assignments or expectations, lest they become "super personnel offices."[34] Thus, not only is it hard for many women to realize at the outset that they may not, in fact, be doing the same job under the same conditions as their male comparators, but courts, even once presented with a case for sex-based discrimination, will tend to find that the more consistent assignment of projects that require caretaking in some form to women is simply not cognizable.[35] Courts, while generally receptive to the idea that women should not be denied promotions more frequently or paid less than men who are considered to be their equals, tend to want to stay out of the business of evaluating "petty" things. These things can include clocking how much time was expended on emotional labor or clearing tables, or quibbling over which associate was asked to take notes at a meeting or spend time heading up a mentor program instead of being assigned to a new project.

And yet this disparate modality of assignment may inure to women's detriment professionally as they spend more time with interns and less time with partners and clients, and as they spend more energy on things like manual cleanup or service, note-taking, or event planning, with less energy left for substantive work, meeting deadlines, and networking. It may also inure to women's financial detriment as their assignments that revolve around caretaking or housekeeping disproportionately keep them away from more lucrative professional opportunities or work that may yield things like promotions and commissions.[36]

Further compounding the harm sustained by women in the face of these situations, as discussed, is the also-unspoken fact that when women do push back against extra work, they are judged more harshly than men for doing the same thing. This harm/pain is demonstrable. In fact, a 2005 study published in

---

[34] *See, e.g.,* Cathcart v. Flagstar Corp., 155 F.3d 558 (4th Cir. 1998); Ulreich v. Ameritech Cellular Commc'ns, Inc., No. 97 C 4281, 1999 WL 160838, at *6 (N.D. Ill. Mar. 16, 1999), *aff'd,* 202 F.3d 275 (7th Cir. 2000).

[35] *See* Kathy Caprino, *The "Glass Cliff" Phenomenon That Senior Female Leaders Face Today and How to Avoid It,* FORBES (Oct. 20, 2015 12:40 PM), www.forbes.com/sites/kathycaprino/2015/10/20/the-glass-cliff-phenomenon-that-senior-female-leaders-face-today-and-how-to-avoid-it/#7aobfofb79c6.

[36] Moran, *supra* note 10.

the JOURNAL OF APPLIED PSYCHOLOGY concluded that men are disproportionately praised and applauded for exhibiting altruism in the workplace as compared to women, and women, for their part, are criticized disproportionately more ardently when they fail to go above and beyond, as compared with their male colleagues.[37]

In any event, it is worth considering that whether a woman volunteers for invisible or emotional labor, or she is selected for it as a simple function of the fact that she has fewer clients than a man on her level, the question ought to be asked as to *why* she has fewer clients or less work so as to free up her time in the first place. The harms attendant to the belief that women ought to be grateful just to be in their workplaces and the conferral of office housekeeping and emotional labor on them can compound easily. Indeed, if unspoken historically sexist expectations, even women's own, are bound up in their heavy "volunteering," or in unspoken cues from others that precipitate their stepping forward, this is problematic.[38] Further, since this labor is deleterious over the long term, women disproportionately finding themselves less occupied or sought-after as a group and thus more available for invisible or emotional labor may be a function of compounded harm that is unacceptable.[39] And the vicious cycle that is women being overburdened, siphoned away from important work, exposure, and opportunities, having visibility, productivity, or demand for them decline, and then being seen as available for more invisible or emotional labor is permitted to continue until more scrutiny of the unspoken occurs.

MANIFESTATIONS

There is a host of proof, anecdotal and data-based, that many in society believe on some level or in some way that women are somehow responsible for or should be responsible for the physical and emotional comfort of others, even in the workplace. In the September 2017 HARPER'S BAZAAR article "Women Aren't Nags. We're Just Fed Up," writer Gemma Hartley broached the issue of the toll that emotional labor and sexist unspoken expectations take on a marriage and a family.[40] In that article, gender sociologist Dr. Lisa Huebner was quoted as saying:

---

[37]   Heilman & Chen, *supra* note 25.
[38]   Babcock et al., *Why Women Volunteer for Tasks That Don't Lead to Promotions, supra* note 19.
[39]   *See* Guarino & Borden, *supra* note 30.
[40]   Gemma Hartley, *Women Aren't Nags. We're Just Fed Up*, HARPER'S BAZAAR (Sept. 27, 2017), www.harpersbazaar.com/culture/features/a12063822/emotional-labor-gender-equality/.

In general, we gender emotions in our society by continuing to reinforce the false idea that women are always, naturally and biologically able to feel, express, and manage our emotions better than men . . .. I would argue that we still have no firm evidence that this ability is biologically determined by sex. At the same time . . . we find all kinds of ways in society to ensure that girls and women are responsible for emotions and, then, men get a pass.

Anecdotal evidence of this belief abounds, but often, it is hard to discern because it is so taboo to tell a woman outright: "You are window dressing. You may seem like another employee here, but you are not like other employees. You are here to do your job, but also to serve any number of other discrete functions, whether that be physically looking a certain way, putting others at ease, or any number of other accommodations." People don't tend to verbalize these thoughts, if they even acknowledge to themselves that they are having them. However, caretaking is so frequently ascribed to women societally that courts were able to take judicial notice of this fact and accept it as a given without evidence, carving out a cause of action under Title VII for family responsibility discrimination – as will be discussed later in this chapter. It does not take a huge inferential leap to realize that women are seen as caretakers not only of children outside the workplace, but also of adults inside it.

In 1993, not one, but two of President Clinton's nominees for Attorney General of the United States saw their nominations derailed after they were asked, during the vetting process, about the immigration status of the childcare givers that they had hired to watch their children while they worked.[41] This came to be known as "Nannygate," but it wasn't until feminists started to complain[42] that male nominees for important government jobs were not traditionally asked and wouldn't necessarily be expected to know the answers to these questions, that the unspoken belief was unearthed: "Women can hold the same jobs as men, but we will still see you as caretakers, and we will ask you questions we would never think to ask men during the vetting process, like 'And just who was watching our kids while you achieved these great things?'"[43]

More recent news shows examples of how women are seen as responsible for the comfort of those around them, even to the detriment of their own comfort and bodily integrity. In 2018, New Orleans Saints cheerleader Bailey Davis and Miami Dolphins cheerleader Kristen Ware filed complaints alleging sex discrimination that they both said was rife in the treatment of NFL

---

[41] Claudia Wallis, *The Lessons of Nannygate*, TIME (Feb. 22, 1993), http://content.time.com/ti me/magazine/article/0,9171,977802,00.html.

[42] Pay Wingert, *Nannygate II: A Women's Backlash?*, NEWSWEEK (Feb. 14, 1993, 7:00 PM), www .newsweek.com/nannygate-ii-womens-backlash-195214.

[43] *See Id.*

cheerleaders.[44] Davis alleged that she had been asked to resign after she posted what she considered to be a pretty innocuous picture on Instagram. As she relayed the story, after she posted the headshot of herself in a black lace bodysuit that did not show cleavage, she was inexplicably told that she was in violation of a rule forbidding the cheerleaders (but not the football players) from posting images of themselves in clothing that was too revealing and asked to resign. She even alleged that the official who asked this of her told her that he would never permit his granddaughter to post something like she had posted. Ware alleged in 2018 that she was told to stop discussing her virginity and her religious values publicly as this, too, failed to comport with the public image that an NFL cheerleader should have.

Both Davis and Ware have bemoaned the paternalism displayed by their teams and decried the double standard displayed by teams who pay cheerleaders wages like the mere $10 an hour that Davis said she earned while extensively regulating nearly all aspects of their appearance (on and off the job), expression, and social media presence, all in a way that the male football players are not regulated. Specifically, Davis alleged that, pursuant to the anti-fraternization policy imposed on the Saints cheerleaders, they were not permitted to so much as speak to the football players, or even to follow them on social media. Inexplicably, Davis alleged, the burden of avoiding the players fell on the Saints cheerleaders; even when they were already in a public place when one or more players showed up, the cheerleaders were expected to leave.

Davis, Ware, their lawyers, and their supporters continued to maintain that football players enjoy greater latitude than cheerleaders when it comes to expressing their religious, political, and other beliefs publicly and on social media and appearing as they wish in public. The cheerleaders made more headlines when they later offered to drop their claims against the NFL for a dollar and a meeting with NFL commissioner Roger Goodell and league lawyers, maintaining that, for them, the legal claims were never about money to begin with.[45] But the spark had been ignited. More and more came out

[44] K. D. Drummond, *Former Saintsations Dancer Files Discrimination Complaint against Saints, NFL*, SAINTSWIRE (Mar. 26, 2018, 5:31 PM), https://saintswire.usatoday.com/2018/03/26/former-new-orleans-saints-cheerleader-bailey-davis-discrimination-complaint/; ESPN, *Ex-Dolphins Cheerleader Alleges Religion and Gender Discrimination* (Apr. 12, 2018), www.espn.com/nfl/story/_/id/23132793/former-miami-dolphins-cheerleader-files-complaint-team; John Branch, *Another Former N.F.L. Cheerleader Files a Complaint*, N.Y. TIMES (Apr. 12, 2018), www.nytimes.com/2018/04/12/sports/football/nfl-cheerleaders.html.

[45] Nicole Pelletiere, *Ex-cheerleaders Offer to End Lawsuit against NFL for $1: "This Was Never About Money,"* ABC NEWS (Apr. 25, 2018, 9:28 AM), https://abcnews.go.com/GMA/News/cheerleaders-offer-end-lawsuit-nfl-money/story?id=54715086.

about the treatment of NFL cheerleaders. In 2018, the NEW YORK TIMES reported that one team, rather than take an aggressive stance on the verbal and physical abuse of their cheerleaders by fans, opted to instruct their dancers and cheerleaders in "what to say to people who said offensive things or touched them inappropriately. The women were told never to upset the fans."[46] Cheerleaders were told to show restraint, out of gratitude, if nothing else, "[b]ecause, if [it were] not for the fans, we wouldn't be here."[47]

While most women who work do not have to deal with the extreme restrictions, pageantry, and oversight that NFL cheerleaders do, women in workplaces all over America report dealing with everything from microaggressions,[48] to sexual harassment, to assault in the workplace every day. Most salient, studies have shown that it is likely that instances of sexual harassment go grievously underreported and unreported.[49] Rather, women report that they are tacitly (if not openly) taught that they must navigate these situations with politeness, grace, humor, or whatever it will take to make as few waves as possible. They are made to feel lucky just to be there, reflecting the unvoiced belief's impact and proving its existence.

The Society for Human Resource Management has reported that while 11 percent of nonmanagement employees claimed to have been the victim of a form of sexual harassment over the course of the prior year, 76 percent claimed that they failed to report it because they either feared retaliation or believed that reporting it would not remedy anything.[50] According to the Equal Employment Opportunity Commission (EEOC), almost a third of the charges it received in the fiscal year 2015 contained a workplace harassment claim, but the least common reaction of victims is to take a formal

---

[46] Juliet Macur & John Branch, *Pro Cheerleaders Say Groping and Sexual Harassment Are Part of the Job*, N.Y. TIMES (Apr. 10, 2018), www.nytimes.com/2018/04/10/sports/cheerleaders-nfl.html.

[47] *Id.*

[48] *See* Alan Henry, *How to Succeed When You're Marginalized or Discriminated against at Work*, N.Y. Times (Oct. 1, 2019), www.nytimes.com/2019/10/01/smarter-living/productivity-without-privilege-discrimination-work.html; Kevin L. Nadal, *A Guide to Responding to Microaggressions*, 2 CUNY FORUM 71–76 (2014), https://advancingjustice-la.org/sites/default/files/ELAMICRO%20A_Guide_to_Responding_to_Microaggressions.pdf.

[49] Chai R. Feldblum & Victoria A Lipnic, *Select Task Force on the Study of Harassment in the Workplace*, EEOC (Jun. 6, 2016), www.eeoc.gov/eeoc/task_force/harassment/report.cfm; *SHRM Research Finds Some Employees Unaware of Company Sexual Harassment Policies* SOCIETY FOR HUMAN RESOURCE MANAGEMENT, (Jan. 31, 2018), www.shrm.org/about-shrm/press-room/press-releases/pages/sexual-harassment-survey.aspx; Tara Golshan, *Study Finds 75 Percent of Workplace Harassment Victims Experienced Retaliation When They Spoke Up*, VOX (Oct. 15, 2017, 9:00 AM), www.vox.com/identities/2017/10/15/16438750/weinstein-sexual-harassment-facts.

[50] SOCIETY FOR HUMAN RESOURCE MANAGEMENT, *supra* note 49.

action, like reporting their harassment. Victims are far more prone to forget or endure harassment. Indeed, roughly 75 percent of victims never even initiated a discussion about their harassment with someone like a supervisor or union representative.[51]

The social, the scientific, and the legal literature all agree: women at work are often sent the largely unspoken message that they will fare better personally and professionally if they are accommodating in a host of ways. Being a "team player" who is not "defensive," "hysterical," "sensitive," or any other handy stereotype in the face of workplace abuse is seen as crucial for women hoping to ascend the power structure in any enterprise in which promotion depends upon others' opinion of them.

But when the unspoken message transmitted to women who feel unwelcome and underrepresented at the highest levels of prestige, power, and compensation at work is that they, too, need to be grateful for where they are and mindful of how they come across, is that much different? Professional cheerleaders were told outright that there would be zero tolerance for insubordination when it came to these archaic, asymmetrical rules; but do the unwritten rules imposed on women in other jobs render them any less powerless in other ways in the workforce? To the extent that the argument is advanced that the teams are merely trying to "protect" their cheerleaders, we must wonder why it feels like we are burdening or even punishing women for the undesirable behavior of those around them. Rape shield laws that prevent a rape victim from being assailed with queries about what she might have done to "get herself raped," and backlash against sexist school dress codes that restrict girls so as not to tempt boys, among other things, show that this phenomenon is not new. Women at work, too, are too often blamed or stigmatized for the unwanted attention they draw from those around them, while powerful harassers are retained and insulated from consequences by shrouds of secrecy.

TAKEAWAYS

This book lays absolutely no blame or responsibility for remediation at the feet of the women harmed by the beliefs, behaviors, and practices described here. Women should not have to fight these things off. It may be useful, however, as a practical matter, to set forth some thoughts about ways in which women, themselves, may stave off emotional labor, office housework, and other burdens that accompany the misguided perception that they should be grateful merely to

---

[51] Feldblum & Lipnic, *supra* note 49.

have a seat at the table. Everyone from renowned feminist scholars sharing tactical advice to self-help authors has promoted a set of responses for those who do not want to become casualties of the double bind. These responses aim subtly, but powerfully, to remind those who assign this type of work that women are, in fact, the professional equals of the men around them, deploying humor, and maybe even some passive aggression where necessary. Professor Williams recalls a woman who said, "I'm not sure you want someone with my hourly rate making coffee."[52] They might also, if they fear reprisal for refusing or protesting the assignments, cognizant of the trend toward assigning them such work, situate themselves, physically or conceptually, far from the task they fear being asked to do ("I'd love to stay and help clean, but I have a meeting right after this.") Suggesting a rotation with respect to a task, or a more junior person who might be more appropriate for the job, may help as well, according to Williams.[53]

It is incumbent upon employers, however, to take the lead in dispelling the unspoken belief that women should be grateful to simply be where they are and work disproportionately hard to ensure that their workplace is happy and comfortable for others. In the first place, discussing invisible and emotional labor in training sessions will go a long way toward raising awareness of a problem that has eluded capture because it usually blankets a workplace so transparently. Even a small dose of conscious thought about these phenomena can go a long way toward individuals making concerted efforts to assign tasks that might fall into these categories more mindfully. In the second place, employers, supervisors, and managers ought to employ best practices in giving conscious, explicit thought to tasks that are often assigned "unofficially," on the spot, undocumented, and with little thought. Developing processes for thoughtfully assigning tasks like setting up for parties or events, note-taking, serving food, or counselling employees, when these tasks and others fall outside of employees' job descriptions, can go a very long way. Cultivating a culture in which open discussion of assignment patterns, personal experiences with disparate expectations, and other issues that typically go undiscussed can also go a long way toward engendering a healthier workplace that affords sex and other equality to all workers.

---

[52] Williams, *supra* note 8; *see also* Feintzeig, *supra* note 7; Monica Torres, *How Women Can Say No to "Office Housework,"* CAREER CONTESSA (Dec. 18, 2018), www.careercontessa.com/advice/how-women-can-say-no-to-office-housework/; Ruchika Tulshyan, *How to Say No to "Office Housework,"* LANDIT (Apr. 15, 2018), https://landit.com/articles/how-to-say-no-to-office-housework; Lysa Myers, *For Women to Avoid "Office Housework, Work from Home,"* CSO (Apr. 28, 2015, 12:40 PM), www.csoonline.com/article/2915354/for-women-to-avoid-office-housework-work-from-home.html.

[53] Williams, *supra* note 8.

On the employer front, a more explicit discussion about sex-based tacit assumptions and expectations should also be able to lead to more mindfulness and uniformity when it comes to employee evaluations and standards. If women are being judged, whether it is part of their job criteria or not, on their demeanor, tone, or feelings created in others, are men? Are extraneous comments or critiques beyond those specified being meted out to men and women equally – orally and in writing? Perhaps the biggest boost that explicit discussion of emotional and invisible labor can yield is an awareness at the forefront, rather than the recesses, of employers' and supervisors' minds that they are susceptible to cultivating and acting on disparate expectations without being fully cognizant of the fact that this is what they are doing.

Judges charged with interpreting and applying employment discrimination law walk a fine line, as they tend to be, rightfully, wary of encroaching too far into the minutiae of any one workplace. It is not, in fact, tenable to have judges habitually inserting themselves to pass upon barely perceptible slights or enmeshing themselves in nuanced and complex decisions about things like how clients are assigned or how projects or cases are staffed. On the other hand, the Supreme Court has acknowledged that the objective of Title VII is to "strike at the entire spectrum" of discrimination,[54] and to the extent that systemic sex inequality can be discerned in or across workplaces as a sort of death by a thousand paper cuts, those paper cuts may warrant a second look, or at least some awareness. So, for example, if a plaintiff in a case can identify a pronounced pattern of disparate treatment between the sexes expressed in disparate expectations when it comes to invisible or emotional labor, it may behoove a court to take judicial notice of the fact that this behavior is not atypical; it is pernicious.

It is important that society and employers remain vigilant about actions that look like they are addressing the problem of inequality but are really just adding to it. For example, women may be given a seat at the table on certain committees (especially those dealing with mentoring, employee development, and other personnel issues) to showcase, both internally and to customers and others externally, that women are involved in decision-making functions. For example, a law firm may seek to appoint a diverse group of members to its attorney recruiting committee, and this may be useful for public relations purposes, and potentially if there is a need to rebut a claim that the hiring process was discriminatory. Although this inclusion may be viewed positively in some respects, would a woman or any other member of an underrepresented group

---

[54] L.A. Dep't of Water & Power v. Manhart, 435 U.S. 702, 707 n.13 (1978) (quoting Sprogis v. United Air Lines, Inc., 444 F.2d 1194, 1198 (7th Cir. 1971)).

trying to make partner or ascend to the highest levels of the partnership be better served by perennially visiting law schools for thirty-minute screening interviews, followed by lengthy evaluation sessions, or by having some time freed up for pursuing client matters and building a book of business? Perhaps employers should think about a more equitable distribution of these types of appointment and assignment that may have marginal professional returns but appear cloaked in an appearance of prestige. Perhaps they ought to also think about giving more meaningful credit to such assignments when it is time to discuss promotions and bonuses. Organizations can and should do more to recognize the detriment of devoting time to working on certain administrative committees and be careful that they are not disproportionately using female employees on these types of committee as "window dressing" for the organization.

In the end, it is unacceptable that, with respect to the unspoken belief that women should just be grateful for their job in the workplace or seat at the table, women would ever have to craft a response to discriminatory expectations or disproportionately burdensome, dead-end assignments. It is equally unacceptable that they would have to do so while worried that the stridency with which they reply or the emphasis they place on their own professional well-being will further taint the waters of the workplace against them. However, until those charged with establishing and maintaining true, not merely surface, equality in the workplace, from those who act on this belief to those who regulate and adjudicate claims against them, start confronting directly both the belief and the elusive behavior it engenders, this advice is needed. Change and awareness simply cannot dawn soon enough.

7

"Don't Burden Us with Your (Impending) Motherhood" (Because)

Shortly after my supervisor found out that I was pregnant, he took away a professional opportunity that I had been looking forward to when he excluded me from a high-profile event/exhibition, attended by our CEO, that would have boosted my visibility and presented me with an opportunity to promote our brand and myself in a way that could have led to financial and status gains for me at work. Above my protestations, I was explicitly told that my supervisor was doing this because as a pregnant woman, I couldn't handle the long hours and hard work that the event entailed. I was explicitly told that they offered [valuable growth opportunities] to a guy, instead of me, because I had small kids and he didn't have any kids, and "It would be easier."

—Rachel, thirty-three, retail manager

It never relents. You struggle to get pregnant and to have your boss not notice that anything's amiss. And then, once you are, you struggle under the weight of their projections onto you and what that will mean. And then, once you give birth, you're rushed back, pumping milk in a bathroom, and feel their scrutiny of you always. Feeling like you cannot make one misstep. Because that's all they're waiting for.

—Beth, thirty-six, accountant

THE BELIEF

With companies from all over the S&P 500 touting their family-friendly policies and support of mothers,[1] and everywhere you look, from public

---

[1] Pregnancy and motherhood are not the exclusive province of women, as "[t]rans[gender], non-binary and intersex people can and do get pregnant, too, and they have a place . . . in the parenting world." As with many topics in this book, those discussed in this chapter are predominantly experienced by, though not confined to women. Kim Wong-Shing, *Why women aren't the only people who can get pregnant*, CNET (Sept. 10, 2021), https://www.cnet.com/health/parenting/women-arent-the-only-people-who-can-get-pregnant/. *Matching Mothers to Mentors: Working Moms Get the Support They Need*, WASH. POST (Mar. 23, 2019), www.washingtonpost.com/sf/

relations (PR) campaigns to job search websites, the public lauding the support of mothers who work, it would seem downright foolish to admit to seeing motherhood as a burden or an inconvenience on a woman's employer. And yet a look at the dearth of effective policies – legal, corporate, or cultural; formal or informal – in this country that actually allow expecting and new mothers to thrive and progress in their jobs, speaks for itself.

It would appear that, irrespective of the lip service given, the PR dollars spent, and the hearts warmed in service of the *idea* that accommodating and supporting mothers at work translates into the retention and growth of talented women in the workforce, a very ugly unspoken belief still inheres. Motherhood is, when it comes to the day-to-day operations of the workplace, a burden or an inconvenience whose costs are to be minimized and whose unsightliness – taking the form of everything from the need to take time away from the office, to the need to express milk in the office – is to be shielded from sight.

In society and in the workplace, words may extol flexibility, accommodation, and understanding, but our laws, policies, and culture reveal how far too many ultimately feel: "Don't Bother Us With Your (Impending) Motherhood." And yet, much has been written about how, economically, it is fallacious to think that by pushing the costs of childbirth and child-rearing onto individual mothers, this does not impact families and, ultimately, society.[2] And while we herald the two working parent household, the rise of

---

brand-connect/JPMC/wp/enterprise/mothers-navigate-new-whirl-with-mentors-aid/;   7 *Ways Johnson & Johnson Supports Working Mothers*, JOHNSON & JOHNSON (Oct. 17, 2016), www .jnj.com/latest-news/7-ways-johnson-johnson-supports-working-mothers; *Parental Paid Time Off for U.S. Employees*, EXXONMOBIL (last visited Nov. 3, 2019), https://corporate.exxonmobil.com /Company/Careers/Parental-paid-time-off-for-US-employees; Rachel Gillett, *14 Useful Perks for New Parents Beyond Paid Parental Leave*, INC. THIS MORNING (Aug. 18, 2015), www.inc.com /business-insider/14-popular-perks-for-new-parents-that-go-beyond-paid-parental-leave.html   ("At certain Silicon Valley tech companies, baby showers and on-site child care are the norm.").

[2]   *How Workplace Discrimination Impedes Economic Growth*, COUNCIL ON FOREIGN RELATIONS (Oct. 26, 2017), www.cfr.org/event/how-workplace-discrimination-impedes-economic-growth ("Childcare is not a women's problem. Childcare is a societal problem. And we in this country are in – so in the dark ages as it comes to how we think about that. And the burden that is placed on women to figure out what and how, and how to pay for it, and how to deal with the disruptions that come from that."); *For Too Many Women, Having a Baby Still Means Losing Your Job or a Promotion*, NAT'L P'SHIP FOR WOMEN AND FAMILIES (last visited Nov. 17, 2019), www.nationalpartnership.org/our-work/economic-justice/pregnancy-discrimination.html ("Every time a woman is fired, forced to take leave, denied a promotion or not hired because she is pregnant or because an employer fears she might become pregnant, she is experiencing discrimination – and it hurts her, her family and our economy."); New America Foundation Weekly Wonk, *It's Time to Start Talking about Pregnancy Discrimination*, VOX (Jan. 31, 2015), www.vox.com/2015/1/31/7953641/pregnancy-discrimination ("The bottom line is that women comprise a significant proportion of the nation's talent pool, and when their

the "hands-on" dad, and the advent of paternity leave, where there used to be only maternity leave, we now know that women continue to be the ones who take longer leaves,[3] who spend more time with their children,[4] and who ultimately suffer the economic and professional losses.[5] It is women that are harmed when childbirth and child-rearing are ignored by employers as part of the ordinary life cycle for many, in the name of a false "neutrality." All is expected to carry on as usual in the workplace, with no allowances made for the inconveniences of reality when it comes to having children.

The stark fact is that pregnancy has been seen as an impediment to women since their entry into the workplace. And the fact that society has ascribed the primary responsibility for parenting and child-rearing to women is so well accepted that courts have taken judicial notice of it.[6] And each pregnancy incurs costs, no matter how devoted to her job the employee is, and no matter how trouble-free the pregnancy, itself, is.[7] These costs come in the form of time that must be taken during the day to deal with check-ups, complications, and testing. They come in the form of physical restrictions that may accompany a pregnancy. They come as clients, patients, and co-workers anticipate that the employee will take a period of leave following the baby's birth. And

---

contributions are constrained by patronizing and outmoded notions of what motherhood should look like (even well-intentioned ones), our workforce, our economy and our families suffer.").

[3] Juliana M. Horowitz et al., *Americans Widely Support Paid Family and Medical Leave, but Differ Over Specific Policies*, PEW RSCH. CTR. SOC. & DEMOGRAPHIC (Mar. 23, 2017), www .pewsocialtrends.org/2017/03/23/americans-widely-support-paid-family-and-medical-leave-but-differ-over-specific-policies/ (finding that, among fathers who took at least some time off from work following the birth or adoption of their child in the past two years, the median length of leave was one week; about seven in ten (72 percent) say they took two weeks or less off from work. In contrast, the median length of maternity leave was eleven weeks).

[4] Kim Parker & Wendy Wang, Chapter 5: *Americans' Time at Paid Work, Housework, Child Care, 1965 to 2011*, PEW RSCH. CTR. SOC. & DEMOGRAPHIC TRENDS (Mar. 14, 2013), www .pewsocialtrends.org/2013/03/14/chapter-5-americans-time-at-paid-work-housework-child-care-1965-to-2011/#fn-19096-22 (finding that American mothers still spend about twice as much time with their children as fathers do).

[5] YoonKyung Chung et al., *The Parental Gender Earnings Gap in the United States*, U.S. CENSUS BUREAU (Nov. 2017), www2.census.gov/ces/wp/2017/CES-WP-17-68.pdf (finding that between two years before the birth of a couple's first child and a year after, the earnings gap between opposite-sex spouses doubles; the gap continues to grow for the next five years).

[6] *See* Akin-Taylor v. Kaiser Found. Health Plan, Inc., 2013 U.S. Dist. LEXIS 116571, at *16 (N.D. Cal. Aug. 16, 2013) (holding that the Plaintiffs claims for Title VII discrimination based on "family responsibility," and violation of the FMLA should be dismissed); Childers v. Trs. of the Univ. of Pa., 2016 U.S. Dist. LEXIS 35827, at *1 (E.D. Pa. Mar. 21, 2016) (explaining that the plaintiff did not achieve tenure because of stereotypes relating to the career focus of women with childcare responsibilities, or family responsibility discrimination).

[7] Jennifer Bennett Shinall, *The Pregnancy Penalty*, 103 MINN. L. REV. 749, 764 (2018) ("An employer's assumption that the primary caretaking burden of a new child will fall on the woman will, more often than not, have some validity.").

once the employee returns to work, they come in the form of both the perceptions and expectations of others, as well as reality when it comes to additional time, effort, and resources that the employee redirects to the baby. These can be for anything from check-ups to expressing milk (pumping), to the infinite ways that parenting impinges upon the work life of an adult – especially when that adult is an American mother.

No; for all of the grand gestures and lip service that we pay, the unspoken belief that having children produces unsightly, costly, and inconvenient burdens that should be absorbed by working mothers with minimal intrusion into the workplace still thrives.[8] This belief may, for some, be rooted in the conviction that women, once they become mothers, belong in the home and not in the workplace. For some, it may be about feeling discomfited, or even disgusted, by the physical changes that accompany women's bodies through pregnancy, childbirth, lactation, etc. For others, on some level, there may be an unspoken issue with the idea that pregnancy indicates that a woman has, ostensibly, engaged in sexual behavior.

THE PANE

This chapter will cover a wide range of legal issues and obstacles created for women at all stages of planning and experiencing motherhood. The failings of the social safety net, laws, and policy when it comes to parenthood are abundant and pervasive from the point in time at which a working woman tries to become a mother to the point in time at which she attempts to thrive back at work while parenting.[9] Most employers' health insurance plans do not cover infertility treatments.[10] Once a woman is pregnant, although the Pregnancy Discrimination Act (PDA) does render discrimination "on the basis of pregnancy, childbirth, or related medical conditions" to be discrimination "because of" sex, in violation of Title VII, no accommodation of the pregnancy per se is required by law.[11] This means that an employer may not

---

[8] *See* Valerie Wilson, *African American Women Stand Out as Working Moms Play a Larger Economic Role in Families*, ECON. POL'Y INST. (May 11, 2017, 10:00 AM), www.epi.org/blog/african-american-women-stand-out-as-working-moms-play-a-larger-economic-role-in-families/.

[9] Natalie Kitroeff & Jessica Silver-Greenberg, *Pregnancy Discrimination Is Rampant Inside America's Biggest Companies*, N.Y. TIMES (Jun. 15, 2018) www.nytimes.com/interactive/2018/06/15/business/pregnancy-discrimination.html?smid=fb-share ("The number of pregnancy discrimination claims filed annually with the Equal Employment Opportunity Commission has been steadily rising for two decades and is hovering near an all-time high.").

[10] *Infertility Coverage by State*, RESOLVE, https://resolve.org/what-are-my-options/insurance-coverage/infertility-coverage-state/ (last visited Feb. 7, 2020).

[11] Title VII of the Civil Rights Act of 1964, 42 U.S.C. § 2000e(k).

single out a woman for inferior treatment because of her pregnancy, and as the Supreme Court held recently, an employer cannot refuse to accommodate a pregnant woman because she is pregnant, when it freely grants similar accommodations to others limited in similar ways (such as a light-duty lifting restriction on the job, for example).[12] However, there is no affirmative legal mandate in the law requiring that an employer must accommodate a pregnant employee.

Moreover, while federal law grants twelve weeks of unpaid parental leave to some employees, this is, for most people, insufficient.[13] Finally, while judicially crafted doctrines afford protection to women from *unfounded* prejudice against women with small children, nothing affords women any actual entitlement to flexibility or accommodation that they might actually *need* once they have children.

The Law and Policies that Regulate Working Moms: Legal Institutions and Individuals Show Their Beliefs

A look back at the pronouncements of federal courts on the issue of pregnancy discrimination and accommodation shows a history marked by the construction of legal fictions. Some of these have been recognized as fallacious and corrected; others have not. From the basic fallacy that pregnancy discrimination is (somehow) not sex discrimination, but simply discrimination against those who happen to fall pregnant,[14] to characterizations of pregnancy as (somehow) something that need not be accommodated, as a disability would be, because it is a "voluntarily undertaken and desired condition,"[15] convenient, but false or incomplete narratives have always abounded.

And then there is the persistent fiction that "neutrality" means that an affirmative grant of an accommodation to a pregnant woman to help her keep or perform her job, which nonpregnant employees are *not* given, accords her, as the Supreme Court put it, "most favored nation status," and is thus unacceptable.[16] The accommodation of an employee's disability under the Americans with Disabilities Act of 1990 (ADA) or religion under Title VII is

---

[12]   Young v. United Parcel Serv., Inc., 575 U.S. 206 (2015).

[13]   Quinn Fish, *Second-Time Mom Nails Why Maternity Leave Must Be Longer Than 12 Weeks*, WORKING MOTHER (Aug. 21 2019), www.workingmother.com/maternity-leave-must-be-longer-than-twelve-weeks.

[14]   General Elec. Co. v. Gilbert, 429 U.S. 125, 132–33 (1976).

[15]   *Id.; see also Young*, 575 U.S. at 223 (discussing the EEOC's guidelines on pregnancy related to temporary disabilities).

[16]   *Young*, 575 U.S. at 207.

traditionally viewed as leveling the playing field. While Title VII does not extend accommodations in cases brought "because of sex," it arguably should have been added in 1978 when pregnancy discrimination was formally acknowledged to be sex discrimination. In any event, the Supreme Court's view of "neutrality" when it comes to reasonable accommodation makes no sense. These fictions are costly and have conspired, over time, to systemically disadvantage women.

Fictions cobbled together by workplace decision-makers are no less pernicious. In fact, they are arguably more invidious because they are so much more frequently left unvoiced. Thus, we have a record of much of the reasoning employed by Congress and the courts over time, but no way of ever *knowing* just how many times a manager has looked at a pregnant woman and, on some level, concluded that her abilities or commitment were compromised or diminished.[17] Rarely admitted to or revealed "smoking gun evidence," these unspoken assumptions have been widely hypothesized.

Underlying these fictions, and the failure of legal institutions to craft meaningful protections, is the unspoken belief that pregnancy, rather than being a reasonably anticipated experience in most women's lives, is some unforeseen, haphazard burden whose costs are typically best shouldered by the woman who chose it.[18]

There is enough to say about the indignities and inequities of the workplace when it comes to working mothers and the complete history of the treatment of working mothers to fill an entire book on that subject. There is also much to consider and some great literature and legal analysis about the plight of the "working father," and issues like employers' discomfort with paternity leave, among other things.[19] This, however, is a book about women in the workplace and the unspoken beliefs that engender law, policy, and behaviors that disadvantage them. In the rest of this chapter are some selected highlights of moments at which legal institutions, like the Supreme Court or Congress, produced case law or legislation that appeared to be marked by a certain

---

[17] *See* Kitroeff & Silver-Greenberg, *supra* note 9 (finding that managers often regard women who are visibly pregnant as less committed, less dependable, less authoritative, and more irrational than other women).

[18] Deborah A. Widiss, *Gilbert Redux: The Interaction of the Pregnancy Discrimination Act and the Amended Americans with Disabilities Act*, 46 U.C. DAVIS L. REV. 961, 1036 (2013) (explaining that those who opposed the PWFA believed that it would allow pregnant women "to 'shift the burdens' of their 'lifestyle choice' to others").

[19] *See, e.g.*, Kelli K. García, *The Gender Bind: Men as Inauthentic Caregivers*, 20 DUKE J. GENDER L. & POL'Y 1, 35 (2012). Alison Koslowski, *When Workplace Cultures Support Paternity Leave, All Employees Benefit*, HARV. BUS. REV. (Jun. 14, 2018), https://hbr.org/2018/06/when-workplace-cultures-support-paternity-leave-all-employees-benefit.

hesitation and motivated by one or more unspoken beliefs about mothers in the workplace, and how and when their needs are to be met.

Gilbert: *The Supreme Court Says Pregnancy Discrimination Is Not Sex Discrimination*

When presented with the opportunity, in 1976, to determine whether pregnancy discrimination is generally tantamount to sex discrimination at all, the Supreme Court inexplicably and emphatically said that it is not.[20] In *General Electric Company* v. *Gilbert*, the Supreme Court failed to acknowledge that pregnancy is a common and pervasive part of the life cycle that simultaneously creates a unique and systemic impediment to many women's careers.[21] There, the Supreme Court held that General Electric's disability benefits plan's failure to cover pregnancy-related disabilities did not violate Title VII, so long as there was no indication that the exclusion was specifically a pretext for sex discrimination.[22]

This holding appeared to many to be almost willful blindness toward the absolutely discriminatory effects of pregnancy discrimination. Approximately 75 percent[23] of working women can expect to be pregnant over the course of their lifetimes, most more than once. In 1976, approximately 50 percent of women worked part-time during their pregnancies, while about 60 percent worked full-time while pregnant.[24] Yet, the Supreme Court persisted in its disregard of these realities and the impact on women when divested of protection against pregnancy discrimination at a time when they are perhaps most physically and professionally vulnerable.[25] The Court inexplicably maintained: "While it is true that only women can become pregnant, it does not follow that every legislative classification concerning pregnancy is a sex-based classification."[26] Indeed, the Court treated pregnancy as a sex-neutral condition, nonsensically noting that, while it was admittedly "confined to women," it was "not a 'disease' at all, and is often a voluntarily undertaken and desired condition."[27] The Court

---

[20] General Elec. Co. v. Gilbert, 429 U.S. 125, 136 (1976).
[21] *Id.*
[22] *Id.*
[23] Maya Sequeira & Katherine Kimpel, *Women Work and They Get Pregnant*, SHATTERING THE CEILING (Dec. 2, 2014), www.shatteringtheceiling.com/women-work-and-they-get-pregnant/.
[24] Bourree Lam, *Yes, There Really Are More Pregnant Women at the Office*, THE ATLANTIC (Apr. 8, 2015), www.theatlantic.com/business/archive/2015/04/yes-there-really-are-more-pregnant-women-at-the-office/389763/.
[25] *Gilbert*, 429 U.S. at 135.
[26] *Id.* at 134.
[27] *Id.* at 136.

sounded almost willfully blind regarding its professed limited understanding of the unity of identity of pregnancy discrimination and sex discrimination when it described the employer's challenged insurance coverage program as separating "potential recipients into two groups—pregnant women and nonpregnant persons," and inexplicably seeming to give weight to the fact that "[w]hile the first group is exclusively female, the second includes members of both sexes."[28]

Congress Responds with the PDA

This holding created the impetus for Congress to step in two years later and state the obvious: pregnancy discrimination is sex discrimination.[29] The enactment of the PDA was crucial to the protection of women as a class in the workplace, but the need for it appears to evince the attitude on the part of so many, including Supreme Court Justices, that pregnancy, rather than being seen as a statistical probability, could be viewed as anomalous, even surprising to come across, inconvenient, and burdensome to an employer.

The ensuing PDA expressly amended Title VII's definition of sex discrimination to encompass discrimination because of pregnancy, childbirth, or related medical conditions.[30] It also stated that "women affected by pregnancy, childbirth or related medical conditions must be treated the same as other persons not so affected but similar in their ability or inability to work."[31] When the proper construction of the PDA and Title VII was finally placed before the Supreme Court in 2015, the Court acted to uphold principles of formal equality between the sexes, but somehow still telegraphed the unspoken belief that pregnancy was not an ordinary event in the lives of most women, but rather an inconvenience or a burden to employers.[32]

Young: Must Employers Accommodate Pregnancy?

In the 2015 Supreme Court case of *Young v. United Parcel Service, Inc.*,[33] the plaintiff, Peggy Young, was a part-time driver for UPS who became pregnant, and was subsequently advised by a doctor to restrict her lifting of objects to no more than twenty pounds. Her job, however, required that she be able to lift

---

[28] *Id.* at 135.
[29] Pregnancy Discrimination Act of 1978, 42 U.S.C. § 2000e-(k).
[30] *Id.*
[31] *Id.*
[32] *Young,* 575 U.S. 206.
[33] *Id.*

up to seventy pounds, and she was denied a requested restriction on her lifting, meaning that she was unable to work for as long as she was medically restricted.[34] She brought suit under Title VII, alleging discrimination on the basis of her pregnancy and highlighting the facts that UPS's policies allowed it to accommodate similar "light-duty-for-injury" requests by its workers with on-the-job injuries. These workers were disabled and thus covered by the ADA, or had lost their Department of Transportation (DOT) certifications.[35] Her theory was that she had been singled out for the denial of something given freely to others; UPS's theory was that it had cordoned off special categories of people to accommodate, and Young was being treated like everybody else.[36]

Interestingly, the Supreme Court took issue with both sides' characterizations of what had occurred and their respective readings of Title VII and the PDA.[37] On one hand, the Court rejected the notion that pregnant employees could be presumptively entitled to any accommodation, such that they would be seen to enjoy, as the Court phrased it, "most-favored-nation" status.[38] Noting that Young's interpretation of the PDA and when it was violated "proves too much,"[39] the Court expressed "doubt[] that Congress intended to grant pregnant workers an unconditional 'most-favored-nation' status, such that employers who provide one or two workers with an accommodation must provide similar accommodations to all pregnant workers, irrespective of any other criteria."[40]

However, the Court similarly rejected UPS's argument that the PDA "simply defines sex discrimination to include pregnancy discrimination,"[41] noting that a plaintiff like Young could succeed if she were able to prove that her employer "provided more favorable treatment to at least some employees whose situation cannot reasonably be distinguished from hers."[42] The Court ultimately held that the PDA "requires courts to consider the extent to which an employer's policy treats pregnant workers less favorably than it treats non-pregnant workers similar in their ability or inability to work. And ... it requires courts to consider any legitimate, nondiscriminatory, non-pretextual justification for these differences in treatment."[43] In the end, while the law would scrutinize a decision to deny a pregnant woman an accommodation that an employer had given to

[34]   *Id.* at 211.
[35]   *Id.* at 216.
[36]   *Id.*
[37]   *Id.* at 219.
[38]   *Id.*
[39]   *Id.* at 207.
[40]   *Id.*
[41]   *Id.*
[42]   *Id.* at 230.
[43]   *Id.* at 210.

a nonpregnant employee with similar restrictions, it conferred no affirmative entitlement to that accommodation upon pregnant women.[44]

The Court's aversion to conferring what it termed "most favored nation status" on pregnant women speaks volumes. At oral argument, Justice Anthony Kennedy challenged the plaintiff's attorney: "You make it sound as if the only condition that was not accommodated was a lifting restriction because of pregnancy," observing that it was "really giving a misimpression."[45] Justice Antonin Scalia then made the accusation, "You're calling for 'most favored nation treatment,' for pregnant employees," referring to the plaintiff's contention that, as he put it, if you grant an accommodation to any other employee class, "you have to give it to the pregnant worker too."[46]

Young's Aftermath

But many didn't see it that way. Justice Ruth Bader Ginsburg later derided the challenged policy in *Young* as conferring "least favored" status upon pregnant women.[47] And many were not satisfied with the somewhat tortured attempt at line drawing by the Court in *Young*. Multiple members of Congress did not feel that it effectuated the policies of workplace equality embodied in Title VII and the PDA. Congress introduced the Pregnant Workers Fairness Act (PWFA) in 2012 as an attempt to promote nondiscrimination of pregnant workers.[48] The PWFA, however, has been reintroduced, but has yet to be passed.[49] This Act would affirmatively mandate reasonable employment accommodations (that do not engender hardships for the employer) for employees requiring them due to pregnancy, childbirth, or a related condition, who work for employers with four or more employees.[50] Other protections would include a prohibition on employers compelling a pregnant employee to take unwanted leave so long as alternative accommodations can

---

[44] *Id.* at 232.

[45] Transcript of Oral Argument at 1, Young v. United Parcel Serv., Inc., 575 U.S. 206 (2015) (No. 12–1226).

[46] *Id.*

[47] Adam Liptak, *UPS Suit Hinges on an Ambiguous Pregnancy Law*, N.Y. TIMES (Dec. 3, 2014), www.nytimes.com/2014/12/04/us/politics/in-ups-case-justices-tackle-ambiguity-in-pregnancy-law.html.

[48] *The Federal Pregnant Workers Fairness Act*, A BETTER BALANCE (last visited Nov. 3, 2019), www.abetterbalance.org/our-campaigns/pregnant-workers-fairness/.

[49] *The Federal Pregnant Workers Fairness Act*, A BETTER BALANCE (last visited Nov. 1, 2019), www.abetterbalance.org/resources/the-federal-pregnant-workers-fairness-act/.

[50] *Id.*

be afforded, and an antidiscrimination mandate with respect to terms, conditions, and privileges of employment.[51]

Twenty-seven states have passed laws similar to the PWFA, often with comprehensive and bipartisan support.[52] Many scholars support the passage of the PWFA, while others believe that other measures, like paid leave before and after childbirth, would be more effective for pregnant women who find themselves boxed out of the workplace by physical limitations and restrictions surrounding pregnancy.[53]

The Issue of Leave and Support for New Parents

In recent years, everyone from Ivanka Trump, to Marco Rubio, to Hillary Clinton, has come up with strategies and proposals for procuring paid parental leave.[54] American support for some sort of paid family leave has recently been estimated to be as high as 82 percent in support for maternity leave, and 69 percent in support of paternity leave.[55] Yet, the United States stands virtually alone in the industrialized world as a country that does not entitle its workers to paid family leave.[56] California, New York, Rhode Island, and New Jersey have all enacted state legislation that grants paid family leave, with entitlements as high as ten weeks in New York.[57] In 2017, a Pew Research Center survey found

---

[51] *Id.*

[52] *Reasonable Accommodations for Pregnant Workers: State and Local Laws*, NAT'L P'SHIP FOR WOMEN & FAMILIES (Jun. 2019), www.nationalpartnership.org/our-work/resources/economic-justice/pregnancy-discrimination/reasonable-accommodations-for-pregnant-workers-state-laws.pdf.

[53] Shinall, *supra* note 7, 753.

[54] *See* Paige Winfield Cunningham, *The Health 202: Ivanka Trump Pushes "Bipartisan Agreement" on Paid Family Leave*, WASH. POST (Feb. 13, 2019), www.washingtonpost.com/news/powerpost/paloma/the-health-202/2019/02/13/the-health-202-ivanka-trump-pushes-bipartisan-agreement-on-paid-family-leave/5c633d391b326b71858c6b6c/; *see also Rubio, Romney, Wagner, Crenshaw Introduce Bill Giving Parents an Option for Paid Family Leave*, MARCO RUBIO US SENATOR FOR FLA. (Mar. 27, 2019), www.rubio.senate.gov/public/index.cfm/2019/3/rubio-romney-wagner-crenshaw-introduce-bill-giving-parents-an-option-for-paid-family-leave; *Paid Family and Medical Leave*, THE OFFICE OF HILLARY RODHAM CLINTON (last visited Nov. 3, 2019), www.hillaryclinton.com/issues/paid-leave/.

[55] Renee Stepler, *Key Takeaways on Americans' Views of and Experiences with Family and Medical Leave*, PEW RSCH. CTR. (Mar. 23, 2017), www.pewresearch.org/fact-tank/2017/03/23/key-takeaways-on-americans-views-of-and-experiences-with-family-and-medical-leave/.

[56] Christopher Ingraham, *The World's Richest Countries Guarantee Mothers More Than a Year of Paid Maternity Leave. The U.S. Guarantees Them Nothing.*, WASH. POST (Feb. 5, 2018), www.washingtonpost.com/news/wonk/wp/2018/02/05/the-worlds-richest-countries-guarantee-mothers-more-than-a-year-of-paid-maternity-leave-the-u-s-guarantees-them-nothing/.

[57] *State Paid Family and Medical Leave Insurance Laws*, NAT'L P'SHIP FOR WOMEN & FAMILIES (Aug. 2019), www.nationalpartnership.org/our-work/resources/economic-justice/paid-leave/state-paid-family-leave-laws.pdf.

that 51 percent of respondents said that the paid leave should be compelled by the federal government.[58]

The Family and Medical Leave Act (FMLA), heralded as progressive and remedial when it was enacted in 1993, affords many (but not all) employees twelve weeks of leave, though it does not have to be paid leave.[59] It also mandates that employers continue to provide the benefits of those who take leave pursuant to the Act and have either their job or a reasonably equivalent job for them to return to after the leave is over.[60] But it does not do nearly enough. For one thing, while many employers do, in fact, grant longer parental leave than the law requires and/or make that leave paid, this is typically out of a desire to foster goodwill and remain competitive in the market, rather than because they are required to do so.[61] Moreover, the twelve weeks are simply not enough time for many women to handle the swath of time that they may need both prior to and after the birth of their children, when their physical capabilities to work are diminished and the demands of self- and newborn care preclude working.[62] Numerous studies have pointedly demonstrated the benefit of time spent after the birth or adoption of a new child to engage in bonding, feeding, and other necessary activities.[63] In the case of a birth mother, the amount of time deemed necessary for her own physical healing typically exceeds both what the law permits and what employers are willing to cede.

It also bears noting that only "qualified employees" are protected, meaning that employees need to be employed by the government or any company that

---

[58] Stepler, *supra* note 55.
[59] Family and Medical Leave Act, 29 U.S.C. § 2612.
[60] Family and Medical Leave Act, 29 U.S.C. § 2614.
[61] Adam C. Uzialko, *Why Offering Paid Leave Is Good for Your Business*, BUSINESS.COM (Feb. 16, 2018), www.business.com/articles/paid-leave-is-good-for-business/.
[62] *See* Fish, *supra* note 13.
[63] Ask Rex Huppke: I Just Work Here, *Let's Get on Board with Paid Leave*, CHI. TRIBUNE (May 6, 2012), http://articles.chicagotribune.com/2012-05-06/features/ct-biz-0507-work-advice-huppke-20120506_1_national-partnership-women-families-women-and-work ("A 2005 study published in THE ECONOMIC JOURNAL found that children whose mothers return to work within 12 weeks of giving birth 'are less likely to receive regular medical checkups and breastfeeding in the first year of life' or get all their immunizations by 18 months of age."); Meredith Melnick, *Study: Why Maternity Leave Is Important*, TIME (Jul. 21, 2011), http://healthland.time.com/2011/07/21/study-why-maternity-leave-is-important/ (finding that women with three-month-old infants who worked full-time reported feeling greater rates of depression, stress, poor health, and overall family stress than mothers who were able to stay home); Pinka Chatterji & Sara Markowitz, *Family Leave after Childbirth and the Mental Health of New Mothers*, 15 J MENTAL HEALTH POL'Y ECON. 61, 72 (2012) (finding that women who took longer than twelve weeks' maternity leave reported fewer depressive symptoms, a reduction in severe depression, and improvement in their overall mental health).

has fifty or more employees employed within seventy-five miles of the workplace. A qualified employee must have also worked for the employer for at least 12 months and for at least 1,250 hours during the previous year. It is estimated that the FMLA affords leave only to some 60 percent of the workforce.[64] State laws sometimes afford more generous leave and/or protections, but only a few states mandate a period of paid parental/family leave beyond what the federal law provides,[65] and leave as afforded generally across the board by law is paltry as compared with what it should be. In fact, a House Report provided expert testimony showing that twelve weeks is the minimum time needed for a parent and child to grow accustomed to one another.[66]

In early 2019, Senator Kirsten Gillibrand of New York and Representative Rosa DeLauro of Connecticut reintroduced the Family Act, which had previously been introduced in 2013, and every year subsequently, but has never been enacted.[67] The Family Act, which builds on the foundation of the FMLA, would afford American workers up to twelve weeks of *paid* family leave at a rate of 66 percent of what they would earn in a month.[68] Family leave is construed as leave surrounding becoming a parent through birth or adoption, as well as to handle serious health conditions that might afflict oneself, or one's child, parent, spouse, or domestic partner.[69] This leave would be funded via employer and employee payroll contributions of 2 cents per $10 in wages.[70] It is estimated that it will cost an ordinary worker approximately $2 per week.[71]

Also in early 2019, Senators Marco Rubio and Mitt Romney introduced the New Parents Act, which would allow parents to use a portion of their Social Security after the birth or adoption of a child as a voluntary option of paid parental leave.[72] A companion bill would also provide new parents with paid

---

[64]   *A Look at the U.S. Department of Labor's 2012 Family and Medical Leave Act Employee and Worksite Surveys*, NAT'L P'SHIP (Feb. 2013), www.nationalpartnership.org/our-work/resourc es/economic-justice/fmla/dol-fmla-survey-key-findings-2012.pdf.

[65]   *State Paid Family and Medical Leave Insurance Laws, supra* note 57.

[66]   *See* H.R. Rep. No. 103–8, pt. 2, at 12–13 (1993) (discussing the inadequacy of parental leave for pregnancy in the United States as compared to other countries).

[67]   *FAMILY Act Reintroduced*, J.J. KELLER (Feb. 1, 2019), www.jjkeller.com/learn/news/022019/ FAMILY-Act-reintroduced.

[68]   *The Family and Medical Insurance Leave (FAMILY) Act*, NAT'L P'SHIP FOR WOMEN AND FAMILIES (Sept. 2019), www.nationalpartnership.org/our-work/resources/economic-justice/ paid-leave/family-act-fact-sheet.pdf.

[69]   *Id.*

[70]   *Id.*

[71]   *Id.*

[72]   New Parents Act of 2019, S. 920, 116th Cong. (2019); Stephen Miller, *GOP Rolls Out "New Parents Act" to Provide Paid Family Leave*, SHRM (Mar. 28, 2019), www.shrm.org/resource sandtools/hr-topics/benefits/pages/gop-rolls-out-new-parents-act-for-paid-family-leave.aspx.

leave that lasts one, two, or three months, in exchange for delaying or reducing future Social Security benefits.[73] Alternatively, parents would be able to choose to keep working full-time or part-time and utilize the Social Security funds for childcare expenses.[74] With bipartisan support for more desperately needed relief for new parents, but no new legislation, it seems clear that some legislative reform is needed.

Once Working Moms Return from Leave

And then there arrives the issue of the way in which new mothers are treated upon their return to work. Prior to the 2000s, new mothers typically could be discriminated against with impunity upon their return to work, the thinking being that no disparate treatment was on the basis of sex but, rather, on the basis of the actual or perceived responsibilities that they had undertaken. While US courts heard approximately eight Family Responsibility Discrimination (FRD) cases in the 1970s, these cases rose exponentially in the first half of the 2000s.[75] In 2007, the Equal Employment Opportunity Commission (EEOC) issued its publication regarding FRD, and jurisdictions around the country finally came to recognize as cognizable this discrete form of discrimination, which identifies women with small children as a subset of the protected class of all women and renders discrimination against them discrimination "because of" sex.[76] This was a watershed moment in law in that the maneuver to identify the class, as the courts did, entailed judges taking judicial notice, or acknowledging, on the basis of their observations of life outside of the cases before them, the societal tendency to ascribe child caretaking responsibilities to women in families. A supervisor who, upon finding out that an employee will be having triplets, says "Bless her heart" and promptly divests her of substantial responsibilities, clients, or opportunities upon her return from work is thus seen as having discriminated against her because of her sex, even though he may have conferred those things upon one of her female colleagues.[77]

---

[73] Miller, *supra* note 72.
[74] *Id.*
[75] Mary C. Still, *Litigating the Maternal Wall: U.S. Lawsuits Charging Discrimination against Workers with Family Responsibilities*, WORK LIFE LAW, UC HASTINGS COLLEGE OF THE LAW, http://worklifelaw.org/publications/FRDreport.pdf (last visited Nov. 16, 2019).
[76] Debra S. Katz, *Recent Developments: Sex Discrimination and Family Responsibility Claims*, KATZ, MARSHALL & BANKS, LLP (Mar. 5, 2009), www.kmblegal.com/publications/recent-developments-sex-discrimination-and-family-responsibility-claims.
[77] *See generally* Spees v. James Marine, Inc., 617 F.3d 380 (6th Cir. 2010); Rafeh v. University Research Co., L.L.C., 114 F. Supp. 2d 396 (D. Md. 2000); Kitroeff & Silver-Greenberg, *supra*

The FRD doctrine, however, is severely limited in that it affords an employee protection only from the *unfounded prejudices* that an employer deploys in taking an adverse employment action without any cause, but in *anticipation* of future failings precipitated by competing childcare responsibilities. It does not insulate an employee from adverse actions taken due to their *actual* failings, no matter how slight, so long as they are not disproportionately punished in comparison with similarly situated employees who are not new mothers. In other words, once a new mother actually *does* falter or require the slightest accommodation due to a sick child, a dance recital, the failure of a caregiver to show, or any other childcare responsibility, she is, essentially, outside the ambit of the law's protection. While this is not irrational, it is worth noting because women do tend to most often be the ones both tasked with childcare within the family unit and assumed to be responsible for childcare by those outside the family unit – and often in the workplace. This makes issues like a lack of affordable and convenient childcare in this country a women's workplace equality issue, among other things.

The issue of expressing milk at work has become yet another issue that beleaguers women returning from leave as they struggle to resume their responsibilities and be viewed as unflaggingly ready to do so. Under the Patient Protection and Affordable Care Act (Affordable Care Act, or ACA), which amends the Fair Labor Standards Act (FLSA), employers must grant an employee "reasonable break time for an employee to express breast milk for her nursing child for 1 year after the child's birth each time such employee has need to express the milk."[78] This time must be afforded in "a place, other than a bathroom, that is shielded from view and free from intrusion from coworkers and the public, which may be used by an employee to express breast milk."[79]

However, this law was enacted only in 2010, and in order to be entitled to the breaks, a worker must be a "nonexempt" employee who works for an employer that is covered by the FLSA.[80] Employers need to have annual sales totaling $500,000 or more or be engaged in interstate commerce to be covered under the FLSA; and, even then, employers with fewer than fifty employees are not subject to the break time requirement when they can show that their compliance with the provision would confer an undue

note 9 ("There is a cultural perception that if you're a good mother, you're so dedicated to your children that you couldn't possibly be that dedicated to your career."); YoonKyung Chung & Robert Graham, *Center the Parental Gender Earnings Gap in the United States*, U.S. CENSUS BUREAU (Nov. 2017), www2.census.gov/ces/wp/2017/CES-WP-17-68.pdf.

[78] Patient Protection and Affordable Care Act, § 4207, 29 U.S.C. § 207.
[79] *Id.*
[80] *Id.*

hardship on them.[81] Further, numerous employees are deemed "exempt" from the law's protections in light of their being any number of things, including highly compensated, executive/managerial, administrative, or professional.[82] "Besides," notes Nina, a thirty-one-year-old medical professional, "if you have to resort to researching Obamacare to see what you're legally entitled to, without your employer stepping forward to offer you something workable and humane, you're kind of in a bad situation to begin with."

To be clear, even if an individual is not accorded accommodations to express milk under the FLSA, individual states' laws may nonetheless mandate protection.[83] However, these laws vary widely, and nearly half of states have no applicable laws mandating entitlements beyond those afforded by the ACA.[84] Even nearly a decade after the ACA's passage, many women remain without the protection of the law on this issue, and many more find themselves either: (1) given subpar accommodations that technically comply with the law; and/or (2) uncomfortable with how they may be perceived for having asked for, taken, or balked at an accommodation. A thirty-nine-year-old consultant recalls being sent to a supply room to express milk:

> The room was tiny, and because there was a safe in it, there needed to be a camera on in the room at all times. I worked with a co-worker to find a small corner of the room out of the camera's line of vision, and I knelt against a wall, knowing that if I leaned forward more than three inches, I'd be on camera. But the room was in compliance.

Parenting in a Pandemic

Perhaps no modern event has demonstrated the inadequacies of the American workplace when it comes to parenthood, and often motherhood in particular, more than the COVID-19 pandemic, the subsequent lockdown, and the shift to remote work for so many, starting in the spring of 2020.[85] According to

---

[81] *Fact Sheet #14: Coverage under the Fair Labor Standards Act (FLSA)*, U.S. DEP'T OF LAB. (Jul. 2009), www.dol.gov/whd/regs/compliance/whdfs14.htm.

[82] Alison Doyle, *Difference between an Exempt and Non-exempt Employee*, CAREERS (Oct. 21, 2019), www.thebalancecareers.com/exempt-and-a-non-exempt-employee-2061988.

[83] *Breastfeeding State Laws*, NAT'L CONF. OF STATE LEGISLATURES (Apr. 30, 2019), www.ncsl.org/research/health/breastfeeding-state-laws.aspx.

[84] Summer S. Hawkins et al., Breastfeeding and the Affordable Care Act, THE NAT'L CTR. FOR BIOTECH. INFO. (Jul. 10, 2015), www.ncbi.nlm.nih.gov/pmc/articles/PMC4555840/.

[85] AJMC Staff, *A Timeline of COVID-19 Developments in the First Half of 2020*, AJMC (Jul. 3, 2020), www.ajmc.com/view/a-timeline-of-covid19-developments-in-2020; CNN Editorial Research, Coronavirus Outbreak Timeline Fast Facts, CNN (Aug. 3, 2020, 10:55 AM), www.cnn.com/2020/02/06/health/wuhan-coronavirus-timeline-fast-facts/index.html.

a Stanford economist, there was "an incredible 42 percent of the U.S. labor force . . . working from home full-time. About another 33 percent [we]re not working — a testament to the savage impact of the lockdown recession. And the remaining 26 percent — mostly essential service workers — [we]re working on their business premises."[86] This fundamental shift in how things are being done accomplished a number of things.

In the first place, it has shown everyone what is possible in terms of the flexibility and remoteness of work. And while things like commercial office space and a fixed workday or workweek have not yet become obsolete, the perceived need for them has been somewhat obviated.[87] This has shown, in dramatic fashion, the ways in which old, fixed notions of what is essential or indispensable to a successful workplace or workforce are hollow and can be toppled.

In the second place, this shift to remote work, compounded with schools having shifted to online learning (largely compulsory for all students in the spring of 2020), has rendered pronounced the ways in which it is difficult to parent while working.[88] With the advent of legislated "equality in the workplace" somehow came the myth that women, now seemingly allowed a seat at

---

[86]   May Wong, *Stanford Research Provides a Snapshot of a New Working-from-Home Economy*, STANFORD NEWS (Jun. 29, 2020), https://news.stanford.edu/2020/06/29/snapshot-new-working-home-economy/. Many sources vary on those workers reportedly being required to transition from in-person to remote work. Rani Molla, *Office Work Will Never Be the Same*, VOX (May 21, 2020, 7:30 AM), www.vox.com/recode/2020/5/21/21234242/coronavirus-covid-19-remote-work-from-home-office-reopening (estimating that 34 percent of workers are working from home); *Ability to Work from Home: Evidence from Two Surveys and Implications for the Labor Market in the COVID-19 Pandemic*, U.S. BUREAU OF LAB. STAT., (Jun. 2020), www .bls.gov/opub/mlr/2020/article/ability-to-work-from-home.htm (estimating that at least 31 percent of workers transitioned to remote work between March 2020 and the end of April 2020); *When Everyone Can Work from Home, What's the Office For?*, PwC (Jun. 25, 2020), www .pwc.com/us/en/library/covid-19/us-remote-work-survey.html; (estimating that 70 percent of workers are working remotely due to COVID-19).

[87]   *See* Rani Molla, *This Is the End of the Office as We Know It*, VOX (Apr. 14, 2020, 8:00 AM), www .vox.com/recode/2020/4/14/21211789/coronavirus-office-space-work-from-home-design-architecture-real-estate; Mark C. Perna, *How to Keep Working from Home after COVID-19*, FORBES (May 1, 2020, 6:50 AM), www.forbes.com/sites/markcperna/2020/05/01/how-to-keep-working-from-home-after-covid-19/#23b537b361a4; Carrie Rich, *The Pandemic Is Wrecking the Typical 9-to-5 Workday. Good Riddance.*, BUS. INSIDER (Jul. 9, 2020, 10:32 AM), www.businessinsider.com/co vid-19-pandemic-ended-normal-work-week-9-5-workday-2020-7; Joseph Coughlin, *How COVID-19's 168-Hour Workweek Is Changing Work in Retirement*, FORBES (Aug. 9, 2020, 8:00 AM), www .forbes.com/sites/josephcoughlin/2020/08/09/how-covid-19s-168-hour-workweek-is-changing-work-in-retirement/#5a1484a54502.

[88]   Herminia Ibarra et al., *Why WFH Isn't Necessarily Good for Women*, HARV. BUS. REV. (Jul. 16, 2020), https://hbr.org/2020/07/why-wfh-isnt-necessarily-good-for-women.

the proverbial table, could "have it all" (meaning often doing the lion's share of parenting while ascending professionally), provided that they were talented and hardworking enough.[89] This meant, in the minds of many, that they were now permitted or "free" to put in a full day of work and then return home to their households to parent. And yet, this conveniently overlooks the unspoken truth, even recognized – as described in this chapter – by courts, namely that responsibility for child-rearing and household maintenance tends to be ascribed, societally and individually, to women.

This means that, on the whole, women are more likely to do the lion's share of housework and more likely to be expected to and to actually handle childcare responsibilities like feeding, dressing, and bathing children. They are also more likely to miss work than are men for things like school recitals and conferences, and children's sick days or doctor's visits. This comes into sharp tension with one of the biggest unspoken dynamics about sex and the American workplace: the myth of the ideal worker. According to Joan C. Williams: "Market work is structured around an ideal worker who takes no time off for childbearing, has no daytime child rearing responsibilities, and is available 'full-time' and for overtime at short notice."[90] Lip service about working mothers being able to "have it all" is thus belied by this tension. And in the wake of the pandemic and the shift to remote work and school, parents found themselves working from home, but also expected to supervise their remote-schooled children, in addition to undertaking regular housekeeping responsibilities.[91] This became the point at which the tacit shading of "women's work" as domestic work and the tacit shading of "ideal work" as all-consuming could be clearly seen as on an irreversible collision course.

It is therefore not at all surprising that while the pandemic has all but eviscerated national and family economies alike, and parents at all

---

[89]   Michelle King, *Why Working Hard Is Not Enough to Get Ahead*, Forbes (Jan. 9, 2018, 10:14 AM), www.forbes.com/sites/michelleking/2018/01/09/why-working-hard-is-not-enough-to-get-ahead/#1a60b5144b67.

[90]   Joan C. Williams, *Restructuring Work and Family Entitlements Around Family Values*, 19 Harv. J. of L. & Pub. Pol'y 753 (1996).

[91]   Ana Homayoun, *How To Actually Do This Remote-Learning Thing While Also Working from Home*, Wash. Post (Apr. 2, 2020, 11:30 AM), www.washingtonpost.com/lifestyle/2020/04/02/homeschool-working-home-coronavirus/; Jeremy Engle, *How Is Your Family Dividing Responsibilities during the Quarantine?*, N.Y. Times (May 15, 2020), www.nytimes.com/2020/05/15/learning/how-is-your-family-dividing-responsibilities-during-the-quarantine.html ; Jocelyn Frye, *On the Frontlines at Work and at Home: The Disproportionate Economic Effects of the Coronavirus Pandemic on Women of Color*, Ctr. for Am. Progress (Apr. 23, 2020, 9:00 AM), www.americanprogress.org/issues/women/reports/2020/04/23/483846/frontlines-work-home/.

socioeconomic levels have seen their morale and productivity suffer, women have borne the brunt of the time, space, and resources crunch brought on by the pandemic.[92] In May 2020, it was reported that 14 percent of women were contemplating leaving employment as a result of the constraints placed upon their time by COVID-19-related increased family responsibilities, whereas only 11 percent of men were.[93] Moreover, as per FAST COMPANY, despite the shift to remote work, more and more employers permitting remote work are nonetheless compensating for the increased flexibility afforded by ratcheting up expectations with respect to things like around-the-clock availability on email or teleconference, "face time," and alacrity.[94] This crisis has laid bare the inequitable division of work outside of the workplace, and women have disproportionately encountered impediments to their professional success that have made the dual (sexist) notions of the "ideal mother" and the "ideal worker" appear more mutually exclusive than ever. To add insult to injury, in the wake of the shift to at-home work, reports started to surface that, at least in certain industries, parents who *were* afforded resources or accommodations by employers as they attempted to negotiate their now complicated existences actually received backlash and resentment from their colleagues.[95]

All Connected to Unspoken Beliefs

Whether it has been Congressional inaction or insufficient action, willful blindness shown and legal fictions crafted by courts, or employers' own rigidity and refusal to afford women more than the law demands, it is easy to see how the ways in which working mothers have been systemically disadvantaged stem from the belief that pregnancy is a burden and an inconvenience.

Whereas the Supreme Court had once shown, in *Gilbert*, what looked almost like willful blindness to the fact that pregnancy discrimination is sex

---

[92]   Joan C. Williams, *The Pandemic Has Exposed the Fallacy of the "Ideal Worker,"* HARV. BUS. REV. (May 11, 2020), https://hbr.org/2020/05/the-pandemic-has-exposed-the-fallacy-of-the-ideal-worker.

[93]   *Id.*

[94]   Zoran Latinovic & Sharmila C. Chatterjee, *3 Reasons Why the Workplace Can't Return to Normal after COVID-19,* FAST CO. (Jun. 18, 2020), www.fastcompany.com/90517966/3-reasons-why-the-workplace-cant-return-to-normal-after-covid-19.

[95]   *See* Kylie Ora Lobell, *Accommodating Working Parents during the COVID-19 Pandemic,* SHRM (Jul. 30, 2020), www.shrm.org/resourcesandtools/hr-topics/employee-relations/pages/accommodating-working-parents-during-the-covid-19-pandemic.aspx; Daisuke Wakabayashi & Sheera Frenkel, *Parents Got Time Off. Then the Backlash Started,* N.Y. TIMES (Sept. 5, 2020), www.nytimes.com/2020/09/05/technology/parents-time-off-backlash.html.

discrimination, it seemed to, in *Young*, construct a whole new legal fiction surrounding the idea that it was in danger of conferring an unwarranted "most favored nation status" on pregnant women, should it construe the statute as the plaintiff urged.[96] What does it mean; moreover, what does it say when commentators herald a "victory" for pregnant women when all the Supreme Court did was mandate accommodation only when the plaintiff can prove discriminatory intent?[97] It arguably means that the Court persists, as it did in 1976, in seeing pregnancy as a burden or inconvenience whose costs ought not plague a woman's employer unduly.[98]

On the legislature's part, the failure to pass legislation like the PWFA contrasts with Congress recognizing the need to allow the reasonable risks and costs associated with accommodating disability to reside with employers so that those who become disabled are not siphoned from the workforce. This cost, of course, gets passed along to everyone from the employer's owners or shareholders, who will see less profit, to co-workers, who will see less salary, to customers and clients, who will see higher prices. Congress was fine with all of this because it saw the societal benefits of ensuring a diverse and inclusive workforce with respect to the disabled, who had suffered systemic exclusion and discrimination.[99] Its failure to ensure the same for pregnancy speaks to the unspoken belief that pregnancy is a private inconvenience that, at most, warrants an antidiscrimination mandate – but no affirmative accommodation.

THE PAIN

It took a Supreme Court case in 1976 that held that employer discrimination against pregnant women was *not* sex discrimination – and merely discrimination against people who happen to fall pregnant – to serve as the impetus for Congress to pass the PDA in the first place.[100] With the advent of the FRD doctrine, and the passage of the ACA in 2010, among other legal advances, the courts and the legislature recognized the ineluctable need for the protection and accommodation that women who have children while working *still* need. But to the extent that these advances have not been enough, and the

---

[96] *Young*, 575 U.S. at 207.
[97] Tom Spiggle, *Why Young v. UPS Is a Big Win for Pregnant Workers*, HUFFPOST (May 27, 2015), www.huffpost.com/entry/why-young-v-ups-is-a-big_b_6956498?utm_hp_ref=tw; Rebecca Leber, *The Supreme Court Just Sided with Pregnant Working Women*, THE NEW REPUBLIC (Mar. 25, 2015), https://newrepublic.com/article/121376/supreme-court-hands-pregnant-workers-win-young-vs-ups.
[98] *See Gilbert*, 429 U.S. 125.
[99] Americans with Disabilities Act of 1990, 42 U.S.C. § 12101(b).
[100] *Gilbert*, 429 U.S. at 134.

incompatibility of a smooth, successful career trajectory and motherhood persists, it is imperative to examine why.

Numerous books have been written about the many ways in which the American legal system and the typical American workplace have failed women who seek to hold down a job while becoming pregnant, having a baby, and then raising a newborn, toddler, etc.[101] Scholars like Professor Joan C. Williams have decried employers' practices of discriminating against pregnant women, promulgating restrictive, rigid policies when it comes to parental leave, and failing to afford the kinds of accommodation that would permit new mothers adequate time and space to nurse, bond with, and otherwise be with their new children, among other things.[102] These scholars have lamented the failure of the US government to mandate free or subsidized childcare in the workplace, the way other countries do, or to guarantee parental leave with more generous terms than those in the FMLA. Scholars have even critiqued judges for not interpreting the existing laws that are supposed to provide somewhat of a safety net for mothers broadly enough to afford meaningful protection.[103] The actions and the failures of employers, legislators, and judges have, as many agree, been nothing short of inimical to the successful recruitment, professional development, promotion, and retention of talented women in the workplace. This has laid down yet another pane of the glass ceiling.

It has never been easy for a working woman to become and be a mother while holding down a job or pursuing a profession. From the process of trying to conceive a baby, when a woman finds out that fertility treatments are not (typically) covered by her insurance, to being pregnant and requiring accommodations to which she may not be entitled by the law, to giving birth and not being given ample leave to heal and take care of her baby, the gaps and flaws in the laws and protections afforded are seemingly endless. Men and women who seek to adopt often encounter similar frustrations in the process of becoming parents. And then, once parenthood has started, there is no mandated accommodation by law for any parent who has a problem with childcare arrangements, sick children, or any other parenting obligation. Women are the usual caregivers of children, evidenced by the fact that women still spend twice the

---

[101] Shani Orgad, Heading Home: Motherhood, Work, and the Failed Promise of Equality (2019).

[102] Joan C. Williams, *The Maternal Wall*, Harv. Bus. Rev. (Oct. 2004), https://hbr.org/2004/10/the-maternal-wall.

[103] Joan C. Williams, *Pregnant Workers Have Rights, No Matter What the Supreme Court Says about UPS*, Harv. Bus. Rev. (Dec. 18, 2014), https://hbr.org/2014/12/pregnant-workers-have-rights-no-matter-what-the-supreme-court-says-about-ups.

amount of time with their children that men do,[104] and women are also those to whom caregiving responsibilities are ascribed primarily by society.[105] Thus, any attitude, spoken or not, that parenthood is an intolerable inconvenience, that the physical state of being pregnant, the physical act of giving birth, or post-natal recovery and infant care are somehow unsightly, unseemly, or uncomfortable to be around, will disproportionately harm women. So will the expectation, spoken or unspoken, that a woman who gives birth should "bounce back," physically and mentally, and care for her child quickly, silently, and in a way that does not disrupt her work or inconvenience anyone.

And what of pregnant women who need slight tweaks to their daily work routine or physical labor assigned, but who do not have complications that rise to the level of a disability as defined by the ADA? They will fall through the cracks in the law, finding themselves neither protected under the ADA nor presumptively entitled to any accommodation due to their pregnancy. Most people do not expect to become disabled, especially during their prime working years, but the law keeps the ground from being ripped out from beneath them if they do, by mandating reasonable employer accommodations that can keep employees working, vital, and earning a living. On the other hand, most women get pregnant during their prime working years. Pregnancy ought to be reasonably anticipated – not the sort of surprise that disability winds up being for most working people who need to seek accommodation. It should certainly be accommodated like a disability would be, and not only when an employee can prove that the employer "did accommodate others similar in their ability or inability to work."[106]

Finally, it needs to be noted that the aforementioned issues – leave time, accommodation for milk expression, being divested of work or privileges, etc. – are all concrete. They happen, or they don't; and they are capable of legal resolution, one way or another. Nothing has been said of the intangible detriments of being pregnant and/or a parent in the workplace. The almost imperceptible looks, the subtle comments unaccompanied by a concrete adverse employment action, the negative or even less than glowing subjective evaluations that don't reference a worker's status as a mother but seem inextricably tied to it. At the end of the day, the tangible and less tangible slights, and the failures of legislation and judicial interpretation to adequately enable and protect women at work, may all be seen to emanate from an

---

[104] Parker & Wang, *supra* note 4.
[105] Kim Parker & Gretchen Livingston, *6 Facts about American Fathers*, PEW RSCH. CTR.: FACTTANK (Jun. 15, 2017), www.pewresearch.org/fact-tank/2017/06/15/fathers-day-facts/.
[106] *Young*, 575 U.S. 206.

unspoken belief that (1) pregnancy and motherhood are unsightly and inconvenient; and that (2) women are obligated to do all they can to shield the world at large from pregnancy and motherhood's impact on everything from their appearance to their productivity.

MANIFESTATIONS

It is not hard to find voiced expressions of the belief that a woman's pregnancy is a burden on her employer – and one that she ought best shoulder without resort to her employer – as well as related beliefs. Federal case filings alleging sex or pregnancy discrimination are rife with allegations that firm partners, factory foremen, and other supervisors of all kinds regularly voice beliefs like this in the workplace.

One such case, reported on by thenation.com, was filed by Kristine Webb, who began working at a cellular phone company store in South Dakota in 2014.[107] She became, by her own account, a successful sales representative, and was even accepted into the company's training program, intended to prepare employees for advancement.[108] She finished the program in 2017, just as she discovered that she was pregnant.[109] While she was initially very positive about her professional future there, she developed hyperemesis gravidarum, which consisted of debilitating, persistent "morning sickness," and wound up in the emergency room due to pregnancy-related complications.[110]

Dehydrated, she was kept by doctors in the emergency room to receive fluids and wound up missing work.[111] This caused her, she recounted, to be penalized, despite her explanation.[112] She was told, she claims, that the sole way to avoid a penalty would be for her to have her absence excused by filing paperwork under the FMLA.[113] This caused her to attempt to work while very sick, and she told thenation.com that when she asked other managers to cover for her while she excused herself periodically, they "made it seem like it was a burden on them to have to do that."[114] She went on to say that, as her

---

[107]   Bryce Covert, *The American Workplace Still Won't Accommodate Pregnant Workers*, THE NATION (Aug. 12, 2019), www.thenation.com/article/pregnant-workers-discrimination-workplace-low-wage/.
[108]   *Id.*
[109]   *Id.*
[110]   *Id.*
[111]   *Id.*
[112]   *Id.*
[113]   *Id.*
[114]   *Id.*

pregnancy progressed, she "definitely felt like [she] was being almost targeted," as people increasingly refused to assist her.[115]

She recalled: "It went from a job that I absolutely loved and I thought that I was going to make a career out of into something that you wake up every day and have to talk yourself into wanting to go to work," but "[q]uitting a job when you're seven, eight months pregnant—financially, I didn't know if we would be able to do it."[116] However, as her penalties mounted, she attempted to find another job and leave, but, she alleges, she was fired instead.[117] She filed a suit in the summer of 2019, alleging pregnancy discrimination.[118] Her story is one of many in which employees recall that they went from being in excellent professional standing to being seen as burdensome or even a liability by their employers.[119]

Former President Donald Trump has been quoted in an October 2004 interview with NBC's Dateline, as saying that pregnancy is "a wonderful thing for the woman, it's a wonderful thing for the husband, it's certainly an inconvenience for a business. And whether people want to say that or not, the fact is it is an inconvenience for a person that is running a business."[120]

TAKEAWAYS

An overhaul of the vast array of beliefs that underlie the various indignities and injustices that expecting and new mothers suffer in the workplace would require vast ideological and policy changes at every level from the legislature to the courts to the inside of decision-makers' heads. Much has already been written on what could and should happen, from sweeping policy changes and legislation regarding paid maternity leave, to changing employers' perception of working mothers.[121] While a majority of Americans now say that they believe

---

[115]   *Id.*
[116]   *Id.*
[117]   *Id.*
[118]   *Id.*
[119]   *Id.*
[120]   Ali Vitali, *Trump in 2004: Pregnancy Is an "Inconvenience" to Employers*, NBC News (May 26, 2016), www.nbcnews.com/politics/2016-election/trump-2004-pregnancy-inconvenience-employers-n580366.
[121]   *See* Maya Rossin-Slater & Lindsey Uniat, *Paid Family Leave Policies and Population Health*, Health Affairs (Mar. 28, 2019), www.healthaffairs.org/do/10.1377/hpb20190301.484936/full/?utm_source=Newsletter&utm_medium=email&utm_content=Health+Policy+Briefs%3A+Paid+Family+Leave+and+Food+Support+Programs%3B+Standard+Episode+Definitions%3B+GrantWatch&utm_campaign=HAT+3-28-19&; *see also* Julia Isaacs et al., *Paid Parental Leave in the United States: Time for a New National Policy*, Urban Inst. (May 2017), www.urban.org/sites/default/files/publication/90201/paid_family_leave_0.pdf;

that employers ought to furnish their employees with paid family leave, there is not the same strong consensus when they are asked whether it should be required of employers.[122]

At the end of the day, there are a multitude of good proposals – some more realistic than others in terms of their cost-effectiveness and the support that they have managed to garner – that are out there to help society grapple with a range of the harms and burdens that accrue to women in the workplace because of motherhood. Some are legal proposals in the form of bills that have languished and failed to pass; others are corporate policies that need to be considered by more employers who claim that they want to change the culture and composition of their workforces. Some involve paid parental leave or defrayed or free childcare. Some entail funds being drawn from tax revenue or from corporate profits. These all hold great potential to effect change when it comes to the retention and advancement of women in the workplace.

However, one of the most overlooked ways to approach the problems bound up in this country's treatment of working mothers is a reexamination of the unspoken belief that underlies so much of it. Companies ought to, in the formation of their corporate ethos, cultures, and policies, expressly consider their stance on motherhood. At a minimum, companies ought to make one of their corporate values the view that motherhood is not a burden, an imposition, or anything else that needs to be mitigated, hidden away, or apologized for. Irrespective of whether an employer has the resources to afford employees long periods of paid leave or private offices with doors, there are things that it can do to adhere to the view that motherhood is not a source of inconvenience or shame. Much of this can be done with (1) pervasive mindfulness of the employer's stance on motherhood when it comes to training, or to drafting an employee handbook's policies, and (2) viewing the law as a floor and not a ceiling when it comes to what can be done to support employees who become mothers.[123]

What might this look like? The Affordable Care Act compels employers to furnish "reasonable break time for an employee to express breast milk for her

---

Donatus I. Amaram, *Attracting and Retaining Women Talent in the Global Labor Market: A Review*, 7 J. Hum. Res. Mgmt. Lab. Stud. 1 (Jun. 2019).

[122] Horowitz et al., *supra* note 3 ("Americans are divided when it comes to government mandates on employer-paid family and medical leave: 51% say the federal government should require employers to pay their employees when they take leave from work for family or medical reasons, and a similar share (48%) say employers should be able to decide for themselves.").

[123] Joan C. Williams & Nancy Segal, *Beyond the Maternal Wall: Relief for Family Caregivers Who Are Discriminated Against on the Job*, 26 Harv. Women's L.J. 77, 121 (2003).

nursing child for 1 year after the child's birth each time such employee has need to express the milk," as well as "a place, other than a bathroom, that is shielded from view and free from intrusion from coworkers and the public, which may be used by an employee to express breast milk."[124] However, "a place, other than a bathroom," can refer to a variety of locations, and "reasonable break time" can be interpreted in various ways under various circumstances. Moreover, the law only covers employers covered by the FLSA when dealing with employees who are not exempt from section 7 of the FLSA,[125] though state analogues of this mandate may dictate protection anyway. Generous, across-the-board interpretation of the above terms, along with provision of clean, private, and spacious rooms and ample time for all who need it, is a great place for a committed employer to start. A corporate culture, fostered through training, written policies, and top-down informal policies, can reinforce support from supervisors, clients, and coworkers, while deterring those who would show impatience, annoyance, or dissatisfaction with those in need of breaks to express milk or the incursions these breaks could reasonably be expected to make into their work.

What else might this look like? The FMLA mandates, among other things, twelve weeks of unpaid parental leave, as well as continuity of benefits and employment for qualifying employees who work for covered employers.[126] Committed employers can view this as a floor, rather than a ceiling, and see an investment into expanding these entitlements in any way and to any degree (paid leave, more time, extending the accommodations to those not legally entitled to them) as an expression of their belief that, far from an inconvenience, parenthood, is something to invest in so that employees feel appreciated and able not only to simply navigate their careers as their lives move forward, but to thrive.

---

[124] Patient Protection and Affordable Care Act, § 4207, 29 U.S.C. § 207.
[125] Doyle, *supra* note 82.
[126] Family Medical Leave Act, 29 U.S.C. § 2612.

8

"He Has a Family to Support" (And Besides ...)

"He has a family to support." That's what one of my mentors said she literally heard her boss say in the 1990s when he gave a promotion and raise to a guy in her starting class who hadn't done anything more than anyone else to distinguish himself. My mentor told me this while we were discussing the fact that I had recently found out that I made less money than a guy with my same job title who had started the same year that I had started. "You know," she said, "you don't hear many people say things like that anymore." But you have to wonder how often they're thinking it—on some level. And then you hear all of this about how systemic this all is ... how little women make per dollar that men earn for doing the same work—across the board! And you start to think, it can't be all of us. We can't all lack ambition and talent. There has to be something else going on. We can't be valued so low so consistently without something else going on.

—*Farrah, thirty-seven, advertising executive*

THE BELIEF

The belief that a man should, or needs to, earn more than a woman because he probably has a family to support – like so many other beliefs explored here – is one that most modern people would not admit to harboring. It is one that many people may not even process consciously. Despite more than half a century of legislation and several waves of social and political movements to compel sexual and other equality in employment, women still, on the whole, make less money for doing the same work as men. And when attitudes, assumptions, and history are probed for explanations, it appears that, to some extent and on some level of consciousness, many people still see male employees as "serious" breadwinners with families to support who should receive, or need to receive, higher wages. This stands in contrast to their heterosexual cohabitating female colleagues, who risk being perceived as a "second income" (either because they are, in fact, part of a two income household with the male partner earning more, or because people believe that they should be the lower income in a two income family if they work outside of the home at all). This chapter aims to unpack the "should" and "need" elements of this belief, which is both heteronormative and antiquated; nearly half of all U.S. households are headed by women.[1]

Both the "need" and the "should" elements are rooted in historical gender roles and stereotypes. Men have historically and heteronormatively been perceived to be the "breadwinners," meaning the provider and the head of the household.[2] Women have been cast as mothers and homemakers, subordinate to their husbands.[3] If women worked outside of the home, they were thought to have somehow accessed a man's world, distracted from their proper homemaking duties.[4] Women may have, the thinking went in certain circumstances, brought home a "second" income in order to, the thinking went, help make ends meet, or to purchase luxuries that were beyond their husband's earning capacities, or even simply because they had personal ambitions that they wanted to fulfill. But the common misperception, especially early on, was decidedly not that women had mouths at home to feed with their paycheck.

Even among women who wanted to work, there was often a perception that those of means, which usually meant that their husbands had means, were somehow less deserving of earning a wage in the workforce. A 1930 article entitled "Should Women Earn Pin Money[:] Status of Those Who Are Not Bound to Work and Their Effect on [the] Labor Market Is Discussed by Economists," went so far as to announce that "[once] more the question of the woman of independent or semi-independent means, and her right to a niche in industry is up for discussion. Opinions on her as a social phenomenon seem to vary."[5] The article went on to quote Frances Perkins, who was the New York State Commissioner of Labor, as "insist[ing]" that "the woman 'pin-money worker' who competes with the necessity worker is a menace to society, a selfish, shortsighted creature, who ought to be ashamed of herself," and that

[u]ntil we have every woman in this community earning a living wage—and by that I mean not less than $20 a week for the City of New York—until we

---

[1]   Laurie Goodman et al., *More Women Have Become Homeowners and Heads of Household. Could the Pandemic Undo That Progress?*, Urban Inst. (March 16, 2021), https://www.urban .org/urban-wire/more-women-have-become-homeowners-and-heads-household-could-pan demic-undo-progress.

[2]   Angélique Janssens, *The Rise and Decline of the Male Breadwinner Family? An Overview of the Debate*, 42 Int'l Rev. of Soc. History 1, 5–7 (1997).

[3]   Melissa Walker, *Women in the 1930s: Workers or Homemakers?*, H Net: Humanities and Soc. Sciences Online (Jul. 1996), www.h-net.org/reviews/showpdf.php?id=499.

[4]   *Id.*

[5]   U.S. Press, *Should Women Earn Pin Money?*, Macleans (Apr. 1, 1930), at 60, http://archive .macleans.ca/article/1930/4/1/should-women-earn-pin-money.

have a firmly established habit of short working hours and some kind of old-age security, I am not willing to encourage those who are under no economic necessities to compete with their charm and education, their superior advantages, against the working[ ]girl who has only her two hands.

This was just the tip of the iceberg. In the 1930s, this country experienced a sharp uptick in employer policies and legislation that prohibited married women from working. In fact, while fewer than ten states had laws like this before the Great Depression, no fewer than twenty-six states ultimately acted to curb the employment of married women.[6] As one commentator put it, in that economically turbulent era, "[a]s women around the country struggled to make ends meet during the nation's deepest economic crisis, they became an easy scapegoat for people looking for someone to blame."[7] And the vilification of the women who sought to work was explicit, with Wisconsin lawmakers passing a resolution in 1935 declaring that married women whose husbands worked and who chose to enter the workforce were the "calling card for disintegration of family life."[8]

Sometimes, a woman serving in the workforce was even seen as a *deficiency* on the part of her husband, because he could not earn enough income, on the part of the woman herself, or a combination of both. Today, many persist in the belief that a man's status within society is elevated if his wife does not "need" to work, and, therefore, he serves as the sole breadwinner, reinforcing the notion that women typically do not want to work outside the home but are forced to do so. Women who did work were traditionally limited to certain professions, such as teachers, secretaries, waitresses, and nurses,[9] which were often lower paying and conformed with the view that women were exclusively to hold caretaker roles in the workforce.

At the end of the day, we are arguably left with a range of pervasive beliefs in and around the workplace that men are presumptively more serious, more committed, and more deserving of a better paycheck than are women. Women, the belief goes, are, for their part, susceptible to being seen as dilettantes and hobbyists, perhaps at work merely for personal fulfillment, and perpetually in danger of leaving the workplace for greener, or at least more domestic, pastures.

---

[6] MEGAN MCDONALD WAY, FAMILY ECONOMICS AND PUBLIC POLICY, 1800S–PRESENT 152 (2018).

[7] Erin Blakemore, *Why Many Married Women Were Banned from Working During the Great Depression*, HISTORY, www.history.com/news/great-depression-married-women-employment (last updated Jul. 21, 2019).

[8] *Id.*; S. Res. 018–158, 1935 Leg., 62nd Sess., at 2403 (Wis. 1935), https://books.google.com/books?id=mZJsAAAAMAAJ&lpg=PA2403&dq=married%20women%20work&pg=PA2403#v=onepage&q=married%20women%20work&f=false.

[9] U.S. DEP'T OF LABOR, CHANGES IN WOMEN'S OCCUPATIONS 1940–1950, https://fraser.stlouisfed.org/files/docs/publications/women/b0253_dolwb_1954.pdf (1954).

And, again, while these thoughts may sound extreme, they exist along a spectrum and at various levels of the thinker's consciousness. Several articles have discussed a complaint filed in the Southern District of New York in 2011, in which a terminated female law firm associate alleged that her male supervisor made comments that voiced beliefs like these.[10] Among the things he was alleged to have said were that Harvard was a place to "meet some pretty women pretending to get a legal education," and that women "just get pregnant and leave. Out of every three years you only get one good year out of them."[11] While the case never went to trial, for every supervisor who *does* voice things like these, how many more are thinking them? There is mounting evidence that as pay inequality persists across time, states, and sectors of employment, there are defined, albeit often less than conscious, beliefs that underlie this phenomenon.

According to Pew research, Americans persist in viewing men as financial providers, despite the fact that women's contributions to household earnings have grown over the years, with women bringing in half or more of the family income in roughly a third of couples who are married or live together.[12] In 2017, about 71 percent of adults said that it was "very important for a man to be able to support a family financially to be a good husband or partner," but only 32 percent said the same of women.[13] And, indeed, men out-earn their female spouses or partners with whom they live about two-thirds (69 percent) of the time.[14]

While the belief that it is important for men to be breadwinners for their partners and families exists across swaths of the population, it is most predominant among people who, themselves, have less education, earn less income, and are older.[15] Moreover, studies have shown that women employed in fields that have historically been male-dominated may actually be perceived negatively by both sexes if they are successful.[16] One study actually showed that

---

[10] Michele Henry, *Woman Alleges Sexual Discrimination in Lawsuit Against Toronto-Based Firm*, THE STAR (Feb. 15, 2011), www.thestar.com/news/gta/2011/02/15/woman_alleges_sexual_discrimination_in_lawsuit_against_torontobased_firm.html/; Debra Cassens Weiss, *Fired NY Associate Sues Firm, Claims "Hostile and Demeaning" Environment*, AM. B. ASSOC. J. (Feb. 16, 2011, 1:40 PM), www.abajournal.com/news/article/fired_ny_associate_sues_firm_over_hostile_and_demeaning_environment/.

[11] Henry, *supra* note 9.

[12] Kim Parker et al., *Americans See Men as the Financial Providers, Even as Women's Contributions Grow*, PEW RSCH CENTER: FACT TANK (Sept. 20, 2017), www.pewresearch.org/fact-tank/2017/09/20/americans-see-men-as-the-financial-providers-even-as-womens-contributions-grow/.

[13] *Id.*

[14] *Id.*

[15] *Id.*

[16] S. Dingfelder, *Women Who Succeed in Male-Dominated Careers Are Often Seen Negatively, Suggests Study*, 35 AM. PSYCHOL. ASS'N 12 (2004), www.apa.org/monitor/julaug04/women.

people asked to evaluate employees who enjoy varying levels of success will impose a "success penalty" for women who excel, by downgrading their likability factor. The study's coauthor reported that the female employees who were portrayed to subjects (evaluators) as excelling were perceived as being "more selfish, manipulative and untrustworthy—your typical constellation of 'bitchy' characteristic." Male employees in the study who excelled, by contrast, were viewed as increasingly likeable as their perceived competence level was raised. However, this has not proven to be the case when women "stay in their lane," succeeding in careers that have traditionally attracted and been dominated by women, like teaching. The study's coauthor noted: "Success for women is OK, it seems, unless it is in an area deemed off-limits for them."[17] Unsurprisingly, where employee performance was presented as ambiguous for employees of both sexes, the male employees were adjudged to be competent while the female employees were seen as struggling.[18] Moreover, other studies have concluded that women deemed attractive who work in corporate America are often perceived as less trustworthy, more deserving of termination, and all around more "dangerous."[19]

It is a popularly held belief that men often get promoted to higher levels of power within a workplace than do their female colleagues because they exude more confidence and "know their worth" in the course of navigating their careers in a way that women simply do not.[20] But this may tell only part of the story. In a recent study of three European business schools, researchers concluded that while male employees' success correlated positively with their perceived levels of self-confidence, women, on the other hand, were held liable for coming across as too self-promoting or confident for not displaying an ample amount of corresponding altruism, humility, and graciousness toward those around them.[21] The

---

[17]   Madeline E. Heilman et al., *Penalties for Success: Reactions to Women Who Succeed at Male Gender-Typed Tasks*, 89 J. OF APPLIED PSYCHOL. 416–27 (2004).

[18]   *Id.*

[19]   Leah D. Sheppard et al., *The Femme Fatale Effect: Attractiveness Is a Liability for Businesswomen's Perceived Truthfulness, Trust and Deservingness of Termination*, SEX ROLES: J. RSCH. 1–18 (2019); Maya Salam, *Pretty Can Hurt Women's Careers*, N.Y. TIMES BUS. (Apr. 23, 2019), www.nytimes.com/2019/04/23/business/beauty-women-careers.html.

[20]   Katty Kay et al., *The Confidence Gap*, THE ATLANTIC (May 2014), www.theatlantic.com/magazine/archive/2014/05/the-confidence-gap/359815/; Jack Zenger, *The Confidence Gap in Men and Women: Why It Matters and How to Overcome It*, FORBES (Apr. 8, 2018, 4:22 PM), www.forbes.com/sites/jackzenger/2018/04/08/the-confidence-gap-in-men-and-women-why-it-matters-and-how-to-overcome-it/#30ffa5fd3bfa.

[21]   Stéphanie Thomson, *A Lack of Confidence Isn't What's Holding Back Working Women*, THE ATLANTIC (Sept. 20, 2018), www.theatlantic.com/family/archive/2018/09/women-workplace-confidence-gap/570772/ (citing Laura Guillen, *Is the Confidence Gap Between Men and*

result was their accomplishments being dimmed by a backlash they'd experience for behavior that, on them, is too unseemly, immodest, unlikable, and masculine.[22] A second study confirms that many women who are seen as failing to possess enough confidence are often simply afraid of this backlash and desirous of remaining likeable and nonthreatening enough to be seen as promotable.[23]

Meanwhile, women are being exhorted to "lean in,"[24] watch their intonation to ensure that they don't sound juvenile, and follow many other pieces of advice that cast them, as a group, as deficient in the professionalism department. However, the key to their not being taken seriously enough arguably lies more in their feeling the need to hold back than in their inability to do anything else. And further compounding the problem, the cacophony of advice is seen by some experts as having an effect of confirmation bias: women are receiving the message that they are lacking, and they begin to feel as though everything from their voices to their assertiveness to their confidence truly is flagging.[25] To be sure, there is nothing wrong with exhorting any employee who wants to advance and be taken seriously to be more prepared, proactive, and engaged at work. But we must also take care to understand how much of what we are seeing in terms of reticence at work is a product of societal pressures, negative stereotyping, or merely misapprehension and misperception of what is occurring.

Finally, it should be recalled that while equal pay for equal work is a noble ideal, it ensures equality only where men and women are given the same jobs and tasked precisely with the same work. Where men receive promotions, power, equity, and other advancements that women do not because of the unspoken belief that they "have a family to support," or some other iteration of their being more serious about their work, unspoken beliefs prop up a whole other dimension of pay inequality that is premised on sex-based power inequality.[26]

Women a Myth?, HARV. BUS. REV. (2018), https://hbr.org/2018/03/is-the-confidence-gap-between-men-and-women-a-myth).

[22] *Id.*

[23] Meghan I. H. Lindeman et al., *Women and Self-Promotion: A Test of Three Theories*, 112 PSYCHOL. REP. 219, 221, 228 (2018).

[24] Sheryl Sandberg & Neil Scovell, LEAN IN: WOMEN, WORK, AND THE WILL TO LEAD (2013).

[25] Karen Morley, *Women's Confidence: Lacking, or Just Another Example of Confirmation Bias?*, www.karenmorley.com.au/womens-confidence-lacking-or-just-another-example-of-confirmation-bias/ (last visited Feb. 14, 2020); DeEtta Jones, *Confirmation Bias: How It Hurts Your Organization* (Nov. 21, 2018), https://deettajones.com/confirmation-bias-hurts-organizations/; Heather Murphy, *Picture a Leader, Is She a Woman?*, N.Y. TIMES (Mar. 16, 2018), www.nytimes.com/2018/03/16/health/women-leadership-workplace.html.

[26] Parker et al., *supra* note 11.

THE PANE

There is no denying pay inequality in this country.[27] While many can quote the old refrain that women earn 77 cents on the dollar, this understates the actual pay disparity. As per the Bureau of Labor Statistics, as of January 2020, women across all professions experience a "wage gap" of being paid a mere 81.5 cents for every dollar that a man is paid for doing the same work. According to the Bureau, women make just 85.29 percent of what men make as attorneys, 81.65 percent of what male civil engineers are paid, and a mere 80.41 percent of what male accountants are paid. This phenomenon is not limited to white-collar professions; women earn 87.05 percent of what men earn as bus drivers, 83.33 percent of what men earn driving taxi cabs, and 71.71 percent of what men earn working in retail sales.[28]

As a direct result of the wage gap, a typical woman who works full-time will lose $406,280 of her salary in wages over a forty-year period,[29] and it is estimated that millennial women with college educations will lose an astonishing $1,066,721.[30] According to research announced by the Institute for Women's Policy Research, if the progress made toward pay equity between the sexes keeps up the same pace it has kept over the past fifty years, women will not achieve pay parity until 2059.[31] For women of color, the wait will be even longer – until 2224 for Hispanic women and until 2119 for African American women.[32]

The pay gap is even more extreme if one focuses on women of color and how relatively little they earn as compared with their white male colleagues doing the same work.[33] This underscores the significance of the impact of

[27] *See* Valerie Wilson & Williams M. Rodgers III, *Black-White Wage Gaps Expand with Rising Wage Inequality*, Econ. Pol'y Inst. (Sept. 20, 2016), www.epi.org/publication/black-white-wage-gaps-expand-with-rising-wage-inequality/; Courtney Connley, *Reminder: Today Isn't Equal Pay Day for All Women*, CNBC (Apr. 2, 2019, 11:58 AM), www.cnbc.com/2018/04/10/today-isnt-equal-pay-day-for-black-latina-or-native-american-women.html.

[28] U.S. Bureau of Labor Statistics, *Labor Force Statistics from the Current Population Survey*, www.bls.gov/cps/cpsaat39.htm (last updated Jan. 22, 2021).

[29] *The Lifetime Wage Gap by State for Women Overall*, Nat'l Women's L. Ctr (Mar. 25, 2019), www.catalyst.org/research/womens-earnings-the-wage-gap/.

[30] Jeff Hayes et al., *Wage Gap Will Cost Millennial Women $1 Million over Their Careers*, Inst. for Women's Pol'y Rsch (Apr. 10, 2018), https://iwpr.org/publications/wage-gap-cost-millennial-women-1-million-over-careers/.

[31] *Pay Equity and Discrimination*, Inst. for Women's Pol'y Rsch, https://iwpr.org/issue/employment-education-economic-change/pay-equity-discrimination/.

[32] *Id.*

[33] Andy Kiersz et al., *7 Charts That Show the Glaring Gap Between Men and Women's Salaries in the US*, Bus. Insider (Aug. 26, 2019, 9:16 AM), www.businessinsider.com/gender-wage-pay-gap-charts-2017-3#cities-show-an-even-bigger-discrepancy-especially-for-people-of-color-2.

intersectionality on sexual inequality and highlights the need to look at the impact of pay and other inequality on women of color uniquely. In 2016, the Economic Policy Institute noted that the wage gap was a mainstay of employment in America, even when the gap was adjusted for factors like workers' inexperience, educational backgrounds, or industry.[34] It also observed that the pay gap persists despite the fact that women, as a group, are now better educated than men.[35] Moreover, it should be underscored that "by both race and gender, a higher percentage of black women (9.7 per cent) is enrolled in college than any other group, including Asian women (8.7 per cent), white women (7.1 per cent) and white men (6.1 per cent)."[36] Furthermore, the American Association of University Women's report on the gender wage gap is evidence that pay inequality is greater in higher-paying employment sectors.[37]

Introducing motherhood into the equation only widens the wage gap. The resultant loss of status and compensation that comes from taking time off from working after giving birth looks nothing less than punitive. As per the Institute for Women's Policy Research, between 2001 and 2015, women who took even a year off made 39 percent less in wages than women who worked for the entirety of that time.[38] Further, the Economic Policy Institute has concluded that mothers make less than both women without children and men, whether or not the men are parents,[39] as has a study conducted at the City University of New York that analyzed the incomes of New Yorkers in 1990 and 2010.[40] This conclusion proved steady and consistent irrespective of the employees' occupations or ethnic, racial, or educational backgrounds.[41]

[34] Elise Gould et al., *What Is the Gender Pay Gap and Is It Real?*, ECON. POL'Y INST. (Oct. 20, 2016), www.epi.org/publication/what-is-the-gender-pay-gap-and-is-it-real/.

[35] Anthony P. Carnevale et al., *Women Can't Win: Despite Making Educational Gains and Pursuing High-Wage Majors, Women Still Earn Less than Men* (2018), https://cew .georgetown.edu/wp-content/uploads/Women_FR_Web.pdf.

[36] Samuel Osborne, *Black Women Become Most Educated Group in US*, INDEPENDENT (Jun. 3, 2016) www.independent.co.uk/news/world/americas/black-women-become-most-educated-group-in-us-a7063361.html; *Degrees Conferred by Race and Sex*, NAT'L CENTER FOR EDUCATION STATISTICS, https://nces.ed.gov/fastfacts/display.asp?id=72.

[37] *The Simple Truth About the Gender Pay Gap*, AM. ASS'N OF U. WOMEN (2018), www .aauw.org/research/the-simple-truth-about-the-gender-pay-gap/.

[38] Stephen J. Rose et al., *Still a Man's Labor Market: The Slowly Narrowing Gender Wage Gap*, INST. FOR WOMEN'S POL'Y RSCH (Nov. 26, 2018), https://iwpr.org/publications/still-mans-labor-market/.

[39] Gould et al., *supra* note 33.

[40] Laura Montini, *Study: Men with Families Make More Money*, INC. (May 23, 2014), www .inc.com/laura-montini/study-men-with-families-make-more-money.html.

[41] Gould et al., *supra* note 33; Montini, *supra* note 39; Rose et al., *supra* note 37.

This persistent sex-based pay gap is odd in light of the fact that not only does Title VII mandate equality regarding the sexes' terms and conditions of employment[42] but so does the Equal Pay Act of 1963.[43] This Act, passed as an amendment to the 1930s New Deal era Fair Labor Standards Act, predated the passage of Title VII by a year and was crafted to eradicate sex-based disparities in pay for the same work. The Act forbids a covered employer from discriminating against employees by

> paying wages to employees . . . at a rate less than the rate at which he pays wages to employees of the opposite sex . . . for equal work on jobs[,] the performance of which requires equal skill, effort, and responsibility, and which are performed under similar working conditions, except where such payment is made pursuant to (i) a seniority system; (ii) a merit system; (iii) a system which measures earnings by quantity or quality of production; or (iv) a differential based on any other factor other than sex . . . .[44]

The four affirmative defenses listed in this provision, especially the last "catch-all" provision, have provided avenues for employers to elide liability time and time again. The requirement that the work be "equal" and demand "equal skill, effort, and responsibility," and "under similar working conditions," leaves space and the potential for what some might think of as slight variances in any of these things to remove a claim from the ambit of protection. The defenses, especially the last "catch-all" defense, have been called a "[j]udicially [c]reated [l]oophole" by the National Women's Law Center.[45] Indeed, the wording of the defenses leaves open a space for employers to assert that a host of things, including women's failure to negotiate as vociferously as a man for a higher salary, renders a seemingly sex-correlated pay differential "neutral." The law is not settled on this issue, although there is much research and many scholars' and commentators' arguments that posit and support the idea that categorizing "failure to negotiate" as a "reason other than sex" is wrong. In the first place, according to studies, women don't actually ask for raises or negotiate less well or less often than do men, but they have their requests denied more often.[46] Additionally, to ignore the social stereotypes

---

[42] Title VII of the Civil Rights Act of 1964, 42 U.S.C.S. § 2000e-2.
[43] The Equal Pay Act, 29 U.S.C. § 206(d).
[44] The Equal Pay Act, 29 U.S.C. § 206(d)(1).
[45] *Closing the "Factor Other Than Sex" Loophole in the Equal Pay Act,* NAT'L WOMEN'S L. CTR (April 2011), https://nwlc.org/sites/default/files/pdfs/4.11.11_factor_other_than_sex_fact_sheet_update.pdf.
[46] Benjamin Artz et al., *Research, Women Ask for Raises as Often as Men, but Are Less Likely to Get Them,* HARV. BUS. REV. (Jun. 25, 2018), https://hbr.org/2018/06/research-women-ask-for-raises-as-often-as-men-but-are-less-likely-to-get-them.

that women are less assertive, confident, and willing to negotiate, which result in their unjustly being seen as less deserving, is to ignore a crucial sex-based component of the dynamic at play. Finally, social norms that dictate that women are supposed to be "nice" and not aggressive can operate to socially and professionally disincentivize women from negotiating in the first place. The fact is that when it comes to negotiation, in the words of one scholar, "an assertive woman, no matter how well she presents her arguments in a negotiation, risks decreasing her likeability and therefore her ability to influence the other side to agree with her point of view," and so, "men do not face the same social disincentives as women when they make the decision whether or not to negotiate."[47]

There is also currently a circuit split raging, and thus a debate over whether an employer's factoring in past salary when setting a current salary is actually a neutral, permissible "factor other than sex."[48] Each time a woman gets a new job and her new employer uses her prior salary to determine her new salary and to value her work, any discrimination that went into calculating any past salaries carries over and serves to replicate and build upon that discrimination.[49] Despite this, discrimination-tainted past salaries used to set new salaries have been proffered to courts as neutral "factors other than sex" to justify paying a woman less than a man for doing the same work.[50] Again, scholars and other commentators have decried this.[51]

The federal government and several states have introduced legislation to close some of these loopholes and to effectuate paycheck equality.[52] For example, the Paycheck Fairness Act, introduced by then-Senator Hillary Clinton in 2005, sought, among other things, to limit the "any factor other than sex" language to factors proven to be job-related or in service of some legitimate business interest of the employer.[53] Despite many attempts, it was

---

[47] Christine Elzer, *Wheeling, Dealing, and the Glass Ceiling: Why the Gender Difference in Salary Negotiation Is Not A "Factor Other Than Sex" Under the Equal Pay Act*, 10 GEO. J. GENDER & L. 1, 6 (2009) (internal quotations and citation omitted).

[48] Arianne Renan Barzilay, *Discrimination Without Discriminating? Learned Gender Inequality in the Labor Market and Gig Economy*, 28 CORNELL J.L. & PUB. POL'Y 545, 565 (2019).

[49] *Asking for Salary History Perpetuates Pay Discrimination from Job to Job, supra* note 44.

[50] *See* Elzer, *supra* note 46 at 10 (citing the Equal Pay Act of 1963, 29 U.S.C. § 206(d)(1)).

[51] *See, e.g., id.* at 3; Sabrina L. Brown, *Negotiating Around the Equal Pay Act: Use of the "Factor Other Than Sex" Defense to Escape Liability*, 78 OHIO ST. L. J. 471, 472 (2017).

[52] DEL. CODE ANN. tit. 16, § 709B (2017); COLO. REV. STAT. ANN. § 8-5-102 (effective Jan. 1, 2021); ALA. CODE § 25-1-3 (2019); HAW. REV. STATE. ANN. § 378-2.4 (2019); 820 ILL. COMP. STAT. ANN. 112/10 (West 2019); ME. REV. STAT. ANN. tit. 5, § 4577 (2019); CONN. GEN. STAT. ANN. § 31-40z (2019); Chapter 688, CAL. LAB. CODE § 432.3 (2017); N.Y. LAB. Law § 194-a (2020).

[53] Paycheck Fairness Act, S. 841, 109th Cong. (2005).

never signed into law. There are currently at least seventeen so-called salary history bans that have been passed by states and at least twenty that have been passed by localities.[54] In 2009, the Lilly Ledbetter Fair Pay Act was signed into law by President Obama.[55] This Act helped plaintiffs who were faced with expiring statutes of limitations by rendering each sex-unequal paycheck a fresh violation of the law.[56]

And yet the wage gap persists. And many are content to reduce the gap to the confluence of individual choices made by employees, choices too diffuse and individually explainable to form a systemic problem with a single remedy. In fact, a 2007 study commissioned by the Department of Labor on the wage gap concluded:

> Although additional research in this area is clearly needed . . . the differences in the compensation of men and women are the result of a multitude of factors and that the raw wage gap should not be used as the basis to justify corrective action. Indeed, there may be nothing to correct. The differences in raw wages may be almost entirely the result of the individual choices being made by both male and female workers.[57]

Only later, in 2014, did the Department of Labor concede that "gender discrimination may be responsible for some portion of the unexplained wage gap."[58]

Interestingly, popular discourse still tosses around causes for the gap that range from women negotiating their salaries less vociferously than their male colleagues, to their "opting out" of a traditional career trajectory to have children and go on the "mommy track."[59] The Pew Research Center has posited that it is probably the least ascertainable factors, like discrimination, that bear the most responsibility for the gap. According to the Pew Research

---

[54] *Salary History Bans*, HR Drive (Dec. 6, 2019), www.hrdive.com/news/salary-history-ban-states-list/516662/.

[55] Lilly Ledbetter Fair Pay Act, 42 U.S.C. 2000(a).

[56] *Id.*

[57] Charles E. James, Sr., Deputy Assistant Secretary for Federal Contract Compliance, *Introduction to An Analysis of Reasons for the Disparity in Wages Between Men and Women* 1, 2 (2009).

[58] *Breaking Down the Gender Wage Gap*, Dep't of Lab. (2014), www.dol.gov/wb/resources/b reaking_down_wage_gap.pdf.

[59] Justine Calcagno, *The "Mommy Tax" and "Daddy Bonus,"* Ctr for Latin Am., Caribbean & Latino Stud. (May 2014), www.gc.cuny.edu/CUNY_GC/media/CUNY-Graduate-Center/PDF/Centers/CLACLS/Parenthood-and-Income-in-New-York-City-1990 -2010.pdf; Jackie Bischof, *New York City's Working Fathers Get Daddy Bonus*, Wall Street J. (May 16, 2014, 12:46 PM), https://blogs.wsj.com/metropolis/2014/05/16/new-york-citys-working-fathers-get-daddy-bonus-study/.

Center, 42 percent of women were the victims of sex-based discrimination at work in 2017.[60]

THE PAIN

The pain of the pay gap is as vast as it is intricate. As a multitude of factors and beliefs, like the ones discussed already, result in women being paid less for doing the same work as men, a spiral is produced whereby women's lack of morale, training, opportunities, and positive perception all conspire to siphon them off into lower-paying positions down the road.[61] The gap also works to manage women's expectations so that they are less likely to fight for equal pay as they progress in their work lives. The pain manifests itself in the lives of real people, often entire families, who suffer from the depressed income and career paths of women, which may be especially pronounced where a woman is a single parent or otherwise the main breadwinner of the household.

As stated, although some state and local governments nationwide have prohibited employers from soliciting prior salary information from job applicants in order to stop the proliferation of the wage gap and prevent the disparities of the past from muddying equality in the present, the majority of states and localities have no such laws.[62] Some laws also ban reliance on an applicant's compensation history to set salaries, and still others forbid employers from banning employees from or retaliating against employees for discussing pay amongst one another. However, some courts have said that governments violate the First Amendment when they bar employers from asking certain questions of interviewees. Notably, while the Court of Appeals for the Third Circuit reversed the case, a district court initially found Philadelphia's law that made it unlawful for employers to ask job candidates about their past salaries to be violative of the First Amendment.[63] Meanwhile, employers' ability to discourage discussion of salaries, once set, among employees who could discover inequities creates a virtual code

---

[60] Kim Parker & Cary Funk, *Gender Discrimination Comes in Many Forms for Today's Working Women*, PEW RSCH CTR (Dec. 14, 2017), www.pewresearch.org/fact-tank/2017/12/14/gender-discrimination-comes-in-many-forms-for-todays-working-women/.

[61] Gould et al., *supra* note 33.

[62] *Salary History Bans, supra* note 53.

[63] Chamber of Commerce for Greater Phila. v. City of Phila., 319 F. Supp 3d, 773 (E.D. Pa. 2018) *aff'd in part, rev'd in part* Greater Phila. Chamber of Commerce v. City of Phila., 949 F.3d 116 (3d Cir. 2020); Roy Mauer, *Philadelphia Salary History Ban Violates Free Speech*, SHRM (May 3, 2018), www.shrm.org/resourcesandtools/hr-topics/talent-acquisition/pages/philadelphia-salary-history-ban-violates-free-speech.aspx.

of silence on a topic that requires discussion and aeration to foster greater equality. This allows for the near-unfettered replication of skewed and disparate pay rates.[64]

Additionally, as stated, there is evidence that while women's lack of negotiating prowess is often said to be a cause of the pay gap, this isn't the case at all.[65] A 2014 study in Australia found that women actually ask for raises just as often as their male colleagues do; they simply receive them far less often.[66] Case in point: the study's own authors admitted to being surprised to conclude that women requested raises as often as men did.[67] The women in the study, however, received the requested raises 15 percent of the time, while the men received the requested raises 20 percent of the time.[68] Until society can disabuse itself of these long-held, but false beliefs – like the one that women's lack of assertiveness is the real reason for wage inequality between the sexes – and acknowledge the way in which women are stereotyped, vilified, and socialized differently from men, paycheck equality may remain elusive.

MANIFESTATIONS

The connection between the pay gap and the perception of women as somehow less serious about or less desirous of doing hard work and earning money is made clearer when one examines history.

Numerous women in the inaugural and first few coed classes admitted to Harvard Law School in the 1950s and 1960s, including Supreme Court Justice Ruth Bader Ginsburg, have lamented the indignities that they were forced to suffer as students there. Significant among these was the rumored habit of Law Dean Erwin Griswold, meeting with the few women admitted each year, of asking them, among other things, whether and how they could justify occupying a place in the class that, ostensibly, could have gone to a man who would have

---

[64] *See* Tim Herrera, *Why You Should Tell Your Co-Workers How Much Money You Make*, N.Y. Times (Aug. 31, 2018), www.nytimes.com/2018/08/31/smarter-living/pay-secrecy-national-labor-rights-act.html.

[65] Benjamin Artz et al., *Research: Women Ask for Raises as Often as Men, but Are Less Likely to Get Them*, Harv. Bus. Rev. (Jun. 25, 2018), https://hbr.org/2018/06/research-women-ask-for-raises-as-often-as-men-but-are-less-likely-to-get-them; Claire Wasserman, *Women DO Ask for Raises—We Just Aren't Getting Them*, InStyle (May 6, 2019, 12:00 PM), www.instyle.com/news/women-ask-for-raises-dont-get-them-harvard-study.

[66] Artz et al., *supra* note 64.

[67] *Id.*

[68] *Id.*

the burden of supporting a family.[69] In a 1993 interview done by the Harvard Crimson, Dean Griswold vehemently denied opposing women's presence in the class, claiming that Justice Ginsburg was "dead wrong" about him, and that by asking for women's justifications, he was merely playing "devil's advocate," and garnering support for his own beliefs that the women would, in fact, become lawyers.[70]

Even this defense, given nearly forty years after the events, bespeaks his fear that the women might avail themselves of, but fail to use, the scarce resource that was a Harvard Law education. This abiding belief that women are somehow more liable to bypass or exit the workforce to live a more domestic life is still evident in many today.[71] Men and women alike often seem to subscribe to the belief that women are more likely to need to leave their professional track upon becoming parents in a way that men simply are not.[72] The sexes are thus often paid, trained, and treated accordingly. As this stigma takes hold, it likely fuels the belief held by 37 percent of women that motherhood is going to prove a disruption to their careers; a mere 13 percent of men believe that fatherhood will similarly disrupt their careers.[73]

In 2007, a Harvard study concluded that mothers were perceived to be less committed to their work than were female employees who were not mothers.[74] Conversely, fathers were perceived to be even more committed than their male colleagues who were not fathers.[75] This reinforces the notion, still pervasive throughout American culture, that working moms' priority cannot (or should not) be their work, while working dads' priority must be their work and the income on which their families rely. Moreover, that same study found

---

[69] *See* Dahlia Lithwick, *"It's Amazing to Me How Distinctly I Remember Each of These Women,"* SLATE (Jul. 21, 2020, 5:06 AM), https://slate.com/news-and-politics/2020/07/ruth-bader-ginsburg-interview-transcript.html#griswold.

[70] Ira E. Stoli, *Ginsberg Blasts Harvard Law*, HARV. CRIMSON (Jul. 23, 1993), www.thecrimson.com/article/1993/7/23/ginsburg-blasts-harvard-law-pin-testimony/.

[71] Felix Salmon, *Why Women Leave the Workforce*, AXIOS (Nov. 4, 2018), www.axios.com/why-women-leave-the-workforce-profession-66341a45-a2b8-49bf-ba26-e7181fdb837f.html; Alex Mahadevan, *Women Are Leaving the Workforce at a Staggering Rate — Here's Why*, THE PENNY HOARDER (Mar. 1, 2019), www.thepennyhoarder.com/make-money/career/shrinking-number-of-women-in-the-workforce/; Liz Elting, *Why Women Quit*, FORBES (Aug. 21, 2019, 3:32 PM), www.forbes.com/sites/lizelting/2019/08/21/why-women-quit/#44904f8216fa.

[72] Calcagno, *supra* note 58; Bischof, *supra* note 58.

[73] Farha Khaliadi, *The Trust About Women Who "Choose" to Leave the Workforce*, WOMEN'S MEDIA CTR (Dec. 8, 2017), www.womensmediacenter.com/fbomb/the-truth-about-women-who-choose-to-leave-the-workforce.

[74] Shelley J. Correll et al., *Getting a Job: Is There a Motherhood Penalty?*, 5 AM. J. OF SOC. 112, 1297 (2007), available through HARV. KENNEDY SCH. at http://gap.hks.harvard.edu/getting-job-there-motherhood-penalty.

[75] *Id.*

that pregnant workers are seen as less capable than their colleagues.[76] Working dads, by contrast, often receive a pay bump, ostensibly because of some unspoken desire to ensure that they can provide for their families, and because they are seen as being more committed to their work.[77]

TAKEAWAYS

The pay gap between the sexes has been so stark and so persistent that, unlike other issues, there is reason to think there may be a legislative or other organized movement to combat it, perhaps *without* a discomfiting probe into the unspoken beliefs that might underlie it. That said, it is worth thinking about the assumptions that tacitly underlie the expectations, valuations, and understandings that employers bring into pay-setting negotiations or processes.

Is it the case that a male candidate for hire or promotion is seen, on some level of consciousness, as one who either needs or deserves to make more money than his female colleagues? Is he, as a result of this perceived "provider" or "breadwinner" status, somehow seen as being more serious or committed? Does his status as a father make him seem more responsible, earnest, likeable, or sympathetic, whereas his colleague who has become a mother is perceived as more distracted, distant, and perhaps resentful or "on the way out" – for no other reason than the simple juxtaposition of their sexes and life events? These are questions worth considering, and it may be that the simple introduction of these thoughts into the conscious minds of those who might struggle with these stereotypes subconsciously may be beneficial in terms of fairer outcomes. Thus, again, conversation, education, and training may be an employer's first line of defense against inequality.

But, as mentioned, legislatures have already started to take up the mantle – attempting to ban employers from inquiring about or weighing information regarding prior salary when calculating future earnings. Even though not all of these bans have been upheld by courts, and even though many states and localities do nothing to ban this behavior, there is nothing to stop employers from undertaking to cease the practice on their own initiative. In light of the fact that such queries and factoring in of past salary can simply replicate the discriminatory practices of other employers and other inequalities, it would seem to be a good business practice to avoid inquiring. At the very least, employers who insist on asking can calculate future salaries for new or

[76] *Id.*
[77] *Id.*

promoted employees armed with knowledge of and vigilance with respect to the phenomenon.

In a 2011 survey conducted by the Institute for Women's Policy Research, half of the adults responding said that talking about salary was either prohibited or discouraged by their employers.[78] These discussions are, of course, a great way of affording the pay gap problem – shrouded as it is in opacity – some transparency and light. In this vein, several states, including Colorado, Michigan, and Illinois, as well as the District of Columbia and California, have passed measures designed to curb this employer behavior, and in 2014, President Obama signed an executive order pertaining to wage transparency for federal contractors.[79]

Additionally, employers should be mindful that the National Labor Relations Act (NLRA),[80] which governs almost all employers when it comes to certain things, affords most employees the unfettered right to "engage in concerted activities for their mutual aid or protection."[81] Interestingly, the National Labor Relations Board (NLRB), the body that, along with courts, interprets and enforces the NLRA, has been interpreting this provision as covering the right of employees to discuss their wages, as a term or condition of their employment, as an effort to act in concert to better their employment lot.[82] Thus, employers' policies that constrain the ability of employees to openly discuss salary are susceptible to being found to be violative of the NLRA's section 7.[83] While it should be noted that the NLRA's process is notoriously clunky, and its remedies notoriously limited, cases brought under it have resulted in the scrutiny and sometimes rejection of policies promulgated by employers like Lowe's, for example.[84] It is thus a good (if not best) practice for employers to refrain from discouraging salary discussions and disclosures among employees.

---

[78] Ariane Hegewisch et al., *Pay Secrecy and Wage Discrimination*, INST. FOR WOMEN'S POL'Y RSCH (Jun. 9, 2011), https://iwpr.org/publications/pay-secrecy-and-wage-discrimination/.

[79] Exec. Order No. 13673, 79 Fed. Reg. 45309 (2014).

[80] National Labor Relations Act, 29 U.S.C. §§ 151–69.

[81] *Id.*

[82] Flex Frac Logistics, L.L.C. v. NLRB, 746 F.3d 205, 211 (5th Cir. 2014) (enforcing the NLRB's order that Flex Frac Logistics violated the National Labor Relations Act by maintaining a policy prohibiting employees from discussing wages).

[83] Nancy Owen, *Is It Illegal to Prohibit Employees from Talking Salary?*, EAST COAST RISK MGMT, https://eastcoastriskmanagement.com/is-it-illegal-to-prohibit-employees-from-talking-salary/ (last visited Mar. 3, 2020).

[84] Lowe's Home Centers, LLC, 368 N.L.R.B. 133 (2019).

From an employee's point of view, it is clear that knowledge is power; arming oneself with accurate information enables one to make compelling arguments for equal pay to one's employer. Lara, a professor, recommends approaching an employer with the question "What do I need to do to earn as much as X man?" "This way," she explains,

> [y]ou're not playing defense—making a case for your own worth and leaving the choice to them. You're starting with your own "unspoken" premise—that the employer has a cogent and ... abiding belief in compliance with the dictates of equal pay for equal work—and you're asking the employer to articulate to you what the contours and nuances of their fair structure look like. Where do you fit in to what should be their coherent framework?

9

"Bad People Don't Do Good Things, but Good People Frequently Say Bad Things" (and Employment Discrimination Plaintiffs Can't Be Fully Trusted)

I complained to my mentor at work that I felt like my department chair spoke to me in ways that he wouldn't speak to one of my male colleagues and that he seemed to really have it in for me lately. He had recently made some references to whether I had my "head in the game" now that I was back from my honeymoon, and when he spoke to me about the partnership track, he wasn't encouraging to me like he was to my male colleagues. He seemed to have doubts about my "commitment," even though there was no factual basis for concern — my work was objectively exceeding expectations. When I complained to my mentor that I had a nagging feeling about being held back in his head by my sex, she seemed really surprised, and quickly said "That's not possible. He is literally the one who pushed to hire you, and he fought to get you on his team when you started here four years ago. You shouldn't even think that."

— Devin, twenty-eight, management consultant

THE BELIEF

The law and the judicial system are a mystery to many who rely somewhat on the knowledge that legal protections exist, but don't necessarily follow cases or truly understand how, exactly, the law works. As a result, there are widely held misconceptions about the law's content, interpretation, and capacity, especially in the area of employment discrimination law.[1] As misplaced reliance on nonexistent protections becomes complacence, people stop questioning inequality. The fact of the matter is that while many believe that Title VII affords blanket protection against sex- and other types of discrimination, the law and the legal system fail sex discrimination plaintiffs regularly due to the vague dictates of Title VII itself, coupled with faulty

---

[1] Rosa Ehrenreich Brooks, *Dignity and Discrimination: Toward a Pluralistic Understanding of Workplace Harassment*, 88 GEO. L.J. 3, 8 (1999).

judge-made doctrines, which were intended to serve as adjudicatory devices and streamline interpretation.[2]

Courts craft and rely upon adjudicatory frameworks to aid them in weighing evidence, applying the law, and resolving legal questions before them; but these devices are supposed to launch and streamline analysis, not substantively supplement or alter the law. To further confuse things, courts too often muddy their Title VII analyses with specious and clumsy doctrines and devices that vary wildly, leading to inconsistent adjudication of cases nationwide.[3]

These doctrines, moreover, are often asymmetrical or lopsided, meaning that the bedrock principles behind them do not seem to apply consistently across the board to both exonerate *and* implicate accused discriminators. To put this simply, we must review briefly: a case survives summary judgment and goes to trial when a court decides that, viewed in the light most favorable to the non-movant (usually the plaintiff), the case presents open, triable issues – in other words, a demonstrable version of what happened that, if believed by a trier or jury, entitles the plaintiff to win her case.[4] Judges and juries are supposed to consider evidence that is relevant, meaning, according to the Federal Rules of Evidence, any testimony or other evidence that has "any tendency to make the existence of any fact that is of consequence to the

---

[2] *See* Suzette M. Malveaux, *Front Loading and Heavy Lifting: How Pre-dismissal Discovery Can Address the Detrimental Effect of Iqbal on Civil Rights Cases*, 14 LEWIS & CLARK L. REV. 65, 95 (2010); Kevin M. Clermont & Stewart J. Schwab, *Employment Discrimination Plaintiffs in Federal Court: From Bad to Worse?*, 3 HARV. L. & POL'Y REV. 103 (2009); Wendy Parker, *Lessons in Losing: Race Discrimination in Employment*, 81 NOTRE DAME L. REV. 889, 897–900, 899 n.49 (2006); Kevin M. Clermont & Stewart J. Schwab, *How Employment Discrimination Plaintiffs Fare in Federal Court*, 1 J. EMPIRICAL LEGAL STUD. 429 (2004); Michael Selmi, *Why Are Employment Discrimination Cases So Hard to Win?*, 61 LA. L. REV. 555, 574–75 (2001); Ruth Colker, *The Americans with Disabilities Act: A Windfall for Defendants*, 34 HARV. C.R.- C.L. L. REV. 99, 109 (1999); Ann C. McGinley, *Credulous Courts and the Tortured Trilogy: The Improper Use of Summary Judgment in Title VII and ADEA Cases*, 34 B.C. L. REV. 203, 205–06 (1993).

[3] *See* Robert A. Kearney, *The High Price of Price Waterhouse: Dealing with Direct Evidence of Discrimination*, 5 U. PA. J. LAB. & EMP. L. 303, 320 (2003) ("When a vague standard is passed out to hundreds of federal court judges, the results are exactly what one might expect: inconsistency and confusion."); *see also* Hopkins, 490 U.S. at 291 (Kennedy, J., dissenting) ("Lower courts long have had difficulty applying McDonnell Douglas and Burdine. Addition of a second burden-shifting mechanism, the application of which itself depends on assessment of credibility and a determination whether evidence is sufficiently direct and substantial, is not likely to lend clarity to the process."); Brian W. McKay, *Mixed Motives Mix-Up: The Ninth Circuit Evades the Direct Evidence Requirement in Disparate Treatment Cases*, 38 TULSA L. REV. 503, 520 (2003) ("There can be little doubt that the direct evidence requirement has led to some bewilderment among the lower courts and a lack of uniformity even within single circuits.").

[4] FED. R. CIV. P. 56.

determination of the action more probable or less probable than it would be without the evidence."[5]

However, as will be explained, when accused discriminators say or do things that lawyers seek to have considered as evidence of discrimination, courts are shockingly inclined to impute significance into the "good" deeds and words of these individuals, while attenuating any connection between the "bad" deeds and words of these individuals and whether they engaged in unlawful sex- (or other) discrimination under Title VII. This practice, which has the effect of streamlining case dockets by disposing of cases, seems to be an outgrowth of the inexplicable, unspoken belief that "Bad people don't do good things, but good people frequently say bad things."

This belief joins with other illogical and inconsistent beliefs about the people who sue their employers ("Employment discrimination plaintiffs can't be fully trusted") and the people who stand accused of discriminating ("People are either 'good' or 'bad,' and it's easier to believe that they are good") to cultivate what scholars have referred to as judicial "shortcuts" to summary judgment. This often means prematurely winnowing out of the legal system many a meritorious case – layering another pane onto the glass ceiling. Courts have also persisted, despite there being no basis for their doing so, in bifurcating evidence of employment discrimination into "direct" and "indirect" evidence, and then using the spurious classifications to cram cases into adjudicatory frameworks that may or may not result in a fair evaluation of the sole relevant question: whether a reasonable juror could ever reasonably conclude that the plaintiff was discriminated against or harassed because of her sex.

THE PANE

Legal scholars have long bemoaned the multitude of seemingly special and sometimes logically inconsistent requirements that judges nationwide have imposed upon employment discrimination plaintiffs. These requirements seem to fly in the face of how most other traditional litigation is conducted.[6] A review of some of these, in contrast with the plain task before a court adjudicating a Title VII discrimination case, would be appropriate.

---

[5] FED. R. EVID. 401.
[6] *See* Michael J. Zimmer, *A Chain of Inferences Proving Discrimination*, 79 U. COLO. L. REV. 1243 (2008); *see also* Charles A. Sullivan, *Plausibility Pleading Employment Discrimination*, 52 WM. & MARY L. REV. 1613 (2011); Sandra F. Sperino, *Rethinking Discrimination Law*, 110 MICH. L. REV. 69 (2011); Suzanne B. Goldberg, *Discrimination by Comparison*, 120 YALE L. J. 728 (2011); Michael J. Zimmer, *Title VII's Last Hurrah: Can Discrimination Be Plausibly Pled*, 2014 U. CHI. LEGAL F. 19 (2014).

To review, a Title VII case, like any case filed, is theoretically supposed to survive a defendant employer's motion for summary judgment and proceed to trial, *unless* a judge decides that all of the evidence that's been collected for trial – all of the testimony, documents, recordings, emails, and any other evidence – viewed in the light most favorable to the plaintiff – renders the plaintiff *legally incapable* of winning.[7] That is to say, to dispose of the case before trial and declare it won by the employer, the judge must find that *no rational juror* could possibly look at all of the evidence presented by both sides, apply the relevant law and legal standards, and find that the plaintiff could win. Only when it is determined that no reasonable juror could possibly find for the plaintiff should a case terminate with no chance to go to trial.[8] And, in theory, under Title VII, there is no one clear path toward the answer. No singular adjudicatory framework, doctrine, or "shortcut" ought to be able to short-circuit or otherwise bypass this central and broad query.

This would seem to indicate that lots of cases would be deemed capable of proceeding to trial so that a judge or a jury could resolve them and come to a conclusion on the ultimate question – in a Title VII suit, the question of whether the employer unlawfully discriminated against the plaintiff because of her protected class status (here, sex). It would seem to indicate that a fair amount of cases could and would be won. In 2018, some 24,655 charges of sex discrimination under Title VII were filed with the Equal Employment Opportunity Commission (EEOC)[9] (a preliminary step to getting a case properly filed in court), but, in that same year, only 111 lawsuits were filed alleging sex discrimination under Title VII.[10] The cases are simply not making their way into court, and when they do, outcomes are dubious; studies have concluded that roughly a mere third of plaintiffs with workplace sex discrimination cases are emerging victorious.[11]

---

[7] See FED. R. CIV. P. 56; *see also* John V. Jansonius, *The Role of Summary Judgment in Employment Discrimination Litigation*, 4 LAB. LAW. 747 (1988).

[8] See McGinley, *supra* note 2, 247.

[9] Sex-Based Charges filed with EEOC, EEOC, www.eeoc.gov/eeoc/statistics/enforcement/sex .cfm.

[10] EEOC Litigation Statistics, EEOC, www.eeoc.gov/eeoc/statistics/enforcement/litigation .cfm.

[11] Laura Beth Nielsen et al., *Individual Justice or Collective Legal Mobilization? Employment Discrimination Litigation in the Post Civil Rights United States*, 7 J. OF EMPIRICAL LEGAL STUD. 175 (2010); Joseph A. Seiner, *Workplace Sex Discrimination Claims Are Common – But They're Not Making It into Court*, THE NAT'L INTEREST (Oct. 10, 2019), https://nationalinter est.org/blog/buzz/workplace-sex-discrimination-claims-are-common-%E2%80%93-they%E2 %80%99re-not-making-it-court-87006.

Recall that Title VII as applied to sex discrimination merely asks whether a plaintiff has been discriminated against with respect to the terms, conditions, or privileges of her employment "because of" her sex. It expressly allows for a gauging of whether there has been discriminatory disparate treatment, as well as for a cause of action predicated on a disparate impact theory, under which the plaintiff need not prove intent. But other than that, the statute contours no special evidentiary requirements or doctrines for a trier to employ while weighing the facts to get to an answer to the central question of discrimination. So, why aren't more cases proceeding to trial? Why are so many cases getting dismissed each year, over plaintiffs' protestations that they can adduce evidence that is relevant (and relevancy is a low bar to meet)? What is going on here? Well, it turns out that there are several things going on.

Special Evidence Requirements? The Rise and Fall of the "Mixed Motive Case"

The Supreme Court introduced "mixed motive" analysis in Title VII cases in 1989.[12] Located in Justice O'Connor's concurrence, the mixed motive theory of a case permitted a plaintiff to establish discrimination when additional, lawful motivations for an adverse employment action exist alongside unlawful discriminatory reasons and motivations.[13] Subsequently, lower courts started to bifurcate cases, shunting them into frameworks based on their assessment of the strength of the evidence presented. Cases with "indirect evidence" proffered by the plaintiff typically were assessed using the *McDonnell Douglas* pretext framework (the plaintiff sets up a prima facie case of discrimination, the employer proffers a legitimate, nondiscriminatory reason for what it did, and then the plaintiff shoulders the burden of proving that this "reason" is a pretext for discrimination). By contrast, if a plaintiff proffered "direct evidence" of discrimination, a straight mixed motive analysis was employed.

In 1991, Title VII was amended to clarify, among other things, that a plaintiff could prevail in a Title VII suit where she was able to prove that "race, color, religion, sex, or national origin was a motivating factor for any employment practice, even though other factors also motivated the practice."[14] Courts nonetheless persisted in the bifurcation of cases and the rigid shunting of

---

[12] *Hopkins*, 490 U.S. 228.
[13] *Id.* at 261 (O'Connor, J., concurring).
[14] Title VII of the Civil Rights Act of 1964, 42 U.S.C. § 2000e–2(m).

cases into different frameworks, depending on the evidence proffered by the plaintiff.[15]

This approach, though widely adopted, was met with a good deal of criticism. After all, neither the statute nor the Supreme Court had either required or defined any different types of evidence.[16] Heightening the threshold for proof of the issue to be determined based on a preliminary assessment of the strength of the evidence struck many as arbitrary and circular.[17]

In 2003, the Supreme Court basically said as much in *Desert Palace, Inc.* v. *Costa,* which held that a plaintiff with a Title VII individual disparate treatment claim was not required to proffer "direct evidence" to merit a "motivating factor" jury instruction.[18] The Supreme Court noted that "[s]ince the passage of the 1991 Act, . . . a number of courts have held that direct evidence is required to establish liability under" a mixed motives theory.[19] It reasoned, however, that nothing in the plain language of the statute or in Congress's intent (evinced by the way in which it defined relevant terms in the statute) seemed to call for a heightened proof requirement.[20] Finally, highlighting the way in which indirect evidence is entirely permissible in proving criminal law cases, let alone a violation of Title VII, the Supreme Court observed: "The reason for treating circumstantial and direct evidence alike is both clear and deep rooted: 'Circumstantial evidence is not only sufficient, but may also be more certain, satisfying and persuasive than direct evidence.'"[21] In short, there was no basis to impose a heightened requirement on plaintiffs, and there was no reason to insist upon "direct evidence," whatever that meant, for any particular treatment of one's case under Title VII.

---

[15]   *See* Troupe v. May Dep't Stores Co., 20 F.3d 734, 737 (7th Cir. 1994); Mickens v. Penn Mut. Ins. Co., 1994 U.S. Dist. LEXIS 10464 (E.D. Pa. Jul. 29, 1994); Victory v. Hewlett-Packard Co., 34 F. Supp. 2d 809 (E.D.N.Y. 1999); Starceski v. Westinghouse Elec. Corp., 54 F.3d 1089 (3d Cir. 1995); Azar v. TGI Friday's, 945 F. Supp. 485 (E.D.N.Y. 1996); Jackson v. Georgia-Pacific Corp., 296 N.J. Super. 1 (1996); Demick v. City of Joliet, 135 F. Supp. 2d 921, 933 (N.D. Ill. Mar. 29, 2001); Wilson v. Russell-Stanley Corp., 2002 U.S. Dist. LEXIS 24268, at *8 (N.D. Ill. Dec. 13, 2002); Chi. Hous. Auth. v. Human Rights Comm'n, 325 Ill. App. 3d 1115 (2001); City of Austin Police Dep't v. Brown, 96 S.W.3d 588 (Tex. 2002); Watkins v. Nabisco Biscuit Co., 224 F. Supp. 2d 852 (D.N.J. 2002).

[16]   Kearney, *supra* note 3, at 308–09 ("there have been some cracks in the bifurcated approach and calls for reform . . . the [Civil Rights Act of 1991] does not use the term 'direct evidence' nor explicitly confine the 'motivating factor' standard to a subset of discrimination cases").

[17]   Zimmer, *supra* note 6, 1259.

[18]   Desert Palace, Inc. v. Costa, 539 U.S. 90, 92 (2003).

[19]   *Id.* at 95.

[20]   *Id.* at 97.

[21]   *Id.* at 100.

Courts, however, continued to bifurcate cases, as described above, despite the fact that, as discussed, neither Title VII nor the Supreme Court has mandated any special treatment of certain "types" of evidence when deciding Title VII cases. These courts have, over time, taken it upon themselves to define "direct evidence" as "evidence that proves the existence of a discriminatory motive ... without inference or presumption,"[22] and "indirect evidence" as circumstantial evidence or evidence that requires some inferential leap in order to get to the conclusion sought to be proven.[23] Thus, many courts have determined that if an employment discrimination plaintiff cannot proffer what they term "direct evidence," or "smoking gun" evidence of discrimination, they then must have their case shunted through the *McDonnell Douglas* burden-shifting framework.[24]

There are, however, a few notable incursions that have been made into the artificially ramped-up evidentiary requirements for discrimination cases that have led to haphazard, tentative, and inconsistent treatment by the courts. In 2016, Judge Easterbrook of the Seventh Circuit Court of Appeals launched an out-and-out offensive against his jurisdiction's "convincing mosaic" requirement for employment discrimination cases, as well as the baseless bifurcation of evidence into "direct" and "indirect" evidence.[25] The court of appeals held that courts' attempts "to shoehorn all evidence into two 'methods,' and [their] insistence that either method be implemented by looking for a 'convincing mosaic,' detracted attention from the sole question that matters: Whether

22 *See* Bergene v. Salt River Project Agric. Improvement & Power Dist., 272 F.3d 1136, 1141 (9th Cir. 2001); Carter v. Miami, 870 F.2d 578, 581–82 (11th Cir. 1989); Lopez v. River Oaks Imaging & Diagnostic Group, Inc., 542 F. Supp. 2d 653, 661 (S.D. Tex. 2008).

23 *See* Chavez v. Credit Nation Auto Sales, LLC, 641 F. App'x 883, 884 (11th Cir. 2016); *see also* Cross v. Marshalls of MA, Inc., 2019 U.S. Dist. LEXIS 147801, at *20 (N.D. Cal. Aug. 29, 2019); Townsend v. United States, 2019 U.S. Dist. LEXIS 145794, at *27 (D.D.C. Aug. 27, 2019); Maynard v. Bd. of Regents of Div. of Univ., 342 F.3d 1281, 1289 (11th Cir. 2003); Helfrich v. Lehigh Valley Hosp., 2005 U.S. Dist. LEXIS 14792 (E.D. Pa., Jul. 21, 2005).

24 Palmer v. Pentair, No. 18–02638-CM-TJJ, 2019 WL 3239350, at *2 (D. Kan. Jul. 18, 2019) ("A plaintiff lacking direct evidence of discrimination may rely on indirect evidence under the McDonnell Douglas burden-shifting framework."); Townsend v. United States, 2019 U.S. Dist. LEXIS 145794, at *24 (D.D.C. Aug. 27, 2019) ("Absent direct evidence of discrimination, a plaintiff may prove discrimination through circumstantial evidence using the familiar three-part burden-shifting framework of McDonnell Douglas"); Cross v. Marshalls of MA, Inc., 2019 U.S. Dist. LEXIS 147801, at *25 (N.D. Cal. Aug. 29, 2019) ("Plaintiff has not presented direct evidence of discrimination, and thus the Court must evaluate the evidence under the *McDonnell Douglas* framework."); Singh v. Cordle, 2019 U.S. App. LEXIS 25968, at *24 (10th Cir. 2019); Bryant v. McAleenan, 2019 U.S. Dist. LEXIS 145463, at *35 (D. Md. Aug. 27, 2019); Nunan v. Cty. of Chester, 2019 U.S. Dist. LEXIS 143321, at *17 (E.D. Pa. Aug. 22, 2019); Iyoha v. Architect of the Capitol, 927 F.3d 561, 566 (D.C. Cir. 2019).

25 Ortiz v. Werner Enters., Inc., 834 F.3d 760, 764 (7th Cir. 2016).

a reasonable juror could conclude that [the plaintiff] would have kept his job if he had a different [protected class status], and everything else had remained the same."[26]

Judge Easterbrook lambasted courts for their arbitrary and baselessly harsh approach to employment discrimination cases, noting: "The use of disparate methods and the search for elusive mosaics has complicated and sidetracked employment-discrimination litigation for many years. ... During the last decade, every member of this court has disapproved both the multiple methods and the search for mosaics."[27] Referencing "legal kudzu," he noted the wild inconsistency and the seeming lack of understanding of the relevant analysis on the part of courts that "occasionally treat[] 'convincing mosaic' as a legal requirement, even while cautioning in other opinions that it must not be so understood."[28] He declared: "The time has come to jettison these diversions and refocus analysis on the substantive legal issue."[29] The Court thus clarified the analysis for future cases, noting that its sole issue was "with the treatment of 'convincing mosaic' as if it were a legal requirement."[30] It held that courts in the Seventh Circuit needed to cease "separating 'direct' from 'indirect' evidence and proceeding as if they were subject to different legal standards."[31] Rather, "all evidence belongs in a single pile and must be evaluated as a whole."[32]

Scholars and commentators agree that, while it is still relatively early, this opinion should be impactful beyond the Seventh Circuit.[33] However, the Seventh Circuit seemed to create confusion in *Ortiz* when it noted that nothing in its decision was to affect the *McDonnell Douglas* or any other framework.[34] In any event, courts nationwide persist in conflating and confusing evidentiary standards, erecting and invoking frameworks that serve to erode and eclipse evidence, and misconstruing a Supreme Court directive[35] to refrain from labeling and distinguishing mechanically among different

---

[26]   *Id.* at 765.

[27]   *Id.* at 764.

[28]   *Id.* at 764–65.

[29]   *Id.* at 765.

[30]   *Id.*

[31]   *Id.* at 766.

[32]   *Id.*

[33]   Jason R. Bent, *Hope for Zimmerism: Overcoming the Empathy Problem in Antidiscrimination Law*, 20 EMP. RTS. & EMP. POL'Y J. 277 295–97 (2016), https://heinonline.org/HOL/LandingPage?handle=hein.journals/emplrght20&div=15&id=&page= (last visited Jun. 10, 2018); Zachary J. Strongin, *Fleeing the Rat's Nest: Title VII Jurisprudence after Ortiz v. Werner Enterprises, Inc.*, 83 BROOK. L. REV. 725, 749 (2017).

[34]   *See* Ortiz v. Werner Enters., Inc., 834 F.3d 760, 766 (7th Cir. 2016).

[35]   *Costa*, 539 U.S. at 101.

types of evidence.[36] They continue to ignore their mandates to (1) grant summary judgment to a defendant and dispose of a case only when it appears unwinnable to a reasonable person who construes all contested facts in the light most favorable to the plaintiff and (2) focus on the overarching question of whether the plaintiff was discriminated against because of her sex without becoming distracted by premature presumptions, evidence labeling or valuations, or excuses to wholly disregard evidence, rather than merely assign it a lesser weight or consider it in context.

Asymmetry in the Same Actor Inference and the Stray Comment Doctrine

In the course of routinizing ways of adjudicating employment discrimination cases, many courts seem to feel secure and even emboldened in their some-times-wanton dismissal of cases that might, if thoroughly assessed, be permitted to get to trial.[37] Two doctrines that have not only enabled courts to prematurely winnow out potentially meritorious cases over the decades but also, when examined alongside one another, evince an asymmetry that reveals a systemic bias against employment discrimination plaintiffs are the "same actor inference" and the "stray comments doctrine."[38]

It is truly surprising that so many sex discrimination cases get disposed of on summary judgment. A study conducted by Lex Machina revealed that, from January 2009 through July 2017, 54,810 employment cases were filed and closed.[39] Between those years, employees won just 1 percent of the time and employers prevailed on summary judgment about 13 percent of the time.[40] After all, discriminatory intent is at the core of every case brought under Title VII's prohibition against discrimination "because of" an individual's sex. In theory, it should take an awful lot for a defendant to convince a court, prior to trial, that there is no way that unlawful discrimination took place. Further, the Federal Rules of Evidence, the rules that govern what evidence may be

---

[36] *See* Troupe v. May Dep't Stores Co., 20 F.3d 734, 737 (7th Cir. 1994); Mickens v. Penn Mut. Ins. Co., 1994 U.S. Dist. LEXIS 10464 (E.D. Pa. Jul. 29, 1994); Victory v. Hewlett-Packard Co., 34 F. Supp. 2d 809 (E.D.N.Y. 1999); Chi. Hous. Auth. v. Human Rights Comm'n, 325 Ill. App. 3d 1115 (2001).

[37] *See* Natasha T. Martin, *Immunity for Hire: How the Same-Actor Doctrine Sustains Discrimination in the Contemporary Workplace*, 40 CONN. L. REV. 1117, 1121 (2008).

[38] *See* Kerri Lynn Stone, *Taking in Strays: A Critique of the Stray Comment Doctrine in Employment Discrimination Law*, 76 MO. L. REV. 149, 167 (2012); Kerri Lynn Stone, *Shortcuts in Employment Discrimination Law*, 56 ST. LOUIS U. L.J. 111 113, 114 (2011).

[39] Sean Captain, *Workers Win Only 1% of Federal Civil Rights Lawsuits at Trial*, FAST CO. (Jul. 31, 2017), www.fastcompany.com/40440310/employees-win-very-few-civil-rights-lawsuits.

[40] *Id.*

presented to a jury for consideration at trial, define relevant evidence broadly as evidence that "has any tendency to make a fact more probable or less probable than it would be without the evidence," and "the fact is of consequence in determining the action."[41] There seems to be little reason to disregard relevant evidence at any stage of a proceeding.

But this is not how employment discrimination cases tend to go. There is a widespread fear, expressed by judges and commentators alike, of an opening of the "floodgates" of litigation, whereby too many people flood the court system with inconsequential complaints.[42] Moreover, many legal scholars have suggested that judges view employment discrimination plaintiffs with skepticism, even more so than they view other plaintiffs.[43] And this skepticism, it has been posited by scholars, is reflected by the practice of prematurely disposing of cases through the mechanism of summary judgment, before a trial can be had.[44] Judges do this by promulgating and deploying legal doctrines to aid in interpretation. These doctrines may include inferences to be made under certain circumstances and rules about when to factor in evidence and when to disregard it. These doctrines evolve with the common law, and, often, courts take cues from one another, as the doctrines spread.

Rooted in societal beliefs about what discrimination looks like and when it is evinced or belied, these doctrines have taken hold despite having been widely criticized.[45] Some have been in use for decades, but because (1) they are not very well known outside of employment litigation circles[46] and (2) they disadvantage all employment discrimination plaintiffs, not just women,[47] they are not often commonly attributed to or correlated with the problem of the glass ceiling.

---

[41] FED R. EVID. 401.

[42] *See* Toby J. Stern, *Comment: Federal Judges and Fearing the "Floodgates of Litigation,"* 6 U. PA. J. CONST. L. 377 (2003); Marin K. Levy, *Judging the Flood of Litigation,* 80 U. CHI. L. REV. 1007 (2013).

[43] *See* Stephen Plass, *Private Dispute Resolution and the Future of Institutional Workplace Discrimination,* 54 HOW. L.J. 45, 67, 68–69 (2010); Sandra F. Sperino, Disbelief Doctrines, 39 BERKELEY J. EMP. & LAB. L. 231, 233–36 (2018); Nancy Gertner, *Losers' Rules,* 122 YALE L. J. ONLINE 109 (Oct. 17, 2012), http://yalelawjournal.org/forum/losers-rules (last visited Jun. 10, 2018); Selmi, *supra* note 2.

[44] *See* Trina Jones, *Anti-discrimination Law in Peril?,* 75 MO. L. REV. 423, 425 (2010); *see also* Gertner, *supra* note 44.

[45] *See* Stone, Shortcuts in Employment Discrimination Law, *supra* note 39; *see also* Martin, *supra* note 37, at 1121.

[46] *Id.*

[47] *See, e.g.,* Martin, *supra* note 37, at 1122.

The Stray Comments Doctrine

The "stray comments" doctrine originated in an offhand comment about a concurrence authored by Justice O'Connor in a 1989 Supreme Court case.[48] She noted that "stray remarks in the workplace, while perhaps probative of sexual harassment, cannot justify requiring the employer to prove that its hiring or promotion decisions were based on legitimate criteria. Nor can statements by non-decision-makers, or statements by decision-makers unrelated to the decisional process itself, suffice to satisfy the plaintiff's burden in this regard."[49]

Under this doctrine, courts, usually deciding motions for summary judgment, wholly disregard as "stray" evidence of decision-makers' comments proffered by plaintiffs to support their claims of discrimination. They do this for any number of reasons, including that: (1) the comment was too removed in time from the alleged discrimination; (2) the comment was too contextually isolated or attenuated from the alleged discrimination; or (3) the comment was not made specifically in the context of the adverse action alleged to be discrimination.[50] Many jurisdictions thus insist that in order for a remark to be probative of discrimination at all, "the decision makers themselves[] or those who provide input into the decision [must] express such feelings (1) around the time of [the decision], and (2) in reference to[] the adverse employment action."[51] It is typical for a court to insist that a comment proffered as evidence actually have been made by the decision-maker and not by anyone else, even if the goal of the proffer is to demonstrate a culture or environment rife with discriminatory beliefs and attitudes.[52]

The ramifications of this are immense. Plaintiffs don't get to choose their evidence, and the comments that they are able to document and submit as evidence, if any at all, are rarely "smoking gun"-type insights into the minds of people who have no motivation to disclose their discriminatory beliefs.[53]

[48] *See Hopkins*, 490 U.S. at 261–279 (O'Connor, J., concurring).
[49] *Id.* at 277 (O'Connor, J., concurring).
[50] Sanders v. Kettering Univ., No. 07–11905, 2009 WL 3010849, at *15 (E.D. Mich. Sept. 17, 2009) (referring to factors involved in state actions brought under the Elliott-Larsen Civil Rights Act), *aff'd in part, rev'd in part on other grounds*, 411 F. App'x 771 (6th Cir. 2010) (reversing only judgment with respect to the breach of contract claim); *accord* Medina v. Ramsey Steel Co., 238 F.3d 674, 683 (5th Cir. 2001) ("Remarks may serve as sufficient evidence of age discrimination if they are: 1) age related, 2) proximate in time to the employment decision, 3) made by an individual with authority over the employment decision at issue, and 4) related to the employment decision at issue.").
[51] Hunt v. City of Markham Ill., 219 F.3d 649, 652–53 (7th Cir. 2000).
[52] Bennett v. Saint-Gobain Corp., 507 F.3d 23, 29 (1st Cir. 2007); McKay v. U.S. Dep't of Transp., 340 F.3d 695, 699 (8th Cir. 2003).
[53] *See* Natasha T. Martin, *Pretextin Peril*, 75 MO. L. REV. 313, 315 (2010).

Other plaintiffs are permitted to adduce, at trial, virtually any facts that they have that tend to make a fact in dispute more or less likely to be true. Employment discrimination plaintiffs who set forth slurs, epithets, or jokes told by those whom they accuse of discrimination, or their close cohorts, are told under this doctrine that unless the remarks were made at precisely the right times and under precisely the right circumstances, the remarks will be completely disregarded, and, without more, the case will likely never even get to trial.[54] Employment discrimination attorneys are all too well aware of this, and, logically, may turn away cases in which these "stray" comments may be close to all the plaintiff has in support of her claims.

The stray comments doctrine is as arbitrary as it is harsh. When it comes to naming a cut-off for a temporal proximity requirement, courts have been all over the map. Some courts have held that the comments must have been made within a year of the challenged adverse action;[55] others have held that they must be made within a few months.[56] Moreover, sometimes courts will invoke the stray comments doctrine in order to dismiss as irrelevant comments that are somewhat vague or ambiguous but which the judges have determined cannot possibly be anything other than innocuous in the mind of a reasonable juror.[57] Then, insofar as one might question whether a juror might, in fact, see the comment as evincing bias or animus, that question and the whole case are consequently foreclosed.

It is readily apparent that courts' divorcing what could be insight-yielding, probative words from their spoken and social contexts and substituting their own interpretations for the range of interpretations a jury might give them is not sound jurisprudence. Nor is summarily denying a jury the chance to assign them weight.

The Same Actor Inference
The same actor inference is another judge-made adjudicatory tool or "short-cut" that deploys evidence of benign, or even beneficent, motivations of an

---

[54] *See, e.g.,* Stone v. Parish of E. Baton Rouge, 329 F. App'x 542, 546 (5th Cir. 2009).
[55] *See* Hemsworth v. Quotesmith Com, Inc., 476 F.3d 487, 491 (7th Cir.2007); Petts v. Rockledge Furniture LLC, 534 F.3d 715, 721 (7th Cir. 2008).
[56] *See* Almonord v. Kingsbrook Jewish Med. Ctr., No. 04-CV-4071 NGG/RML, 2007 WL 2324961, at *9 (E.D.N.Y. Aug. 10, 2007) (holding that a comment made five months before termination was too remote to support a finding of pretext); Bauer v. Metz Baking Co., 59 F. Supp. 2d 896, 909 (N.D. Iowa 1999) (holding that five months between an employer's stray remark and the employee's firing was too remote to support a finding of pretext for intentional discrimination).
[57] *See, e.g.,* Ortiz-Rivera v. Astra Zeneca LP, 363 F. App'x 45, 48 (1st Cir. 2010); Phelps v. Yale Sec., Inc., 986 F.2d 1020, 1025 (6th Cir.1993).

accused discriminator in order to protect or exonerate him from accusations of employment discrimination. With its genesis dating back to 1991, the same actor inference is a rebuttable presumption, recognized in some form in many jurisdictions, that one who hired or promoted a member of a protected class, and then subsequently took an adverse action against that employee, could not have possibly taken the action "because of" the employee's protected class status.[58] The Second, Fourth, Fifth, and Ninth Circuits have all held that the same actor doctrine erects a "strong inference" that the defendant did not engage in discrimination, especially if the firing happens within a relatively short time span. These federal courts, clearly compelled by the inference, sometimes mandate that claimants come forward with "an extraordinarily strong showing of discrimination" to overcome the "strong inference" of nondiscrimination.[59] Even the Seventh and Eleventh Circuits, which have rejected the application of the same actor inference at the summary judgment stage, have stated that the same actor inference may be probative of nondiscrimination that can be argued to a jury.[60]

So, for example, in a sex discrimination case, if the defendant employer can show that the decision-maker accused of discrimination was, in fact, the same

---

[58] *See* Proud v. Stone, 945 F.2d 796, 798 (4th Cir. 1991).

[59] *See* Grady v. Affiliated Cent., Inc., 130 F.3d 553 (2d Cir. 1997); Soto v. Marist Coll., 2019 U.S. Dist. LEXIS 94225 (S.D.N.Y. Jun. 5, 2019); Leon v. Columbia Univ. Med. Ctr., 2013 U.S. Dist. LEXIS 177728 (S.D.N.Y. Dec. 17, 2013); Schnabel v. Abramson, 232 F.3d 83 (2d Cir. 2000); Fazzari v. Cohen, Pontani, Lieberman, & Pavane, LLP, 2019 U.S. Dist. LEXoIS 45120 (S.D. N.Y. Mar. 19, 2019); O'Connor v. Bank of New York, 2008 N.Y. Misc. LEXIS 8338; Proud v. Stone, 945 F.2d 796, 797 (4th Cir. 1991); Smith v. Premier Prop. Mgmt., 2019 U.S. Dist. LEXIS 33500 (M.D.N.C. Mar. 4, 2019); Xunian Liu v. Bushnell, 2018 U.S. Dist. LEXIS 105152 (D. Md. Jun. 22, 2018); Georges v. Dominion Payroll Servs., LLC, 2018 U.S. Dist. LEXIS 76110 (E.D. Va. May 4, 2018); Johnson v. BAE Sys. Land & Armaments, L.P., 2014 U.S. Dist. LEXIS 59637 (N.D. Tex. Apr. 30, 2014) (holding that plaintiffs have produced evidence of sufficiently egregious facts to overcome the same actor inference); Brown v. CSC Logic, Inc., 82 F.3d 651 (5th Cir. 1996) (holding that the plaintiff did not put forward facts "sufficiently egregious" to overcome the same actor inference); Kocienski v. NRT Techs., Inc., 2018 U.S. Dist. LEXIS 42461 (D. Nev, Mar. 15, 2018); Bradley v. Harcourt, Brace & Co., 104 F.3d 267, 270–71 (9th Cir. 1996); Ford v. Maricopa County Superior Court Dep't of Adult Prob., 2010 U.S. Dist. LEXIS 56132 (D. Ariz. Jun. 3, 2010) (holding that the same actor inference also applies to the treatment of women taking pregnancy-related leave and that the court must take the inference into account at summary judgment).

[60] *See* Perez v. Thorntons, Inc., 731 F.3d 699 (7th Cir. 2013); Nwanna v. Ashcroft, 66 F. App'x 9 (7th Cir. 2003); Moore v. Life, Inc., 2015 U.S. Dist. LEXIS 123214 (N.D. Ind. Sept. 15, 2015); Artunduaga v. Univ. of Chi. Med. Ctr., 2015 U.S. Dist. LEXIS 79672 (N.D. Ill. Jun. 19, 2015); FirstMerit Bank, N.A. v. Ferrari, 71 F. Supp. 3d 751 (N.D. Ill. 2014); Williams v. Vitro Servs. Corp., 144 F.3d 1438 (11th Cir. 1998); Thomas v. Home Depot U.S.A., Inc., 2017 U.S. Dist. LEXIS 218804 (N.D. Ga. Mar. 23, 2017); Sneed v. Ken Edwards Enters., 2009 U.S. Dist. LEXIS 135287 (N.D. Ga. Aug. 18, 2009).

person who hired and/or promoted the plaintiff, absent some additional evidence to bolster the discrimination claim, the court will presume that the adverse action could not possibly have been motivated by any kind of unlawful sex-based discrimination.[61] Some courts have held that not even the involvement of multiple decision-makers will preclude the application of the same actor inference.[62]

As the Fourth Circuit inexplicably concluded in 1991, it makes sense to operate under such simplistic assumptions because "[o]ne is quickly drawn to the realization that claims that employer animus exists in termination but not in hiring seem irrational. From the standpoint of the putative discriminator, it hardly makes sense to hire workers from a group one dislikes (thereby incurring the psychological costs of associating with them), only to fire them once they are on the job."[63]

There are a multitude of things wrong with the same actor inference. In the first place, it appears to presume that people are monolithic and simple, rather than nuanced and complex.[64] People, however, are rarely ever simply "good" or "bad." Moreover, there are many reasons why someone who initially did something "good" would subsequently discriminate with no change in character. A man who believed in the hiring and advancement of women, generally, might hire a woman but nonetheless fire her if she became pregnant or once she became the mother of small children.[65] However, pregnancy discrimination has been recognized via an Amendment to Title VII as sex discrimination in contravention of Title VII,[66] and family responsibility discrimination (FRD) has been recognized as an actionable brand of sex discrimination by judges in virtually every jurisdiction.[67]

---

[61] *Id.*; *see* Katharine T. Bartlett, *Making Good on Good Intentions: The Critical Role of Motivation in Reducing Implicit Workplace Discrimination*, 95 Va. L. Rev. 1893, 1923 n.99 (2009).

[62] *See* Campbell v. Alliance Natl. Inc., 107 F. Supp. 2d 234, 250 (S.D.N.Y. 2000) (stating that the decision-makers in the hiring and firing need not mirror each other exactly as long as one management-level employee played a substantial role in both decisions); *see also* O'Connor v. Bank of N.Y., 2008 NY Slip Op 30614(U) (Sup. Ct., NY County 2008); Ralkin v. NYCTA, 62 F. Supp. 2d 989, 1000 (E.D.N.Y. 1999) (holding that the same actor inference applied where the manager, who may not have actually hired the employee-plaintiff, interviewed the plaintiff and made the recommendation to hire her and played a significant role in the decision to fire her).

[63] Proud v. Stone, 945 F.2d 796, 797 (4th Cir. 1991).

[64] Stone, Taking in Strays, *supra* note 39, at 167.

[65] Ford v. Maricopa County Superior Court Dep't of Adult Prob., 2010 U.S. Dist. LEXIS 56132 (D. Ariz. Jun. 3, 2010) (holding that the same actor inference also applies to the treatment of women taking pregnancy-related leave and that the court must take the inference into account at summary judgment).

[66] 95 P.L. 555, 92 Stat. 2076 (1978); Title VII of the Civil Rights Act of 1964, 42 U.S.C. § 2000e(k).

[67] Joan C. Williams et al., *The Evolution of "FReD": Family Responsibilities Discrimination and Developments in the Law of Stereotyping and Implicit Bias*, 59 Hastings L.J. 1311, 1313 (2008), available at http://scholarship.law.ufl.edu/facultypub/499.

Conversely, a "bad" person, conceived by the presumption as one who harbored animus or bias against anyone because of their protected class status and who would never act favorably toward them, might nonetheless hire or promote someone in that class merely to evade being accused of discriminatory practices, to appease shareholders, customers, or the public who might demand diversity, or simply in an act of tokenism. This person may, however, still hold the employee to different standards than others or judge them more harshly because of their animus or bias. And, finally, people may change over time, becoming prejudiced and willing to discriminate in a way they were not previously. The generous time spans afforded by many jurisdictions do not take this into account.

The same actor inference will inhere despite what are often great passages of time in between the "good" act of hiring or promoting the employee and the adverse act (typically a firing).[68] So, for example, in the Fifth Circuit, a time span or lapse of five years will still invoke the inference,[69] while in the Sixth Circuit, a span of seven and a half years will do so.[70] The inference, in other words, seems to suggest that, absent some additional compelling evidence to support the plaintiff's claim, the fact that the accused discriminator did something "good," like help launch, advance, or support a woman's career or job means that, as a matter of law and without resort to a jury, they would be incapable of doing something "bad," like acting against the employee because of her sex.[71]

Asymmetry and Unfairness

But perhaps the greatest flaws in the same actor inference, enshrined though it has been in employment discrimination jurisprudence for decades, become most evident when it is examined alongside the stray comments doctrine,

---

[68] Hansen v. Clark Cnty., No. 2:05-CV-672-BES-VPC, 2007 WL 1892127, at *2, 8 (D. Nev. Jun. 27, 2007) (seven-year); Hollingsworth v. Henry Cnty. Med. Ctr. EMS, Inc., No. 05–1272 B, 2007 WL 1695303, at *1, 5 n.3 (W.D. Tenn. Jun. 12, 2007) (six-year).

[69] See Brooks v. Lubbock Cty. Hosp. Dist., 373 F. App'x 434 (5th Cir. 2010); Boyd v. State Farm Ins. Cos., 158 F.3d 326 (5th Cir. 1998).

[70] Buhrmaster v. Overnite Transp. Co., 61 F.3d 461, 464 (6th Cir. 1995).

[71] Bradley v. Harcourt, Brace & Co., 104 F.3d 267, 270 (9th Cir. 1996) (quoting Proud v. Stone, 945 F.2d 796, 797 (4th Cir. 1991)); Muhleisen v. Wear Me Apparel LLC, 644 F. Supp. 2d 375, 386 (S.D.N.Y. 2009) (finding it "quite difficult to reconcile" the defendant's "willingness to hire [the] plaintiff while she was on maternity leave in January 2006 and to provide her three months' paid maternity leave a year later with [the] plaintiff's allegation that he discriminatorily fired her because she was pregnant or because of her gender in March 2007"); Buhrmaster v. Overnite Transp. Co., 61 F.3d 461, 464 (6th Cir. 1995) ("An individual who is willing to hire and promote a person of a certain class is unlikely to fire them simply because they are a member of that class.").

discussed above, that enables courts to excise entirely what may be probative, insight-yielding comments from consideration of a case's fate. The illogic and the asymmetry are striking. Whereas the same actor inference implicitly posits that people have some innate (good) character that may be discerned or somehow cemented by an initial act, far back in time from the one that gives rise to a lawsuit, the stray comments doctrine stands in stark contrast. It, jarringly, demands that judges pay *no* heed and derive absolutely *no* insight into the motivations placed at issue by the suit from comments, jokes, or even epithets uttered by the decision-maker at issue as close as weeks, or even days, before the adverse act occurred.

Think about this: when it comes to employment discrimination cases, motivation and intention are typically the central questions. Courts will infer good or benign motivations from an act as basic as hiring someone, even *years* before their firing.[72] Paradoxically, some of these same courts will declare statements evincing animus or bias against a group wholly worthless and irrelevant when they are made by a decision-maker even just before action is taken because that would somehow unfairly ascribe "bad" motivations to one who was not expressly discussing the plaintiff and her fate at that given moment.[73] Why do we allow words and actions so remote in time to be so probative of who someone is and how they think when the words and actions make them out to be unbiased, but ignore so quickly words and actions closer in time when they might show bias or animus?

In both cases, the fate of the case itself could be at stake. Summary judgment may be granted unjustly and prematurely in a case that deserves to be tried before a jury when the same actor inference is invoked to dispose of a case. The stray comments doctrine, for its part, may be used to, in the words of renowned law professor Michael Zimmer, "slice and dice" away what may be probative evidence until the case is stripped of all that may be used to persuade a jury, and it is dismissed without proceeding to trial.[74] The arbitrariness of the time span restrictions imposed by courts invoking the same

---

[72] Jetter v. Knothe Corp., 324 F.3d 73, 76 (2d Cir. 2003); Schreiber v. Worldco, LLC, 324 F. Supp. 2d 512, 519–20 (S.D.N.Y. Jul. 9, 2004).

[73] Reilly v. Revlon, Inc., 620 F. Supp. 2d 524, 545 (S.D.N.Y. May 12, 2009) ("Further[,] the stray comments made by Krasner during Reilly's pregnancy, while objectionable, are too innocuous and temporally removed from Reilly's termination to infer that they were causally connected to the decision to fire her six months later."); Sheridan v. N.Y. Live Inv. Mgmt., No. 09 Civ. 4746(KBF), 2012 WL 474035, at *7 (S.D.N.Y. Feb. 9, 2012) (finding that a single stray comment was insufficient to be a motivating factor when the adverse action occurred four months after the comment).

[74] Michael Zimmer, *Slicing & Dicing of Individual Disparate Treatment Law*, 61 LA. L. REV. 577, 591 (2001).

actor inference and the stray comments doctrine only adds to their perceived unfairness, and both doctrines have been criticized profusely by legal scholars and other commentators alike.[75]

Why?

So, the question remains, why would courts set up shortcuts and doctrines that seem to cut against one another and be so logically inconsistent as to benefit only the employer? Some scholars have read some judges' special treatment of employment discrimination cases as reflecting those judges' perception that such cases, born of a statute passed in the 1960s, are still somewhat new-fangled and to be treated with an extra dose of skepticism.[76] Others have alluded to courts' desire to clear their dockets.[77] It is difficult to know what is driving this aberrant treatment, but it is clear that the treatment is replete with arbitrariness and a perceived emphasis on "rules" to streamline and winnow out "unworthy" cases; this has contributed to the glass ceiling for decades. In the worst interpretations of these acts, courts are systemically cutting off plaintiffs' cases; even through a more charitable lens, they appear to be acting pursuant to unspoken beliefs.

When courts craft and deploy adjudicatory "shortcut" devices like those discussed above in an attempt to weed out unworthy cases on summary judgment, what, exactly, is going on? Because these devices can reflect tens or hundreds of judges' misapprehension of the queries before them and oversimplification of the analyses, a variety of societally-held unspoken beliefs can underlie them in different combinations. It would be a huge mistake to ascribe a discriminatory or singular mindset to every judge who crafts or unquestioningly uses these shortcuts. This is especially true because many judges are simply applying precedent when they invoke these shortcuts. That said, as discussed, there is an array of societally-held beliefs about employment discrimination plaintiffs and about those whom they accuse of discrimination that arguably underlies some of the creation and sanctioning of these devices in some sense, and to overlook them would be a mistake.

---

[75] *See* Victor D. Quintanilla & Cheryl R. Kaiser, *The Same-Actor Inference of Nondiscrimination: Moral Credentialing and the Psychological and Legal Licensing of Bias*, 104 CAL. L. REV. (2016); Gertner, *supra* note 44.

[76] Henry L. Chambers, Jr., *The Cost of Non-compensable Workplace Harm*, 8 FIU L. REV. 317, 325 (2013); *see* Leland Ware, *Inferring Intent from Proof of Pretext: Resolving the Summary Judgment Confusion in Employment Discrimination Cases Alleging Disparate Treatment*, 4 EMP. RTS. & EMP. POL'Y J. 37, 68 (2000).

[77] Richard Seymour, *16 Summary Judgment Commandments*, 36-DEC Trial 28, 28 (2000).

The notion that employment discrimination plaintiffs ought to be viewed with additional skepticism derives from the ideas that those who sue their employers for discrimination, who are often members of marginalized and/or historically underrepresented groups in the American workplace, are somehow illegitimate, out for gain, vengeful, untrustworthy, or have an axe to grind.[78] These unflattering depictions have been applied to women as well as others in and outside the workforce.[79]

As stated, many scholars and commentators have levied charges that courts' harsh doctrines and inconsistent application of standards when granting summary judgment against employment discrimination plaintiffs, in particular, stem from everything from sheer ignorance to outright hostility toward employment discrimination plaintiffs.[80] Some have posited that judges may feel as though the relative newness of antidiscrimination legislation, combined with its unique queries that rest so heavily on people's undisclosed mindsets, distinguishes employment discrimination claims from other claims. Therefore, the thinking goes, traditional standards are best eschewed in favor of more judge-crafted adjudicatory devices and more exacting vetting of cases at their outset.

THE PAIN

As has been discussed, employment discrimination plaintiffs do not fare well in court. In federal court, about 14,000 employment civil rights cases are filed each year.[81] Of those, 18 percent are dismissed on motions for summary judgment. At trial, only 2 percent of cases are won by the plaintiff.[82] When, because of judge-made doctrines and adjudicatory devices, cases slip through the cracks and are prematurely dismissed, yet another pane of the glass ceiling is set. Women as a class are disadvantaged not only because those particular litigants are not afforded the substantive protections that the law is intended or presumed to confer but also because those losses are high-profile

---

[78] See Gertner, *supra* note 44; Selmi, *supra* note 2, at 557–61.

[79] *Id.*

[80] Hon. Bernice B. Donald et al., *Trial by Jury or Trial by Motion? Summary Judgment, Iqbal, and Employment Discrimination: Bringing Back Reasonable Inferences: A Short, Simple Suggestion for Addressing Some Problems at the Intersection of Employment Discrimination and Summary Judgment*, 57 N.Y. L. Sch. L. Rev. 749, 757 (2012–13); Clermont & Schwab, *Employment Discrimination Plaintiffs in Federal Court, supra* note 2, at 119.

[81] Ellen Berrey et al., Rights on Trial: How Workplace Discrimination Law Perpetuates Inequality (2017).

[82] *Id.*

representatives of all of the cases that might have been brought, but were not, and of future cases.

Those lost cases are data points-dots on the larger landscape that creates the common law interpretation of Title VII as it is understood by those who might run afoul of its protections, those charged with enforcing it in the workplace, and those who must decide whether they have rights to vindicate under it. Those lost cases will come to define the parameters of the law's reach and contour the scope of human behavior, including when a person will identify as a victim of Title VII discrimination or harassment, when a Human Resources executive or other internal personnel will intervene to remediate perceived wrongs, and when a perpetrator of perceived wrongs will repeat the behavior versus when they will modulate their behavior.

When you think about how relatively few people expend the energy, resources, and time to pursue an employment discrimination case, versus the total number of people who identify as victims of sexual harassment or discrimination, you can really see how few people actually vindicate their rights under the law in court.[83] You can also see how unfair or arbitrary rules that prematurely shut down cases before they get to trial can have a devastating effect on the relatively few cases that are filed and come to be emblematic of the state of protection available. This devastation sends a clear message to all those guided by the law as to what is acceptable. When it becomes clear that, absent a veritable smoking gun, the law will treat sex discrimination victims dismissively and with undue skepticism, so will individuals at every level of the system responsible for the prevention and remediation of workplace wrongs. And so is laid another pane of the glass ceiling.

MANIFESTATIONS

Most of the beliefs discussed in this chapter can be distilled down into the unspoken belief that "people are either 'good' or 'bad,' and it's easier to believe that they are good," and that "good people can't do bad things." This belief is found throughout society, from the allure of the redemptive "comeback" in popular culture, to the cartoonish simplification of character.

The Good/Bad Binary

Once you stop and think about the beliefs described just now, it becomes clear that they are backed up by psychological and other socioscientific research, as

---

[83] Nathan Koppel, *Job-Discrimination Cases Tend to Fare Poorly in Federal Court*, WALL ST. J. (Feb. 19, 2009), www.wsj.com/articles/SB123500883048618747.

well as ample anecdotal evidence. The idea that human nature is binary – that people are either "good" or "bad" – is naïve, simplistic, and patently false, but it is a belief that people nonetheless seem to cling to.

It is easy to see where the beliefs that people are inherently well intentioned, and that people fit into a binary of being "good" or "bad," come from. There is science to support the notion that human beings naturally veer toward narratives of redemption and an abiding belief that most people (especially people who resemble these same human beings) are "good" at their core. There is science to bolster the idea that human beings believe that which they want to believe, and, along the way, they mediate their encounters with the outer world to root out evidence that corroborates their desired beliefs and to filter out evidence that negates or invalidates them.[84]

Confirmation bias is what makes humans seek, analyze, and compartmentalize information in a way that only corroborates their own preexisting beliefs.[85] As a result of confirmation bias, people tend to seek out, accord greater weight to, interpret favorably, and selectively recall information that cements their preexisting beliefs.[86]

This cognitive bias is pervasive throughout society, and there are numerous studies that demonstrate the ways in which this phenomenon shows up and infiltrates everything from data analysis, to investing, to diagnosing maladies, often yielding results that are less than rational.[87] Scientists have posited that cognitive bias stems from people's innate desire to discover and confirm that they are right about things and avoid having to discover that they have been wrong about something.[88] Essentially, people naturally want to mitigate an effect called cognitive dissonance, which is the tension and discomfort that result when humans attempt to hold attitudes or beliefs that are inconsistent or contradictory.[89]

---

[84] Elizabeth Kolbert, *Why Facts Don't Change Our Minds*, NEW YORKER (Feb. 19, 2017), www .newyorker.com/magazine/2017/02/27/why-facts-dont-change-our-minds; Shahram Heshmat, *What Is Confirmation Bias?*, PSYCHOL. TODAY (Apr. 23, 3015), www.psychologytoday.com/us/ blog/science-choice/201504/what-is-confirmation-bias.

[85] Heshmat, *supra* note 85.

[86] *Id.*

[87] *See, e.g.*, Saty Satya-Murti & Joseph Lockhart, *Recognizing and Reducing Cognitive Bias in Clinical and Forensic Neurology*, NAT'L CENTER FOR BIOTECH. INFO. (Oct. 5, 2015), www .ncbi.nlm.nih.gov/pmc/articles/PMC5762024/; Ben Yagoda, *The Cognitive Biases Tricking Your Brain Science Suggests We're Hardwired to Delude Ourselves. Can We Do Anything about It?*, THE ATLANTIC (Sept. 2018), www.theatlantic.com/magazine/archive/2018/09/cog nitive-bias/565775/.

[88] Kendra Cherry, *10 Cognitive Biases That Distort Your Thinking*, VERYWELLMIND (May 10, 2019), www.verywellmind.com/cognitive-biases-distort-thinking-2794763.

[89] Saul McLeod, *Cognitive Dissonance*, SIMPLYPSYCHOLOGY (Feb. 5, 2018), www .simplypsychology.org/cognitive-dissonance.html.

It makes sense, then, that simply being human may predispose a person to ignore information or evidence that opens up the possibility of many conclusions when it comes to employment discrimination. These possible conclusions, like "He loves his wife and generally respects women, but became irrationally annoyed/skeptical/uncomfortable on a less than conscious level by some facet of her being a woman," are uncomfortable, and arguably harder to reach. To the extent that a judge or fact-finder somehow, on some level, identifies with a decision-maker, who may very well have engaged in the initial hire of the plaintiff (where the same actor inference comes up) or come across as a basically "good" person who "misspoke" or had a "joke" unrelated to the adverse action fall flat, the asymmetry that emerges from doctrines that favor evidence of goodness in others and minimizes other insights may feel comforting or natural. To the extent that cognitive dissonance can be resolved by selectively looking at "good" acts, no matter how old or how motivated, and disregarding "bad" communications as irrelevant, perhaps the doctrines and courts' adherence to them make sense.

But the fact of the matter is that people are complex and nuanced. They experience perceptions and insights at sometimes such a visceral level as to render them imperceptible. Strands of thought that are "permissible" – socially, ethically, or legally – become inextricably intertwined with those that are "impermissible." And the query posed by workplace antidiscrimination law, despite the contorted frameworks that have spiraled out from it, is whether a plaintiff experienced workplace discrimination "because of" her protected class status. This is the sole question to be answered, and it is not supposed to hinge on the intent, or even the awareness of any actor. When the unspoken belief that undergirds these doctrines and the human tendency toward redemption are voiced, it becomes apparent that some of our legal doctrines may be failing us.

It is thus not surprising that the depictions of employers as they are animated by doctrines like the same actor inference, or even by frameworks like the *McDonnell Douglas* burden-shifting framework, are oversimplified – even cartoonish. The same actor inference makes it a rebuttable presumption that you are "good" because you did a "good" thing by hiring someone from a protected class that you might have been "bad" to and discriminated against. Absent proof sufficient to overcome your presumption of "goodness," you remain steadfastly "good." Even the *McDonnell Douglas* burden-shifting framework seeks to determine whether you are "good" and acted adversely to the plaintiff for, as you claim, a "legitimate, nondiscriminatory reason," or you are "bad," having crafted a "pretext" for your discriminatory motives. There is rarely an allowance made for anything in between.

The Romance of Redemption

Similarly, there is the notion that we, as humans, would prefer to see people as "good," even if their virtue is "hidden down deep." Who doesn't love a good comeback? Society's love affair with redemption as a virtue and a form of extreme makeover is also easily documented, with the bias of human nature to find and reinforce the positive everywhere.

Indeed, even the courts' persistence in bifurcating cases and relegating those plaintiffs without "direct" evidence to the pretext analysis instead of the more holistic, "substantial motivating factor" analysis, is illustrative of this belief. As the courts read it, despite admonitions by Congress and the Supreme Court that this reading is baseless, if, *and only if* a plaintiff has "direct evidence" (which, essentially, if believed, is "smoking gun" evidence) can their case be considered holistically because . . . Why? Because if an alleged discriminator is obvious or admits the discrimination, only *then* do we regard him as a complex person with a bouquet of rationales and motivations for his actions? And only if the unlawful motivation emerges as "substantial" do we want to condemn him?

But if a plaintiff only has "indirect" or more circumstantial evidence, then . . . what? *McDonnell Douglas?* We filter the judgment of the alleged discriminator through a binary framework where he can be only a "good" person who employed his legitimate, nondiscriminatory reason for his actions or a "bad" person who erected a pretextual lie to cover his tracks? That's it?

And what about the asymmetry of the same actor inference, which attaches so much import to the deeds and words of alleged discriminators, even years out, and the stray comment doctrine, which cuts off any plausible nexus of relevance between a person's words and his actions, except in the narrowest of circumstances? Certainly, this can be construed as a decidedly anti-plaintiff disparity. Can it also be somewhat rooted in the notion that people want to believe the best about the accused? If you do something "good," we rush to attach "goodness" to you and resist the idea that you could have had unlawful, discriminatory motivations.

The Villainous Employment Discrimination Plaintiff Belief

The unspoken view that employment discrimination plaintiffs generally are shifty, entitled, feckless, dishonest, or lazy may also underlie some of why and how they are and have been systemically disadvantaged by the law through the promulgation of legal doctrines and interpretations. While, clearly, this overt sentiment cannot be ascribed to all judges who craft and abide by these "shortcuts," scholars have suggested that judges have sometimes shown a disproportionate skepticism toward employment discrimination plaintiffs.[90] The baseless heightened evidentiary burden that judges persisted in reading into Title VII for so long is illustrative of this. The temptation to vilify these plaintiffs, whether consciously or subconsciously, is an applied belief that harms women and other minorities trying to vindicate their rights everywhere from HR offices to courtrooms.

This would seem to reflect a larger societal odious unspoken belief that employment discrimination plaintiffs, and minorities, including women are especially likely to file unworthy claims because they are somehow vindictive, untrustworthy, or misguided.[91] Thus, judges have crafted and perpetuated asymmetrical rules that supplement, and sometimes contravene, the Federal Rules of Evidence and the Federal Rules of Civil Procedure.[92] The Federal Rules of Evidence have broad allowances for what constitutes relevant evidence worthy of submission to and consideration by a jury. The shortcuts and frameworks discussed earlier artificially limit consideration of evidence that may yield insight into a decision-maker's discriminatory motivations, and permit broad assumptions that a single act done years prior can yield insight into benign or positive intentions. The Federal Rules of Civil Procedure, as discussed, specifically call for the dismissal of only those cases that cannot possibly be won with a rational jury evaluating evidence in the light most favorable to the plaintiff. The baseless classification of evidence to create heightened standards for the

---

[90] Thomas J. Crane, *Employees Fare Worse in Federal Lawsuit Study*, SAN ANTONIO EMPLOYMENT LAW BLOG (Jan. 11, 2010), www.sanantonioemploymentlawblog.com/2010/01/articles/general/employees-fare-worse-in-federal-lawsuit-study/ ("federal trial level judges are skeptical toward discrimination claimants. Discrimination plaintiffs are among the least successful sorts of claimants in federal court."); Hon. Denny Chin, *Summary Judgment in Employment Discrimination Cases: A Judge's Perspective*, 57 N.Y.L. SCH. L. REV. 671 681, (2012–13) ("[J]udges must avoid the temptation to engage in fact-finding when they are skeptical about a case. The task of the lawyers is to educate the judges, and to do a better job of telling a compelling story."); Elizabeth M. Schneider, *The Changing Shape of Federal Civil Pretrial Practice: The Disparate Impact on Civil Rights and Employment Discrimination Cases*, 158 U. PA. L. REV. 517, 525–26 (2010) ("[M]any federal judges appointed over the last several years appear to be deeply skeptical of civil rights and employment cases ... Many judges apparently tend to view these cases as petty, involving whining plaintiffs complaining about legitimate employment or institutional matters, rather than important civil rights issues.").

[91] Selmi, *supra* note 2, at 562 ("Courts often analyze race cases from an anti-affirmative action mindset, one that views both the persistence of discrimination and the merits of the underlying claims with deep skepticism."); Damon Ritenhouse, *Where Title VII Stops: Exploring Subtle Race Discrimination in the Workplace*, 7 DEPAUL J. FOR SOC. JUST. 87, 92–93 (2013) ("Judges may believe that plaintiffs bringing these cases have already received too many breaks along the way and are merely whining about treatment that does not amount to actionable discrimination.").

[92] *See, e.g., Costa*, 539 U.S. 90.

survival of many plaintiffs' cases substitutes a heightened suspicion and vigilance for this standard. There is no reason to treat these cases differently from other cases, absent the operation of unspoken beliefs about sex and other discrimination plaintiffs. Yet, many judges have felt compelled to sort and label evidence in an attempt to erect artificially demanding frameworks that quickly degrade and dispose of cases in which the evidence is prematurely deemed too weak, rather than allowing a jury to pass upon it.

But there are other unspoken beliefs that may be at work here in some cases, and to some degree. Even a judge who is not skeptical, on any level, of employment discrimination plaintiffs may unquestioningly subscribe to judicial shortcuts that cut off cases prematurely. An unspoken belief that may underlie such situations may be that "People are either good or bad, but it is easier to use clues about their character to believe that they are good than that they are bad." Thus, the same actor inference is propped up by the notion that a single act, unexplained, in the past can shield a person from being declared "sexist" or "racist." But the stray comment doctrine unjustly removes a critical question from the hands of a jury because judges, like others, are loath to believe the worst about someone because of a comment or joke that they might have made that they are believed to have not really meant.[93]

TAKEAWAYS

More than one legal scholar has posited that courts' opinions evince judges' beliefs that instances of discrimination are somehow "one-offs" committed by people who are outliers and acting antithetically toward their employer's interests or workplace culture.[94] At the most basic level, it would behoove courts to take heed of Judge Easterbrook's admonition that judges, especially on summary judgment motions, should never lose sight of the forest (being the precise question of triable issues of fact before them) for the trees (being the numerous adjudicatory framework, devices, and shortcuts). The adjudicatory framework, devices, and shortcuts promulgated by courts to aid in their interpretation of the law ought not amount to courts' rewriting of the law,

---

[93] Stone, Taking in Strays, *supra* note 39, at 184–86 ("The asymmetry between the same actor inference on the one hand, and the stray comment doctrine and the temporal nexus requirement between protected activity and an adverse action in retaliation cases on the other hand, is striking."); Sperino, *supra* note 44, at 233–36; Donald et al., *supra* note 81, at 760.

[94] Sandra F. Sperino, *A Modern Theory of Direct Corporate Liability for Title VII*, 61 ALA. L. REV. 773, 787–88 (2010); Tristia K. Green, *Insular Individualism: Employment Discrimination Law after Ledbetter v. Goodyear*, 43 HARV. C.R.-C.L. L. REV. 353, 356 (2008).

and they should be in service only of the larger goal of cogent, thoughtful analysis of relevant issues. The kind of deliberate mindfulness evinced by Judge Easterbrook in the *Ortiz* case would benefit many judges who seem to find themselves waylaid and otherwise distracted by the devices that are supposed to focus them.

Mindfulness is key all around. Employment discrimination plaintiffs face the unspoken, often unconscious belief that they are shifty or otherwise deserving of skepticism at all levels of lodging their complaints.[95] It would benefit everyone, from HR officers, to judges and legislators – whether or not they consciously harbor the belief – to engage with and confront it before performing their jobs.

Professional training that focuses on Title VII and other antidiscrimination laws, whether for new judges or corporate executives, might be better off focusing not just on the dictates of the laws, as most does, but also on the purpose, need for, and effects of antidiscrimination laws.[96] This would cement them in people's minds not only as necessary shapers of at-work behaviors and policies but also as engendering beneficial ends for employers, employees, and society at large. While such an approach will not work to make everyone more cognizant of and committed to the ends of antidiscrimination law and its proper functioning, it will certainly operate to probe beliefs that are held at a less than conscious level.[97]

When women are taken seriously and have their cases, at all levels of concern- and complaint-lodging, treated as other cases are when it comes to the evidentiary burdens imposed on them and their chances of being dismissed before they get to trial, their rights will be vindicated.

---

[95] Gertner, *supra* note 44; Selmi, *supra* note 2.

[96] *See* JoAnna Suriani *Reasonable Care to Prevent and Correct: Examining the Role of Training in Workplace Harassment Law*, 21 N.Y.U. J. LEGIS. & PUB. POL'Y 801 (2018); Chai R. Feldblum & Victoria A. Lipnic, *Breaking the Silence*, HARV. BUS. REV. (Jan. 26, 2018), https://hbr.org/2018/01/breaking-the-silence; Susan M. Heathfield, *Tips for Providing Mandatory HR Training*, THE BALANCE CAREERS (Jun. 25, 2019), www.thebalancecareers.com/tips-for-providing-mandatory-hr-training-1919288; Susan M. Heathfield, *Prevent Employment Discrimination and Lawsuits*, THE BALANCE CAREERS (Sept. 4, 2018), www.thebalancecareers.com/prevent-employment-discrimination-and-lawsuits-1917923.

[97] *Id.*

Conclusion

The Biggest Unspoken Belief is That it's not Worth it to Engage with Unspoken Beliefs.

The glass ceiling is about women having qualities projected onto them that are not discernible or prone to being noticed in men. It is about women being held responsible for the feelings of those around them in a way that men aren't. Above all, it is about none of this being articulated to their faces. A 2018 article on the well-known blog site Above the Law by an anonymous law professor who goes by the moniker "Lawprofblog" recounts the frequency with which female professors receive student evaluations that fixate on how they make students feel, or their perceived personality, demeanor, or even looks, rather than on germane aspects of their class and teaching:

> "I don't like her as a professor but she'd be great to grab dinner with."
> "Definitely would want to hang out with her, or do yoga . . .."
> "I Know! We Can Go Shopping Together!"
> "She's a bitch but she wears great shoes."
> "You have the best clothes of any professor at the law school! Where do you shop?"
> "I love your outfits!"[1]

Unnecessary critiques of how these women made students feel, rather than their effectiveness at teaching, pervaded the sample reviewed for the article. The author posited that, indeed, this was a problem experienced much more frequently by female professors than by male professors, a fact which he said has been supported by the literature on the subject. Other comments included:

> ". . . literally one of the sweetest professors . . ."
> "Great teacher, too nerdy for me."

---

[1] Lawprofblog, *Weaponizing Student Evaluations (Part II)*, ABOVE THE L. (Oct. 2, 2018), https://abovethelaw.com/2018/10/weaponizing-student-evaluations-part-ii/.

"Sweet and helpful."

"Catty and Unapproachable."

"She frequently comes across as a bully."

"Very nice and caring."

"Her California accent is annoying and makes her sound dumb."

"She was a good professor until her pregnancy got in the way."

"Boring but hot."[2]

THE GLASS CEILING IS ABOUT WHEN THESE PROJECTIONS CONSPIRE TO CREATE REALITY.

I got into a heated argument with a male colleague in front of others at work. I was definitely keeping a cooler head than he was, but he was saying some really provocative things. At a certain point, he said, almost as if to everyone else there, "You're really getting hysterical." The funny thing was that I had not been, until then. I grew frustrated and embarrassed once he said that, and I actually did start to get emotional. I felt like I was on display, being judged. And I felt like there was no way out.

—*Simone, thirty-one, attorney*

The glass ceiling is about the near-invisible, but filmy lens through which women are uniquely evaluated and through which expectations for them are uniquely shaped, even by well-intentioned people. In September 2018, Republican Senator Orrin Hatch seemed to attempt to give some credence to the testimony of Dr. Christine Blasey Ford, who famously accused then-Supreme Court nominee Brett Kavanaugh of sexual assault, saying that he didn't "think she's uncredible," but rather "an attractive, good witness."[3] When questioned about his use of the word "attractive," he responded, "[i]n other words, she's pleasing."[4]

The glass ceiling is about the expectation that women peddle and transact in emotions, making those around them feel comfortable and at ease, appearing pleasant and pleasing. The glass ceiling is about the noxious confluence of unspoken beliefs that we as a society lack the courage and humility to own and confront, saying to ourselves (on some level, anyway), "It's just not worth it."

---

[2] *Id.*

[3] Elizabeth Landers, *Republican Senator on Kavanaugh Accuser: "She's an Attractive, Good Witness,"* CNN POLITICS (Sept. 27, 2018), www.cnn.com/2018/09/27/politics/orrin-hatch-kavanaugh-accuser-attractive/index.html.

[4] *Id.*

Billy Bush is the former host of *Access Hollywood*, who, in 2005, famously laughed and encouraged a not yet president Donald Trump as *he* famously engaged in what he would later term "locker room" talk about groping women and about a female actress that the two were about to meet up with.[5] In October 2016, this tape was released, and the backlash was swift and, ultimately, propelled by momentum-gaining social movements that promoted reckoning for perpetrators and enablers of sexual assault or abuse.[6]

Bush would later claim that he was not under the belief that the tape was "going to be weaponized" against him the way he felt it was, noting "I got taken out, but I wasn't the target."[7] Specifically, he later revealed to an interviewer that he was reassured that professional and reputational harm would not come to him because he "didn't say anything."[8] But, as Bush recounted, "it was leaked on a Friday," and by Sunday morning he was unceremoniously let go when he left his home to be taken to work and was informed that the car sent by his employers had been canceled.[9]

Many proponents of the #MeToo movement were quick to focus on Bush's role as an enabler of the unchecked "locker room talk" – and quick to warn that the cowed silence and forced support of those who wish to curry favor with wrongdoers can be as devastating as the wrongdoing itself. On one hand, this is a fair and necessary conclusion. Enablers harm women (and others) by placing their own social comfort, professional prospects, and social standing above acting responsibly to exert social pressure to halt and stem the harmful speech and actions that prop up the glass ceiling.

---

[5]   Billy Bush, *Billy Bush: Yes, Donald Trump, You Said That*, N.Y. TIMES (Dec. 3, 2017), www .nytimes.com/2017/12/03/opinion/billy-bush-trump-access-hollywood-tape.html.

[6]   Julie Miller, *Billy Bush, Access Hollywood Respond to Lewd Trump Tape*, VANITY FAIR (Oct. 7, 2016), www.vanityfair.com/hollywood/2016/10/billy-bush-donald-trump-access-hollywood; Alex Johnson, *Billy Bush Reaffirms Trump's "Access Hollywood" Comments Are Real*, NBC NEWS (Dec. 7, 2017, 9:45 PM), www.nbcnews.com/news/us-news/billy-bush-reaffirms-trump-s-access-hollywood-comments-are-real-n826146; *NBC News Fires Billy Bush after Lewd Donald Trump Tape Airs*, CHI. TRIBUNE (Oct. 17, 2016, 8:22 PM), www.chicagotribune.com/entertainment/ct-billy-bush-fired-20161017-story.html.

[7]   Eric Todisco, *Billy Bush Says Infamous Trump Tape Was "Weaponized": "I Got Taken Out, but I Wasn't the Target*," YAHOO! FINANCE (Sept. 10, 2019), https://finance.yahoo.com/news/billy-bush-says-infamous-trump-184726267.html.

[8]   *Id.*

[9]   Chris Spargo, *Billy Bush Learned NBC Had Fired Him When His Car Service Was Cancelled as He Stood Outside His NYC Pad to Go to Work—Two Days after "P***ygate" Audio Was Leaked by One of His Co-workers*, DAILY MAIL (Sept. 10, 2019, 2:21 PM), www.dailymail.co.uk/news/article-7449077/Billy-Bush-learned-NBC-fired-car-service-cancelled-stood-outside-work.html.

On the other hand, noxious unspoken beliefs are products of the norms and culture from which they sprang. In other words, confronting them is thorny precisely because they are the product of societal values, tradition, and humor, among other things. In 2019, three years after his exile from the entertainment industry, Billy Bush railed against the heat he took for his role in the tape after interviewer Gail King asked him, point blank, whether at that precise moment in 2005, he felt as though he needed to "go along to get along," and questioned why he did not "feel [he] could challenge him, and say, 'You know, that's not cool.'"[10] Providing context, Bush noted that it was his first year cohosting the show, musing, "You know, you want people to like you, and you're a little eager."[11] His apprehension and the pressure he felt, he maintained, were well-founded:

> Trump's the kinda guy who would say, you know, "Forget Billy Bush . . . ." And then, I might have gotten, "Hey, why did you lose Trump? He's the biggest guest we ha —?" I mean, it was — there was always a little bit of, you're a little anxious around him because you just want it to end well and get out.[12]

This sets forth some evidence of what might be the most uncomfortable unspoken belief: so many people are susceptible, under the right conditions and at the right time, to being cowed into silence or acquiescence in the face of speech or actions that, no matter how inperceptively, can reflect or promote certain noxious unspoken beliefs. How many decent adults in the year 2005, male or female, in the privacy of that van, trying to curry favor with a powerful interviewee, would have actually rebuked Mr. Trump, without fearing or actually being seen as antisocial, unprofessional, or both? This does not excuse Billy Bush, but more pervasive interrogation of unspoken beliefs makes it easier to avoid their promotion and enabling. When we subscribe to the aspirational fiction that Bush was an outlier who was either exceptionally weak or exceptionally supportive of the speech he was hearing, we deceive ourselves all over again, shrouding and burying the truth about human nature, popular culture, and what it will take to start to erode misogyny and the glass ceiling.

The social change that will educate, shame, or otherwise discourage silence and enabling in individuals must stem from the understanding that these individuals are not inherently shameful or aberrant "others," but potentially anyone. There are fictions and lies that we espouse, if only within ourselves, daily, and truths about what we believe that we leave unspoken. But just as the

---

[10] *Billy Bush: The Access Hollywood Tape Was "Weaponized,"* CBS NEWS (Sept. 10, 2019, 10:19 AM), www.cbsnews.com/news/billy-bush-access-hollywood-tape-everybody-knew-says-donald -trump-tape-was-going-to-be-weaponized-exclusive-interview/.

[11] *Id.*

[12] *Id.*

implicit bias that society instills in humans without regard for how good or fair we each think we are is best combated when we confront it, so must we start interrogating unspoken beliefs. Confrontation of and reconciliation with implicit bias when it comes to race, for example, may be achieved through engagement with antiracist literature[13] or training,[14] or widely available tests like the Implicit Association Test[15] that measure often unspoken attitudes, beliefs, and biases. Confronting unspoken beliefs will also aid in the battle of many varieties of discrimination. Confronting unspoken beliefs unflinchingly starts with rejecting the unspoken belief that it's not worth the trouble.

WHAT NOW?

And so, we shame those who don't speak up without questioning why they don't or whether we, ourselves, would, in the face of "locker room talk," bullying, pay inequality, or any other workplace or social injustice. We are willfully blind when a victim tries to explain why she "went along to get along" with strained laughter, smiled through gritted teeth, or was cowed into silence. We, as women, may be momentarily emboldened to click "like" when a famous actress uses a hashtag to promote a movement advancing truth telling, but all too aware of how tenuous our own professional and social prospects may become if we speak out for ourselves or on behalf of another. And we realize that these problems are so much bigger than our individual horizons let us see. So, what now?

This book is intended to serve as a springboard. It is a project – far from complete. The researched cited in it focuses largely on white-collar women, and while it emphasizes the compounding of challenges that intersectional discrimination engenders for women, whole books have and should continue to be written on more of the specifics of sex discrimination in the workplace for women who are of color, members of the LGBTQIA+ community, disabled, or who identify with any number of additional minority statuses in addition to their sex. This book – ultimately – is an invitation to give voice to and confront the innumerable additional unspoken beliefs that comprise the "panes" of the glass ceiling, and to identify their manifestations in society and popular culture,

---

[13]   *See, e.g.,* IBRAM X. KENDI, HOW TO BE AN ANTIRACIST (2019).

[14]   *See, e.g.,* Maura Judkis, *Anti-racism Trainers Were Ready for This Moment. Is Everyone Else?,* WASH. POST (Jul. 8, 2020, 7:00 AM), www.washingtonpost.com/lifestyle/style/anti-racism-trainers-were-ready-for-this-moment-is-everyone-else/2020/07/07/df2d39ea-b582-11ea-a510-55b f26485c93_story.html.

[15]   *See* Implicit Bias Test, AM. BAR ASS'N, www.americanbar.org/groups/litigation/initiatives/ task-force-implicit-bias/implicit-bias-test/.

as well the phenomena they give rise to in the legal and legislative arenas. Once the beliefs are voiced, society has something palpable to confront and to reckon with, rather than something too slippery, invisible, and insidious to wrap its collective mind around and contend with. And though some of the beliefs are ugly and extreme, it is important to recall that they are not necessarily universally believed or subscribed to, but rather present in a range of forms across swaths of society.

Perhaps there has never been a time in history when women who have been victimized by everything from sexual assault to sex discrimination at work have been so emboldened to speak out. We have seen the toppling of powerful men in virtually every industry from Hollywood to Washington, D.C., and from Madison Avenue to Silicon Valley, by their harassment and assault victims, who are taking their stories to the court of public opinion, if not to a court of law. This is a constant and instructive reminder of what some are calling a "reckoning" in this country. And these once powerful men retreat, often divested of their jobs, wealth, and legacies, seemingly by the public, amid increasingly echo-y chatter from all segments of society and professions that "they too" can relate.

But the propulsive social movements, like #MeToo, that continue to call for social justice and public reckoning when it comes to sex and other inequality have the advantage of playing out on public stages with protagonists whose bank accounts are typically full, and whose lives are usually public.[16] They have the ability to capture the public interest and imagination that regular people typically do not. Often, their vindication is sealed with a barrage of advertising boycotts, celebrity tweets of support, or even the filing of criminal charges. Too often, though, the glory of the movements' triumphs as they play out on our social media pages or are splashed across headlines is aspirational, but inaccessible to those who cheer them from their cubicles. Until that fourth wall starts to be dismantled, and these conversations about the beliefs that erode our more mundane work experiences can be had more comfortably, the success of these movements cannot fully translate to effect change for most ordinary people.

Anecdotally and numerically, it appears as though women are suffering as many or more indignities at work because of their sex than ever before.[17] The

---

[16] *See* Lupita Nyong'o, *Lupita Nyong'o: Speaking Out about Harvey Weinstein*, N.Y. Times (Oct. 17, 2017), www.nytimes.com/2017/10/19/opinion/lupita-nyongo-harvey-weinstein.html.

[17] *See, e.g.*, Robert Sheen, EEOC Sees Increase in Gender Pay Discrimination Cases, Pay Parity Post (Apr. 23, 2019), https://payparitypost.com/eeoc-sees-increase-in-gender-pay-discrimination-cases/; Khadija Murad, *Sexual Harassment in the Workplace*, NCSL (Feb. 17, 2020), www.ncsl.org/research/labor-and-employment/sexual-harassment-in-the-workplace.aspx (reporting a 14 percent increase in sexual harassment claims between 2018 and 2019).

backlash has been swift, too. High-profile men in power lament that they are afraid to mentor or, in some cases, to even appear in public with female mentees, associates, or colleagues, for fear of winding up on the wrong end of a misunderstanding, a vitriolic lie, or an exploitation of some unwitting gaffe that they might make. Hate groups of all sorts, including those who hate women, have been proceeding with impunity.

This book seeks to draw the subtlety of sex inequality in the workplace into sharper focus by giving voice to the uncomfortable, unspoken beliefs that undergird a host of injustices in the workplace – the "panes" of the glass ceiling. You can probably identify many more unspoken beliefs and their nexus to problems – social and legal – that prevent sex equality at work. Once they are identified, it is easy to discern these beliefs everywhere from published studies to human interest articles spawned by popular news headlines. And once they are voiced, it is easier to begin to engage, confront, and vanquish them.

Index

CPSIA information can be obtained
at www.ICGtesting.com
Printed in the USA
LVHW051417120422
715965LV00005B/307